D1614703

Music
Analysis
Experience
New Perspectives in Musical Semiotics

MUSIC ANALYSIS EXPERIENCE

New Perspectives in Musical Semiotics

Edited by
Costantino Maeder and Mark Reybrouck

LEUVEN UNIVERSITY PRESS

ISBN 978 94 6270 044 4
D / 2015 / 1869 / 44
NUR: 663

Cover images: Ancient Chinese character Yue (music) on front cover;
Yan (speech), Yin (tone), and Yuan (rhyme) on back cover.
Cover design: Griet Van Haute
Typesetting: Friedemann Vervoort

Table of Contents

Preface   9
Costantino Maeder and Mark Reybrouck

**Part One. Setting the Stage: Music-In-Action, Semiotics,
and Intermediality**   17

Music, Speech and Meaning in Interaction   19
Ian Cross

Capturing the Music: The Thin Line Between Mediation and
Interference   31
Zelia Chueke and Isaac Chueke

Performativity Through(out) Media: Analyzing Popular Music
Performance in the Age of Intermediality   43
Maurizio Corbella

Part Two. Representation, Interpretation, and Meaning   59

Reading a Work of Music from the Perspective of Integral Interpretation   61
Mieczysław Tomaszewski

La musique au second degré: on Gérard Genette's Theory of
Transtextuality and its Musical Relevance   83
Paulo F. de Castro

Semiotic Narrativization Processes   97
Nicolas Marty

Musical Understanding: Wittgenstein, Ethics, and Aesthetics   115
Paulo C. Chagas

Where to Draw the Line? Representation in Intermedial Song Analysis   135
Lea Maria Lucas Wierød

Part Three. Experience, Cognition, and Affect   149

The Ability of Tonality Recognition as One of Human-Specific
Adaptations   151
Piotr Podlipniak

Musical Semiotics and Analogical Reference   167
Lawrence M. Zbikowski

The Other Semiotic Legacy of Charles Sanders Peirce:
Ethology and Music-Related Emotion   185
David Huron

Part Four. Intermediality and Transdisciplinarity   209

The Death of Klinghoffer: From Stage to Screen   211
Maarten Nellestijn

The Perception of Art Songs Through Image: A Semiotic Approach   225
Mônica Pedrosa de Pádua

"What Kind of Genre Do You Think We Are?" Genre Theories,
Genre Names and Classes within Music Intermedial Ecology   239
Gabriele Marino

Part Five. Analysis and Beyond   255

A Story or Not a Story? Pascal Dusapin's Opera *Roméo & Juliette*
and New Ways of Musical Narratives   257
Małgorzata Pawłowska

Authorship, Narrativity and Ideology: The Case of Lennon-McCartney   277
Dario Martinelli

The Sublime as a Topic in Beethoven's Late Piano Sonatas   301
Jamie Liddle

Melodic Forces and Agential Energies: An Integrative Approach to
the Analysis and Expressive Interpretation of Tonal Melodies   315
Robert S. Hatten

The Embodiment of Yearning: Towards a Tripartite Theory of
Musical Agency   331
Rebecca Thumpston

Editors   349

Contributors   351

Preface

Costantino Maeder and Mark Reybrouck

Studying music, in all its forms and uses, contributes to the understanding of how our brains work and how (and why) we communicate, interpret and judge. Western music has undergone several centuries of profound unification and common exchange and development. Today, most of us are continually exposed to music. Music has become all-pervasive. We listen to music, even unwillingly, in shops, on TV shows, on the radio, when strolling through a town, when sitting next to an audiophile in a plane. The very absence of music in a TV serial creates a kind of surreal, alienated effect. Even in the womb of our mothers music probably conditioned our growth and the development of our brain. We get accustomed to clichés, to correlation of particular musical *signifiers*, closely tied to *signifieds*: even today in Hollywood movies, in pop music, classical music and TV serials, we encounter musical "words" that were forged very early in Western musical history. Common structures and musical solutions within an intermedial and transmedial framework were repeated for centuries and this cultural preparation and imprinting allowed the creation of a common ground that enables the listener to understand music. This very understanding, however, stems from some basic, cognitive faculties that define us.

Poetry, narration, paintings are crucial to the understanding of what we are, and certainly not superfluous and negligible hobbies. From the very beginning, these art forms were typical of our *human being*, as archeological and historical data suggest. This is also true for music, which, more than any other art form, is all-pervasive. It serves as *muzak* in stores, as apparent and often unnoticed background in movies, serials, documentaries, and even on the news. Only one century ago, music was rather rare. People could sing when working or perhaps in their leisure time, but they had few opportunities to actually listen to a wealth of music. Today, music has conquered our complete human sphere: people listen and make music, enjoy TV serials, make photos, create interactive web pages with their homemade movies. Semiotics and

9

cognitive sciences, therefore, do not relegate music, poetry, narration and painting out of what is really important (hard science, economy) but study these forms of human behavior and human being as basic and essential aspects of what defines us. It is about what we are, how creativity works, how we could transform the world we live in.

It does not come as a surprise that semiotics no longer studies music as a structure by itself. Music could be studied as a closed and self-sufficient system, but it is much more: it is embedded in a broader context that embraces performance, literature, linguistics, staging, etc., as exemplified in opera, pop music, happenings, advertizing, movies, and so on. Understanding semiotics as the theory of signs and communication prompts us to develop analytical strategies that can cope with this complexity. Just imagine a layman, who listens to a concept album, or who enjoys a musical, an opera or a piano concert without being a musicologist, a specialist in Italian or English literature and poetry. This person will be able to understand a very complex object that does not include only music, but also cultural memory, his own experience, interpretative skills and mindset, as well as the enunciative setting. But how is this possible? Which interpretative strategies are triggered and which generative strategies are developed by a composer, a poet or an opera producer in order to catch the attention of the layman? All the participants in this complex communication act rely probably on some very basic semiotic strategies and cognitive faculties. Semiotics should be able to answer these questions. It should provide the tools for developing a theoretical and interpretative framework that enables us to deal with this complexity by integrating elements that stem from cognitive sciences, cultural studies, complexity science, systems theory or transmedial studies. What is happening in the field of musical semiotics can be compared to what happened in many other disciplines, such as linguistics. We can analyze single sentences or texts from a purely syntactical and semantic point of view. However, any sentence can change its apparent sense completely in function of the situation in which it is used. The simple sentence "it is cold", e.g., can have different meanings dependent upon the communicative context, the pronunciation and the disposition of the addresser and the addressee at the moment of the utterance. In a particular situation, this sentence can mean that the addressee should close a window or should leave the room together with the addresser because both do not like a third person present in this very room. Many other meanings are possible in function of different situations and pragmatic contexts. This is not advocating the *lability* of the sign or the *impossibility* to communicate meaning, as it was quite common to pretend in literary studies in the nineties; we do not claim that everything is possible or that there is no "sense" that can be transmitted. We simply state that musical semiotics has to continue also to develop analytical strategies that take into account input that does not stem (directly) from non-semantic and non-syntactical data.

Communication as a complex, *multi- and transmedial phenomenon,* does not rely solely on language as a closed system—be it musical or linguistic—but includes several other dimensions (Eco 1975, 1979, 2000). Grice and many other pragmaticians and recent cognitivists (for example Grice, 1975; Sperber & Wilson, 2005) claim that the interpretation of the outer world and most communicative means (production and reception) relies on a handful of basic cognitive faculties and acquired skills that stem from them. When making music or listening to music, be it alone or within an intermedial context, we negotiate the outcome by comparing what we perceive to what we know already (norm, cultural memory, expectancies); we make use of our mind-reading abilities (the so-called theory of mind, or ToM described for example in Zunshine, 2006); we divide percepts into categories and construe systems; we identify patterns, we try to foresee the future, and we expect and look for sense-giving difference. When we listen to music, our behavior is not different from what we do when we try to make sense of a dialog or any discourse we are listening to; we assume that the counterpart wants to communicate with us—Grice's principle of cooperation—and we assume that in one way or another what we perceive is significant, to us or to others. This allows us to develop interpretation strategies, even for cases where our usual schemes apparently do not work, as is the case with violation of conversational maxims, such as "be pertinent" or "give as much information as needed". If this is not the case, we will proceed with hypotheses that will enable us to find a convincing explanation for a possible puzzling answer. We will consider the context of enunciation, we will try to attribute mental states (emotions, intents, beliefs, etc.) to our counterpart, and so on. When we listen to music, we conjecture that what we listen to is significant to us and that the interpreters want to express something; we assume as well that the principle of cooperation is valid here. By virtue of simple mechanisms, the audience can make meaningful and sound hypotheses on the sense of the music, the possible meanings it transports (Maeder, 2011; Reybrouck, 2012, 2015).

The ideas promoted in this book pay tribute to these claims. They are about musical sense-making and the way music works. They aim at providing new ways of musical understanding in defining music as a phenomenon that calls forth an integral experience. As such they are not restricted to structural descriptions of canonical music (the common practice tradition) but aim at encompassing also ways of capturing the music-in-action as exemplified in popular and intermedial kinds of musical performances. In semiotic terms this means a shift from *musical syntax* over *musical semantics* to *musical pragmatics*. Music, in fact, is not merely a sounding structure but something that impinges upon our body and our mind. This *pragmatic turn*, so typical of cognitive sciences, is also characteristic of today's semiotics. It points to a paradigm that turns away from the traditional representation-centered framework toward a paradigm that stresses the role of *action* and *experience* and which was also the starting point for an international conference on musical signification (ICMS XII) that was held in Louvain-la-Neuve and Brussels in Belgium in 2013 with *Music, semiotics and intermediality* as its conference theme. The conference had six major topics:

- the tension between traditional musicology with its emphasis on a structural approach to music (music as structure, score analysis) and sense-making by the listener (music as heard, music as experienced),
- the working of music within this context,
- musical sense-making, narrativity and music reception,
- the role of the semiotic point of view: moving from syntactics over semantics (self-reflective or extramusical) to pragmatics (effect on listener),
- encompassing actual and emerging new topics of music research such as music and emotion, music as experience, music and the body, musical universals and music and evolution,
- interdisciplinary and transdisciplinary approaches to music in an attempt to bring together traditional musicology, musical semiotics, cognitive sciences and (neuro)biology.

The present volume is an outcome of this conference. It is not a proceedings book but a self-sufficient and coherent contribution that should be accessible also to a broader readership. It contains 19 contributions, selected from about 120 submissions. The contents were chosen on the basis of their generic and innovative character; the authors were selected with the aim of presenting a balanced mixture of music theorists, music analysts, composers, conductors and performers. The list of contributors, further, shows both established and renowned scholars as well as young and promising scholars with challenging and provoking new ideas, in order to guarantee some fruitful dynamics in the choice and elaboration of the overall contents.

The selection of the contributions was no easy task, but still more demanding was the ambition to make something coherent out of them. The first idea was to split the book into two major parts: a theoretical part with broad generic claims and an analytical part with case studies in the domain of music, movies, stage, songs and popular music. This division, however, was not tenable as many of the contributions are theoretical as well as analytical, abstract and concrete, partly due to the interdisciplinary background of many of the contributors, but also due to the typical challenge of musical semiotics. Semiotics, in fact, holds a symbolic approach to cognition. It is concerned with sense-making and principles of cognitive economy, and relies on signs rather than on sensory realia. Music, on the contrary, is a sounding art with the sounding realia as concrete instances of more general ideational concepts. As such, there is always a tension between the abstract and the concrete and between the tendency to generalize or to particularize. Many of the contributions are exemplary of this tension. Yet, there are some general claims, which are threaded throughout the overall contents, such as how music works, how we can capture the music, music as a medium for interaction, as a communicative and inductive medium, music as a source of emotions and affect, and the intermedial character of musical performances.

The book is organized in five parts. Contrary to previous contributions in the field of musical semiotics, there is much more emphasis on the role of *intermediality, musical performance* and the *living experience of sounding music in the real world*. It is also *inter-* and *transdisciplinary* by bringing together insights from other disciplines such as cognitive sciences, biology, ethology, linguistics and musicology.

Part one sets the stage with contributions by Ian Cross, Isaac and Zelia Chueke and Maurizio Corbella. It broadens the definition of music by defining music-in-action as compared to language-in-action, by stressing the role of performance studies and by introducing the crucial investment in intermediality. Reflections about media have shaken the basis of music disciplines and have demanded a deep reassessment of the key notions of musical understanding. The fundamentals of text-based musicology have been seriously questioned by ethnomusicology, popular music studies and new musicology.

In part two Mieczysław Tomaszewski, Paulo F. de Castro, Nicolas Marty, Paulo C. Chagas and Lea Maria Wierød investigate music from a receptive point of view. Their main focus is on musical representation, interpretation and meaning. They stress the role of the listener's responses to music and the resultant processing of the musical experience. It is often stated that music does not function referentially, but what does music represent? How do we read the musical work and what are the levels of sense-making in the imposition of meaning on the music?

Musical experience and its relation to cognition and affect are covered in part three. Piotr Podlipniak, Lawrence M. Zbikowski and David Huron explore the origin and nature of the thoughts and feelings that are connected with various aspects of experience, relying on biological, ethological and analogical sources of musical meaning and affect. They go beyond a merely acoustic description of sound. Starting from music-as-heard they inquire into music's possibility of summoning phenomena that are not themselves sonic.

In part four, Maarten Nellestijn, Mônica Pedrosa de Pádua and Gabriele Marino deal with the medial properties of music mostly from a perceptual point of view. They question the traditional borders between different media, according to recent investigations in intermedial and transdisciplinary approaches to the arts. Relying on musical performance and movie productions, which combine elements from the fields of the visual, advertising and web semiotics, they make it obvious that musicology can gain in scope by going beyond standard aesthetics. Their multimedial approach shows that, beside voice and instruments, gestures, lighting, scenery, and many other non-musical means are key in understanding how music actually works in the real world.

Part five, finally, provides a number of musical analyses by Małgorzata Pawłowska, Dario Martinelli, Jamie Liddle, Robert Hatten and Rebecca Thumpston. They all focus on the interaction between musical analysis and extramusical interpretation by going beyond a mere acoustical description of the sound. Combining theoretical insights with music analysis, they argue for a kind of hermeneutics that relies on the concepts of musical topic, musical allusions, narrativity, discourse analysis and the anthropomorphic concept of musical agency.

References

Eco, U. (1975). *Trattato di semiotica generale*. Milano: Bompiani.

Eco, U. (1979). *Lector in fabula: la cooperazione interpretativa nei testi narrativi*. Milano: Bompiani.

Eco, U. (2000). *Kant and the platypus: Essays on language and cognition*. New York: Harcourt Brace.

Grice, H. P. (1975). Logic and conversation. In J. L. Morgan & P. Cole (Eds.), *Speech acts* (pp. 41-58). New York: Academic Press.

Maeder, C. (2011). Argumentative, iconic, and indexical structures in Schubert's *Die schöne Müllerin*. In P. Michelucci, O. Fischer, & C. Ljungberg (Eds.), *Iconic investigations* (pp. 389-404). Amsterdam, New York: Benjamins.

Reybrouck, M. (2012). Musical Sense-Making and the Concept of Affordance: An Ecosemiotic and Experiential Approach. *Biosemiotics, 5*(3), 391-409.

Reybrouck, M. (2015). Real-time listening and the act of mental pointing: deictic and indexical claims. *Mind, Music, and Language, 2*, 1-17.

Sperber, D., & Wilson, D. (2005). Pragmatics. In F. Jackson & M. Smith (eds), *Oxford Handbook of Contemporary Philosophy* (pp. 468-501). Oxford University Press, Oxford.

Zunshine, L. (2006). *Why we read fiction: theory of mind and the novel*. Columbus: Ohio State University Press.

PART ONE

Setting the Stage: Music-In-Action, Semiotics, and Intermediality

---

This part reflects on the nature of music. It broadens its definition as a mere description in terms of a sounding structure by comparing it to language and speech. By stressing their roles in action and performance, both music and language in action establish social bonds that afford listeners and performers the feeling of a genuine and shared experience. The figure of the performer who acts as a mediator between music and audience is a crucial element in understanding the mutual relationship between theoretical approaches to music and its possible, actual performances. Ethnomusicology, popular music studies, new musicology and (post-)semiotics, for example, have shown that audio and video documents are highly efficient in providing data that transcend a mere transcription of sounding music, typical of standard and traditional, text-based approaches. They enrich performance studies and contribute substantially to the understanding of how listeners construct their musical meaning. The rediscovery in recent years of the intrinsic intermedial dimension of music is crucial in this context. It has shaken the basis of music disciplines and has demanded a deep reassessment of the key notions of musical understanding.

The following three contributions deal with these main topics, to wit: the relation between language and speech, the role of the performer, and the importance of intermediality for recent approaches to musical understanding.

Ian Cross explores the relation between music, speech, language and meaning. Music and speech (language-in-action) are culturally-particularizable manifestations of the same human communicative toolkit. They rely on cognitive and behavioral resources and mechanisms that are common to both. Cross investigates in particular the phatic dimension of both language and music, which establishes and reaffirms social bonds. Music, accordingly, can be experienced as though it is an honest signal that means the way it sounds. It affords listeners the impression that their experience of music-in-action is both genuine and shared, especially when their attention and actions rely on a common temporal framework. To share each other's time, in fact, entails a type of joint affiliation.

Isaac and Zelia Chueke explore the role of the performer and his or her particular approach to the music as a mediator, by examining the thin line between mediation and interference. They focus on the interaction between analysis and interpretation. They also highlight the way performers imagine the sound and find ways to perform it. They distinguish two general performance situations: those that contribute to the artistic mediation and those, which disturb it. As such, they emphasize the role of gestures and visual aspects of music making and claim that the physical and aural aspects of the performance cannot be disconnected from one another.

Corbella's contribution, finally, tries to gather musicologists and semioticians around the question of how notions of grammar, language and style are entangled with musical meaning. In practices such as film music and popular music the production of meaning depends substantially upon intermediality in all its aspects. Musicology, ethnomusicology, popular music and sound studies have converged with media and performance studies, semiotics and aesthetics to generate not one but several grammars, which are commensurate with the plural nature of multimedia artifacts. The question of which grammar (the musical grammar? The grammar of mass-media?) is appropriate to read musical intermediality can challenge the status of text-based music analysis. Semiotics might be capable of taking charge of such multimodal approaches to musical intermediality.

Music, Speech and Meaning in Interaction

Ian Cross
University of Cambridge

Music and language seem, in our western conceptions, distinct spheres of human activity. Each has features that the other does not: language can refer, and is of paramount importance in our transactions with each other; music lacks any referential exactness and seem limited to the domain of affect, having powers to elicit emotions and their concomitant personal memories and meanings to a degree to which language, outwith the domain of poetry, rarely aspires. But seen, heard and understood from the perspective of cultures other than our own, the distinctness of music and language blurs. Music, for us primarily an aesthetic and presentational form, can be instrumental and participatory: a medium for interaction, just as is language. Music may fulfill functions in some cultures that, in our own, are the preserve of language, while in other societies language and music are almost indistinguishable. Indeed, even in cultures such as our own, many attributes of language in action—speech—seem as musical as they are linguistic. Music shares cognitive and behavioral resources and mechanisms with language, or rather, with language in action—speech. Just as is the case for language, music can be the focus of aesthetic experience; but just as is the case for speech, music is optimized to fulfill particular functions in human communicative interaction; these overlap with, but are differentiable from, the functions for which language can be interpreted as optimized.

This paper proposes that music and language can best be understood as constituting culturally-particularizable manifestations of a common human communicative toolkit. I shall review some of the evidence that supports these conclusions, and outline some recent research that suggests that "something-like-music" can best be interpreted as an optimal means of managing situations of social uncertainty, to the extent that it can at times be privileged over, and preferred to, language as a means of regulating social relationships. I shall suggest that the study of language in action cannot and should not be separated from the study of music in action-as-interaction. I shall draw

Ian Cross

on evidence from musicology, ethnomusicology, psychology, linguistics and neuroscience to support this suggestion.

In making the argument, I adopt a functionalist approach, starting by asking the question "What does music—insofar as we can identify 'something-like-music' as a generic human capacity—actually do?" The first problem that we encounter is that music appears to exhibit a startling diversity of form and function across cultures, and across historical time within our own culture. While music in contemporary Western societies appears to be an aural commodity, consumed for pleasure through passive listening, this conceptualization of music can be argued to be of fairly recent origin, having its roots in social, economic, institutional and legal dynamics peculiar to the last few hundred years of Western cultural history. The "work" concept (Goehr, 1988), and the idea of "pure" instrumental music (see, e.g., Hanslick, 1891/1986), both emerging around the turn of the nineteenth century, have shaped the ways in which music is conceptualized and managed in Western culture up to the present. Everyone "knows" what music is. But once outside the iPod, music turns out to be much more multifaceted and slippery as a concept and practice; it is a multimodal activity, at times indissociable from the cultural contexts in which it appears, serving as a focus for social interaction and sometimes as a medium for that interaction. This is not a novel claim; in particular, it comes as no news at all to music sociologists and ethnomusicologists—and, of course, to practicing musicians.

1. Music as a component of the communicative toolkit

Music as a multimodal, participatory activity (as opposed to its typical Western incarnation as presentational display: see Turino, 2008) is central to all musical practice, and is particularly evident in what we, from a Western perspective, might recognize as manifestations of music in many traditional, non-Western, societies. I use this somewhat convoluted form of words here because not only are there many societies where what we might think of as music appears to be entangled in a multitude of other social activities, there are societies where even the "something-like-music" that we can identify appears to overlap with, and shade into, other forms of interaction that are emically distinct. An illustrative case is described by Seeger in his superb study of the musical culture of the Suyá people of Amazonia, *Why Suyá sing* (1987). He suggests that Suyá communicative activities are best conceived of as falling into overlapping categories that span a continuum between two extreme situations: at one pole, the responsibility for an utterance should be accorded to an individual "communicator", while at the other that responsibility is held not to lie with the ostensible communicator but rather with a remote—even non-human—source. In the first of these overlapping categories, *kapérni* (speech), text has priority over melody, with text and melody determined by speaker; *kapérni* may become increasing formalized in public performance, when utterances are addressed to a large group or even the whole community rather than to an individual or small group. In the second and third categories, *sangére* (invocations, which come from a teacher in the past) and *sarén* (narrative and oratory), there is a relative priority of relatively fixed texts over relatively fixed melodies, and both are held to derive from earlier, ancestral times. In the fourth, *ngére* (song), melody has priority over text, with the time, text and melody of the utterance(s) fixed by some non-human source. Hence speech shades into invoking and orating which elide with song; a distinction between what, from a Western perspective, would constitute "speech" and "music" does not appear to exist for the Suyá.

Nevertheless, as Blacking noted (1995, p. 224), "[...] every human society has what trained musicologists would recognise as 'music' "; there are sounds, behaviors, and sometimes concepts that we can identify as "something-like-music" in all world cultures. Why should this be, and what is it that music is doing in all these cultures? Nettl (2005) suggests that it is doing many things; but while music has a multiplicity of uses within cultures, its common functions across cultures are, for Nettl, (2005, p. 253) " [...] to control humanity's relationship to the supernatural [...] and to support the integrity of individual social groups." The second of these two functions is sometimes referred to as "social bonding" (e.g., Freeman, 2000), but I think that Nettl is being more cautious in referring to supporting "the integrity of individual social groups". I shall take my cue from him, and also from the suggestion by McLeod (1974, p. 113), that music, particularly in the context of ritual, is associated with "the public presentation of social uncertainty". I will suggest that music is not just associated with such contexts, but that from a cross-cultural perspective, *music is a communicative medium optimal for managing situations of social uncertainty.*

1.1 The phatic dimension in communication

Situations of social uncertainty are those in which events are unfolding where outcomes are uncertain, for the individual, for the individual as a member of the group or for the group. These events can range from the trivial (such as daily encounters with others) to the life-changing (births, marriages, deaths, revolutions). It may seem strange to put music at the heart of such situations, particularly when we have available another resource—speech—that we can use to navigate the vicissitudes of social life. And of course we do use speech to manage such occurrences, in particular, one facet: the phatic dimension. The word phatic was introduced by Malinowski (1923), and is used to refer to that aspect of speech that is concerned with establishing and maintaining channels of communication between potentially conversational participants. It is sometimes thought of as referring only to greetings and farewells, and is most observable in such contexts. When, on meeting another, one party says "How are you today?", this is *usually* not intended as a substantive question that will elicit an informative answer about the other's state of health; it typically functions as a ritual opening, to which the appropriate (ritualized) response is expected to be "Oh, fine. And you?" With an answering "I'm good, thanks", the exchange is complete, the possibility of communication has been established and channels are now in place for the exchange or sharing of information.

But the phatic dimension of speech is not limited to openings and closings. As Coupland et al. (1992) observe, it permeates everyday conversational interaction, as communicative channels, once established as open, are constantly re-checked by each conversational participant. In Malinowski's view, the phatic dimension of communication constitutes a manifestation of phatic communion, where social bonds are established and reaffirmed. Phatic functions permeate speech, particularly where the purpose of that speech is not particularly to share information but rather to keep the communicative interaction alive—to maintain human communicative contact—particularly when we want to keep interacting with another person for no particular reason (such as sex, money, power, etc.). We could characterize gossip as a type of conversational interaction where the phatic dimension is likely to be particularly salient, where the purpose is not to impart or share information of any great significance but rather to play with the possibilities of conversing with another. The phatic dimension of speech appears to provide us with an excellent means of managing at least some situations of social uncertainty. Why, then, might we use music in such contexts, if we already have a communicative resource that can fulfill the function that I've proposed for music?

I shall suggest that this is because music provides an ideal communicative medium for non-conflictual (or minimally conflictual) group interaction (Cross, 1999, 2012; Cross & Woodruff, 2009). Speech is the only way in which we can exchange information about states of affairs in the world. This requires that each party to a conversation attempts to ensure that the informative context and substance of their utterances is made mutually manifest; in other words, each speaker tries to make clear to the other speaker the information that they are trying to impart. But as we can see from the earlier example of a greetings sequence, there is scope for misinterpretation when speech is employed in the phatic mode; speaker A utters "How are you today?", expecting that this apparent question will be taken as an opening element of a ritualized exchange by speaker B, but it is open to speaker B to (mis)interpret the question literally and respond with unwanted information about how they are. In a communicative interaction that is oriented towards the phatic, speech, by virtue of language's referential dimension, has the potential to break up the common ground of the conversation, albeit that this may be unintentional. And, of course, outside the phatic domain speech can create and escalate conflict, making explicit differences between speakers' interpretations of states of affairs, their wishes in respect of goals, and their feelings about each other.

Music, on the other hand, generally does not serve to communicate referential meaning. While someone engaged with music—as a listener or active participant in music-making—may feel that the music has a quite specific meaning, that meaning is likely to fluctuate as the music progresses. The meanings that may be attributed to, or experienced in respect of, any single musical act are likely to be multiple, varying from listener to listener and from participant to participant. At the same time each person engaged with the music is likely to feel, from moment to moment, that the music "means like it sounds"; music is typically experienced *as though* it were an "honest signal", unambiguously, immediately and accurately expressing some quite specific meaning (in ethological terms, an honest signal "reveals the relevant quality of the signaller to the receiver": Számadó & Szathmáry, 2006, p. 266). Music's presentation of multiple simultaneous meanings— its *floating intentionality*—together with an appearance of communicating directly, truthfully, and honestly, allows participants in a musical act (whether presentational or participatory) to interpret its significances individually and personally. Realizations of meaning in music are likely to be bound specifically to their contexts of occurrence and to participants' own expectations of what may be appropriate or relevant to those contexts—to the participants' cognitive models of the situation. But individual meanings are not reflected back into the public domain; they are not required to be made mutually manifest to all participants by each participant, and thus do not serve to crystallize disagreement.

Concurrently, music's apparent unmediatedness—the immediacy and apparent honesty of the meaning(s) that we impute to it—affords participants the impression that their experience of the music is both genuine and shared. This sense that music's meanings are being commonly experienced by all participants is intensified by music's temporally regular structures, inducing listeners to entrain their attention and actions around a common temporal framework: in effect, to share each others' time, inducing a sense of common affiliation. And finally, music may function as a particularly parsimonious means of managing situations of social uncertainty, in part because it is not restricted to dyadic interactions and is able to mobilize multiple individuals simultaneously, and in part because it can provide an "institutionalized" setting for the repeated rehearsal over long time-scales of non-conflictual communicative interaction amongst group members.

2. The evidence ...

The ideas that I have sketched here are not speculative; they are underpinned by a substantial weight of evidence from a variety of sources. The notion of floating intentionality and immediacy or honesty of musical meanings can be related to analyses of musical meaning in the musicological and ethnomusicological literature. That music can provide a powerful means of regulating social relationships is strongly substantiated by a wide range of ethnomusicological studies. And the idea that music and language—in the form of speech—are overlapping communicative domains is backed by an increasing amount of evidence from the cognitive sciences and neuroscience, as well as by ethnographic cases such as that of the Suyá.

2.1 Musical meaning in musicology and ethnomusicology

The idea that music embodies "natural", direct or unmediated meaning for participants is found in many societies (Feld, 1981; Leman, 1992; Turino, 1999), albeit embedded in different ontologies in different cultures. The idea that music is polysemic—that music's meanings are multifarious and slippery—is similarly common across the spectrum of musicological thought. Writing particularly about listening to instrumental nineteenth century music—the classic presentational context of the Western concert hall—Maus (1988, p. 68) states that "[his] claim is not that different listeners may interpret the music differently (though they undoubtedly will), but rather that a single listener's experience will include a play of various schemes of individuation, none of them felt as obligatory." In a similarly presentational context, but discussing audience responses to the *qawwali* music of the Sufi tradition, Qureshi (1987, p. 80) notes that "[...] the musical code makes it possible to convey a range of different or divergent meanings, simply by uttering each meaning through a different channel [...] music might be seen to operate as an open-ended semantic code which allows both the performer and listener to choose from among, or combine, several meanings, each of which is itself quite specific". And writing of participatory music-making in general (in the context of discussing Small's book *Musicking*), the ethnomusicologist Keil (2000, p. 163) comes close to the notion of floating intentionality when he asserts that he is "[...] convinced that music and musicking are inherently meaningless; all the meanings, deep and powerful ones, are fluctuating in individual heads and hearts, in the moments of playing and listening, and subject to miraculous mergings, shifts, and reversals in each mind within a split second".

2.2 Music and the regulation of social relationships

One of the most ambitious—yet controversial—research programmes in ethnomusicology was the Cantometrics project of Lomax (1976). In that project, he and his team sought to show that consistent relationships tended to hold between social structures and the properties of vocal music in a wide range of cultures. While aspects of Lomax's project were criticized severely (for instance, his apparent conceptualisation of 'musical cultures' as static and discrete entities, and his use of unfeasibly small samples to represent particular cultures), underlying his project was a differentiation between musical styles—across cultures—that tended towards being "individualized and little integrated", or that were "groupy and integrated". That distinction is made more explicit in Turino's (2008) book *Music as social life*, where he draws on a wide range of ethnographic examples in distinguishing between musical styles that tend towards performance and display—in his term, *presentational*—and those that tend towards active musical engagement—which he terms *participatory*. Turino notes that music in the participatory mode—music as active, interactive and socially inclusive—is usually marked by pulse regularity, by movement as well as sound, and by a high degree of synchrony, or entrainment, between participants. These features of the music, he suggests, tend to reinforce social bonds between participants; as he puts it (Turino, 2008, p. 43), "moving together and sounding together in a group creates a direct sense of *being* together and of deeply felt similarity, and hence identity, among participants".

2.3 The neuroscientific evidence

That music and language share at least some behavioral and neural resources and mechanisms is self-evident, at a simple level; both involve sound, hence both depend, to some extent, on the workings of the human auditory system. But several cognitive scientists and neuroscientists have made strong claims about the distinctness of language from music (see, e.g., Peretz, 2003; Jackendoff, 2009); they have claimed, variously that language embodies structures and functions that are wholly distinct from those implicated in music, or that discrete and dedicated—modular—neural resources are involved in processing aspects of music, and of language. However, an increasing number of researchers are interpreting their findings as indicating that common behavioral and neural resources underpin language and music. Patel (2003, 2008) has proposed that at least some aspects of syntactical integration are shared by language and music, though he holds that music and language systems are subserved by different representational resources in the brain. Patel's theories have been partially challenged and partially supported by some recent work, including that of Sammler et al. (2013), who interpret their findings as showing (p. 144) that "local syntactic processes in music and language are subserved by partially shared neuroanatomical regions that differ [...] in their relative weighting and timing". In respect of a different aspect of language, intonation or prosody, the findings of Patel et al. (2008) show that individuals with deficits in the processing of fine-grained pitch relationships (amusics) may also have difficulty in distinguishing between intonational features of linguistic utterances, again suggesting that significant overlaps exist in the neural resources that are involved in processing music and language. It must be noted, nevertheless, that most of the research that has aimed to elucidate the relationships between music and language have explored a somewhat restricted notion of music—as complexly patterned sound, listened to for pleasure—and have tended to compare somewhat formal properties of language with those of music so construed. In other words, there are few, if any, studies that have sought directly to evaluate relationships between the properties of music as an interactive social process with those of what can be interpreted as its linguistic counterpart, speech.

2.4 The cognitive and behavioral evidence

In the domain of human behavior, Brandt et al. (2012) adopt a developmental perspective in reviewing the evidence for shared behavioral resources between language and music, suggesting (p. 13) that "music [...] underlies the way that we acquire language: as 'creative play with sound,' it directs our attention to and amplifies the features of speech that we were paying attention to *before* we were listening for referential meaning." That developmental evidence adds to a growing body of research that is showing that perceptual and productive properties considered to have been unique to language or to music may in fact apply to both domains.

An example is work recently undertaken in Cambridge by Knight and myself, which explored the extent to which speech may exhibit a regular pulse or beat. This work aimed to test the common dictum that speech does not display temporal regularities of the sort that characterize music, i.e., isochronous pulses or beats. It started from the observation that different types of speech seemed to incorporate different degrees of isochrony. Taking its cue from findings that isochrony in music can serve the function of modulating or "capturing" a listener's attention (Large & Jones, 1999), and that joint, periodic behavior between two individuals can lead to judgments of enhanced inter-personal rapport (Hove & Risen, 2009), we postulated that speech registers that were intended to capture attention—such as lecturing—or aimed to enhance a sense of mutual affiliation—such as party political oratory—should exhibit higher degrees of isochrony than should everyday speech. And this is what we found. Listeners rated didactic talk (lecturing) as more temporally regular than everyday speech, and oratory as yet more regular; moreover, our experimental participants were also asked to tap along to the speech stimuli, and we found that they exhibited most irregularity in the everyday speech condition, rather less in the didactic talk, and even less variability in respect of oratory. Hence while all speech is not isochronous, when speech is used for capturing attention, or for increasing the extent to which listeners find the speaker likeable, it will incorporate more and more isochrony—in effect, becoming more like music.

Further work in Cambridge supports and extends the idea that speech and music are underpinned by common processes. In an ongoing study we are recording spontaneous interaction in speech and music to explore whether or not they share a common substrate that enables or facilitates successful joint action and communication. We have amassed a substantial corpus of recordings of quasi-naturalistic interactions between pairs of same-sex friends, and have conducted a preliminary analysis, focusing on the relationships between intonation peaks in speech and the musical pulse during, before and after successful and unsuccessful musical bouts. Our results (reported in Hawkins, Cross & Ogden, 2013) show that in successful musical bouts, pulse variability is about half that in unsuccessful bouts, and that intonation peaks in speech are statistically significantly more likely to fall close to musical pulses in successful than in unsuccessful bouts. It's perhaps not surprising that intonation peaks in speech tend to co-occur while people are interacting musically. What is more interesting is that in several instances, the pulse effectively emerged in the speech intonation peaks across pairs of participants before the first pulse in their musical interaction. Hence it does appear that unscripted talking together and joint music-making share a common resource of mutual temporal alignment that allows successful initiation and continuation of spontaneous interaction.

Two further examples from the empirical literature indicate that music, in managing social uncertainty, may indeed have the capacity to effect a change in the degree to which interacting individuals engage positively with each other in social contexts; music may indeed serve to enhance social bonds. A recent large-scale study by Rabinowitch, Burnard and myself (2013) explored the effect of a long-term (nine-month) programme of Musical Group Interaction (MGI) on the empathic capacities of children aged between 8 and 11 years. We found that the children who had participated in the MGI programme did show a statistically significant increase in their scores on a number of empathy measures over a matched group of children who had not participated. These findings complement those of a study by Gerry, Unrau, and Trainor (2013) conducted with six-month old infants. They found that infants who participated in an active musical experience program (Suzuki Early Childhood Education classes) over a six-month period showed significant enhancement of their capacity for positive social engagement. In contrast, infants who were assigned to a condition where their experience of music was limited to listening showed no such enhancement. Hence active engagement in musical interaction does appear to have the types of social effects that musicians and ethnomusicologists have identified in their everyday practice and in their ethnographic fieldwork, and we are at the stage where we might begin to understand the nature of the mechanisms that drive these effects.

3. Conclusions

So where does all this leave music? I would suggest that this view of music, and the weight of evidence that I believe supports it, puts music on a co-equal footing with speech as an integral element of the human communicative toolkit. Music is not an optional extra but an integral component of our communicative capacities. If we are to achieve anything like a comprehensive understanding of our abilities to communicate with each other, music must be as much the focus of study as is language. While much effort is devoted to the study of languages across cultures, very little of that effort takes into account the ways in which a culture's musical practices may relate to, and inform our understanding of, the ways that language manifests itself for that culture. Fortunately, amongst some linguists—and even some musicologists—there is an emerging acceptance that only through an integrated approach to studying the whole communicative toolkit will we be able to arrive at a meaningful account of the factors that underpin and enable human social life.

References

Blacking, J. (1995). *Music, Culture and Experience*. London: University of Chicago Press.

Brandt, A., Gebrian, M., & Slevc, L. R. (2012). Music and early language acquisition. *Frontiers in Psychology, 3*(327).

Coupland, J., Coupland, N., & Robinson, J. D. (1992). "How are you?": negotiating phatic communion. *Language in Society, 21*(2), 207-230.

Cross, I. (1999). Is music the most important thing we ever did ? Music, development and evolution. In S. W. Yi (Ed.), *Music, mind and science* (pp. 10-39). Seoul: Seoul National University Press.

Cross, I. (2012). Music as a social and cognitive process. In P. Rebuschat, M. Rorhrmeier, J. A. Hawkins, & I. Cross (Eds.), *Language and music as cognitive systems* (pp. 313-328). Oxford: Oxford University Press.

Cross, I., & Woodruff, G. E. (2009). Music as a communicative medium. In R. Botha & C. Knight (Eds.), *The prehistory of language* (Vol. 1, pp. 113-144). Oxford: Oxford University Press.

Feld, S. (1981). 'Flow like a waterfall': the metaphors of Kaluli musical theory. *Yearbook for Traditional Music, 13*, 22-47.

Freeman, W. J. (2000). A neurobiological role of music in social bonding. In N. Wallin, B. Merker & S. Brown (Eds.), *The origins of music* (pp. 411-424). Cambridge, MA: MIT Press.

Gerry, D., Unrau, A., & Trainor, L. J. (2012). Active music classes in infancy enhance musical, communicative and social development. *Developmental Science, 15*(3), 398-407.

Goehr, L. (1989). Being true to the work. *The Journal of Aesthetics and Art Criticism, 47*(1), 55-67.

Hanslick, E. (1891/1986). On the Musically Beautiful: A Contribution Towards the Revision of the Aesthetics of Music (G. Payzant, Trans.). New York: Hackett Publishing Co.

Hawkins, S., Cross, I., & Ogden, R. (2013). Communicative interaction in spontaneous music and speech. In M. Orwin, C. Howes & R. Kempson (Eds.), *Language, Music and Interaction* (pp. 285-329). London: College Publications.

Hove, M. J., & Risen, J. L. (2009). It's all in the timing: interpersonal synchrony increases affiliation. *Social Cognition, 27*(6), 949-961.

Jackendoff, R. (2009). Parallels and nonparallels between language and music. *Music Perception, 26*(3), 195-204.

Keil, C. (2000). Review of *Musicking: The meanings of performing and listening* by Christopher Small. *Ethnomusicology, 44*(1), 161-163.

Large, E. W., & Jones, M. R. (1999). The dynamics of attending: How people track time-varying events. *Psychological Review, 106*(1), 119-159.

Leman, M. (1992). The theory of tone semantics: Concept, foundation, and application. *Minds and Machines, 2*(4), 345-363.

Lomax, A. (1976). *Cantometrics: a handbook and training method.* Berkeley: University of California Extension Media Center.

Malinowski, B. (1923). The problem of meaning in primitive languages. In C. K. Ogden and I. A. Richards (Eds.), *The Meaning of Meaning: A Study of the Influence of Language upon Thought and of the Science of Symbolism* (pp. 267-306). London: Routledge.

Maus, F. E. (1988). Music as drama. *Music Theory Spectrum, 10*, 56-73.

McLeod, N. (1974). Ethnomusicological research and anthropology. *Annual Review of Anthropology, 3*, 99-115.

Nettl, B. (2005). *The study of ethnomusicology: thirty-one issues and concepts* (2nd ed.). Urbana and Chicago: University of Illinois Press.

Patel, A. D. (2008). *Music, language and the brain.* Oxford: Oxford University Press.

Peretz, I., & Coltheart, M. (2003). Modularity of music processing. *Nature Neuroscience, 6*(7), 688-691.

Qureshi, R. B. (1987). Musical sound and contextual input: a performance model for musical analysis. *Ethnomusicology, 31*(1), 56-86.

Rabinowitch, T.-C., Cross, I., & Burnard, P. (2013). Long-term musical group interaction has a positive influence on empathy in children. *Psychology of Music, 41*(4), 484-498.

Sammler, D., Koelsch, S., Ball, T., Brandt, A., Grigutsch, M., Huppertz, H.-J., et al. (2012). Co-localizing linguistic and musical syntax with intracranial EEG. *NeuroImage, 64*(0), 134-146.

Seeger, A. (1987). *Why Suyá sing: a musical anthropology of an Amazonian people.* Cambridge: Cambridge University Press.

Számadó, S., & Szathmáry, E. (2006). Selective scenarios for the emergence of natural language. *Trends in Ecology and Evolution, 21*(10), 555-561.

Turino, T. (1999). Signs of imagination, identity, and experience: a peircian semiotic theory for music. *Ethnomusicology, 43*(2), 221-255.

Turino, T. (2008). *Music as social life: the politics of participation.* London: University of Chicago Press.

Capturing the Music:
The Thin Line Between Mediation and Interference

Zelia Chueke and Isaac Chueke

Universidade Federal do Paraná, OMF/Paris-Sorbonne

Introduction

Over the past years, performance studies have brought up many aspects present in music making. The theme is being explored by numerous domains of research implied in the process of building an interpretation and performing it.

On the other hand it has also to be considered that perceiving and understanding music doesn't necessarily involve performance; while the latter is dependent on these first two premises, the contrary is neither always possible nor mandatory. For this paper's purpose, our focus is the performer and his/her particular approach to the music as a mediator.

Adorno summarizes the main difference between theoretical and practical approaches, saying that one who does not belong to the music making métier will always miss the "concrete familiarity" of "the hand which follows the score" (1982, p. 17). Familiarity leads to conviction: conviction in order to communicate musical ideas and the instantaneous engagement of the physical act/gesture of music making. We might add that Susanne Langer's image of the hands which follow the ears (1953, p. 140) completes Adorno's thoughts.

From a phenomenological standpoint, the process of mediation and its consequences can neither be effectively anticipated nor measured and the numerous series of studies regarding reception are common knowledge (see for instance: Aiello & Sloboda, 1994; Dufourt & Fauquet, 1996; Meric, 2012 ; Grabocz, 2001; Grewe, Nagel, Kopiez, & Altenmüller, 2008).

Our assumption is that if the public's perception of music may be directly influenced by former experiences this applies as well to the performer. The latter's mission is then one of educating the former, opening new horizons for a rewarding listening experience. As described by Schoenberg (1984, p. 347), "expounding motivic relationships to the listener (*performing* them for him), in so far as it genuinely helps him to understand the piece."

Evoking the concept that the performer's relationship with a chosen piece begins with the score,[1] musical narration is thus bestowed upon the performer when displaying the musical events collected from his reading, serving as the *narrator*, weaving the music tapestry. The musical message is conveyed through a *fil conducteur*, satisfying the public's quest—be it conscious or unconscious—for a musical narrative intrinsic to the performance act.

Our understanding of mediation and interference treats these concepts as conflicting points of view that either may lead the listener to the musical and even extra-musical ideas suggested by the composer in the score or instead deviate from those very same aspects. In this line of thought, Alfons Kontarsky considers two categories of pianists: those who enter the stage to show "what music has done to them" and those who go on stage to show "what they had done to the music" (Chueke, 2000, p. 51).

1. Describing music

Daniel Barenboim, who excels both as conductor and pianist, declares on the first pages (Barenboim, 2007, p. 15) of his book *La musique éveille le temps* that it is impossible to talk about music. On the other hand, audio and video illustrations have proven to be quite efficient at enriching performance studies.

Regarding the handicap of mere description, any kind of text will necessarily be read differently when more than one lecture is involved; after all this is what defines the uniqueness of each performance. A single example will suffice.

Exploring the interaction between analysis and interpretation, Joel Lester's article (1995, pp. 197-216) explores, among others, one particular passage: measure 40 of the Mozart Piano Sonata KV 331 (fig.1) in the interpretations given by Vladimir Horowitz and Lili Kraus respectively.

FIGURE I. Mozart KV 331, Minuet, measures 28 - 42[2]

According to Lester, in Horowitz's 1966 Carnegie Hall recital, before going into measure 41, the pianist made a ritenuto and took "a noticeable breath" before ending the passage as a half cadence; consequently, the tonic chord of the next measure sounded as the beginning of a new phrase (1995, p. 202). However, upon listening to the live recording,[3] this is not what we observed: the ritenuto really occurs when going from measure 38 to 39. Measure 40 in fact almost brings the music back to the original tempo ready to plunge into measure 41; regarding the half cadence effect, if it really happens, it is in a very subtle way, a topic which remains to be discussed.

The perfect cadence and consequent overlap are indeed more evident in Lili Kraus' rendition[4] since in her performance, according to the classical tradition, the perfect cadence resolution and consequent overlap effect come out in a more fluent way, with no slowing down. Dominant and tonic chords are undoubtedly connected and the tonic chord is heard both as the end of one phrase and the beginning of the next one. The same effect can be perceived in other great masters' performances such as those of Kempf[5] and Brendel.[6]

Our intent here is not to discuss either the performers' or the analyst's interpretations but rather reinforce the idea that it is almost impossible to describe musical phenomena in words.

1.1 Musical metaphors

In this line of thought analogies and interdisciplinary approaches may also be categorized, from a general perspective, into two groups: one that enriches music making, and a second one, which overemphasizes extra-musical subjects. Considering that technical terminology, although quite precise, may need to be reinforced due to the complex subjectivity of music material, the authors would like to introduce the term *musical metaphors*, even if taking care not to distract ourselves from the priorities normally associated with interpretation.

On measure 298 of his piano score *d'Erikhthon* de Xenakis, French pianist Claude Helffer indicated "give the impression of a boiling sound";[7] in this particular passage when the piano plays an incredible variety of rhythms and chromatic intervals, the instrument truly seems to be in a heated effervescence, an impression that is moreover reinforced by a continuous effect produced by the strings, sounding almost like a *glissando*.

Also, in his orchestral facsimile score, Helffer indicates "beginning of great figures of strings",[8] visually illustrating what Xenakis calls, in French, *effet massal* (1971, p. 19); this mass is delimitated on the page with a pencil. This could serve as another example of a *musical metaphor*.

The sound material moves accordingly to the context and a composer's style. This kind of knowledge, when incorporated by the performer through his experience and immersion in the score influences listening; it cannot be compared to the kind of information obtained through historical musicological research.

1.2 Mediation or interference?

Questions such as fidelity to the score, concerns for authentic performance as well as an active curiosity coupled with awareness of the varied praxis in contemporary music making, are also part of a huge literature with discussions accumulating over the years (cf. Walls, 2002; Rothstein, 1995; Taruskin, 1988; Taruskin, 1982; McAdams & Batier, 2001; Gilly & Samuel, 1991; Chueke, 2003; Bosseur & Michel 2007; Bosseur & Bosseur, 1993; Deliège, 2003). We can perceive thus how, as far as interpretation is concerned, gesture and expression remain of capital importance.

Considering the role of musicological and analytical features present in the preparation of a performance, we are dealing, objectively speaking, with musicians' daily bread: imagining the sound and finding the way to perform it.[9] Research data made accessible by means of papers, communications, conferences, etc., illustrate quite objectively two general performance situations: those that contribute to the artistic mediation and those which disturb, interfere or, worse, betray its purpose.

Avoiding the well-known and long debates on the several implications of performers' access to composers' intentions and the mission to communicate those, why not simply consider that mediation implies serving the music, not occupying its place.

If the main point is, from the performer's side, the appropriation of the music to be communicated, the consideration is that nothing could be in the way, interfering and/or obstructing instead of contributing to this process.

2. Gesture, narration and meaning

Forms of narrativity and musical signification may then converge or diverge not only between the artist and the public but also among musicians. Our choice for this article was to focus on different examples of efficient mediations instead of pointing out controversial interpretations that might be understood as interference.

The activity of a conductor is exemplary in this regard since, quite noticeably both in rehearsals and concert, orchestral musicians and audiences are permanently left with the idea that a statement is being made. The purpose is to leave a proper stamp on the final result, be it a live concert or a recording, symbolizing, after several hours of prior study and thoughts, the last expression of a performer's view upon a particular work.

Here follow some examples where full engagement with the music material can be perceived; physical and aural aspects of performance are never disconnected from one another. This visualization of music making can be important to show how it can affect the perception—both from the orchestra and the public perspectives—of what is being played.

Observing how a conductor tries to convey his ideas, let us investigate how different are the gestures adopted by Carlos Kleiber and Carlo Maria Giulini for the beginning of Brahms' *Fourth Symphony*.

In the case of Kleiber, watching the video with the Bavarian State Orchestra[10] and listening to the audio recording with the Vienna Philharmonic.[11], one perceives his influence upon the two orchestras. Those familiar with the interpretative style of this particular conductor can in fact visualize the connection between the musical and the physical gesture even in the audio recording.

In the first movement, for instance, all the subtleties of the dynamics are quite palpable, the long phrases being designed, alternating the epic character with the sublime. This is confirmed by the video where a delineation of the score is more than visible; a perfect anticipation of the gesture coming from the conductor contributes largely to a better understanding of the music, and this is intended not only for the audience but also (perhaps chiefly, we dare to say) for the orchestral musicians placed in front of him. Particularly effective are those moments representing a sudden change in the musical atmosphere or when a theme is enunciated for the last time; we also notice the *ritenutos* and *accelerandos* splendidly calculated for the best effect. Kleiber places his arms above the level of the shoulders, leading the interpretation at all times; he is in fact 'playing the orchestra' and it helps also for the clarification of the various contrapuntal lines.

Giulini at the helm of the Staatskapelle Berlin[12] adopts another technique— not less influential than that of Kleiber. His arms are placed down, perhaps requiring a more compact sound to come from the orchestra. Also, his eyes, most often than not, are closed. Giulini seems plunged in deep concentration as if he wouldn't like to interfere with the normal emergence of the music. We have the impression that he is searching from within the orchestra. One might argue that after all the musicians more than know the piece…[13]

With so many details to observe on this very same first movement, what about the felt notions of brightness (provided by Kleiber's version) and shade (given by Giulini's)? Their gestures are certainly different, but both are effective.

This is to say that a contrast in the interpretation is perfectly envisioned moreover when we consider internationally renowned artists such as these two conductors. From a delicate beginning it is quite easy in fact to forget how deep this music can prove to be. Again, from Giulini's recording we get the impression that his path is more languid, the spectral of sound is contained and certainly less extrovert, not as affirmative in its rhythmic feature.[14]

A *grand seigneur*, Carlo Maria Giulini, a man of an impeccable elegance, has been known for serving the music almost in a mystical way. An interesting parallel is analyzing his comments when, after a gap of 17 years, he decided to again conduct Beethoven's *Eroica Symphony*, another fundamental column of the symphonic literature; before that period, he had already abandoned it for 15 years, unsatisfied with his own interpretation. He explains that the "strange and extremely dangerous word *eroica* had nothing to do neither with the normal meaning of the adjective *eroico* nor with the even more dangerous reference to Napoleon." In fact, what Giulini really sees in terms of the interpretation of this work is its relationship with the classic Greek concept of the hero that singles out the individual with high ideals of life, a person that fights for men and liberty, ideals frequently attained through the sacrifice of oneself. Giulini's point of view is that the true protagonist in *Eroica* is the human being (Matheopoulos, 1983, p. 181).

The second movement in Brahms's *Fourth Symphony*, in Giulini's interpretation, is absolutely beautiful exactly because of this self-contained attitude, which lets things apppear slowly and progressively. While the authors have better appreciated the first movement in Kleiber's version, concerning the second, preferences tended clearly towards Giulini. This is of course a question of taste.[15]

The conducting of this piece's last movement by Russian conductor Euvegni Mravinsky is energetic, autocratic, incisive to a point that the sonority can at times be a little bit harsh; the orchestra sounds less rounded but it is an interpretation that deserves equal appreciation particularly due to its rhythmic drive.[16]

2.1 Text and music in Mahler

Mahler activates the tonality from within, by simple need for expression, to the point of burning itself (Adorno 1976, p. 37). When one thinks of the several applications of the musical setting of *Des Knaben Wunderhorn*, a compilation of stories and songs written by Arnim and Brentano at the beginning of the 19th century, it so deeply influenced Mahler that he spent 15 years of his life at the turn of the century busy with the composition of 24 lieder gathered under the same title (9 for piano and voice, 15 for orchestra). In addition, he uses it as an indispensable material for his 4 first symphonies, the so-called *Wunderhorn Symphonies*. *Urlicht* is used in its integrality as the 4th movement of Mahler's *Second Symphony*, while in the same work *Des Antonius von Padua Fischpredigt* serves as the material for the Scherzo. *Es sungen drei Engel*, the 5th movement of Mahler's *Third Symphony* is thematically related to *Das himmlische Leben*: present in Mahler's *Des Knaben Wunderhorn* this song has also provided material for the composition of his *Fourth Symphony*.

In terms of technique, the triads used throughout the cycle serve as a close connection to the origins of the songs, the alternation of the modes equally relevant. Most importantly, and even if it seems quite obvious how music in general can be channeled in a very expressive manner through the voice, our principal comment in *Urlicht* is the observation of an articulation between the instrumental playing and the singing that successfully converges to a representation of a plural narrativization, simultaneously capable of unifying the several layers into one. If we wish, a condensation, which leads us then to an important question: is the voice within this setting a soloist or another instrument incorporated into the orchestra?

Briefly considering a possible interpretation of Mahler's *Urlicht*, Fisher-Dieskau stresses the intimate quality between text and music in this work—"the dialectic relationship between semantics and music"—and there is the difficulty, always, of achieving naturalness, which can be done by a strong effort that looks permanently for an utmost familiarity with the text (2010, p. 688). Matter also explores this subject when stating that Mahler uses the

Lied in the symphony not only for what the human voice may contribute to the orchestra but also for what the text itself brings (Matter, 1974, p. 101).

In short, *Urlicht* is made up of 4 sections that carry an incredible power of expression, thanks also to its lyrics. We are not dealing here with the typical setting of a contralto acting as a soloist, but at the same time it sounds as such and we know that Mahler was trying to emulate in his manner, altogether differently, what Beethoven had achieved with the *Ninth Symphony*, i.e. inserting the voice within an instrumental context. We find the key to who should be carrying the flame right at the beginning of the piece thanks to this quite unusual situation of the voice, not the orchestra as normally expected, taking the lead, introducing the music with a first note that puts all (orchestra and audience) in a state of suspense.

This vocal configuration is also particularly impressive, making use of what is not properly a melody, in the sense commonly meant; there are only three notes for this introduction. The voice fashions more a monolog than a dialog to the point that, had the composer in fact chosen the first option, it could prove equally interesting. But of course we are grateful for the presence of the orchestra which colors the scene, reminding us of the melodrama form when music functions as incidental. From the very first call—*O Röschen roth!*—the voice is joined by the strings right after the anacrusis, the orchestra illustrating the singer's plea until the end of the piece. Concrete answers are not necessarily provided even considering the beautiful solos played by the oboe, the violin (playing what could perfectly be the reminiscence of an Eastern European folk melody) and the *piccolo;* those are comments that reinforce the expectation implied by the musical discourse.

It is equally important to observe how the musical sentences are unique, never repeated, and what is mostly amazing is the unfolding of a score that in orchestral terms relies totally on the voice.

3. Capturing the music

How to describe then the process of incorporating a piece that is aimed at a performance? Sergiu Celibidache (2012, p.138) uses the terms transcendence, reduction and appropriation, considering those as essential aspects of the performer's approach to a piece; according to the conductor, appropriation depends on the first two. Summarizing his ideas, there wouldn't be appropriation without reduction since the latter doesn't occur when dealing with multiple aspects.[17] Transcendence could be regarded as the amount of subjectivity that arises from notation's objectivity and perception of the whole piece should thus transcend consciousness.

In performers' daily work, appropriation and transcendence are only possible if there is empathy, connection between the music and the one who is transmitting it. How to prepare a performance without profiting from each phase of this process? How to transcend without plunging into the music, being involved in and seduced by every single note? Only then, after this long term relationship, is reduction possible. Entering the stage, the performer deeply knows the piece that will be communicated from beginning to end, able to access details meant to be emphasized whenever needed. Through appropriation, performers thus reveal what sounds true to them, serving with passion and sincerity as committed mediators.

Notes

1   Even considering Demus' statement that "pianists usually play master works that they have heard in concerts and recordings, and because it has made an impression […] they want to do it themselves", preparation for performance actually begins by approaching the score, which will remain as the ultimate reference, in depth. This becomes more obvious when preparing a premiere, that's to say, music of which there is no auditory memory whatsoever. Cf. Chueke, 2000, p. 31; 72-73.

2   Mozart, W. A. (1878). *Wolfgang Amadeus Mozarts Werke, Serie XX: Sonaten und Phantasien für das Pianoforte, No.11* (p. 124).Leipzig: Breitkopf & Härtel.

3   Retrieved 5 March 2015 from: http://www.allmusic.com/album/the-historic-return-carnegie-hall-1965-the-1966-concerts-mw0001805584.

4   Cf. Kraus, L., *Mozart. The complete piano sonatas*, Columbia legends, Sonny, 2003, CD2, (track 11; 1'09-1'24).

5   Kempff, W., *Wolfgang Amadeus Mozart. Klaviersonaten KV. 331 & 310, Fantasien KV. 397 1 475*. Deutsche Grammophon Gesellschaft, 1962, (1'09 – 1'24").

6   Brendel, A., *Mozart. Piano Sonatas KV 330, 331, 570, Rondo in A minor, KV 511*, Philips, 2000.

7   Xenakis, I., *Erikhthon*, Paris, Ed. Salabert, 1974. Helffer's piano score, *Fonds Claude Helffer*, Bibliothèque Mahler. « *donner* l'impression d'un bouillonnement sonore ».

8   Ibid. « *Début grandes figures de cordes* », page 10, Helffer's orchestral facsimile score. Cf. live recording (at 3'47') *Fonds Claude Helffer*, Bibliothèque Mahler.

9   Oppens, U., interview with Zélia Chueke, New York, January 15th, 2012.

10   Retrieved 5 March 2015 from: http://www.youtube.com/watch?v=yCaaPaQx5zg.

11   Retrieved 5 March 2015 from: http://www.youtube.com/watch?v=wxB5vkZy7nM.

12   Retrieved 5 March 2015 from: http://www.youtube.com/watch?v=wUe6r9UcIkw.

13   "I like to leave something extra, an 'x' factor for the concert. Of course the orchestra must be prepared to its best but there is a *quid misterioso* difficult to define and which however makes an enormous difference. I am convinced that the audience plays an important role. It is not a passive factor during the execution. The emotion that comes from the public

reflects on us. The orchestral musicians have a soul, in general quite sensitive, and are able to perceive the concentration that is directed at them. In the end how can we affirm who gives and who receives?" (Matheopoulos, 1983, p. 190, freely translated by the authors).

¹⁴ Musicians like John Wallace and Martin Jones of the Philharmonia Orchestra in London praise the qualities of this conductor: "Belongs to the old school, where the technique is what counts less. He doesn't succeed in his executions through technique, but via a profound and intense emotional contact with us... A marvelous sound, refined... but sometimes sacrificing to the ensemble... on occasion difficult to sound in a very exact way for Giulini but it is never difficult to sound in a beautiful way!" (Matheopoulos, 1983, p. 186, freely translated by the authors).

¹⁵ Althought the term "preference" might sound too subjective for research purposes, the subject been explored from different perspectives, mostly that of listening, p.e. Lanmont & Webb (2010). Regarding performers' viewpoint, Neuroscience studies begin to explore the relationship between emotion, preference and musical activity, e.g. Grewe et al. (2008).

¹⁶ Retrieved 5 March 2015 from: http://www.youtube.com/watch?v=aaqQL8poWkU.

¹⁷ "[…] que puis-je m'approprier ? Pas la multiplicité !" (Cf. Celibidache, 2012, p. 138).

References

Adorno, T. (1982). *Quasi una fantasia.* Paris: Gallimard.

Adorno, T. (1976). *Mahler. Une physionomie musicale.* Paris: Les éditions de Minuit.

Aiello, R., & Sloboda, J. (1994). *Musical Perceptions.* New York: Oxford University Press.

Baremboim, D. (2007). *La musique éveille le temps.* Paris: Fayard.

Bosseur, D., & Bosseur, J-Y. (1993). *Révolutions musicales: la musique contemporaine depuis 1945.* Paris: Minerve.

Bosseur, J-Y., & Michel, P. (2007). *Musiques contemporaines: perspectives analytiques.* Paris: Minerve.

Celibidache, S. (2012). *La musique n'est rien.* Arles: Actes Sud.

Chueke, Z. (2000). *Three Stages of Listening During Preparation and Execution of a Piano Performance.* Universtiy of Miami. UMI 9974800. Retrieved 5 March, 2015, from http://www.ams-net.org/ddm/fullResult.php?id=237.

Chueke, Z. (2003). Music never heard before: the fear of the unknown. *Revista Musica Hodie, 3*(1-2), 100-104.

Deliège, C. (2003). *Cinquante ans de modernité musicale: de Darmstadt à l'Ircam.* Sprimont: Mardaga.

Dufourt, H., & Fauquet, J.-M. (1996). *La musique depuis 1945. Matériau esthétique et perception.* Sprimont: Mardaga.

Fisher-Dieskau, D. (2010). La musica vocale di Mahler. In G. Fournier-Facio (Dir.), *Gustav Mahler. Il mio tempo verrà* (pp. 685-697). Milano: Il Saggiatore.

Gill, C., & Samuel, C. (1991). *Acanthes an XV: composer, enseigner, jouer la musique d'aujourd'hui.* Fondettes: Van de Velde.

Grabocz, M. (2001). *Approche herméneutique de la musique.* Strasbourg: Presses Universitaires.

Grewe, O., Nagel, F., Kopiez, R., & Altenmüller, E. (2008). Listening to music as a re-creative process: physiological, psychological and psychoacustical correlates of chills and strong emotions. *Musicae scientiae, 12*(1), 101-113.

Langer, S. (1953). *Feeling and Form.* New York: Scribner.

Lanmont, A., & Webb, R. (2010). Short- and long-term musical preferences: what makes a favourite piece of music? *Psychology of Music, 38*(2), 222- 241.

Lester, J. (1995). Performance and analysis. interaction and interpretation. In J. Rink (Ed), *The practice of performance: studies in musical interpretation* (pp.197-216). Cambridge: CUP.

Matheopoulos, H. (1983). *Maestro: Incontri con i grandi direttori d'orchestra.* Milan: Garzanti.

Matter, J. (1974). *Mahler.* Lausanne: L'âge d'homme.

McAdams, S., & M. Battier. (2001). *Creation and perception of a contemporary work: the angel of death by Roger Reynolds.* Paris: Ircam-Centre Pompidou.

Meric, R. (2012), *Appréhender l'espace sonore. L'écoute entre perception et imagination.* Paris: L'Harmattan.

Rothstein, W. (1995). Analysis and the act of performance. In J. Rink (Ed.), *The practice of performance: studies in musical interpretation* (pp. 217-238). Cambridge: CUP.

Schoenberg, A. (1984). *Style and idea: selected writings.* California: UCP.

Taruskin, R. (1982). On letting the music speak for itself: some reflections on musicology and performance. *The Journal of Musicology, 1*(3), 338-349.

Walls, P. (2002). Historical performance and the modern performer. In J. Rink (Ed.) *Musical performance. A guide to understanding (*pp.17-34). Cambridge: CUP.

Xenakis, I. (1971). *Musique architecture.* Tournai: Casterm.

Performativity Through(out) Media: Analyzing Popular Music Performance in the Age of Intermediality

Maurizio Corbella

Università degli Studi di Milano

In this paper I will focus on performance analysis in popular music from the standpoint of intermediality. Furthermore, I will trace some methodological trajectories that, to be truly tested, should be substantiated by a wide selection of case studies. Since there is no room to extensively concentrate on case studies, this contribution should be considered as a methodological introduction to upcoming new chapters. I claim that the study of how ideas of performativity are translated throughout the web of media in the process of the production, circulation and consumption of a musical artifact can contribute to point out common traits of different media grammars and eventually locate semantic nodes. I will stress how the multi-layering of performative elements allows one to access, although indirectly, issues of musical performance that are otherwise unattainable by textual analysis. Media performativity, in other words, is useful to bypass dead ends of the analytical discourse on musical performance, which too often either dismisses performance upfront or considers media documents as performance's transparent and neutral records.

The question underpinning this contribution is in fact an old one: to what extent can media "documents" be means to access the transitory characters of musical performance? If we treat them as texts—however expanded such a concept can be—we have to accept that they cannot disclose much more than the textual properties of performance. If we treat them, instead, as performances, as I will suggest, we can attempt to point out those processual traits that mediatization shares with the transitory events that predate it.

1. Beyond text: performance and media experience

Music analysis appears to be radically mutated after the notion of music as text has been destabilized in favor of that of music as experience. Borio (2012) observes that the shift from text to experience can be interpreted as an emphasis on the acts of musical consumption. I would add that in this change of paradigm a central relevance needs to be accorded also to performance. My argument is indeed that performance demands a repositioning of the kernel of meaning production from the conception to the enactment of musical ideas. Although in western art music enactment was sublimated and then marginalized by paradigms of "musical literacy", it still remains as a prominent feature in many musical practices worldwide.

"Traditional" musicology fairly overlooked performance as not consistent with the triumph of the musical score as "reification of the 'work' or 'text'" (Tagg, 2012, p. 149). As Gary Tomlinson put it, "the notated music came to be viewed less as a preliminary script for performance than as the locus of the truest revelation of the composer's intent, the unique and full inscription of the composer's expressive spirit which was elsewhere—in any one performance—only partially revealed" (2003, p. 39). These fundamentals of text-based musicology have been seriously questioned by ethnomusicology, popular music studies and "new" musicology. Cook is among the main advocates of overcoming the notion of text in favor of that of "script" in the study of western art music: musical works should be seen "as scripts in response to which social relationships are enacted," instead of "as texts within which social structures are encoded" (2003, p. 213). In a recent contribution, Cook comes to juxtapose what he calls autonomy mentality with "multimedia mentality," two "alternative systems for the conceptualization and practice of music, the difference between which is ultimately ontological: autonomy mentality is based on understanding music as a thing, multimedia mentality is based on understanding it as an experience" (2013). In the framework of a multimedia mentality, "the idea of music as performative multimedia goes together with a belief that meaning is negotiated, that it emerges from both media and social interactions and is constituted in the experience of hearing and seeing" (*ibid.*).

As much as Cook's demand for a historical and cultural relativization of the concept of musical autonomy can be viewed as an impulse for a new interdisciplinary field of research in which not music alone, but multimedia compounds, gain the favor of attention, musicology still faces the problem of how to address an enormous archive of mediatized musical artifacts which characterized 20th and 21st century production within and outside the boundaries of western culture. In order to respond to similar challenges, musicology has in the last decades developed methodologies that more and more frequently borrow tools and models from other disciplines: I should mention here in particular Tagg's semiotic perspective (Tagg & Clarida, 2003; Tagg, 2012), Clarke's ecological approach (2005) and Moore's integrated method of analysis for recorded song (2012). It is not a coincidence that popular music stands as a pillar in the three mentioned methodologies.[1] As Tagg has it, "due to the importance of non-notatable parameters in popular music and to the nature of its storage and distribution as recorded sound, notation cannot function as a reliable representation of the musical texts circulating in the mass media" (2012, p. 150). Besides bypassing notational centricity, popular music artifacts, mainly taking the form of records, films, videoclips, footage and so on, are subjected to another reification compelled by the technological media, which on one hand restores a less restrictive conception of text that stresses the discursive articulation of the meaning production, rather than allocating meaning in a mere alignment of signs (Borio, 2012), on the other brings back to the fore (even in western art music practice) the performative paradigm. As Anno Mungen put it, audio-visual recording returns to music its visual qualities: "Music is [also] visual, and certain aspects of the film are musical" (2003, p. 4).

2. From scripting performance to designing experience

While, as Cook suggests, "script" could encompass "text" and thus allow the dismantlement of the latter's authority, the textual becomes but one of the possible paradigms of musical experience, ostensibly the most historically entangled with western art culture but also amongst the least characteristic of popular culture. By contrast, other configurations of experience, such as the meta- and hyper-textual, the flux and the immersive (Eugeni, 2010, pp. 50-52; Albert, 2012), seem more remarkably intertwined with what semioticians have started to address as the media experience. For Ruggero Eugeni, media experience (*esperienza mediale*) differs from ordinary experience in the fact that "it is activated and regulated by technological devices [and] has its trends and articulations pre-constituted from outside," thus becoming "a supra-personal and serial experience" (2010, p. 43, translation by the author). Media experience is subjected to operations of projectual designing, "an activity of pre-planned regulation of some areas of ordinary experience" (*ibid.*), in which media are involved as "generators" and "catalysts" of experience.

A distinction between "ordinary" and "media" experience is perhaps useful as a cognitive model but less effective as a concrete analytical tool with regard to performance: medial experience seems to be more rigid and less transformative than ordinary experience because it relies heavily on technology, and yet, as there are fewer and fewer experiences that do not imply any sort of technological apparatus, there is certainly no medial experience that does exclude human agency. I thus propose to partially conflate the notions of "script" and "design" in order to grasp the differences between the two. Both stress projectuality as a form of experience organization and meaning production; both imply some sort of mediation. However, they trigger different configurations in the subject-object relation: script alludes to inter-subjective relations to musical objects, while design to super-subjective structures that pre-exist and underpin music making.

In the field of music performance, the mediation fostered by script usually consists in embodiment (Born, 2005, p. 9), for example that of a musician physically interpreting a set of codified instructions (e.g. under the form of notation), or interacting with other musicians and the audience in accordance with (or in opposition to) the framework of shared, rehearsed or conventionalized dynamics. In the case of design, the mediation is instead superimposed by an apparatus that responds to a regulated model of communication: a musical instrument is in this sense as much a compelling experiential design as a system of sound amplification, for they both act as super-subjective apparatuses, defining, organizing, shaping and circumscribing the horizon of music making within a set of definable parameters.

In this respect, analyses centered on musical gesture may be read as attempts to detect performative and gestaltic structures embedded in performance scripts (scores) as well as in experiential designs (instrumental praxis) (Hatten, 2004, p. 94). In analyzing the progressions of thirds that characterize what Stravinsky called *Leit-Harmony* in *The Firebird*, Locanto (2011, pp. 171-172) advocates for an interconnection between such musical figures and the piano improvisatory patterns that the composer had arguably introjected following his earlier studies of Rimsky-Korsakov's *Practical Manual of Harmony*: this enables the author to define an embodied-cognitive gesture that produces meaning when set into context. The analytical relevance of musical gesture is of crucial importance also when considering non-western musical traditions. In considering a series of sequences played by a Nande flautist from Butembo, Zaire, Blacking overturns Eurocentric interpretational schemes by observing the performer's physical interaction with the instrument (Blacking, 1973, pp. 18-20): while a western ear would detect a relaxation-tension-relaxation pattern by abstracting the melodic contour from that performative context, the anthropologist stresses the ergonomic features of the flute that "design" the musician's gestures, with the result that "tension" for western ears becomes "relaxation" for the Nande musician's fingers and vice versa.

These extremely condensed examples serve to stress that, for a projectual experience to be musically transmitted from composers to performers, to audiences, there are mediation passages which are loaded with performative values. Today we accept that, when performing a western classical composition

> [there] are decisions of dynamics and timbre which the perform-
> er must take but which are not specified in the score; there are
> nuances of timing that contribute essentially to performance
> interpretation and that involve deviating from the metronom-
> ically-notated specifications of the score (Cook, 2001, par. 11).

And yet, many interpreters would agree that those performance decisions, albeit free, are not arbitrary but rather influenced by the projected experience that the composer has, so to speak, encrypted in her/his score—they are latent gestures whose meanings are (inter-)subjectively determined. At the same time, in dealing with a historical repertoire, interpreters usually make decisions on how to relate to the technological design within which a composition was conceived: to perform Bach on a piano or on a Moog synthesizer has consequences for it dislocates music to different experiential designs than the original.

Every technological mediation bears an experiential design which stems from historical and cultural processes. Therefore, the relationship between script and design must be understood on a cyclical schema of reciprocal generation: individual scripts, tied together as social practices, produce designs which encompass new scripts, and so forth. Typical examples of design in the field of aurality are models of sound amplification, synthesis, delivery, digital encoding and portability. Stereophony offers a paradigmatic case: stereophonic configuration of aural experience is based on technologies shaped on bio-physical and cultural models of listening which historically superseded other models of sound spatialization and embodiment, due to functional, economic and contingent factors.[2] In the framework of the stereophonic "design", it is possible to "script" several aural experiences by operating—on the part of musicians and sound engineers—different choices on the texture, movement and distance of sound (Moore, 2012, chap. 2); each of these decisions implies various grades of subjectivity and creativity and is further informed by social, economic and historical trends (Zak, 2001). Musicology has demonstrated that it is possible to contribute to the understanding of these phenomena at the level of exegesis, or in proposing heuristic models of interpretation of media design to be tested on broader historical and cultural grounds.

In this line of thought, the sound-box model introduced by Moore (Moore, Schmidt & Dockwray, 2009; Moore & Dockwray, 2010; Moore, 2010) effectively grasps the "designed" level of stereophony and interrogates its "scriptural" occurrences throughout the history of Anglo-American popular song, thus providing historical ground for semiotic theorization.

3. How to do things with songs: song as medium, media as performance

As a synecdoche of popular music (Fabbri, 2001, p. 554), song offers a vantage point to observe the ways mediatization intertwines with musical meaning. On the one hand mediatization is co-substantial to the spreading of popular song as a global practice; on the other song itself imposes a "multimedia mentality" *ante litteram* even in its pre-technological existence, due to its composite nature of literary, verbal and musical medium.

Being a short, condensed and syncretic compound of expression and content (Spaziante, 2007, pp. 33-47), song qualifies as a particularly adaptable trans-historical and cross-cultural entity to be easily subsumed in wider frames, each of which implies diverse projects of experience. Fabbri (2001) delineated two of the most spread structures informing 20th-century western song's experiential design, namely the verse-refrain and the chorus-bridge forms; these two forms enact functions at three levels: (1) a deep anthropological level "concern[ing] behavioral and gestaltic schemas [as well as] motor stimuli" which are allocated "somewhere in between the pre-semiotic [...] and the semiotic"; (2) a middle level "concern[ing] behaviors and expectations imbricated in the history of relationships within and outside the community"; (3) a "surface" level that is "closely linked [...] to cultural movements and trends" (p. 561; translation by the author).

Prior to the 20th century, song with its above-mentioned multi-layered implications, played a central role within larger artifacts (e.g. operas, operettas, vaudevilles and, later, movies and albums), social venues (e.g. salons, cafes, clubs, concerts) and events (e.g. rites, cults, parades, fairs, sport and political celebrations). Similarly, long before the coming of recordings, song could circulate through time and space in different typologies of written re-mediations, such as collections, treatises, broadsides, brochures, drawings, librettos and scores, each configuring a parallel existence of songs as "transcriptions" and "translations" outside the realm of performance.

It is true that these sorts of remediations involved any other musical form and not song in particular, but what makes song a privileged subject of a multimedia mentality is that notation did not become an "avatar" (Tomlinson, 2003, p. 39) for song as it did for instrumental "classical" music in the western world. To put it differently, with the exception of cultivated and localized varieties of song such as the Romantic Lied—a genre that indeed had to rely on a well-codified singing style and performance context in order to accomplish an autonomous "notated" existence—song did not undergo the process of autonomization which instead characterized western art instrumental music.

The resistance exhibited by song to paradigms of musical autonomy can be sought in the centrality of *performativity*. I use this term drawing on Austin's definition of "performative utterance" (1962): a performative utterance is a speech act that implies an action, *doing* something through saying it, and in this differs from the majority of utterances, which are acts of memory and description. *Song means*, as Moore pragmatically entitles his last book (2012); but, while meaning, it undoubtedly *does*. By crossing Austin's seminal title *How to do things with words* with Moore's, I aim to simply recall that the act of singing automatically triggers something wider than the song itself, that is, the creation of a performing persona and a space of enactment. For Frith, "the 'act' of singing is always contextualized by the 'act' of performing" (1996, p. 211). Moreover, this *act* is multimodal because it combines different regimes of communication, from the verbal and phonatory, to the musical and gestural, mediated by embodiment. The trouble is that this eminently performative aspect cannot be grasped by analysis if not under forms of further mediation, which in the terminology of the semiotics of text would be labeled as discursive categories, or interpretants (Spaziante, 2007, pp. 40-43).

Quoting Bauman, Frith reminds us that "a performance is 'an emergent structure' [, which] comes into being only as it is being performed" (1996, p. 208). Neither script nor design ultimately coincides with meaning, but with projects of signification, deep structures to convey meaning on the "tracks" of communication; it is performance that makes them *come into being*. We need thus to reassess the specificity of popular music performance and try to judge how, if at all, mediatization discloses aspects of it.

With the coming of recording technologies, when, so to speak, songs became *tracks*, song's performative features were translated to the new medium and song obtained new potentialities in return from them, especially in enhancing those key qualities, described by Fabbri, and fostering them into new dimensions of everyday experience, with the option of entering houses, cars and, later, virtually every moment of our lives thanks to mobility and portability.

For Moore (2012, ch. 1) the *track* is the only way for the analyst to access structural and discursive categories that are identified by *song* and *performance*. These categories exist as crystalized configurations of parameters that bear only an indirect relationship with what a song and a performance are in reality. *Song* can be defined as the set of formal features (chord structure, lyrics, melody, meter) ensuring that a particular composition remains recognizable throughout different interpretations or covers, while *performance* is what marks by difference the uniqueness of each version of the same song, hence concerning issues of "instrumentation, speed and tone, production value or style" (*ibid.*). In Moore's definition, crystalized *performance* results in a sum of the performative agencies incorporated by the medium, which both display traces of evanescent real-time events (e.g. the band playing their piece in the recording room) and of technical operations concerning the phases of studio recording, postproduction and mixing.

4. The live, the mediatized and the intermedial imagination

To put it bluntly, every mediatization has something more and something less than live performance; conversely, only in limited cases is it possible to establish a genetic relation of determinacy between live performance and track. Values associated with live performance "migrate" onto the recorded track as virtual properties, in which the level of proximity to a supposed real-time event (the "live") demands assessment each and every time: there are tracks that openly call for autonomy from the live (e.g. the Beatles's *A Day in the Life*) and tracks that explicitly claim a transparent and direct connection to the extemporary energy of live (e.g. most concert recordings). It goes without saying that, in the record making process, recordists are well aware of the paradox of performance's fleetingness: technology represents a means of "poetic collaboration" (Zak, 2001, p. 1) for the recordist to displace her/his particular idea of musical performance. What recordings can do, in terms of suggesting imaginary performances, is extraordinary to the point of being deceptive: examples are plenty, starting from Stokowski and Gould's well-known experimentations with studio facilities (pp. 7-9) to experimental works of tape music and *musique concrète*; but even an epitome of improvisatory spontaneity such as *Bitches Brew* (Miles Davis, Columbia, US, 1970) managed to accomplish such characteristic blend of improvisatory freedom and formal solidity through combining a carefully pondered plan of performance sessions, pre-composed material and open improvisations, with an uncommon (for the standards of jazz recordings) use of invasive studio editing techniques (Merlin & Rizzardi, 2009).

The assessment of the liveness demanded by tracks is not so much a matter for scholarly speculations, as in fact every listener re-elaborates/translates in her/his own experience an imagined performance, no matter how fantastical, of the sound event (s)he is listening to. To borrow Frith's words:

> I listen to records in the full knowledge that what I hear is something that never existed, that never could exist, as a "performance", something happening in a single time and space: it is thus a performance and I hear it as one (1996, p. 211).

Even if we are venturing into the realm of subjectivism, we learn from ecological approaches to music listening that a certain degree of invariability is retained among listeners belonging to the same or comparable socio- and geo-cultural environment (Clarke, 2005, pp. 32-36). As Clarke explained:

> the principle of invariance [consists in] the idea that within the continuous changes to which a perceiver is exposed there are also invariant properties. As the ecological approach emphasizes, these invariant properties are those of the stimulus information itself—not a representational projection by the perceiver (p. 34).

From this last passage it appears that the ways in which processes are codified and understood in a particular environment, are crucial to ensuring the sharing of performative values among communities of listeners and spectators.

However stressed the discrepancies between the live and the mediatized may be, it is fair to note that developments of contemporary media such as online feedback and interactivity are disclosing scenarios of openness and unpredictability even in medial experience, where the borders between subjective script and super-subjective design appear to be extremely blurred. New media might be opening up the possibility for individuals to script their own agencies within highly mediatized contexts, thus substantiating Auslander's warning against ontological divides between the live and the mediatized (2008, pp. 43-63). Nonetheless, what (at least for now) still marks a gap between the live and the mediatized is the irreducibility of co-presence: a live concert can presuppose a great deal of technological mediation but, differently from its mediatized recording, depends on bodily presence rather than on the signal generated by the medium. While one can put mediatized performance to an end by simply switching off the signal generator, short-circuiting the technological apparatus in a live performance does not mean annulling it, but potentially transforming it.

Performance theory has long demonstrated the ability of staged performance to actively focus the audience's attention and thus direct their reactions and responses. The impression of unpredictability that comes along with the participation in a live rock concert is in fact deeply oriented by how the experience is "scripted" by the performer. However, as "scripted" an experience can be, a live audience will always be free to contravene their "script" by choosing, for example, to focus on different details or, in certain extreme cases, to impress their own mark on the course of the performance (by crashing onto the stage, interrupting the concert, etc.). Such occurrences, of which the histories of performance art and rock culture provide ample evidence, express the key attributes of live performance that Fischer-Lichte extensively examined: "first, the role reversal of actors and spectators; second, the creation of a community between them; and third, the creation of various modes of mutual, physical contact that help explore the interplay between proximity and distance, public and private, or visual and tactile contact" (2008, ch. 3). Fischer-Lichte stressed these processual properties as transformative, and thus transformation becomes the prominent outcome of performance. In introducing a recent collection of essays, Inglis similarly wrote about "the possibility of the unexpected" as the main feature distinguishing live performance from records (2006, pp. xiii-xvi) and, by qualifying the history of rock'n'roll as "turbulent, unpredictable and constantly surprising" (2006, pp. xvi), he prospected a somehow close bond between values of "unexpectedness" and the essence of rock'n'roll. In Inglis' view, and as we will see in much of the mediatizations of rock performance, unexpectedness and unpredictability become cultural values, rather than inherent properties, of live performance which are closely tied with notions of the authenticity of rock expression.

But what happens to those transformative traits when performance is filmed and then consigned to a dislocated space-time? We can readily assume that the issue of focalization is emphasized by the meddling of the recording apparatus between the "internal" performers (we include in this category also the internal audience) and the media spectators. Recording implies discretional choices of the personnel within an inventory of more or less established practices (rhythm of montage, choice of point of view, special effects, etc.) and of the particular designing devices afforded by the medium apparatus (number of cameras, types of lenses, typology of sound recording etc.): these elements have a direct impact on the audience's competence in reading a particular experience as unitary. This complex set of factors entails that the focalization issue must be seen as a result of negotiations between the performer's live script, his awareness of the media—modern music performers, not differently from athletes, are used to extemporaneously interact with cameras and thus to orient their focalization—and the choices of the director, who can decide to indulge in, emphasize, or even contradict the performed scripts.

From this awareness stems the attention that especially film ethnographers accord to their own *performing* bodies while recording (Ferrarini, 2009), a modality that could be interpreted as a major example of negotiation between two orders of mediations: the *scripting* body and the *designing* machine.

Despite being appointed for theorizing the great ontological divide between the live and the mediatized, Phelan acutely acknowledged in her seminal contribution (1993) the indisputable performative power of media artifacts. She fostered the idea that, while no documentation of performance can retain the latter's ephemeral essence, it can nonetheless activate a performative possibility within textuality: "Performance's challenge to writing is to discover a way for repeated words to become performative utterances, rather than [...] constative utterances" (1993, p. 149). For Phelan, performance and its media writings cannot coincide; however, this does not impede media artifacts in creating room, once activated, for new performances. We are in the field that Auslander defines as "the performativity of performance documentation" (2006). In other words, media work at a time as writing *and* performative devices: they write *while* performing and they perform *while* writing.

This last aspect has a particular relevance for the issue of recording rock. Embodiment and focalization are among the pivotal notions of the poetics of direct cinema, among the champion currents for the theory of documentary film, which in the second half of the 1960s profoundly intermingled with the imagery of rock culture through films such as *What's Happening! The Beatles in the U.S.A.* (Albert and David Maysles, 1964), *Dont Look Back* (Donn Alan Pennebaker, 1967), *Monterey Pop* (D. A. Pennebaker, 1968), *Woodstock* (Michael Wadleigh, 1970) and *Gimme Shelter* (Albert and David Maysles, Charlotte Zwerin, 1970). Direct cinema filmmakers extensively theorized about not altering the environmental conditions within which they were expected to film. This can be interpreted as a form of resistance against the experiential design of film facilities and a program to adhere to the "direct" experience, which in terms of filming rock events translated into committing to the performative values of the event. Still, in addressing Pennebaker's insistence on close-ups of women in *Monterey Pop*, Dave Saunders noted that "the visual approach of [the movie] unquestionably colours our perception of the filmmakers' relation to the historical world" (2007, p. 87), thus disclosing the gender contradictions embedded in the hippie culture.

Interestingly, Pennebaker's gendered perspective is consistent with his placing Hendrix's performance of *Wild Thing* almost at the exact golden section of the film (minutes 47-53 of 75, whereas Hendrix's set had originally taken place towards the end of the third and last day of the Festival) thus setting the groundbreaking guitar rape/sacrifice as the climax and crystalizing it as a powerful synecdoche of rock culture contradictions as a whole.

A very similar trajectory can be pursued through quite opposite means than those of direct cinema: *Shine a Light* (Scorsese, 2008) is a film of the Rolling Stones double concert at the Beacon Theatre on October 29 and November 1, 2006. The first extensive sequence of the movie is a sophisticated and self-ironical representation of the huge deployment of energy necessary to prepare such a kind of hybrid event, a live concert specifically conceived to become a movie. Director Scorsese elaborates on his struggles to discover the set-list of the concert in advance and offers evidence of arguments between Jagger and himself concerning for instance the invasiveness of cameras. Jagger complains that the cameras "whizz around all the time and [...] are very annoying to the audience and to everyone on the stage," and a half annoyed Scorsese replies: "it'd be good to have a camera that moves, that swoops down and in... and out... and tracks us, you know, along the sides somehow." This opening sequence indulges in disclosing what the whole poetics of direct cinema had historically disguised: the fact that every filmed music performance demands careful and exhaustive preparation and negotiation between filmmakers and performers. At the same time Scorsese plays once more with the mythology of rock by fabricating an (apparent) friction between the frivolous and moody nature of the rock-star and the methodical rehearsal of the film director. Naturally this results in a perfectly pondered dramatic strategy: the more Scorsese's role as a director seems undermined by the indiscipline of Jagger and his fellows, the more the film's "recipe" succeeds in pointing at the "essence" of a Rolling Stones concert: a perfect blend between discipline and indiscipline, between industry and spontaneity, between rehearsal and improvisation. Scorsese's operation can be fully understood by considering his historical vantage point on the whole tradition of rockumentaries. Filming in the 2000s, he can rely on the mythology of the Rolling Stones' mediatized personae, piled up over four decades. Their aged yet still powerfully active bodies offer themselves as a half-ironic, half-nostalgic and half-cynical retrospective of the "values" they have been representing.

From a different standpoint, branches of ethnomusicology and anthro-pology of music superseded the ideology of documentation in favor of the acceptance of the direct and creative intervention of media in field research. Since *Voices of the Rainforest* (Smithsonian Folkways, US, 1991), Feld has referred to his fieldwork recordings either as soundscape compositions or films, and has shown interest in reflecting upon "the interface between listening and recording across cultures" (Feld, 2013). The problem of the anthropologist is to convey *histories of listening* through recording, histories that are both his own and those of the people he interacted with in the fieldwork. Feld recently commented also on the researcher's interaction with the recorded material as a process of memory and re-creation articulated in three double-headed phases: (a) recording/re-listening, (b) selection/assemblage, (c) montage/mix (Scaldaferri & Feld, 2012, p. 79). In each of these three phases the people involved as subjects of the recording may contribute with their personal feedbacks to the making process. This tripartite process by all means configures an analysis in progress that presents itself to the listener in the form of a mediatized performance, entertaining a meaningful (*not* faithful) relationship with the "original" experience. It is this time-space rift between the event and its creative reconstruction—a rift of mnemonic recollection and technological creation at the same time—that needs to be filled by the audio-spectator, who supplies the missing data with his own baggage of experience. This act of "creative supply", abstracted from the anthropological terrain, characterizes what Montani calls the *intermedial imagination* (2010), the recipient's faculty of re-connecting pieces of media footage and digging into the interstices between media in order to authenticate experience.

To conclude, it is perhaps possible at this point to infer the goals of musical analysis. With reference to mediatized performance, analysis becomes first of all a meta-discourse, an analysis of the analytical processes already encapsulated in the multimedia artifact. Analysis is indeed already contained in the artifact: a track is an analysis per se, insofar as it stems from complex operations of recording, dissection, selection and montage of elements that (re-)create a unitary experience and engender a new performance. Between each new added layer of recording/performance/analysis there lies a mechanism of reciprocal *illumination* between different media, in the bakhtinian sense already outlined by Cook (2001, par. 24).[3] In this meta-discourse, the analyst's specific goal (distinct from the performer's or the recordist's) probably consists in tracking and setting into dialog the technical operations enacted by performers and media along the uninterrupted process of negotiation of musical meaning.

Maurizio Corbella

Notes

[1] Clarke does not deal primarily with popular music; his most important study (2005) includes an analysis of Jimi Hendrix's Star Spangled Banner. We can also consider the relevance popular music has had in shaping Cook's idea of multimedia mentality (starting from analysis of Led Zeppelin to YouTube mashups, passing through Madonna: see Cook 1995-6; 1998; 2013).

[2] For a cultural foundation of binaurality and stereophony, see Sterne, 2003, in particular pp.111-113 and 156-157.

[3] Cook himself retrieves the bakhtinian setting from performance theory, and in particular from Korsyn: "This image of different languages being brought into contact with one another [...] provides a fertile framework for the analysis of musical performance, and indeed it is hard to think of an area in which the Bakhtinian concepts of heteroglossia and double-voiced discourse might be applied in a more literal manner" (2001, par. 24).

References

Albert, G. (2012). Immersion as category of audiovisual experience: from long beach to hollywood. *Worlds of AudioVision*. Retrieved September 5, 2013, from http://www-5. unipv.it/wav/pdf/WAV_Albert_2012_eng.pdf.

Auslander, P. (2006). The performativity of performance documentation. *PAJ: A Journal of Performance Art, 84*, 1-10.

Auslander, P. (2008). *Liveness. Performance in a mediatized culture.* 2nd Edition. Abingdon & New York: Routledge.

Austin, J. L. (1962). *How to do things with words.* London et al.: Oxford University Press.

Baker, D. (2005). "I'm glad i'm not me!" marking transitivity in *Don't look back. Screening the past.* 18. Retrieved September 5, 2013, from http://tlweb.latrobe.edu.au/humanities/ screeningthepast/firstrelease/fr_18/DBfr18b.html.

Blacking, J. (1973). *How musical is man?* Washington: University of Washington Press.

Borio, G. (2012). The indeterminate status of audiovisual experience. Paper presented in the panel "Image-Sound Structure and the Audiovisual Experience" at the 19th International Musicological Society Congress (Roma, July 1-7). Retrieved September 5, 2013, from http://www.italianacademy.columbia.edu/publications_working.html.

Born, G. (2005). On musical mediation: ontology, technology and creativity. *Twentieth-Century Music, 2*(1), 7-36.

Bratus, A. (2010). Popular music and cinema: how the rock artist is represented on the big screen. *Worlds of AudioVision*. Retrieved September 5, 2013, from: http://www-5.unipv.it/ wav/pdf/WAV_Bratus_2010_eng.pdf.

Clarke, E. F. (2005). *Ways of listening. An ecological approach to the perception of musical meaning.* Oxford & New York: Oxford University Press.

Cook, N. (1995-6). Music minus one: rock, theory and performance. In N. Cook. *Music, performance, meaning. Selected essays* (pp. 119-138). Aldershot: Ashgate, 2007.

Cook, N. (1998). *Analysing musical multimedia*. Oxford & New York: Oxford University Press.

Cook, N. (2001). Between process and product: music and/as performance. *Music Theory Online*. *7*(2), September 5, 2013, from http://www.mtosmt.org/issues/mto.01.7.2/mto.01.7.2.cook.html#FN69REF.

Cook, N. (2003). Music as performance. In M. Clayton, T. Herbert and R. Middelton (Eds.), *The cultural study of music: A critical introduction* (pp. 204-214). New York: Routledge.

Cook, N. (2013). Beyond music: mashup, multimedia mentality, and intellectual property. In J. Richardson, C. Gorbman and C. Vernallis (Eds.). *The Oxford handbook of new audiovisual aesthetics*. Oxford & New York: Oxford University Press (ebook version).

Eugeni, R. (2010). *Semiotica dei media. Le forme dell'esperienza*. Roma: Carocci.

Fabbri, F. (2001). La canzone. In J-J. Nattiez (Ed.), *Enciclopedia della musica*, (Vol.1, pp. 551-576). Torino: Einaudi.

Feld, S. (2013). Paper presented at the panel "Audiovisual Footage as a Source for Ethnomusicological Research". International conference "Musical Listening in the Age of Technological Reproducibility: Giovanni Morelli *in memoriam*", March 23-24, Fondazione Cini, Venezia. Now forthcoming as Listening to histories of listening: collaborative experiments in acoustemology. In G.Borio (Ed.). *Musical listening in the age of technological reproduction*. Aldershot: Ashgate.

Ferrarini, L. (2009). Registrare con il corpo: dalla riflessione fenomenologica alle metodologie audio-visuali di Jean Rouch e Steven Feld. *Molimo. Quaderni di antropologia culturale ed etnomusicologia*, *4*, 125-155.

Fischer-Lichte, E. (2008). *The transformative power of performance. A new aesthetics*. London & New York: Routledge (ebook version) (original work published *Ästhetik des Performativen*. 2004).

Frith, S. (1996). *Performing Rites. Evaluating Popular Music*. Oxford & New York: Oxford University Press.

Hatten, R. S. (2004). *Interpreting musical gestures, topics and tropes: Mozart, Beethoven, Schubert*. Bloomington (IN): Indiana University Press.

Inglis, I. (2006). History, place and time: the possibility of the unexpected. In I. Inglis (Ed.), *Performance and popular music: history, place and time* (pp. xiii-xvi). Aldershot: Ashgate.

Locanto, M. (2011). L'*Oiseau de Feu* e *Le sacre du printemps* di Igor' Stravinskij nella prospettiva del 'gesto musicale'. *Europa Orientalis*, *30*,161-187.

Merlin, E., & Rizzardi, V. (2009). *Bitches Brew. Genesi del capolavoro di Miles Davis*. Milano: Il Saggiatore.

Moore, A. F., Schmidt, P., & Dockwray, R. (2009). A hermeneutics of spatialization for recorded song. *Twentieth-century Music*, *6*(1), 81-112.

Moore, A. F., & Dockwray, R. (2010). Configuring the Sound-Box 1965-1972. *Popular Music*, *29*(2), 181-197.

Moore, A. F. (2010). Where is here? An issue of deictic projection in recorded song. *Journal of the Royal Musical Association*, *135*(1), 145-182.[2]

Moore, A. F. (2012). *Song means. Analysing and interpreting recorded popular song*. Farnham: Ashgate (ebook version).

Montani, P. (2010). *L'immaginazione intermediale. Perlustrare, rifigurare, testimoniare il mondo visibile*. Roma & Bari: Laterza.

Mungen, A. (2003). The music is the message: The day Jimi Hendrix burned his guitar – film, musical instrument and performance as music media. In I. Inglis (Ed.), *Popular music and film* (pp. 60-76). London: Wallflower Press.

Phelan, P. (1993). *Unmarked. The politics of performance*. London & New York: Routledge.

Scaldaferri, N., & Feld, S. (2012). Documentazione e rappresentazione sonora: un dialogo sulla festa del *Maggio*. In N. Scaldaferri & S. Feld (Eds.), *I suoni dell'albero. Il Maggio di S. Giuliano ad Accettura* (pp. 74-91). Udine: Nota.

Spaziante, L. (2007). *Sociosemiotica del pop: identità, testi e pratiche musicali*. Roma: Carocci.

Sterne, J. (2003). *The audible past. Cultural origins of sound reproduction*. Durham & London: Duke University Press.

Tagg, P. & Clarida, B. (2003). *Ten little tunes. Towards a musicology of mass media*. New York & Montreal: The Mass Media Music Scholars' Press.

Tagg, P. (2009). *Everyday tonality: towards a tonal theory of what most people hear*. New York & Montreal: The Mass Media Music Scholars' Press.

Tagg, P. (2012). *Music's meanings: A modern musicology for non-musos*. New York & Huddersfield: The Mass Media Music Scholars' Press.

Tomlinson, G. (2003). Musicology, anthropology, history. In M. Clayton, T. Herbert and R. Middelton (Eds.), *The cultural study of music: a critical introduction* (pp. 31-44). New York: Routledge.

Zak, A. J. III (2001). *The poetics of rock. Cutting tracks, making records*. Los Angeles: University of California Press.

PART TWO

Representation, Interpretation, and Meaning

The contributions to this part deal with reception as a crucial part of the communication process: they stress the issue of internal experience as an integral part of musical understanding. As such, the contributions move from semantic to semiotic and hermeneutic questions: what does music mean and how does it mean? Starting from music's so-called *inability* to function referentially, it could be claimed that music expresses nothing but itself. But what does music represent? How do we read the musical work and what are the levels of sense-making in the imposition of meaning on the music? Contrary to the centrifugal tendency of linguistic meaning, where the attention is directed away from the artwork in order to grasp the meaning outside of the written text, music has a centripetal tendency that directs the listener's attention to the sounding music itself. This is the major distinction between language and music. There are, however, certain commonalities as well, which stress the shared components between words and music. They allow the conducting of an intermedial analysis of both of them.

The first contribution by Tomaszewski provides a framework for an integral interpretation of a work of music that is the result of its *reading*, to wit the combined process of listening and sense-making. Interpreters thus function as competent mediators who inscribe the work into the paradigm of a culture. Starting with an intuitive grasp of its general character, they can listen for its basic tone, look for differential or distinctive categories as aliquots of the basic tone, read its specifying categories such as function, genre and style, and test the work with axiological categories or categories of value; they can add fundamental categories of beauty and truth, complementary categories of expression, and fantasy, and end up with transcendent categories.

De Castro's contribution explores Genette's theory of transtextuality and its musical relevance. It departs from the text as a unitary, self-contained, autonomous and original object toward a conception that emphasizes the relational nature of all cultural productions. Meaning, in this view, is a reader-response with the act of reading or listening tracing echoes and reflections of other texts.

Transtextuality is the network of relations both implicit and explicit with textual transcendence of the text pointing to the deconstruction of the opposition between the inside and the outside. A broader category than intertextuality, it encompasses five types of transtextual relationships with two of them (metatextuality and paratextuality) being transmedial in nature.

Marty emphasizes the receptive side of dealing with music. Stressing the imposition of narrativity by a receiver on an object, he relies on several levels of semiotic processes—such as the proprioceptive, associative and analytical ones—which show different degrees of abstraction and levels of *verbalizability*, and describes the transition from less elaborate to more elaborate levels of sense-making, from proprioception to formal analysis of the music.

The contribution by Chagas explores the issue of musical understanding, relying on Wittgenstein's distinction between what can be said and what can only be shown. Starting from the connections that may exist between the linguistic and the musical phrase, he claims that music expresses nothing but itself. It does not need to express something exterior because it is complete in itself. What emerges is the issue of internal experience, and understanding is not caused by an external factor but is internal.

The same inability of music to function referentially is stressed in Wierød's contribution on representation in intermedial song. In investigating songs as a multimodal phenomenon, she focuses on modalities that poetry and music have in common, with rhythm as the most palpable shared component of word and music. Contrary to the centrifugal tendency of literature to direct the recipient's attention away from the artwork to its referential character, there is a focus on the auditory material of songs as the meeting point for shared modalities of words and melody.

Reading a Work of Music from the Perspective of Integral Interpretation

Mieczysław Tomaszewski

Academy of Music in Krakow

I think one can agree with the idea that the primary task of the theory of music, its foundation and its point of departure irrespective of its methodological orientation consists in interpreting a work of music as a result of its *reading*. A work of music is thus understood as a human product for humans, its task being to delight, to stir emotions and to convey meanings and senses. In this system, the interpreter functions as a competent mediator who, by reading the work in the entirety of its inimitable features, helps others to open their ears and eyes, awakens their memory and imagination, inscribing the works interpreted, endowed with specific qualities and particular values, into the paradigm of a culture.

We are now witnessing brilliant achievements in the interpretation of a work of music based on specific and specialized methods. These achievements, however, usually concern a particular and, more often than not, a formal aspect of the work, ignoring or sidetracking any other facets. This is done irrespective of which aspect of the work was constitutive in the composer's intent and in the principles of his or her place and time. This frequently leads to a rift between the results of interpretation and the ideas and the intents of the composer, and, also, the direct experience of the receiver. To bridge this gap it seems necessary to read the work in the *entirety* of its qualities, with emphasis on its constitutive features. The method of *integral interpretation,* which suggests testing all relevant aspects of the interpreted work, is a tentative reconnaissance in this respect.

To make a long story short: reading a work of music according to the principles of integral interpretation is best begun with an intuitive grasp of its general character, with listening for its basic tone, so that its elementary categories present themselves naturally and obviously. Its *differential* or *distinctive* categories can then be seen, metaphorically speaking, as a series of aliquots of the basic tone. These will mostly concern the particular aspects of the work's inner universe and then its external world that is the work's multifaceted context of biography, history and culture. Reading its *specifying* categories—those of function, genre and style—allows one to correctly place the work within an intersubjective system, within the correct paradigm of culture, the one in which the work was created. A further step, which tests the work with *axiological* categories, is an attempt to discuss it within a given sphere of values to assess the degree and the type of its creative perfection and to read the modification of meaning that it is the vehicle of. Yet the apogee of interpretative action is only achieved when works usually referred to as masterpieces (and, also, at moments in works not referred to as such) come to resonate with the highest and *fundamental* categories of beauty and truth in a peculiar counterpoint with their *complementary* categories: expression and fantasy. In even rarer and even more peculiar moments, *transcendent* categories may appear, including *metaphysical* ones.

1. Elementary or syncretic categories

They appear as the result of the interpreter's first step as heard and read in a direct way through no analytic procedures, with no ready-made formulae and recipes. The importance of this first step was noticed and appreciated by Kurt Huber (1953) when he produced his concept of the so-called sphere experience (*Sphärenerlebnis*), rooted in Gestalt psychology: a sensitive and competent listener needs but a few tones to precisely define the sphere into which he or she has been "transported" by a given piece of music, whether the sphere was pastoral or sacred, springtime or wartime. This recognition is not so much a result of individual elements as of their consistent and syncretic combination. In the several recent decades the categories referred to here as elementary have evoked heightened attention in those trends in the modern theory of music that freed musicology from overly scientistic and autotelic variety. Despite their various appellations, they can be reduced to a single denominator.

Constantin Floros (1987) began his reading of Gustav Mahler's symphonics by defining a repertoire of a dozen or so constitutive elementary categories, which he referred to as *characters*. These obviously included the likes of *Trauermarsch* and *Ländler, das Lied* and *Musik aus weitester Ferne*. Floros took his cue from Guido Adler (1916), who saw Mahler's music as a whole as consisting of changing images and, at the same time, states of the soul ("einander ablösender Seelenstimmungen").

In his quest for the relationships between music and myth, Eero Tarasti (1979) isolated, from a series of significant works by Wagner and Sibelius, a truly peculiar combination of semantically-pregnant elementary categories, such as the magical, the mythical, the fabulous, the legendary, the demonic, ...

Marta Grabócz (2009a, 2009b, 2009c) identified an alphabet of elementary categories that combine into unique and multihued *palettes* of Ferenc Liszt and Bela Bartók, classifying them, in accordance with semiotic practice, according to their levels and types (as semes, classemes and isotopies).

Robert Hatten (1994, 2004), who reads the works by Beethoven and Schubert in terms of hermeneutics and narratology, refers to their elementary categories as topics; they include the tragic, the heroic and the triumphant or the sacred and the transcendent.

I have myself attempted a reading of the alphabets of elementary categories in Chopin (Tomaszewski, 1999) and Beethoven (Tomaszewski, 2006a, 2012); I referred to these alphabets as *stylistic idioms*. Also, the syndromes of both composers have been compared based on the principle of antinomy. In the two composers' highly dynamic *œuvres*, each basic category seems to be confronted by one that is contrastive or complementary.

The problem might arise whether reading a work in the above-mentioned categories is a valid approach. First of all, this is exactly how—through titles and directions—composers themselves have oftentimes described their works and their individual fragments. Secondly, descriptions that expressly define the character of music happen to be of import for their creators. In his famous letter to Hofrat von Mozel, Beethoven described "a work's character" as "its soul" ("Geist des Stückes"). Elsewhere, he termed the types of the music he composed as categories that are referred to here as elementary: "romantisch, ganz ernsthaft, heroisch, komisch, sentimental..."

2. Distinctive or differential categories

The interpreter's next step can be described as a differential testing of the work, following the traces of the initial intuition that might be treated as a working hypothesis. The primary and fundamental task of the testing is to *distinguish* or to differentiate between qualities and relationships most proper to the work. The first differentiation would probably be that into categories of *internal* vs *external* qualities and relationships of the work under interpretation.

2.1 Internal qualities

- The distinctive categories of internal qualities and relationships have been the pivot of all methodologies and philosophies of the theory of music. However, its basic object, the work of music, has not always been treated as an integral whole. This whole can only be relevant when the work of music is discussed in terms of its four primary aspects: substantial, structural, emotive and semantic. Each relates to a different complex of qualities that combine to create a different layer of the work. Significantly, an analogous view of a work of literature or of graphic art allows a compatible treatment of all works of syncretic or synthetic kind (e.g. songs).

- Yet, above all, while every piece of music of every era can be a manifestation of the coexistence between all four layers of the work, the difference between each style or each tendency consists in a different hierarchy of these layers. The domination of one of them places the work within one of the four different genres or types of music.

- The preponderance of the *material* layer (of the phonic layer in the case of music) places the piece in the genre of *a priori phonic* works such as Varèse's *Ionisation*, Penderecki's *De natura sonoris* or *Fluorescences* (fig.1).

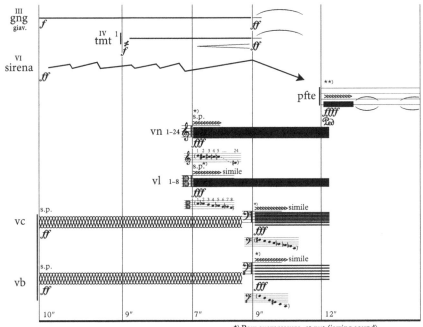

*) Bow overpressure, at nut (jarring sound).
**) Rub the lowest string with a cymbal.

Figure 1. Penderecki: *Fluorescences*

- The preponderance of the *structural* layer is characteristic for *a priori structural* works, such as Mozart's variations, Hummel's rondos or J.S. Bach's fugues (fig. 2).

Figure 2. Bach: *Brandenburg Concerto* No 5 / III

- The dominance of the *expressive* aspect gives rise to an *a priori emotive* work: a nocturne, a serenade or a lament that express or evoke emotion (cf. *Songs on the Death of Children* by Mahler, fig. 3).

FIGURE 3. Mahler: *Kindertotenlieder*, III

- The *clear* presence of the *semantic* makes a work belong to the *a priori semantic* type, such as overtures and program symphonies, symphonic poems or musical landscapes inspired by literature, philosophy or nature (e.g. Beethoven's *Pastorale*, fig. 4).

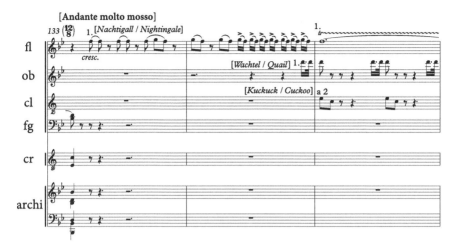

FIGURE 4. Beethoven: *VI Symphonie. Pastorale*. III. Scene am Bach

It is interesting to see the type of relationships that the individual layers have been involved in throughout the history of culture. In phases that emphasized musical autotelism, music was mostly the interplay between categories that belong to the phonic and the structural layers (a situation that found its theoretical basis in Hanslick's ideas). In heteronymous phases—those focusing on intermedial synthesis and at symbiosis between art and the real world—the chief function was performed by the emotive and semantic layers. The relationships between other pairs of layers, between phonic and semantic and between structural and emotive, seem even more interesting. They can be described as running on a single track, except that they are doing it in reciprocal tendencies. Expression is understood as a deformation of structure, and the intensification of semantization as reduction of the significance of the phonic layer.

Thus tones, for instance, gradually become carriers of meaning, only to be discarded in another phase. Similarly, structures are transformed by expression and then get rid of their excess at some point.

This view of a work, differentiating between its layers and testing their functions, is synchronic and vertical in character. A diachronic and linear character appears in a perspective that differentiates a work from an ontological perspective. This allows four different forms of the work which can be described as phases realized in time as texts, namely, *musical text, sonic text, audial text* and *sign text* (cf. Tomaszewski, 2006b).

- A *musical* text, brought to life in a unique act of creativity, constitutes an *intentional object* (Ingarden, 1973). Recorded as a score, it represents a specific work *in potentia*.
- A *sonic* text, repeatedly brought to life by performers in acts of artistic production (*in actu*), is a real, physical object, recorded and registered, over and over again, in its infinitely different forms.
- An *audial* text, a result of an act of aesthetic perception, ever individual and subjective, is a psycho-physical object (a work *in vivo* of sorts), preserved in the audience's memory.
- A *sign* text, a result of generalized and objectivized social and cultural reception, inscribed into a culture with a value judgement as a symbolic object, a particular *in esse*.

In the above differentiation—which is in fact quite necessary for a correct definition of the object of study—the two extreme texts, the musical and the sign, belong, as the coding and decoding properties of a work, to the sphere of *musical culture*, which takes place over the so-called *long time span* (Braudel, 1971) with emphasis on the message. The two other texts, sonic and audial, which coexist in their archetypal situation, i.e. that of the work's musical performance, belong to the sphere called *musical life*. It is characteristic in its repetitiveness and its taking place over *short time spans*. The emphasis here is on genre, quality and perfection of the *medium*.

2.2 External qualities

Distinctive categories that describe and differentiate the relationships between the work and the *outside* world had long been called the *context* of the work. Until recently, this aspect was well-nigh prohibited in scholarly interpretation. The present position is that to ignore this context of the work *from its genesis to its resonance* (cf. Tomaszewski, 2010) would be to preclude its full and true reading. In the most general way, this has been shown by the famous "debunking" text by Joseph Kerman (*How We Got into Analysis, and How to Get Out*) that is itself an interpretation of one of R. Schumann's *Dichterliebe* songs. This was done in a particular way by Tarasti (2012) in his recent semiotic and existentialist reading of another work by the same composer, his mysterious *Fantasia in C major*.

There are many aspects in which a work's context may be viewed: at least and above all *biographical, historical* and *cultural*.

2.2.1 The biographical aspect

To read a work in its *biographical* aspect is above all to discover *"the traces of the author in the work"* and to show the degree of its personalization, although it is not always easy or even possible.

- The relatively most superficial kind of "the author's presence of the author in the work" can be called *autobiographical*. It documents the type and *degree of the author's rootedness in his empirical reality*, in real public life: national, religious, social. This would be true of such pieces as Beethoven's *Wellingtons-Sieg* or Tchaikovsky's *1812 Overture*.
- Works that bear, at times not easily legible, *traces of emotional experience* may be termed *self-expressive*. It is not without reason that C. Floros could entitle the monograph of A. Berg as *Musik als Autobiographie* based on comprehensively-deciphered manuscripts.
- The third degree of *"presence of the author in the work"* may be described as *self-contemplative*. This is true of works that are authentic reflections of *spiritual life*: soliloquies, manifestos, "testaments" witnessed in works such as Brahms's *Vier ernste Gesänge* or the part of Mahler's *Lied von der Erde* entitled *Abschied*.

Otherwise the biographical aspect of a work may be read by discussing its place in the *composer's creative path*. It is not unimportant which phase of this path gave rise to the work or what the relationship is between its own properties and those that are usually ascribed to that phase in its invariant form.

A composer's creative path—in its invariant shape—goes through a sequence of particularly characteristic phases in turn: first, *imitation of one's heritage*; then, *experimentation with the alien and the fascinating*; then, after one's own style has been achieved, comes *monolog*, followed by *dialog* when another's *œuvre* or idea has been encountered and challenged. Finally, after a passage through a "shadow line" in life, an attempt is made to review one's aims and means, which in turn results in a *liberation* from external and internal limitations.

One must not forget the situation when a composer is unable to pass a threshold of a subsequent phase and succumbs to *traditionalism* or *eclecticism*, to *mannerism* or *academism*.

2.2.2 The historical and cultural aspect

Viewing a work from the point of view of its relationships of a *historical and cultural nature* may reveal and explain any of its properties which are otherwise unintelligible and unreadable. This reading should concern the entirety of "being in the universe, in history and culture" that corresponds to the formula "from inspiration through context to resonance."

- The study of the sphere of *inspiration* reveals the type and the degree of a work's roots in the cultural *past*. This is true of adopting specific idioms of a past paradigm as well as its models and systems. The aim is creative *continuation*; contrastingly, in avant-garde trends, the goal is to break away from the traditional and to emphasize novelty.
- The discussion of the sphere of *context* makes it possible to realize the relationships that bind the work to the *present*, to the trends, techniques and modes of the prevailing paradigm. Of particular interest is the moment of encountering (or clashing against), of *entering into a dialog* with the present and the alien. Opposing tendencies prefer *isolation* from the present, a radical autotelism.
- The sphere of *resonance* complements interpretation with the problem of the type and the degree of *influence over future paradigms*. The question arises why some genres of works—such as Haydn's model of the string quartet or the model of symphony as established by Beethoven—produce a resonance of endless duration, while other pieces sound hollow. Works of the avant-garde, happenings, place their bets on uniqueness and consciously *reject the past*.

2.2.3 The intertextual perspective

A view of a work in an *intertextual* perspective leads to the *issue* usually referred to as *music within music*. The remarkable inventiveness of composers in this respect has led to a variety of classifications. One of these identifies three types of the presence of music within music.

- In a *palimpsest* situation, the only new thing in the work is its new sound attire. The "primary", the earlier work, can be easily recognizable under its new instrumentation or intabulation, vocalization or troping.
- *Inspiration* of new music with music that has been brings, on the one hand, works based on cantus firmus, variations and fantasias, and, on the other, stylized or retroversive[1] music.
- *Encrustation* has become, especially since the 20th century, an attribute of music as symbolic speech. The possibilities here include quotation, allusion, reminiscence and also *quodlibet* and collage.

While one might not share the belief in the so-called "death of the author", who is now supposed to create *novum* only according to the principles and basing on *datum*, the intertextual era is a fact. The interpretation of the musical work that does not take into account the aspects and the procedures of intertextuality has lost all sense, at least since Mahler and Ives.

3. Specifying categories

Their discussion is another step in the process of integral interpretation. They are logically bound in a triad that includes three types of categories: (a) their function within the system, (b) their features of genre and (c) their belonging to a given style.

3.1 Function of the work

The archetypal primariness of the *function of the work* in this triadic structure can be accepted without question. Function has always determined the shape and the character of the work according to the requirements of place, time and circumstance. Odes, hymns and paeans to gods, songs praising a hero's victory, threnodies and elegies for his death all came to life under pressure from particular functions.

The repertoire and the hierarchy of the functions, dictated by the time and place within culture, were defined by theorists in ways that spoke volumes of the music of their era. Suffice it to cite the well-known list of 20 functions of the musical work compiled by Tinctoris, beginning with "praise God, chase away the devil" and ending in "cure the ill and induce love." It is a truth generally acknowledged that, since the mid-18th century, so-called highbrow music has abandoned specifying its functions, only settling for the one referred to as aesthetic. A return to the category of the work's function in its interpretation underlies attempts at adapting Jakobson's (1960) concept of functions of language. Seeing music as a language of tones has become the point of departure here. With this assumption, a given work can be described as performing one (or more) of the five functions: *expressive* (emotive), *conative* (appellative), *phatic*, *referential* or *poetic*.

3.2 Categories of genre

The consciousness of their presence and their differentiation has been with European culture since its very origins: the *Old* and the *New Testament*, the

Iliad and the *Odyssey*. They have survived until our times in their division into *lyrical* (hymn, ode, idyll, elegy), epic (novel, ballad, legend) and dramatic (tragedy, comedy). But they have also survived as objects of interest to the history of music. They have been rejected from contemporary theory of music—and that due to formalist tendencies. They have been deprived of their own generic identity and baselessly ascribed to different identities. They have been rechristened as *music forms* and, as such, they have been deprived of their primary attribute, their expressive-semantic character.

Most recently, with the appearance of narratological tendencies and methodologies and their ever-expanding scope, new and promising vistas have opened to the aspect of genre. Yet, curiously and strangely, scholarly interest has concentrated mainly on two of the three traditional types of creativity: the epic and the dramatic. The third, lyrical, seems to have become largely marginalized—and that despite the fact that it has played a particularly significant part in some historical phases, especially those of romantic persuasion.

Obviously, two musical genres have become the main carriers of the lyrical: instrumental miniatures and songs. A modest reconnaissance into the *Romantic love song* seems to suggest that the category of lyricism could be discussed in terms analogous to the categories of the epic and the dramatic, the main object of interest in narratology. Much like a succession of events serves as the point of departure for narratological interpretations, interpretations of lyrical genres could begin with a *timeless lyrical situation*.

Tests on a representative corpus of songs from a repertoire famously running into thousands of works in the genre have yielded some noteworthy regularities. The first of these was a repetitiveness of situations that can be seen as models. Secondly, these can be differentiated into two clearly discrete modes: the acts and the states. Act-like lyrical situations are usually characteristic in their dynamism and spontaneity, in their at times explosive impulsiveness. They are moments that come and go, often leaving a deep traumatic trace. In contrast, state lyrical situations tend to be dominated by static and reflexive moods; they seem suspended in time, or to exist beyond time.

Each of these nine model situations is associated, in a natural way, with a particular and *unique type of expression*. The degree of this naturalness—constantly coherent in character—may be checked thanks to the composers' custom of describing them with performance directions, or *didascalia*. It can also be verified by *reductio ad absurdum*: no composer would ever annotate a situation of first encounter or of confession of true love with the word "wistfulness" (*Wehmut*); nor, conversely, would he describe a moment of separation or loneliness as "fascination" or "euphoria".

The five state-like lyrical situations and the four act-like situations seem to exhaust the means of expression used by the Romantic love song. In terms of *thematic structure*, it ran within the speaker's suspension in *loneliness* or in *a relationship*; *distant* or *close* to the object of his love. N.B. this is a complex of categories that could be tested with a modified version of the Greimas Square (1966). I think however that the validity of such an interpretation should be verified by direct musical presentation of the nine lyrical situations that combine to create the syndrome of the Romantic love song:

- The state of *initial loneliness*, featuring the expression of *a sense of void*. A state of reflexion, expectation, of daydreaming. [Example: Schubert: *Nacht und Träume*]
- The moment of *first encounter* and its accompanying *fascination*. This category is much preferred not only by Schubert (*Schöne Müllerin*) or Schumann (*Im wunderschönen Monat Mai*). [Example: Glinka: *Ya pomnyu chudnoye mgnavenye*]
- The state of *first separation*, corresponding to an expression of *longing* (*An die ferne Geliebte*). This is a truly model situation, present in the song genre since the troubadours and constitutive for the *Sehnsuchtlieder* song type. [Example: Schubert: *Nur, wer die Sehnsucht kennt*]
- The moment of *full love disclosed*, manifested with spontaneity and *euphoria*. [Example: Schubert: *Dein ist mein Herz!]*
- The state of *ultimate closeness,* which is accompanied by a subdued and idyllic expression of emotional and spiritual union, *in delight and adoration* [Example: Schubert: *Du bist die Ruh*]
- The moment of *clash* as a reaction to love's betrayal, to dashed hope. It is associated with an expression of *disappointment*, featuring dynamism and explosiveness. [Example: Rossini: *Mi languerò tacendo*]
- The state of *secondary separation* as a result of the clash. It is realized in an expression of *wistfulness*, constitutive for songs described as *Wehmutslieder*. [Example: Brahms: *Immer leiser wird mein Schlummer*]
- The moment of *final rupture*, an irreversible act. The basic expressive category of this complaint is that of despair rather than rage. [Example: Schubert: *Der Doppelgänger*
- The state of *secondary*, or final, *loneliness*. This is an *experience of irretrievable loss*—rather than that of indefinite void—which results in a state of constant *melancholy.*[Example: Schubert: *Die Einsamkeit*]

Mieczysław Tomaszewski

3.3 Stylistic categories

Reading a work's stylistic category is one of the interpreter's canonical tasks, non-trivial yet necessary. All manner of stylistic elements coexist in each work, and they all deserve to be heard and identified. First, elements that belong to the style of the era and the tendency into which the work has been inscribed by the composer; also, the specific style of the genre that serves to express the work. This includes identifying and differentiating the *genotypic*, i.e. assimilated from tradition, from the *phenotypic*, or the composer's own and individual. Finally, to isolate elements of individual style—a unique idiom— and of the style of the correct phase of the composer's creative path. The discussed work's own idiom may also be a factor.

This is the repertoire of qualities that describe a work in stylistic detail. The most difficult task is to hear the dominating complex of these properties. Does our reception of a work allow us to hear the *voice* of the composer, of the genre, or merely of the era?

4. Axiological categories, or categories of value

A noteworthy essay by Ernst H. Gombrich (1993) poses a rhetorical question: "What good is there in a study that discovers neither meaning nor value?"

It is beyond any doubt that a reading of a work from an integral interpretative perspective must reach a point when it becomes necessary to test the work in a *domain of value*. Two aspects seem of particular import here: the type and the degree of the *perfection* of its composition and the type and the depth of sense that is conveyed by the work.

The aspect of *perfection* would become of particular significance in those moments of the history of music when the poetic or aesthetic function dominated everything else. Perfection as the goal of composing strategy varied from era to era: from the graceful to the fully sublime. We now witness trends and tendencies—ephemeral, let us hope—that see their aim in an escape from perfection into accidental form, into second-best. Also, the borderline between masterpieces, conventional works and kitsch tends to be in flux. An attempt at defining kitsch was once made by Dahlhaus (1967), sadly with few convincing results. In the present-day era of postmodernism, a work described so far as kitsch might actually function with a positive sign of value. Yet despite the various trends in the interpretation of work, it is still crucial to be able to tell if it represents subtlety, nobility and simplicity or vulgarity, crudeness and the chaos of excessive complication.

74

The aspect of the work's *sense* has united conceptions of various provenance, mostly because sense is understood in a variety of ways. In hermeneutic, exegetic and semiotic interpretations, it is usually described in terms of its significance and character. It functions within the work as a message of some sort, as *envoi*, overtone or moral. In autotelic interpretations, sense—understood as a self-referential context—is brought to the limit of its meaningfulness.

Understood in a purely musical way, it can point—as it does, for instance, in Schenkerian analysis—to an organic coherence and logic of individual composing decisions. In a broader humanist sense, the sense of the work carries and conveys—in tones—the artist's reaction to the universe and to life. This reaction can be of *deep* or *shallow* character, *open* or *covert*; its overtone *tragic* or *comic*, its attitude *trusting* or *skeptical*, *optimistic* or *pessimistic*, *serious* or *ironic*.

5. Fundamental categories

Two categories have played a particular and unique part for over 2,000 years of European culture: beauty and truth. They can be seen as fundamental for any work of art. Of course, in the Antique tradition, beauty and truth, together with goodness, were combined into the triad of transcendentals. The tradition behind them dates back to Plato and his *Phaedrus*. It is equally well known that the three concepts have often substituted for one another or have been brought together in *kalokagathia*, the unity of beauty and goodness. It is known, finally, that the two fundamental values, both truth and beauty, have been demoted in some aesthetic circles as unsuitable and inadequate, indeed as embarrassing, in times after the Holocaust. These views are confronted by the authority of creative talents. At the Congress of Independent Culture in Warsaw, on the very eve of the imposition of martial law in Poland, Witold Lutosławski (1999) said: "Beauty is the ultimate goal of art, much like truth is the ultimate goal of science."

He went on to say: "Yet much like one can find a particular kind of beauty in mathematics, astronomy and undoubtedly in many other sciences, there is, in art, the inevitable issue of truth."

Truth's presence in a work is not only not denied but quite emphatically claimed in statements by major authorities on composing and philosophy. According to Mahler, "Ich habe noch nie auch nur eine Note geschrieben habe, die nicht absolut wahr ist" (Floros 1977/1987). "Music is not to be decorative; it is to be true," said Schönberg (1911). Heidegger (1963) was even more extreme: "Dann ist die Kunst ein Werden und Geschehen der Wahrheit." A work's truth has been understood in a variety of ways: as authenticity, originality, appropriateness, accuracy, but also as naturalness, inner coherence and sincerity. For Lutosławski and for many other Polish artists whose fate it was to work in a country enslaved for half a century, this final phrase, "sincerity of artistic expression" was particularly significant. The interpreter of the time was constantly faced with the task of differentiating between works according to their character as representing authentic, rhetorical, hyperbolic or straightforwardly panegyric music—those were the days when cantatas were written to honor Stalin.

6. Complementary categories

No observation of the course of the history of culture, including music, can ignore the fact of an alternation of its character. Classically-minded eras saw a particular emphasis on what has been called here fundamental categories. Conversely, in romantically-minded times, the emphasis would shift from truth and beauty to what could best be termed complementary categories: *expression* and *fantasy*. Expression complemented and transformed absolute beauty in the expressive or into pure expression. Fantasy (also referred to as fiction) complemented and transformed truth that only served as a point of departure. In both cases the emphasis shifted from the objective to the subjective.

I think that a symbiosis of these four categories can be metaphorically denoted as a *tetraxis* that might serve as a framework for the course of the history of music. This history changed in character depending on which components of this system took over as the dominant functions: the fundamental or the complementary.

To see this in some detail:
- The *beauty* of a work of art is a fundamental and major *category* (and value); to quote Lutosławski (1999) again: "ultimate goal of *art*." There has been general agreement as to the type of its effect. Ever since Plato, "beauty *astounds and delights*." It has for its attributes clarity, lucidity, conformity to the principles of Antique and Classical nomos, harmony and proportion.
- *Expression* was subservient to the rules of *ethos*, adequate to the situation and to the function performed by the work: to euphorize or to lament. Thus beauty was to enchant just as expression was *to move and to stir*.
- *Truth*. It is an equally fundamental category of a work, yet one not directly ascribed to it in the first place; it is primarily significant in science and

philosophy. The principle of *adequatio rei et intellectu* has taken all sorts of forms in the history of music: from the Antique and Aristotelian imitation of nature to *all music that evokes,* in its similitude, *a reality beyond the work.*

- *Fantasy.* A category that complements and replaces truth in art as *Dichtung* that complements *Wahrheit.* The true is confronted with the fantastic ("fictional"), derived from imagination rather than from memory. Truth enlightens, explains, identifies, relates to the reality of things. Fantasy *departs from "the here and now,"* inspires, *liberates from immediate reality.*

7. Transcendent categories

There are situations when, faced with a work that has enchanted us or stirred us to the core, we are at a *loss for words.* We feel that the phenomenon we have encountered cannot be described in ordinary, down-to-earth language of any category. We are convinced that in order to come any closer we must attempt some special type of statement that would do justice to the peculiarity of the object of interpretation. More than just peculiarity: *a singularity transcending all barriers, triggering a consciousness of a contact with what seems to be inexpressible, indescribable, impalpable.* Surely, this only happens in confrontation with select works and extraordinary moments, for instance the striking simplicity of the chorale *Wenn muss ich einmal scheiden* in Bach's *St Matthew Passion,* the unfathomable darkness of the *Confutatis* in Mozart's *Requiem,* in the pensive and distant *Adagio* in Schubert's *Quintet in C major,* the epiphanic B major part in Chopin's *Fantasia in F minor,* the first phrase of the broken voice in Gustav Mahler's *Kindertotenlieder.* In all these—and many more—there *is a step beyond, a transgression of, the normal, the everyday, the conventional, the expected;* a momentarily revealed perspective of a different reality.

The aspect I touch upon here has not yet been discussed in any systematic way. What is more, in his *Aesthetic Meaning and Symbolic Message,* Carl Dahlhaus (1992) gives a warning against going in that direction; against attempts at "reaching in open language towards one that is hidden, which constantly eludes our grasp and yet calls for deciphering."

I am not going to go down that road, but I also do not intend to turn a deaf ear to phenomena that beg at least to be approached. To try and grasp the problem in formalized scientific discourse would be self-defeating. Yet it seems that there are languages in culture that might lessen this distance.

It seems that whatever is *par excellence "poetic"*—romantic, oneiric, stirring—in the music of Schubert, Chopin or Schumann can be rendered in the *language of metaphor.* In turn, the *language of rhetoric* would be relatively the most adequate choice for the music of the Bach era and for its *symbolic* qualities. In the words of H. H. Eggebrecht (1973), "due to its symbolic message, the music of Bach is inexhaustible in its aesthetic sense." Sacred music, in its use of the categories of sanctum, perfectum, numinosum or epifanicum, usually finds its explication in its own *confessive languages* fitting their transcendent reality.

What remains is the question of those moments of musical masterpieces that are called, at times, the *metaphysical moments of a work*. According to R. Ingarden, the manifestation, in a work, "of metaphysical qualities constitutes the apex and at the same time the ultimate depth of our life and of all that exists" (1960). It is unfortunate that he himself did not develop and complete this idea. So far, I think, Eero Tarasti (2005, 2009) has been the closest to approaching it, if from a somewhat different direction. Of the three narrative categories with which he interprets the music of Wagner, one is of *existential character*. This might make it possible to grasp the essence of music that seems impossible to grasp, to read and to name.

A couple of *tentative ideas* seem to naturally derive from the above-drafted panorama: a need for a shift in emphasis, for a vindication of certain areas of interpretation, for a change in position and style of utterance.

(1) In order to do justice to a work of music that is the subject of interpretation, it is necessary for the practice and theory of *music to shift the emphasis* from interpretation based *solely on the principles of the exact sciences* (such as mathematics and physics) to interpretation that *also relates to humanist and artistic principles*. T. Wiesengrund-Adorno (1992) warned that "treating music as 'tönend bewegte Form' usually ends in blind stimuli or in the trivial fact of ordered musical material, devoid of any association between aesthetic form and the non-aesthetic 'something' that becomes transformed into aesthetic form."

(2) A *shift of emphasis* is also necessary *from the sphere of musical linguistics into that of musical poetics*; this, in fact, is already underway, if at a slow pace. Among other reasons, this is necessary so that the question of a work's *artistry* can become discernible in an act of interpretation. R. Jakobson (1960) reminds us that "the issue of what it is that transforms a linguistic message into a work of art is the subject of poetics." A discussion of a work in its aspects limited to musical linguistics ignores the most interesting and the most significant elements of the work—the moment when *ability* transmogrifies into *creativity*, *téchne* into *poiesis*.

(3) The goal described here requires particular *acts of vindication*, usually tantamount to restoring aspects that have been removed or marginalized in the theory of music due to tendencies towards scientist reductionism. This mainly

denotes introducing, into theoretical studies and analytic-interpretational practice, the problems of *expression and genre,* and of all that is referred to as *the work's organic context* spanning from its origins to its resonance.

(4) A change in the *style of utterance*, in the way a work's interpretation is worded, would be highly desirable. This is connected with another question: who is the addressee of interpretations of works of art? Two main tendencies seem to coexist nowadays, aimed at different audiences: the formalized type that does not go beyond the limits of strictly professional circles, and the essayist type not far removed from journalism. It is to be hoped that the shift of emphasis and the acts of vindication themselves might be enough to lessen the distance between them; that essays acquire a sounder scholarly basis, and that scholarly papers become less arcane and more prone to "reading" the qualities and values, the meaning and the sense carried by the work—rather than dwelling in the self-referential circle of interpretational autotelism.

Finally, it seems important that the reader may share, apart from the knowledge of the work derived from its integral reading, some of the delight and the emotion triggered in the interpreter by his close encounter with the work.

Notes

[1]   A new term created for the needs of music "which turns towards the past" to mimic a style of the past. It differs from epigonism with temporal distance: epigonism refers to imitating a style directly after it has passed, whereas retroversity—a style that passed, for instance, 100 years ago.

References

Adler, G. (1916). *Gustav Mahler.* Leipzig-Wien.

Adorno, Th. W. (1992). *Quasi una fantasia. Essays on modern music.* New York: Verso.

Beethoven, L. van. (1812). Brief an A. von Kotzebue, 28. I.1812.

Beethoven, L. van. (1907). *Briefwechsel. Gesamtausgabe.* Bd. IV Nr 1196. In H. Deiters (Ed.). Leipzig: Breitkopf und Härtel.

Braudel, F. (1971). *Historia i trwanie. (L'histoire de la langue durée.)* Warszawa: "Czytelnik".

Dahlhaus, C. (1967). Über musikalischen Kitsch. In C. Dahlhaus (Ed.). *Studien zur Trivial-musik des 19. Jahrhunderts* (pp. 53-61). Regensburg: Gustav Bosse Verlag.

Dahlhaus, C and Eggebrecht, H.H. (1992). Estetyczne znaczenie i symboliczne przesłanie. *Co to jest muzyka ? (Was ist Musik,* Wilhelmshafen 1985). Warszawa: Państwowy Instytut Wydawniczy.

Mieczysław Tomaszewski

Eggebrecht, H. H. (1973). Uwagi o metodzie analizy muzycznej. *Res facta* 7.

Floros, C. (1987). *Gustav Mahler, I. Die geistige Welt Gustav Mahlers in systematischer Darstellung.* Wiesbaden: Breitkopf & Härtel. (Original work published 1977).

Floros, C. (1989). *Musik als Botschaft.* Wiesbaden: Breitkopf & Härtel.

Floros, C. (1992). *Alban Berg. Musik als Autobiographie.* Wiesbaden, Leipzig, Paris: Breitkopf & Härtel.

Gombrich, E. H. (1993) Patrzeć w skupieniu: rzut oka na sztuki I nauki humanistyczne. "Znak" No 462, p. 23.

Grabócz, M. (2009 a). Stratégies narratives des "épopées philosophiques" de l'ère romantique dans l'œuvre pianistique de Franz Liszt. *Musique, narrativité, signification.* Paris: L'Harmattan.

Grabócz, M. (2009 b). "Topos et dramaturgie": analyse des signifiés et de la stratégie expressive dans deux mouvements symphoniques de Béla Bartók. *Musique, narrativité, signification.* Paris: L'Harmattan.

Grabócz, M. (2009 c). L'influence du modèle épique sur la renaissance de la forme énumérative dans les œuvres pour piano de Liszt. *Musique, narrativité, signification.* Paris: L'Harmattan.

Greimas, A. (1966). *Sémantique structurale.* Paris: Larousse.

Hatten, R. (1994). *Musical meaning in Beethoven.* Bloomington and Indianapolis: Indiana University Press.

Hatten, R. (2004). *Interpreting musical gestures, topics and tropes: Mozart, Beethoven, Schubert.* Bloomington and Indianapolis: Indiana University Press.

Heidegger, M. (1963). *Holzwege.* Frankfurt: Klosterman.

Huber, K., (1953). *Musikaesthetik.* In O. Ursprung (Ed.), Ettal: Buch-Kunstverlag.

Ingarden, R. (1960). *O dziele literackim.* Warszawa: Państwowe Wydawnictwo Naukowe.

Ingarden, R. (1973). *Utwór muzyczny i sprawa jego tożsamości.* Kraków: Polskie Wydawnictwo Muzyczne.

Jakobson, R. (1960). Poetyka w świetle językoznawstwa. *Pamiętnik Literacki, 2.*

Kerman, J. (1994). Jak dotarliśmy do analizy i jak z niej wybrnąć. *Res facta nova 1*(10).

Lutosławski, W. (1999). Wokół zagadnienia prawdy w dziele sztuki. In D. Gwizdalanka and K. Meyer (Eds.). *Postscriptum.* Warszawa: Fundacja Zeszytów Literackich.

Schönberg, A. (1911). Probleme des Kunstunterrichts. *Musicalisches Taschenbuch, II.* Wien.

Tarasti, E. (1979). *Myth and music. A semiotic approach to the aesthetics of myth in music, especially that of Wagner, Sibelius and Stravinsky.* Berlin & New York: Mouton de Gruyter.

Tarasti, E. (1985). Zu einer Narratologie Chopins. *Musik-Konzepte Nr 45: Chopin.* München: Text + Kritik.

Tarasti, E. (1995). A narrative grammar of Chopin G Minor Ballade. *Chopin Studies, 5.* Warszawa: Instytut im. Fryderyka Chopina.

Tarasti, E. (2005). Existential and transcendental analysis of music. *Studi musicali, 34*(2), 223-266.

Tarasti, E. (2009). *Fondaments de la sémiotique existentielle.* Paris: L'Harmattan.

Tarasti, E. (2012). "...ein leiser Ton gezogen..." Robert Schumann's Fantasie in C major (op. 17) in the light of existential semiotics. *Semiotics of classical music. How Mozart, Brahms and Wagner talk to us.* Mouton: De Gruyter.

Tomaszewski, M. (2003 a). La musique de Chopin dans la perspective de la méthode d'interpretation dite intégrale. In A. Szklener (Ed.). *Analytical perspectives on the music of Chopin* (pp. 57-77).Warszawa: Narodowy Instytut Fryderyka Chopina.

Tomaszewski, M. (2003 b). Autour du phénomène de la musique de Chopin. De la provenance à la résonance. I. Poniatowska; & Z. Chechlińska (Eds.). *Chopin and his Work in the Context of Culture*. Kraków: Musica iagellonica.

Tomaszewski, M. (2003 c). Zu den Knotenpunkten in Leben eines Künstlers. Erkenntnis. M. Tomaszewski & M. Chrenkoff (Eds.). *Beethoven 2. Studien und Interpretationen* (pp. 301-311). Kraków: Akademia Muzyczna.

Tomaszewski, M. (2006 a). Beethoven: Inspirationen, Kontext, Resonanz. In M. Tomaszewski & M. Chrenkoff (Eds.). *Beethoven 3. Studien und Interpretationen* (pp. 181-188). Kraków: Akademia Muzyczna.

Tomaszewski, M. (2006 b). The musical work within the space of culture. In E. Tarasti (Ed.). *Music and the Arts. Preceedings from ICMS 7* (pp. 59-75). Imatra: International Semiotics Institute.

Tomaszewski, M. (2010). Das Musikwerk in der intertextuellen Perspektive. Von der Inspiration bis zur Resonanz. L. Navickaitė-Martinelli (Ed.). *Before and After Music. Preceedings from the 10th ICMS* (pp. 93-105). Vilnius: Lithuanian Academy of Music and Theatre.

La musique au second degré: on Gérard Genette's Theory of Transtextuality and its Musical Relevance

Paulo F. de Castro

CESEM/Departamento de Ciências Musicais
FCSH – Universidade Nova de Lisboa (Portugal)

The concept of intertextuality was originally developed in the context of poststructuralist literary theory by Julia Kristeva, who introduced the term (ca. 1966) in the wake of her engagement with Mikhail Bakhtin's notion of dialogism. At around the same time, in *L'archéologie du savoir*, Michel Foucault was writing about the open borders of the book and the way every book is caught up in a system of references to other books (or texts), comparing it to a node within a network (Foucault, 1969, p. 34). The term *intertextuality*, quickly seized upon and given wide currency by Roland Barthes among other French intellectuals and theorists, is at present usually taken to refer to the copresence of different texts within a(ny) given text, that is to say, to the notion that "every text takes shape as a mosaic of citations," that "every text is the absorption and transformation of another text" (Kristeva, 1969, p. 146).[1] Accordingly, in the words of Jonathan Culler, "a work can only be read in connection with or against other texts, which provide a grid through which it is read and structured by establishing expectations which enable one to pick out salient features and give them a structure" (Culler, 1975, p. 139).[2] Generally speaking, the interest aroused by intertextuality reflects a widespread tendency in literary and cultural studies to move away from the inherited notion of the text—or the work of art—as a unitary, self-contained and, in a strong sense, autonomous and original object, toward a view that emphasizes the relational nature of all cultural productions. This tendency in turn accords with the idea that semiosis never emerges from a void: the as-yet-unsaid cannot help but emerge from the already-said (cf. Eco, 1994, p. 319).

Since the 1970s, the notion of intertextuality has been appropriated (if not trivialized) by many other disciplines, including of course musicology. Even at the level of an introductory text, David Beard and Kenneth Gloag (2005, pp. 95-96), for instance, have boldly asserted: "The act of reading or, in the context of music, listening, involves tracing echoes and reflections of other texts. Therefore, all music can in some sense be seen and heard as intertextual," and they go on to suggest that "in the context of twentieth-century music, the inherent intertextuality of music has been enlarged upon as a compositional practice." Whether this is especially true of 20th-century music as opposed to that of other eras would itself be a matter for debate, but I shall not be pursuing this argument in the present essay.

In spite of its ubiquity in musicological discourse, however, it would seem that the notion has not received all the attention it requires from a theoretical and methodological point of view, and the very fact of the term's dissemination remains deceptive, as many authors seem to use it simply as a more fashionable alternative to traditional notions of influence, borrowing, or source-study. Tellingly, we still lack anything like a comprehensive overview of musical intertextuality in the current literature. In this essay, I shall focus on a discussion of some of the categories proposed by French theorist Gérard Genette and their potential musical relevance, with a view to providing some conceptual and terminological clarification of the notion of intertextuality in its possible application to musical objects.

1. Transtextuality according to Genette

In his book *Palimpsestes. La littérature au second degré* (1982), Genette sought to redefine the object of poetics as the study of what he chose to call *transtextuality*, understood as the network of relations, both concealed and explicit, that may exist between a text and other texts, thus subsuming Kristeva's original concept of intertextuality under a broader category. Genette himself defines transtextuality as "the textual transcendence of the text" (Genette, 1982, p. 7), thus—in my reading at least—pointing toward the much-needed deconstruction of the conventional opposition between the *inside* and the *outside* of the text (the intra- and the extramusical, or the introversive and the extroversive semiotics, to use the terminology introduced by the musicologist Kofi Agawu; see Agawu, 1991). Because reference to Genette's ideas is scant in the available musicological literature, I shall briefly survey some of the fundamental tenets of his theory (thus foregrounding a terminology first devised in the field of literature, but not necessarily restricted to literary objects), before I consider some of their possible musical applications. It will be immediately obvious, however, that the majority of Genette's concepts are easily transposed to the musical domain.

Genette identifies five types of transtextual relationships:

- Somewhat confusingly, the first category is termed *intertextuality* (*stricto sensu*), defined as "a relation of copresence between two or among several texts", and signaled, in his view, by the actual (literal) presence of a text within another text (Genette, 1982, p. 8)—a definition that accords well with the Bakhtinian roots of the concept, linked to the presence of different voices within a novel (and by extension, within any kind of text). In the particular sense Genette gives to the term, the practice of intertextuality encompasses what would more commonly be called citation (quotation), plagiarism and allusion (to which one might like to add collage techniques, as exemplified, in music, by certain works of Charles Ives, Luciano Berio, Bernd Alois Zimmermann or Heiner Goebbels; but I am jumping ahead).[3]
- The second category, *paratextuality*, is defined as the frame of a text, consisting of titles, subtitles, chapter headings, prefaces, forewords, footnotes, epigraphs, blurbs, illustrations, etc., which lie on the threshold of the text (a transitional zone without fixed boundaries), aiming to control, or at least to affect, the reader's reception (Genette, 1982, p. 10); the notion of paratext was to become the object of a separate study by Genette, published under the title *Seuils* (*Thresholds*) in 1987.
- The third category is that of the commentary proper, discussion, or criticism, that is to say, of all kinds of text "about" other texts, which Genette places under the rubric *metatextuality* (Genette, 1982, p. 11).
- The fourth category, which makes up the bulk of *Palimpsestes*, is labeled *hypertextuality*, which he defines (somewhat perfunctorily, it must be said) as "a relationship between a text B (which I shall call the *hypertext*) and a pre-existent text A (which I shall obviously call the *hypotext*) upon which it is grafted in a manner that is not that of commentary"; more generally, he adds, hypertextuality is predicated on the principle of transformation (either direct or indirect, in which case he prefers the term "imitation"), as opposed to citation or commentary (Genette, 1982, pp. 13 and 16).
- Finally, he labels *architextuality* the realm of those overarching categories governing a reader's expectations: types and topics of discourse, modes of enunciation, canonic genres, etc. (Genette, 1982, pp. 7 and 12). The notion had previously been expounded in his own *Introduction à*

l'architexte, which deals mainly with the theory of literary genre (1979; also Genette, 2004).

2. The hypertextual principle

Genette's concept of hypertextuality could simply be regarded as a personal variant of the more familiar intertextuality, but, as he takes pains to explain, his approach differs from that of other theorists in that, he claims, they have tended to focus on the "semantic-stylistic microstructures", placing themselves at the level of the sentence, the detail, or the short section of the text, whereas his main interest lies in the work considered as a structural whole (Genette, 1982, p. 9).[4] His perspective is certainly open to discussion in this regard, because it tends to overstate the unitary, homogeneous character of the hypertextual principle operating within a work as a whole; whereas many texts—probably the majority—might best be described as hybrid in this regard, illustrating not just one, but several strands of hyper- (or trans-)textuality. Genette's main concern is with the intended, explicit and self-conscious interrelation among texts, whose production obviously depends to a large extent on authorial intent, and whose recognition demands a considerable degree of competence on the reader's part. Accordingly, one might claim that hypertextuality belongs at least as much to the esthesic as to the poietic plane (if not more). Although Jean Molino's distinction is not particularly relevant to Genette's approach (who, curiously enough, remains quite suspicious of a reader-oriented hermeneutics; cf. Genette, 1982, p. 19), this aspect of the question would be worth pursuing, perhaps in connection with the concept of *interpretive communities* and meaning as reader-response, as developed by Fish (1980). Hypertextuality, or the *literature in the second degree*, as the author of *Palimpsestes* calls it, presents us with an instance of creative *bricolage*, in the sense given to the word by Lévi-Strauss (or, as we might prefer to say, a poetics of appropriation and recycling), inviting in turn a form of relational reading—reading two or more texts in relation to one another: hence the metaphor of the palimpsest, that is, a text superimposed upon another that it does not entirely conceal.[5] Genette's prospective mapping of hypertextuality constitutes an example of the practice he called *open structuralism* (or pragmatic poetics) (Genette, 1982, pp. 556-57), that is to say, "a poetics which gives up on the idea of establishing a stable, ahistorical, irrefutable map or division of literary elements, but which instead studies the relationships (sometimes fluid, never unchanging) which link the text with the architextual network out of which it produces its meaning" (Allen, 2000, p. 100). An obvious taste for the element of play inherent in some forms of hypertextuality leads him to focus primarily on those relationships in which transformation arises from an ironic, satirical or parodical intention,[6] with the corollary that other hypertextual operations tend to remain underexplored in his work, making it necessary to turn elsewhere for inspiration.[7] Genette's basic categories (1982, p. 45) are summarized in table 1:

regime *relation*	ludic	satirical	serious
transformation	parody	travesty	transposition
imitation	pastiche	caricature	forgery[8]

TABLE I. Genette's basic hypertextual categories

The dotted lines in the chart indicate the porous nature of the vertical divisions. Genette is in fact well aware of the oversimplification entailed in the symmetrical precision of his scheme, going as far as to suggest an alternative form of presentation that accommodates three further moods, namely the ironic, the humorous and the polemical, the latter standing for something that could perhaps be described as a negative (or antithetical) imitation of a model (personally, I would advocate the rearrangement of some of the categories in Genette's diagram, as a potentially more satisfying gradation; see figure 1) (Genette, 1982, p. 46).

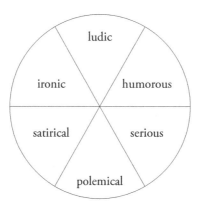

FIGURE I. Alternative presentation of Genette's categories

My suggestion:

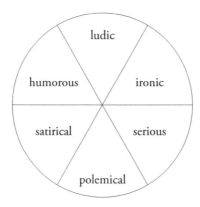

By contrast, Genette insists on the stricter horizontal distinction between the operations he calls *transformation* and *imitation*, respectively (even though he admits the possibility of mixed practices in this area as well). Here, nonetheless, an important objection arises: the distinction between transformation and imitation—or even quotation—remains largely dependent on one's familiarity with a particular hypotext, which may or may not be disclosed by the author, thus implicitly underscoring the prominent role of the reader— or the listener—in the complex economy of hypertextuality.[9] A further distinction is that between the *allographic* and the *autographic* nature of the hypertext, allowing Genette to take into account the peculiar issues involved in the reworking of an author's own (hypo)text, in turn opening up a wide area of genetic criticism (Genette, 1982, p. 73). For those who might find Genette's taxonomic enterprise over-systematic, it is worth quoting one of his refreshingly self-deflationary remarks: 'What follows is, in a sense, nothing but a long commentary on this chart, having as its main effect, I hope, not to justify it, but to blur it, to dissolve it, and ultimately, to erase it' (Genette, 1982, p. 44). The same principle clearly applies to his five basic transtextual categories; he is keen to point out the multiple ways in which those categories tend to overlap or remain codependent (Genette, 1982, pp. 16-17). They should be regarded, first and foremost, as heuristic tools, whose ultimate value can only be gauged in concrete analytic and interpretative situations.

Before we contemplate some of the possible musical applications of Genette's theory, we must forestall the predictable objection that his categories have been devised from within a medium essentially foreign to music, and that music's own semiotic regime should not be equated with a verbal one (as the frustrations arising from a linguistically-oriented music semiotics have made abundantly plain in the past). In particular, the application of the very concept of the *text* to a non-verbal object may cause some discomfort in an age increasingly suspicious (and on occasion, justifiably so) of most text-centric—that is, score-centric—approaches to music. This objection, however, seems to me beside the point (even though Genette himself remains conservative in this regard), not only because the notion of the text here at stake clearly extends beyond the purview of the *written* text (one can easily conceive of transtextuality within an oral tradition, for instance; in fact, one could claim that transtextuality in general is itself constitutive of any definition of tradition), but mainly because the literary uses of the word *text* themselves operate on a metaphorical level that has never been the exclusive province of literature, or even of language: the word, after all, derives from the Latin *textus* (and the verb *texere*: to weave), thus pointing us back to the image of the network, or the fabric (the "textile"), rather than the inscription. From this perspective (itself not unrelated to Clifford Geertz's anthropological paradigm of "culture as text"), music certainly cannot be regarded as being metaphorically less related to texture (a texture made up of many syntactic and semantic threads) than a verbal, or—why not?—a visual, a gestural, a social text. The conceptual figure of the text has, in my view, the additional advantage of emphasizing the complex, multi-layered nature of cultural practices, even as it refocuses attention away from a reductionist construction of meaning based on the atomistic model of the sign. As Umberto Eco, among others, noted long ago, most so-called signs are in fact best understood as texts; more often than not, even a single signifier conveys multiple interwoven strands of content (Eco, 1994, p. 86).

3. Musical applications

Of Genette's five transtextual categories, two—metatextuality and paratextuality—seem to me to be necessarily transmedial in nature; the first owing, perhaps, to the principle, noted by linguist Émile Benveniste, among others, that, for better or worse, language tends to be acknowledged as a privileged interpretant of all semiotic systems (Benveniste, 1974, p. 61); the second, because even in the case of music the paratext tends to assume a verbal (or possibly, a visual), rather than a musical, form. This is not to say that these two categories are any less relevant musically. Quite the opposite: the whole issue of paratextuality, in particular (concerning the status of titles, dedications, prefaces, performing instructions, programs, etc.), seems to me to be crying out for systematic investigation. It seems undeniable that the role of paratext remains poorly understood in musicology, an unfortunate situation given its pivotal role in providing a focus for musical signification, much as titles provide visual images with a semantic anchoring (*ancrage*), as suggested by Roland Barthes in a well-known essay (*Rhétorique de l'image*, 1964; in Barthes, 1982, p. 31). At stake is simply the unavoidably pivotal role of linguistic communication within both kinds of transmedial relationship. One particular situation that is hardly envisioned by Genette, however, arises from the interaction of music and verbal texts in vocal repertoires, prompting the question of whether this kind of symbiotic relationship between two media should require a separate treatment as *the* transtextual (or rather, transmedial) relation par excellence, or whether it might be subsumed under the category of paratextuality—in which case I would propose the designation *embedded paratext* or, if both texts' reciprocal autonomy can be said to prevail, *reversible* or *dialectical paratext*. *Mutatis mutandis*, the same would of course apply to the counterpoint of music and movement in dance and other forms of bodily performance, of music and image in cinema, etc. These are complex intermedial issues, demanding specific and detailed analysis, which lies beyond the scope of this essay.

Meanwhile, we are left with the three remaining categories. Of these, the notion of musical architextuality could be said to encompass the dimensions of genre, form, stylistic and rhetorical typologies, as well as generalized compositional techniques and models, as reflected in a particular musical text, or body of texts. Lastly, musical intertextuality and hypertextuality typically concern the processes through which a concrete musical text enters into a relationship with other concrete musical texts, either in the form of quotation, plagiarism or allusion, at the microstructural level (i.e., intertextuality proper, according to Genette), or in terms of the transformational or imitative relationships to another text, at the macrostructural level (i.e., hypertextuality). Naturally, only a thorough interpretation of individual cases may help determine the degree of interweaving and crossover among different categories. In my own view, as far as musical hypertextuality is concerned, Genette's distinction between the humorous and the serious moods tends to appear far less clear-cut (and perhaps less helpful) than one might be led to expect: is Stravinsky's *Pulcinella* a ludic, a satirical or a serious parody of Pergolesi (or pseudo-Pergolesi)? Is the second movement of Ravel's Violin Sonata a playful or a serious pastiche of the blues? And where in the chart would Mahler's *Bruder-Martin* movement from his 1st Symphony fit, in its uneasy mixture of parody and tragedy? More generally, is modal ambivalence more typical of music than, say, of literature? (Needless to say, performers, through their interpretative choices, can inflect our perception of hypertextual moods in decisive ways.) Maybe the crucial opposition in this respect would simply be that between parody (of a work, or a series of works) and pastiche (of a style). But ultimately, as structuralism recedes into historical perspective, our interest tends to turn away from rigid taxonomies and ideal types toward hybrid forms and perhaps the recognition of the "transitional" nature of most, if not all, hypertextual operations. Still, a basic conceptual equipment of some kind will remain necessary if the study of transtextuality is to move beyond the level of facile generalities. Personally, I would have welcomed a discussion by Genette of distance-enacting strategies, or perhaps an outline of a theory of creative anachronism, which seems integral to many transtextual practices (as in certain forms of so-called neoclassicism): in short, the varying ways in which a composer may choose to achieve the defamiliarization of his/her hypotext, while at the same time underscoring its identity. At any rate, towards the book's conclusion, Genette cites music as a promising field for hypertextual studies, going so far as to suggest that "in music, the possibilities of transformation are without doubt far greater than in painting and certainly, than in literature," owing, as he puts it, to music's freedom from the constraints of linearity (Genette, 1982, p. 539). In his view, transformation is the very soul of composition (not just in the classical mainstream, but also in jazz or contemporary music), and he cites parody, transcription, arrangement, transposition, variation, paraphrase and contamination among typical musical hypertextual procedures (to which, on a contemporary note, one might add the practices of sampling and remixing in rap, hip-hop and various forms of techno); again, the allographic/autographic distinction would apply. Musical imitation too (as distinct from the compositional practice normally understood by the term, which is itself a form of transformation; but including certain varieties of the homage piece and the completion of a composer's unfinished work by another) offers the musicologist a limitless field of exploration: as limitless, probably, as the history of music itself, as one of the most powerful means to convey and negotiate musical meaning.

Genette's own treatment of the issue of musical hypertextuality remains sketchy, however, and musicologists have yet to take up the challenge of developing and complexifying the suggestions offered in those few pages of *Palimpsestes*. Some musical illustrations might be useful at this point, if only in order to remind ourselves that transtextuality may serve vastly different purposes in different contexts.

Examples of intertextuality, narrowly understood, come readily to mind, and these include autographic, or self-quotation, as exemplified by the snatch of Figaro's Aria *Non più andrai* in the Finale of Mozart's *Don Giovanni* (1787) (a kind of in-joke for the discerning spectator). As regards allographic quotation, a particularly intriguing example is prompted by the use of Bach's chorale *Es ist genug* in the concluding Adagio from Alban Berg's Violin Concerto (1935) (whose source melody, incidentally, stems from a third composer, thus—probably unwittingly—emphasizing the continuity of a tradition within a modernist context, and making this a rather intricate case of transtextuality).[10] The quotation's *raison d'être* obviously lies in its role as part of the peroration on the theme of death and transfiguration that forms the symbolic core of the Concerto; the quotation, however (which itself emerges as if by transformation out of the last segment of the work's 12-note row), in turn becomes the focus of a transformational process, thus tending to blur the distinction between quotation and elaboration, inter- and hypertextuality. The quotation of another famous chorale, Luther's *Ein' feste Burg*, once used by Mendelssohn in his '*Reformation*' Symphony (1832) as a proud emblem of the Protestant faith, serves a virtually antithetic purpose in the second piece, *Lent. Sombre*, from Debussy's *En blanc et noir*, for two pianos (1915), in which the chorale, marked "lourd" (heavy) alludes, now in polemical mood, to the German aggressor, in a piece colored by the tense atmosphere of the war years. In other chorale-inspired works, such as César Franck's *Prélude, Choral et Fugue* (1884), Stravinsky's *Histoire du soldat* (1918) or Erik Satie's *Choses vues à droite et à gauche* ("Choral hypocrite") (1914)—among other pieces in the same vein in Satie's œuvre—the chorales can no longer be considered as quotations (although allusions to *Ein' feste Burg* could be argued for in all three examples): together, they illustrate a special category, closely related to imitation, that might perhaps be described as "imaginary quotation". As such, those examples demonstrate the use of the chorale as an easily recognizable musical style, doing service as a veritable topic (the Franck in a highly serious, the Stravinsky in a relatively playful, the Satie in the composer's very own "hypocritical" mood). The discussion of musical topics should obviously take up a prominent place within any general theory of transtextuality, which in Genettian terms should probably be ascribed to the architextual plane. In passing, we may observe how quotation, near-quotation or imaginary quotation all appear to fall roughly under the same functional categories as the hypertext itself, a point also left unexplored by Genette.

4. A summary and a starting point

As to the diverse forms of musical hypertextuality, all I can offer in the space available is the outline of an attempt to fill out Genette's chart with musical examples that might be deemed illustrative of each particular hypertextual category, in order to test the practical musical validity of Genette's taxonomies. Table 2 illustrates the kind of exercise I have in mind:[11]

regime / relation	ludic	satirical	serious
transformation	parody	travesty	transposition
	Offenbach, *La belle Hélène*, "Trio patriotique" [→ Rossini, *Guillaume Tell*]	Berlioz, *Symphonie fantastique*, "Songe d'une nuit du Sabbat" [→ Dies irae]	Bizet, *Carmen*, "Habanera" [→ Sebastián Iradier, *El arreglito*]
	Milhaud, *Le bœuf sur le toit* [→ Brazilian music]	Satie, *Sonatine bureaucratique* [→ Clementi]	Liszt's and Busoni's paraphrases and transcriptions
	Stravinsky, *Pulcinella* [→ Pergolesi, etc.] ...	Fauré/Messager, *Souvenirs de Bayreuth* [→ Wagner, *Ring*] ...	Tchaikovsky, *Mozartiana* ...
imitation	pastiche	caricature	forgery
	Richard Strauss, *Der Rosenkavalier*, the Italian singer's Aria [→ Italian opera]	Berlioz, "Amen" from *La damnation de Faust* [→ church music]	"Adagio of Albinoni" Brahms, "In stiller Nacht" [→ *Volkslied*]
	Hindemith, *Neues vom Tage*, "Duett-Kitsch" [→ Wagner]	Offenbach, *La belle Hélène*, "Tyrolienne avec Chœur" [→ operatic finale]	Prokofiev, *Classical Symphony*
	Kurt Weill, "Alabama Song" [→ American song] ...	Koechlin, *Les Bandar-log* [→ "modern music"] ...	Ravel, Sonata for violin and piano, 2nd movement [→ *blues*] ...

TABLE 2. A chart of musical hypertextuality

Such a chart (which of course can be added to at will) should be regarded as more than just a trivial exercise in pigeonholing. Hopefully, it should provide the starting point for an extended discussion of each individual case, taking into account its irreducible particularity. Concurrently, it should provide a suitable context for a thorough assessment of the purpose and scope of hypertextual operations in general.

To sum up, it seems reasonable to expect the study of hypertextuality to yield deeper insights into the mechanisms of creative influence, a notion that, although widespread in musicological parlance, tends to remain excessively vague in its application. The concept of hypertextuality should widen our perspectives on so-called *Wirkungsgeschichte*, orienting our vision toward the ways in which the history of music is built upon a never-ending dialog among composers, works and styles. Moreover, the study of hypertextual relations should add to our understanding of music signification in general, by refocusing attention away from the isolated masterpiece and helping to recover something of the ecology of musical phenomena, without which the music of the past may risk becoming dangerously "pure"—that is to say, too remote from our experience as listeners. Finally, by uncovering the many layers of accumulated meaning in a musical piece, hypertextuality should make palpable some of the fundamental processes through which new music "grows" out of pre-existing music, thus allowing us to realize how meaning and structure are created, forgotten and recreated in an endless process in which we, in our role as listeners, performers, critics, historians and analysts, are ourselves active players. Maybe a whole branch of music analysis could be envisioned by focusing on a given work's hypotexts and systematically charting their transformations. At any rate, as one begins to develop a feeling for transtextual relations, one quickly becomes aware that musical works talk to one another all the time, and this realization undoubtedly adds a new dimension to one's understanding and enjoyment of music. It is to be hoped that the path opened by Gérard Genette will inspire musicologists to explore further a crucial but far from well-researched field of study.

Notes

1   All translations in the present essay are the author's.

2   Cf. also Michael L. Klein's informal definition of intertextuality: "That constellation of texts speaking both with us and among themselves" (Klein, 2005, p. ix).

3   On the problematics of quotation, cf. Compagnon (1979).

4   Genette includes Harold Bloom's study of the mechanisms of influence and creative misreading ("strong poets make [poetic] history by misreading one another, so as to clear imaginative space for themselves": Bloom, 1997, p. 5) in the category of intertextual relations *stricto sensu*, which seems arguable (Genette, 1982, p. 9). Incidentally, Bloom's approach is entirely governed by an agonistic ("Oedipal") perspective on influence, which has little in common with Genette's own treatment of the subject.

5   The term *hypertext* has acquired a new layer of signification in the era of electronic media, where it designates the means to access multiple texts from any point of a given text through a device known as the *hyperlink*. Although this usage does not exactly agree with Genette's conceptualization of hypertextuality, it has certainly reinforced our perception of texts as semantic networks.

6   One should bear in mind that Genette reserves the term parody for one particular type of hypertextual practice, consisting, to put it schematically, in the association of a "low" object and a "high" style, as opposed to the burlesque travesty, which does the opposite.

7   The musicologist Martha Hyde, for instance, herself drawing on the work of literary theorist Thomas Greene, has explored some of the relevant issues concerning "serious" imitation (or what she calls "metamorphic anachronism"), suggesting four main modes of intertextual operation (which, incidentally, she mainly discusses in the context of 20th-century music): the reverential, the eclectic, the heuristic and the dialectical (see Hyde, 1996). Curiously, Hyde tends to dismiss parody and humorous imitative modes in general, so that her categories (or rather Greene's) may serve as a useful complement to Genette's.

8   Genette's term is *forgerie* (an archaic French word, taken in the sense of "serious pastiche"), which could only be adequately rendered as "forgery" if the connotations of fraudulent imitation might be erased from the English word.

9   Consider Stravinsky's use of folk material in the *Rite of Spring* as a demonstrable hypertextual relation in spite of the composer's somewhat paradoxical efforts to conceal it (perhaps explained by his efforts in later life to present the work's compositional process as a quasi-transcendent "revelation").

10   The original melody (used as the concluding chorale of the Cantata *O Ewigkeit, du Donnerwort*, BWV 60, 1723) is by Johann Rudolf Ahle (1625-1673), one of Bach's predecessors as organist at Sankt Blasius in Mühlhausen. Alban Berg apparently took the chorale from the volume *60 Choralgesänge von Joh. Seb. Bach*, edited by H. Roth (Munich, 1920).

11   My examples come mainly from 19th- and 20th-century art music, but examples from any other historical period or repertoire could of course be envisioned—such as medieval pieces based on pre-existing material, 16th-century parody masses, Baroque choral-preludes or traditional folksongs, among any number of possible examples.

References

Agawu, V. K. (1991). *Playing with signs. A semiotic interpretation of classic music.* Princeton: Princeton University Press.

Allen, G. (2000). *Intertextuality.* London: Routledge.

Barthes, R. (1982). *L'obvie et l'obtus. Essais critiques III.* Paris: Seuil.

Beard, D. & Gloag, K. (2005). *Musicology: The Key Concepts.* London: Routledge.

Benveniste, E. (1974). *Problèmes de linguistique générale* II. Paris: Gallimard.

Bloom, H. (1997). *The anxiety of influence. A theory of poetry* (2nd ed.). New York: Oxford University Press.

Compagnon, A. (1979). *La seconde main ou le travail de la citation.* Paris: Seuil.

Culler, J. (1975). *Structuralist poetics: structuralism, linguistics and the study of literature.* Ithaca, NY: Cornell University Press.

Eco, U. (1994). *Trattato di semiotica generale.* Milano: Bompiani.

Fish, S. (1980). *Is there a text in this class? The authority of interpretive communities.* Cambridge, MA: Harvard University Press.

Foucault, M. (1969). *L'archéologie du savoir.* Paris: Gallimard.

Genette, G. (1982). *Palimpsestes: La littérature au second degré.* Paris: Seuil.

Genette, G. (1987). *Seuils.* Paris: Seuil.

Genette, G. (2004). *Fiction et diction, précédé de Introduction à l'architexte,* Paris: Seuil.

Hatten, R. S. (1985). The Place of Intertextuality in Music Studies. *American Journal of Semiotics, 3/4,* 69-82.

Hatten, R. S. (2004). *Interpreting musical gestures, topics, and tropes: Mozart, Beethoven, Schubert.* Bloomington, IN: Indiana University Press.

Hyde, M. (1996). Neoclassic and anachronistic impulses in twentieth-century music. *Music Theory Spectrum, 18*(2), 200-35.

Klein, M. L. (2005). *Intertextuality in western art music.* Bloomington, IN: Indiana University Press.

Kristeva, J. (1969). *Semeiotikè: Recherches pour une sémanalyse.* Paris: Seuil.

Makaryk, I. R. (Ed.) (1993). *Encyclopedia of contemporary literary theory.* Toronto: University of Toronto Press.

Monelle, R. (2000). *The sense of music: semiotic essays.* Princeton, NJ: Princeton University Press.

Semiotic Narrativization Processes

Nicolas Marty

Université Paris-Sorbonne

Introduction

Fludernik (2002) talked about narrativization as the imposition of narrativity by a receiver on an object. Roughly, this means that narrativity is not a stable characteristic of an object, but rests on the receiver's *experience* of the object.

This point of view can prove somewhat fruitful when applied to the study of acousmatic music listening. In fact, it allows for the distinction between a narrative as a recountal of events and narrativity as the quality of anything *that might be made into a narrative.*

Fludernik (2002) emphasized that for something to be made into a narrative, there needs to be experientiality and/or consciousness at some level. Therefore narrativization, to be effective, implies the centration of experientiality by the receiver, which I coined *focalization.*

In literature, experientiality is often centered on the (pre-defined) character(s) and/or narrator(s). In music, other possibilities are just as likely to be used by the listener. We can therefore distinguish between three kinds of narrativization, relying on three points of focalization:

- *Egocentered* focalization (considering the listener's own experience) induces *embodied* narrativization;
- *Heterocentered* focalization (considering the experience of another being) induces *ecological* narrativization—ecological referring to a sense of analogy to natural world relations;
- and *Exterocentered* focalization precedes *semiotic* narrativization.

Note-based music (i.e. music using discrete parameters and scales) often does not offer ecological, spatial and pictorial perspectives in the same way sound-based music does (because the use of continuous parameters is often accompanied by the similarity and/or contiguity of composed space and sound materials with real-world space and sounds). We can imagine that in note-based music, heterocentered focalization would manifest itself differently, if it is not entirely absent. Leaving aside embodied narrativization, this paper will focus on processes of semiotic narrativization, reliant on propositional/conceptual cognitive representations.

1. Memory, abstraction, semiotization

The following developments are founded on two distinctions made in the field of psychology. As we will see in what follows, it is helpful to distinguish between semiotic narrativization processes according to their degree of abstraction, to the kind of long-term memory they imply, and to their *verbalizability*.

Psychologists distinguished between several kinds of long term memory:

> The first of those distinctions relies on the opposition between our encyclopaedic knowledge and our knowledge relative to personal events. The first is very general knowledge of which recuperation seems to depend very little on contextual indices. This knowledge relies on what is called *semantic memory*. However, the second kind is particular knowledge reliant on our living experience and of which recuperation is intertwined with the context of memorization. It relies on what is called *episodic memory*... In the distinction between implicit and explicit memories, we split data according to whether or not it can be recuperated consciously. (Meunier, 2009, pp. 39 and 41[1])

This is to be taken into consideration since no cognition can rely on immediate experience alone—in other words, cognition is always the product of both immediate experience and its relation to the context, the listener (or any cognizing entity) and his/her past experience. Here we will not be able to study *what* listeners make out of their listening experience, but rather *through which processes* they do so (besides those ecological processes described in Marty, 2012a).

Piaget described several types of processes of abstraction.

> [He] introduces reflecting abstraction as a development mechanism distinct from empirical abstraction. Empirical abstraction consists in extracting data concerning objects (color, weight, shape) or the properties of actions on objects (force or direction). It links back to the equilibrium between subject and object and thus to physical and empirical knowledge. Reflecting abstraction is born neither from objects nor from direct action, but of coordination of actions. [...] Reflecting abstraction evolves, detaching itself from its concrete bases. When the subject becomes conscious of his own operations, it becomes *reflexive* [or *reflected*] abstraction [...] (Bideau, 2007, pp. 53-54)

Empirical abstraction is thus made up of data drawn from perception (I play with rocks, I count them: there are five); reflecting abstraction draws data by linking together several empirical abstractions (I organize the rocks in a circle, I count them; I make a line, I count them; I spread them out sparsely, I count them: in all cases, there are five); and reflexive abstraction consists in drawing data from the relation between several reflecting abstractions, allowing the detachment from perception (I play with rocks, candies, dolls: when I count them, whatever the form, the proportion, there are five: five may then be a value that can exist besides the empirical existence of objects).

We thus obtain three kinds of processes:

- PROPRIOCEPTIVE SEMIOTIZATION PROCESSES, unverbalizable because emanating from implicit memory, reliant on a process of empirical abstraction: I perceive a sonic stimulus, my body reacts in a certain way and I observe this reaction. One could consider those to be the "less semiotic" semiotization processes, because they involve only the listener's body and conscience. *But* once the listener starts to *observe* his/her own experience, rather than *live* it passively, there is an abstracting process at work, that of *meta-cognition*.
- ASSOCIATIVE SEMIOTIZATION PROCESSES, verbalizable without much loss, linked mainly to episodic (implicit or explicit) memory, reliant on a process of reflecting abstraction: I observed my body's reactions and/or constructed an imaginary world/diegesis (through ecological narrativization, which is partly an empirical abstraction, since it cognizes sound into its pictorial form): what do they remind me of?

- ANALYTICAL SEMIOTIZATION PROCESSES, based on (immediate or preceding) verbalization, reliant on semantic (explicit) memory and processes of reflexive abstraction: I realize that this particular sequence of sounds always has the same effect on me and/or reminds me of the same things: maybe the sequence has a value in itself: a perfect cadence?

Let us study in turn each of those kinds of semiotic narrativization.

For now it is quite important to understand that *semiotic narrativization* (or *semiotization*) will refer in this paper to any kind of abstracting cognitive process. Furthermore semiotization (and narrativization) being a mixed, multi-dimensional process, we could wonder what constitutes the relations between the three kinds drafted here: between proprioceptive and associative semiotizations one could hope to find *affect*, whereas between associative and analytical semiotizations there would stand *storification* (the actual making of a narrative, however basic and proto-verbal). In between proprioceptive and analytical semiotization one could hope to find (auto)psychoanalytic processes as well as plain analytical process enlightened by embodied appreciation. All of these will not be developed further here, mainly because they are far too complex.

2. Towards embodiment (proprioceptive semiotization)

> The feature that is [...] most basic to experientiality is embodiment rather than specificity or individuality because these can in fact be subsumed under it. Embodiedness evokes all the parameters of a time and space frame, and the motivational and experiential aspects of human actionality likewise relate to the knowledge about one's physical presence in the world (Fludernik, 2002, pp. 28-30).

We will briefly review the spatial, temporal and morphological semiotics in order to offer several possibilities for the proprioceptive analysis of a work. Proprioceptive semiotization processes being the result of an empirical abstraction of temporal, embodied experience, one could hypothesize that they are the semiotization of a more primary kind of narrativization—kinesthetic proto-narrativization[2]—which is prior to conscious perception and results from empathy (for instance with animal utterances) and dynamic vectors (see below) that are semiotized only as long as the listener places him/herself as an observer of his/her own kinesthetic experience.

2.1 Music, embodiment and the gestural/spatial semiotics

> Let us notice that musical gestures tend to be much more a do-
> ing of something than a saying of things about something. Ges-
> tures are performative. This is, of course, inherent in the nature
> of much gesture, for gesture is a making of sound or movement.
> Gesture is active. […] In its active doing of something, a musical
> gesture directly puts significant events before us and gives us the
> straightforward stimulus of immediate experience (Coker, 1972,
> p. 19).

Other than the attribution of an intention to sound—mentioned in Khosravi
(2012) with the notion of *autonomous spectromorphological entities*, as well as
in Marty (2012a) with the *anthropomorphization* of sounds—there seems to
be an embodied aspect to the movement of sound, whether spatial, melodic
or spectral. Imberty explains the following:

> Psychologists have known for a long time that we have an inter-
> nal representation of our body that relies essentially on the sen-
> sations we have in our daily lives. […] Singing uses the muscles
> of the laryngopharyngeal zone, and hearing sing is finding in
> oneself, at least allusively, a kinesthetic representation of those
> gestures and movements that command the action of singing
> and the melodic gestures it produces (2010a, p. 14).

Moreover, the gestural aspect inherent in the sound's morphology (which
includes melodic, spatial, harmonic, spectral and temporal characteristics) is
emphasized by Faure, who says that

> The discovery of the sound domain and its association with our
> movements during the "musical" experimentation of young
> children (for instance when throwing a fork to the ground until
> the partner who picks up the fork gets bored) would produce
> in memory associations which will "color" every subsequent lis-
> tening with gestures. We could thus follow Delalande when he
> says that "gestures leave an imprint in the sonic form itself and
> contribute to giving it meaning" (Faure, 2000, p. 163).

The question is extremely wide, but seems to rest on the interpretation of stimuli according to embodied criterion: how could I produce this sound? How could I produce this gesture? What would this production do to my body? What *does* it do to my body? All of those questions (and more) would be asked and resolved implicitly at the very moment when sound is perceived.

2.2 The proto-narrative envelope and time semiotics

Imberty focused his research on time perception and its relation to music and musicality. The first thing—which Saint Augustine already understood—is that time has a subjective layer which can be developed in the idea of a *thickness in present*. One could then talk about the *past in present, present in present* and *future in present* (Imberty, 2005, p. 233).

From this grows the idea of a *proto-narrative envelope*, coined by Daniel Stern (1995) as an "intuitive dramatic tension thread" (Imberty, 2005, p. 234) that leads to the narrative perception of self through the association with oneself of the phenomena and experiences with which one is confronted. This proto-narrative envelope develops in early childhood with the repetition and re-presentation of a stimulus that provokes the "after-effect"—i.e. the encoding of a time-oriented phenomenon as a whole in memory (Imberty, 2005, p. 235).

This leads to the idea of the dynamic vector: "Dynamic vectors are the musical events which carry temporal meanings of orientation, progression, diminution or growth, repetition or retrospection" (Imberty, 2010b, p. 2). An experiment with Debussy's *La Puerta del Vino* allowed Imberty to demonstrate the existence of such vectors in music listening: in the piece's coda, with the sudden change to the high register, verbal descriptions of listeners are all relative to a stopping of time, a serenity. It is this change that Imberty qualifies as a dynamic vector, because it seems that listeners' attention is drawn to the suspension of time and to its contrast with what preceded (the whole piece being striated by a continuously repeated habanera rhythm). The dynamics of time may thus be semiotized: sections may acquire temporal meanings, which may become a fundamental element in cognitive form-building. In the Debussy example, rather than focusing on the high register motive as the transformation of an earlier, melodic/rythmic motive, listeners seem to perceive the section it delimitates as a carrier of temporal meaning.

2.3 Six models for a hermeneutical analysis

Baboni formulated a theory that maintains the existence of a hermeneutic circle which rests on need, desire and consideration and is valuable in analyzing the experience of a work of art, on an *embodied model*.

To him, *need* is born from alteration of a state of equilibrium which becomes a state of tension. The logical consequence for a need is to search for its satisfaction. *Desire* is the relation of several needs of which combined satisfactions may provoke pleasure. *Consideration* is the categorization process that allows for the efficient interpretation of a phenomenon through its relation to *marks groups*: "Need, desire and consideration constitute an afferent circle that carries the data of phenomena space to a conscious state. In art, I name this afferent circle, hermeneutic circle" (Baboni, 2008, pp. 48-55). From the circle are drawn six models for a hermeneutical analysis, each of which originates from a bodily experience of early childhood and treats an aspect of the system of the contemplated work of art (Baboni in Marty, 2012b, pp. 211-213). The first two models (*attractivity* and *cyclicity*) study stasis, dynamism and their interactions in the musical system, as observed through an embodied perspective—this is linked, for instance, to the polar nature of the tonic in tonal music. The third model (*corruptibility*) answers to the possibility for the dissolution or disappearance of the system—can the system be contradicted in a way that does not lead to a new understanding of it, but rather to the necessity for a new system?—whereas the fourth and fifth models (*constructivity* and *destructivity*) treat the development and growth, or reduction and shrinking, of the system's rules—toward a new understanding of the system. The sixth model (*excitability*) answers the question of satisfaction in itself, for oneself, which one seeks in contemplation. Baboni is more elusive about this model and seems to leave it at a more abstract stage that the five others.

We are thus in an embodied system. Music, rather than being only "narrating itself", may then be understood as the appraisal of a system's evolution resting on its embodied understanding: "the hermeneutic circle is the search for a [embodied] semantic meaning (verbalizable or not) to the work of art that is contemplated, but also to the system to which the work seems to belong" (Baboni, 2008, p. 65).

Considering briefly an extension of this process toward analytical semiotization, this contemplation of the work's system may be correlated with the making of the (out-of-time) cognitive representation of a work by a listener who evaluates the system's possible states and transitions through a more or less explicitly stochastic view—what Chouvel described using the physics/mathematics concepts of *phase space* and *Markov chains* (2006, pp. 139-145).

3. Towards meaning (associative semiotization)

We saw with proprioceptive semiotization the influence of implicit memory on the apprehension of music. Let us turn to the influence of episodic memory, related to imagination and association of ideas, on semiotic (reflecting—that is, founded on the comparison of several empirical informations) abstraction.

3.1 Verbal induction

As Francès already noted, music's representative effects are polarized by the verbal elements given before or during musical audition (2002, p. 279). This effect is very well-known and plays an important part in the success of programmatic music with children and "naïve" listeners, among others, by allowing them to listen to music through a formal schema that they can easily conceive: instead of being perceived as an abstract, emotional form, musical form is related to images and stories, without *necessarily* becoming a story itself.

For instance, the BBC used verbal induction for the 1978 diffusion of Andrew Sachs' *The Revenge*, the first (and mainly last) radio drama without words. *The Revenge* pictures a man who is probably escaping from a prison, goes into town and kills somebody or gets killed himself at the end, *without a single instance of verbal language.* The title of the piece was announced twice, at the beginning and end of diffusion, evidently to make up for the complete absence of indicators of motivation, aim or goal in the work itself. Indeed, having this idea of *revenge* given to them, listeners may imagine, for instance, that the man escaping from the prison goes to find the person who put him there in order to kill them, which may be paramount to the appreciation of the work.

It seems important to emphasize that narrativization resulting from a title or a program is not necessarily verbalized (either as a narrative, as characters' names or anything else)—it can be manifest only at a pictorial level (we may think of the titles of Debussy's preludes, for instance, which give us a global picture of a scene without implying that any story is *recounted* by their music). But when narrativization actually includes (silent or overt) verbalization, it could be related to symbolism, of which I will talk later.

3.2 Cultural synaesthesia

In 1980 Lakoff and Johnson wrote *Metaphors we live by* (2003), which would become the basis for their subsequent research on the integration of philosophy, perception and cognition in an anthropomorphic, embodied frame. To them,

> The concepts that govern our thoughts are not just matters of the intellect. They also govern our everyday functioning, down to the most mundane details. Our concepts structure what we perceive, how we get around in the world, and how we relate to other people. Our conceptual system thus plays a central role in defining our everyday realities (Lakoff & Johnson, 2003, p. 3).

Those metaphors will be the basis for what can be called *cultural synaesthesia*— that is, a kind of metaphorical correspondence between senses. This way, one can associate (more or less conventionally) colors, smells, textures to sounds, this being different from authentic synesthesia which seems to be the product of a neurological, less cultural phenomenon—though some have hypothesized that both kinds of synaesthesia are closely related and always cognitively cultural (see Rosenthal, 2011).

We will focus here on the most common metaphor in music: the association of pitch height with vertical height—this is what Lakoff and Johnson call an *orientational metaphor*. This kind of metaphor does not seem to be arbitrarily decided, but rather rests on human embodied experience: if HIGH is HAPPY, and LOW is SAD, it may be because (at least in our culture) being happy tends to make one raise one's head, whereas being sad tends to do the contrary, making one lower one's head (Lakoff & Johnson, 2003, p. 18).

Baboni effectively explains our metaphor with an interesting model, differing from the most common "low pitches come from the thoracic cage, high pitches are closer to the head": pitch height being correlated to the bodily tension that produces it (tenser produces higher pitches), this same tension allows us to stand up from the ground, to resist gravity. The more one relaxes, the lower one gets (Baboni in Marty, 2012b, pp. 211-213).

A kind of gravity applied to music (Roy, 2001, p. 458) would thus explain the fact that melodies all around the world tend to descend, even if they often finish at the same pitch as they began because ascending gestures are wider than descending ones (Meeùs in Marty, 2012b, pp. 219-221).

But it may be forgetting the cultural aspect of the orientational metaphor, underlined by Lakoff and Johnson when they say that all cultures do not give the same priority as us to the high/low orientation (Lakoff and Johnson, 2003, p. 24), and that inside a given culture there lie metaphors that do not function together but still apply to the same concepts, emphasizing different aspects of it (pp. 220-221). The metaphor is cultural and built on embodied origins, but also on a social and musical convention that is perfectly established today in the Occident: the spatial-vertical representation (see Duchez, 1979).

Still, many works tend to prove that no matter the culture, acousmatic cognitive images are built in a spatial fashion, higher frequencies corresponding to higher locations (relative to the body of the listener), this being explained by several psychoacoustical factors which are not the topic of this paper (see Khosravi, 2012; Kendall & Ardilla, 2008). Furthermore there are many other *cross-domain mappings* relative to pitch or other dimensions, which do not necessarily imply the verticality metaphor. Moreover, this metaphor could easily be used to make assumptions about metaphorical maps (e.g. UP is GOOD / HIGH PITCH is SPATIALLY HIGH → HIGH PITCH is GOOD) that may have no reality in a listener's apprehension of sound or music (see Eitan & Timmers, 2010). These questions are extremely complex and interesting, but cannot be explored further in this paper (for a more detailed discussion see Khosravi, 2012).

3.3 Unconscious association

Another kind of associative semiotization imposes associative preconceptions on a new musical element in an unconscious fashion. It should be noted that most of the explanations for the cultural synesthesia discussed above would make it an example of unconscious association. However, the discussion of unconscious association that follows focuses on *specific*, value-loaded, images, rather than on *domains* of assocations (as was the case with pitch height).

Any resemblance to a known phenomenon, with no need for verbalization, will aid (or even induce) the same listening strategies used to apprehend the phenomenon the first time. Along with this, images and evocations induced by the first phenomenon will be activated in working memory and will thus be available for easier recuperation by the listener.

Specific activations may happen when a piece of music has been strongly associated by a listener to another stimulus. Such may be the case, for instance, with Ligeti's *Atmosphères* and *Kyrie* (from his *Requiem*), as well as Strauss' *Also sprach Zarathustra*, all of which are repeatedly heard in Kubrick's *2001 Space Odyssey*.

Unconscious associations might also be the reason for what we can call *musical clichés*, acquired through the automation of a symbolism that limits the apprehension of a musical work or sound, such as the "eerie" sound of a flute, or the vampires who come with a cello playing on modal scales with way too much reverberation.

But let's not forget the limit of this trail of thought: every automated thing is not necessarily a cliché. It can also be an archetype, when the symbolic relation is founded on "natural" (human) properties of the symbolic entities. The sound of water may evoke life without being a cliché, because the archetype rests on the necessity of water to survive, a thing common to all humans. However, using water deliberately to evoke life may be considered a cliché. Through more complex associations, a more profound symbolic may be instated.

4. Towards concept (analytical semiotization)

The third kind of semiotic narrativization is necessarily verbalized (though verbalization may be prior to listening, as in the case of guided categorization) because its existence relies fundamentally on its verbalization and/or conceptualization. The consideration of number/letter symbols (i.e. B-A-C-H) is relevant here: even if it is not primordial in the understanding of music, the symbol is the origin of a compositional—poietic—development (Boulez, 2005, pp. 434-435). The sociological and political analysis of musical works is another kind of conceptualism which hypothesizes a link between the creation and its historical context. We will talk here about symbolism, conceptualism and "musical" analysis. "Musicological" listening—identifying tonalities, chords, modulations, etc.—may also enter this frame because, like Schaeffer's typomorphology, it is a (somewhat arbitrary) categorization system that imposes listening to some properties and characteristics as being more relevant than others—which may sometimes lead to a completely unsatisfactory listening experience.

4.1 Conscious association (symbolism)

Beyond unconscious associations appear symbolisms, verbalized and reflexive, which allow one to overcome established clichés in order to apply new meanings to music. The two kinds of associations are closely linked by the possibility for the automation of the symbolism as cliché. Thus the dotted rhythm of a march, before becoming a largely understood cliché (even if it is founded on physical parameters), was a symbolism designating the march itself.

Nicolas Marty

The most explicit instance of reflected symbolism is that of baroque music, particularly in Germany, which was conceptualized in a large number of music dictionaries—a high-pitched note would thus represent height or the sky, for instance, while a chromatic semitone would express suffering and pain, and so on. "With the help of those figures, the text is put into music and interpreted/performed" (Ulrich, 1990, p. 305).

The implicit listener (see Kaltenecker, 2010) thus knows all the correspondences that allow the appreciation of music in its whole and arrives at the concert having studied the theories of *ethos*, *topoï* and other rhetorical figures for music. Listening to music, s/he interprets each melodical, rhythmical figure as being the representation of something that exists in the real world or as having a rhetorical, discursive, or even narrative function. It may be noted that although learning such rules and functions necessarily implies verbal communication, it is not unimaginable that a listener may be so competent that those rules and functions would appear to them as evident and that they would not need to be reflected in a verbal form. Again, this shows how unconscious and conscious associations are linked. I propose, however, that it is the necessity for the listener to explicitly *wish* (at some point) to establish the association that fundamentally distinguishes conscious from unconscious association.

Sometimes, as in Wagner's operas, Prokofiev's *Peter and the Wolf*, or even the TV series *Lost* or *Fringe*, the symbolic may become evident through the simultaneous presentation (verbally or not) of an action, a plot, a narrative and musical motives, themes, which acquire at this point their symbolic or associative value, according to the listener's reception strategies. This question is much more complex than this, of course.

4.2 Conceptualism

We will thus turn to the works in which the *con-text* is just as important as, or even more important than, the *text*. We might call such works "conceptual", if this adjective hadn't taken on a negative and contemptuous connotation for many people (at least in France).

Cage's *4'33"* is such a work, of which the musical/sonic content is not the end in itself, or at least not as much as the concept of music and the presence of silence in a world becoming afraid of it as *muzak*[3] fills the last places where one could hear one's own footsteps. In fact, Cage originally envisioned selling a four-minute silent piece to Muzak Holdings Co. under the name *Silent Prayer*, to give silence to be heard (Kim-Cohen, 2009, pp. 16-17).

In the case of *sound art* or *sound sculpture*, we find Vitiello's 1999 recordings of the World Trade Center to have acquired a very strong conceptual value after 9/11, becoming the last words of the towers, of the pre-9/11 world (Kim-Cohen, 2009, pp. 130-131). In the same vein, Kierkegaard's *Four Rooms* consists of the amplification, by closed-circuiting speakers, of the characteristic sound of four rooms of houses in Chernobyl, where one of the worst nuclear accidents in history took place. Kim-Cohen (2009, p. 132) says: "As listeners, the inflection we hear is not precisely that of radioactive particles and electromagnetic waves but of the story, the history, of them: the radioactive, electromagnetic text. We hear the hum of Kierkegaard's piece through the filter of what we know about Chernobyl." The artist's work is then conceptual in that it demands to be known and understood to allow for the "correct" interpretation (if there is such a thing) of the work. It needs to be understood that even if each musical or sound work has a conceptual aspect, be it only in its style, this aspect is not necessarily discursive and seems to be often treated at the level of unconscious association. In our examples the text is important, but its con-text is even more so, giving a musical/sound vision, but claiming a political/historical perspective.

In Wishart's work, concrete metaphors are excellent examples of concepts asking for verbalization to be understood (1996, p. 166): "The sound-image 'bellow/water-pump' may be interpreted as the functioning of the machine or the functioning of a human body and when our perception of it changes from one to the other, a metaphor is implied." The problem of this conception is its inapplicability to unwarned listeners. I tested the listening of a passage from *Journey into Space* with several listeners, saying or not that there were sonic symbolisms. Even when the listeners are told, it is very rare for them to make the link between the two faces of the sound. We could compare this with the famous rabbit/duck image: even if we perceive the two forms, we generally do not make any conceptualization that would lead us to learn or even infer something about rabbits and ducks.

Still, Wishart's *Red Bird* (1978) makes a bit of a point about this, using mainly animal, human and machine sounds, which may put the listener in a mind to relate those elements and put their relation into question (maybe even more so in the 1980s). But, as Wishart says himself, the point of the piece is elsewhere, in the morphings and interpolations that he used and continues to use today.

4.3 Musical analysis, visual and formal semiotics

We will close with a last kind of analytical semiotization: musical analysis. The question is very large and has led to many critical claims, not the least of which are addressed to serial, algorithmic music, retrogradable rhythms founded on mathematical relations having apparently no perceptive relevance.[4] Questions about macrostructure and its perception were asked more than once.

Meeùs (1994, pp. 22-23) sees three problems in musical analysis:

> The first problem is that of the hierarchy and of levels of obser-
> vations. [...] The second aspect is that of the justification for
> transferring local procedures at the global level, or reciprocally.
> [...] The third major problem to which musical analysis is con-
> fronted today is that of the definition of time. Each cut that is
> made in the linear flux of music must be considered an inter-
> ruption of this flux: segments are identified because of their out-
> of-time characteristics. [...] The segmentation aims to and leads
> to the granulation of the temporal flux, a discretization without
> which, with no doubt, the sound discourse would be senseless.
> If a musical unit is perceived as such, time is blocked with it, the
> present becomes longer.

The notation itself induces the possibility of a segmentation of the work and allows one to study it outside of its time of performance (outside of its musicality?). Sheperd (1980, p. 111) says that it is *because* of notation that the "ideals" of listening and composition are realized on an extremely wide timescale, nearly observed out of time.

Wishart (1980, pp. 144-145) raises the question of the normalization of the listening by the listener, due to the limitation of notation to very general parameters with very few variables:

> Notation banishes the direct, unique, sound-experience from
> the realm considered as *music* and reverses our appreciation of
> a sound-event. We are no longer to respond to the quality and
> articulation of the sound-gestalt in itself. Rather, we are only to
> respond to it as an attempted realization of a conglomerate of
> Ideal (i.e. non-existent) sound-events approximated by proper
> attention to the notes, the counting, and the "correct" instru-
> mental timbre production.

Even if this way of seeing things is really dramatic and not necessarily applicable to all written music nor to all listening situations, it is nevertheless relevant: the repetition of the octave (even if founded on physical/physiological parameters), just like the domination of pitch, is a convention too—let us simply consider our contemporary serious music, in which timbre is often much more important than pitch! Moreover, even melodic orientations are influenced by notation: flats go down, sharps go up. What if we had a 12-note system without alterations?

Regarding narrativization, we can conclude that knowledge of the score (or of its form) may induce in the listener the basis for a semiotization strategy that will correspond to the aspects put forward by the notation used. Form may also be created, parts related, via the score—but all this may influence the listening strategy and its consideration (extended formal listening being glorified while immediate, experienced listening is relegated to "naïve listeners).

5. Synthesis

The model is summarized below (figure 1) in a simplified version. Although arrows, spatial positioning and boxes may give an impression of modular, hierarchized cognitive model, I would like to stress that not one listening mode is "better" than another. The main idea of such a model is to allow for the study of *listening* rather than the study of music pieces. In the long term, I hope to be able to develop an approach for the didactics of acousmatic listening so that—ideally—people may actively find a satisfactory and rich experience in listening to any music or sound phenomenon.

A bit of food for thought: what happens… when we study a score as if studying music? … when we listen to music as if reading a score? … when we segment a piece into themes and motives as if they had an intrinsic existence? … when we listen to acousmatic music searching for variables relevant to tonal music?

What would happen if we considered music as if it were a mode of reception rather than a means of communication?

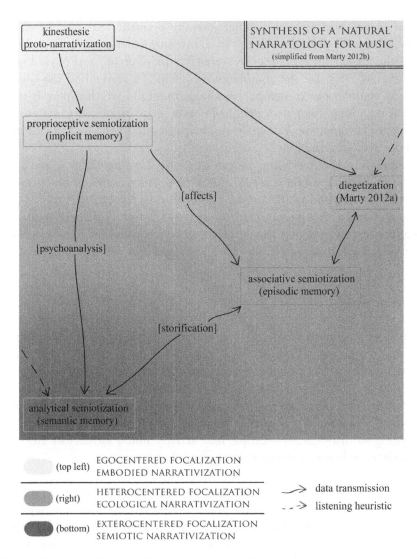

FIGURE 1. Synthesis of a "natural" narratology for music

Notes

112

distinguishes between *kinesthesia* and *proprioception* as follows: just as perception is a cognitive operation applied to the exteroceptive (five) senses, proprioception is a cognitive operation applied to the interoceptive sense (kinesthesia). I use those definitions, because the distinction is not always clear, proprioception being sometimes considered as both kinesthesia and statesthesia (is there or not movement in the body?).

[3]   Muzak Holdings Co. was founded in 1934 and is renowned for the creation and distribution of what is now called *elevator music*, applying abusively the findings of the young music therapy.

[4]   Let us be honest: the point of those musics is not necessarily the immediately perceptible reality for every listener, but maybe, as was the case with Boulez and is often the case nowadays, the blurring of temporal directions to benefit the consideration of larger fields, or just a system to allow formal unity.

References

Baboni-Schilingi, J., & Vallos, F. (2008). *Six modèles d'analyse herméneutique*. Paris: MIX.

Bideau, J. (2007). La théorie piagétienne. In S. Ionescu & A. Blanchet (Eds.), *Psychologie du développement et psychologie différentielle* (pp. 37-57). Paris: PUF.

Boulez, P. (2005). *Regards sur autrui – Points de repère II*. Paris: Christian Bourgeois Éditeur.

Chouvel, J.M. (2006). *Analyse musicale – Sémiologie et cognition des formes temporelles*. Paris: l'Harmattan.

Coker, W. (1972). *Music and meaning: a theoretical introduction to musical aesthetics*. New York: Collier-Macmillan.

Duchez, M.E. (1979). La représentation spatio-verticale du caractère musical grave-aigu et l'élaboration de la notion de hauteur de son dans la conscience musicale occidentale. *Acta Musicologica*, *51*(1), 54-73.

Eitan, Z., & Timmers, R. (2010). Beethoven's last piano sonata and those who follow crocodiles: Cross-domain mappings of auditory pitch in a musical context. *Cognition*, *114*, 405-422.

Faure, A. (2000). *Des sons aux mots : comment parle-t-on du timbre musical ?* PhD thesis in cognitive sciences, dir. S. McAdams. Paris: École des Hautes Études en Sciences Sociales. Retrieved May 1, 2013, from http://tel.archives-ouvertes.fr/docs/00/14/05/21/PDF/These_Anne_Faure.pdf

Fludernik, M. (2002). *Towards a 'natural' narratology*. London / New-York: Routledge.

Francès, R. (2002). *La perception de la musique*. Paris: J.Vrin.

Imberty, M. (2005). *La musique creuse le temps – De Wagner à Boulez : Musique, psychologie, psychanalyse*. Paris: l'Harmattan.

Imberty, M. (2010a). Au-delà de la psychologie cognitive de la musique. In F. Madurell & P. Lalitte (Eds.). *Musique et sciences cognitives* (Conférences et séminaires, n°46, pp. 9-31). Université Paris-Sorbonne: OMF.

Imberty, M. (2010b). Souvenirs et réflexions autour de la perception de la musique. In L. Guirard (Ed.), *50 ans de psychologie de la musique – L'école de Robert Francès* (pp. 34-57). Montauban: Alexitere.

Kaltenecker, M. (2010). *L'oreille divisée : les discours sur l'écoute musicale aux XVIIIe et XIXe siècles*. Paris: MF.

Kendall, G., & Ardilla, M. (2008). The artistic play of spatial organization: spatial attributes, scene analysis and auditory spatial schemata. In R. Kronland-Martinet, S. Ystad & K. Jensen (Eds.), *Computer music modeling and retrieval: sense of sounds* (*LNCS series*, Springer Verlag, *4969*, 125-138.

Khosravi, P. (2012). *Spectral spatiality and the acousmatic listening experience: the birth of autonomous spectromorphological entities*. PhD thesis in electroacoustic composition, dir. D. Smalley. London City University.

Kim-Cohen, S. (2009). *In the Blink of an Ear: Towards a Non-Cochlear Sonic Art*. Continuum International Publishing Group.

Lakoff, G., & Johnson, M. (2003). *Metaphors we live by*. Chicago University Press.

Marty, N. (2012a). Sonic identification and listening strategies – towards a "natural" narratology for electroacoustic musics. *EMS-12 Conference Proceedings*. Stockholm. Retrieved May 1, 2013, from http://www.ems-network.org/IMG/pdf_EMS12_marty.pdf

Marty, N. (2012b). *Identification sonore, stratégies d'écoute et narrativités*. M.Mus. thesis in music and musicology, dir. F. Madurell. Université Paris-Sorbonne.

Marty, N. (2013). Furthering the bases of a 'natural' narratology for music. *Lecture at the ENN2013 Conference*. Paris.

Meeùs, N. (1994). De la forme musicale et de sa segmentation. *Musurgia, 1*(1), 7-23.

Meunier, J.M. (2009). *Mémoires, représentations et traitements*. Paris: Dunod.

Michels, U. (1990). *Guide illustré de la musique (Volume 2)*. Paris: Fayard.

MIM (2009). UST - Modifications. In *MIM website*. Retrieved February 9, 2012, from www.labo-mim.org/site/share/ust/download2.php%3Ffile%3DFiches_ UST_Modifs.pdf

Nattiez, J.J. (2003). La signification comme paramètre musical. In J.J. Nattiez (Ed.), *Musiques - Une encyclopédie pour le XXIe siècle – tome 2* (pp. 256-287). Paris: Actes Sud.

Rosenthal, V. (Ed.). (2011). *Synesthésie et Intermodalité / Synesthesia and Intermodality* (*Intellectica*, n°55).

Roy, S. (2001). *L'analyse de la musique acousmatique : Bilan et propositions*. PhD thesis in musicology, dir. J.J. Nattiez. Université de Montréal.

Sheperd, J. (1980). The musical coding of ideologies. In J. Sheperd (Ed.), *Whose music? a sociology of musical languages* (pp. 69-124). New Brunswick / London: Transactions Publisher.

Stern, D. (1995). *The motherhood constellation*. London: Karnac Books.

Thoresen, L. (assisted by A. Hedman). (2010). Formbuilding patterns and metaphorical meaning. *Organised Sound, 15*(2), 82-95.

Wishart, T. (1980). Musical writing, musical speaking. In J. Sheperd (Ed.), *Whose music? A sociology of musical languages* (pp. 125-154). New Brunswick / London: Transactions Publisher.

Wishart, T. (1996). *On sonic art – aA new and revised edition by Simon Emmerson*. New-York / Oxon: Routledge ('Contemporary Music Studies', Vol. 12).

Musical Understanding: Wittgenstein, Ethics, and Aesthetics

Paulo C. Chagas

University of California, Riverside

1. Wittgenstein, philosophy and music

Ludwig Wittgenstein (1889-1951) is an intellectual myth of the 20th century and certainly one of the most original thinkers that Western culture has ever produced.[1] The philosophy of Wittgenstein reflects on issues of logic, mathematics, language, psychology, ethics, aesthetics, religion, etc. His philosophical method combined the rejection of metaphysics and the scientific spirit with clarity and a simple, colloquial-like language, however pushed to such a level of logical precision that it seems to stretch the limits of thinking. The unorthodoxy of Wittgenstein emerges as much in his life as in his thought. For the reader unfamiliar with him, his writing is almost incomprehensible; Wittgenstein's unusual assumptions, views and inquiries cause surprise, confusion and discomfort. The growing bibliography on Wittgenstein witnesses to the fascination unleashed by his work and life both inside and outside academic circles.[2] The archives of Wittgenstein's work— an enormous body of manuscripts, diaries, correspondence, notes, drafts, aphorisms, etc.—which only recently became available, turned out to be a treasure chest for scholarship.[3] We can expect that the fascination with the myth of Wittgenstein will continue and a profusion of new approaches will appear, seeking to illuminate his legacy through multiple and diversified perspectives and through the connections between his life and philosophy.

Wittgenstein characterized his philosophy as a therapeutic activity. He dismissed the idea that philosophy can serve as a theory to explain the world; he had great antipathy to academic life, which he considered an obstacle to promoting philosophy as a serious and productive activity. No honest philosopher, he said, could treat philosophy as a profession. He encouraged his best students to leave academia and pursue careers such as that of a physician, schoolteacher or gardener. Above all, Wittgenstein abhorred a worldview grounded in science. For him, science and technology have nothing to do with the fundamental problems of the world because "there is no *great* essential problem in the scientific sense" (*CV* 10; 20).[4] Wittgenstein criticized the devastating effect that the scientific method and the cult of science exert on culture as a whole; the view that science would have a "theory for everything" characterizes for him the decline of civilization in the 20th century: "The whole modern conception of the world is based on the illusion that the so-called laws of nature are the explanations of natural phenomena" (*TLP* 6.371). Scientific principles are not appropriate for elucidating, for example, aesthetics and religion; rather they generate distortion, superficiality and confusion.

Wittgenstein had a profound interest in music. He grew up in a family of amateur musicians, who were very active as patrons of Vienna's musical circles. Ludwig's father, Karl, was a businessman who amassed one of the largest fortunes in the iron and steel industry in imperial Austria and also played the violin. His mother was Leopoldine Kalmus, an accomplished pianist who had extraordinary sight-reading ability. Ludwig was the youngest of the family. Of their eight children, two dedicated themselves to music: his brother Hans, the eldest son, was a child prodigy who began composing at age four and had intended to follow a career in music, before committing suicide. His brother Paul Wittgenstein pursued a career as a concert pianist; he had his right arm amputated during the First World War but managed to continue performing only with his left hand. It was for him that Ravel wrote his Piano Concerto in D Major, the concerto for the left hand.

A number of famous artists performed in the salons of the Wittgenstein mansion in Vienna at the beginning of the 20th century, such as the young Pablo Casals, Bruno Walter, Gustav Mahler and the famous violinist Joseph Joachim with his string quartet. Joachim introduced Johannes Brahms to the Wittgenstein family; Brahms gave piano lessons to their two daughters and regularly attended concerts in the house. One of the major works of Brahms's last years, the Clarinet Quintet op. 115, was premiered at the mansion. Growing up among so many musical talents, the young Ludwig became a great admirer of the repertoire of musical classicism and romanticism. He only learned to play the clarinet when he was thirty years old, while pursuing training as a schoolteacher. He had a perfect pitch and showed an exemplary ability to explain music. He was also known for his exceptional talent in whistling; he used to whistle *Lieder* by Franz Schubert, his favorite composer, accompanied by the piano.

Despite his great interest in music, Wittgenstein did not develop any theory or musical aesthetics. However, the references to music, especially the analogies between music and language, pervade his philosophy. A significant body of thoughts on music and musical life appears in *Culture and Value* [*Vermischte Bemerkungen*], a collection of notes, aphorisms and fragments covering the period between 1914 and his death (1951), which was first published in 1977. Wittgenstein addresses themes of philosophy, art, science, culture, religion, etc. Some parts are autobiographical and reveal personal beliefs and traits of Wittgenstein's personality: artistic preferences, identification with certain traditions, and the continuous struggle with the problems of philosophy and man. The observations of *Culture and Value* give clear evidence of Wittgenstein's musical taste and attachment to the music of the 19th century, particularly to the German composers and the Viennese tradition: Bach, Mozart, Beethoven, Schubert, Brahms, Mendelssohn, Mahler and Wagner. There are also many references to Josef Labor (1842-1924), a Czech composer, pianist, and organist who became blind at a young age and whose career was sponsored by Wittgenstein's family. Ludwig greatly appreciated his style of virtuosic interpretation (see below).

1.1 Saying and showing

The *Tractatus Logico-Philosophicus* (*TLP*) was the first and only book by Wittgenstein published in his lifetime. It covers a period of seven years: from 1911, when he was a Russell protégé in Cambridge, to 1918, when he was serving as an officer in the Austrian army during World War I. Published in German in 1921 and in English in 1922, the *Tractatus* reflects on the philosophy of logic and language, metaphysics and ethics. The text is organized under seven major aphorisms, which are each followed by a hierarchy of propositions that give the impression of being increasingly detailed *elucidations* [*Erläuterungen*], but actually function as self-descriptive *commentaries* [*Bemerkungen*]. Wittgenstein's writing is dense and poetic without traps or provocations, without fear of itself appearing incomplete and fragmented. Wittgenstein does not try to seduce the reader with the illusion of an easy solution or a final interpretation.

Contrary to what the title suggests, the *Tractatus* is far from being a work of logical perfection. In the last two paragraphs, Wittgenstein expresses the surprising paradox of his whole philosophy:

> My propositions serve as elucidations in the following way: anyone who understands me eventually recognizes them as non-sensical, when he has used them—as steps—to climb up beyond them. (He must, so to speak, throw away the ladder after climbing up it.)
> He must transcend these propositions, and then he will see the world aright. (*TLP* 6.54)
> What we cannot speak about we must pass over in silence. (*TLP* 7)

What does it mean here to "throw away the ladder"? What is the subliminal message of a text that cancels itself? The reader, who is urged in the beginning to climb the arduous rungs of a treatise on dogmatic metaphysics, discovers at the end that he must discard everything he has learned so far in order to continue. Throw away the ladder is an exhortation to transcend the boundaries of logic and rational thought. Wittgenstein addresses his readers almost like a Zen master that speaks to his disciples by means of paradoxes and nonsense. The master leaves us perplexed, hurls us into the abyss of doubt, literally takes the ground (the stairs) from under our feet, and invites us to swirl in the vortex of the uncertainties of the world. Narrow and winding is the path of knowledge moving upwards from the illusion of metaphysical clarity to the mystical ineffability of existence. Wittgenstein rejects the thesis and philosophical doctrines: "Philosophy is not a body of doctrine but an activity. A philosophical work consists essentially of elucidations" (*TLP* 4.112).

The central and revolutionary idea of the *Tractatus*, which remains intact in Wittgenstein's entire philosophy, is this: any attempt to say something philosophical results in nonsense. The task of philosophy is thus to trace the boundaries between what can be *said* and what cannot be said but only *shown*. The relation between *saying* and *showing* is not a dualism; they are incompatible, mutually exclusive categories: "What can be shown cannot be said" (*TLP* 4.1212). The *saying* is what can be expressed through logical-scientific language using an objective terminology. The *showing* is what cannot be said within the positivist discourse, what is excluded from the objectivity consistent with logical systems. Wittgenstein is concerned with protecting the positivist discourse against metaphysical absurdity. When he refers to the limits of language, he is not evoking ordinary everyday language but the language of science and philosophy. Towards the end of the *Tractatus* Wittgenstein affirms: "There is indeed the inexpressible. This *shows* itself; it is the mystical" (*TLP* 6.522).

For Wittgenstein, the propositions of logic express only imperfectly the aspects of reality. "Logic is not a body of doctrine, but a mirror-image of the world. Logic is transcendental" (*TLP* 6.13). We can logically understand even a proposition that makes no sense because it is not consistent with the reality of the world. Such propositions are, for example, the tautology and the contradiction: "A tautology has no truth-conditions, since it is unconditionally true: and a contradiction is true on no condition. Tautologies and contradictions lack sense" (*TLP* 4.461). Tautologies and contradictions are the limit of language and thought and therefore the limit of the world. The tautology and the contradiction do not say anything, because they are not located in the space between the true and the false: "A tautology leaves open to reality the whole—the infinite whole—of logical space: a contradiction fills the whole of logical space leaving no point of it for reality. Thus neither of them can determine reality in any way" (*TLP* 4.463).

Wittgenstein considered the *Tractatus Logico-Philosophicus* to be primarily a book of ethics. But his conception of ethics is very different from the usual. Ethics is a discourse of human existence that transcends the factual world. The principles of ethics cannot be defined or analyzed by external characteristics. The main function of ethics, according to Wittgenstein, is to give sense to the world: "The sense of the world must lie outside the world. In the world everything is as it is, and everything happens as it happens, in it no value exists—and if it did exist, it would have no value" (*TLP* 6.41). Just as with logic, ethics does not allow itself to be expressed: "Ethics is transcendental. (Ethics and aesthetics are one and the same.)" (*TLP* 6.421). But, in opposition to logic, ethics does not show the structure of the world. The propositions of ethics and aesthetics, as well as of logic, are pseudo-propositions that say nothing of what they want to say, but show something that is not what they give the impression of saying. And unlike logic, ethics and aesthetics are not a "mirror-image" of the world. They do not describe facts, but simply show. Ethics and aesthetics are predicates of the thinking subject and not properties of the world.

Wittgenstein's conception of ethics is influenced by Schopenhauer's philosophy in the sense that for both ethics is a manifestation of a *will*. However, while for Schopenhauer "the thinking subject is *in* the world which is the manifestation of will," for Wittgenstein, "the thinking subject is not a part of the world, but its limit: it is now as metaphysical, as real or unreal as the will" (Griffiths, 1974, p. 103; emphasis in the original). This gives a different view of ethics and aesthetics than Schopenhauer. For Wittgenstein, aesthetics and ethics can be one in a way that was not possible for Schopenhauer: "To view the world *sub specie aeternitatis* is to view it as a whole—a limited whole. Feeling the world as a limited whole—it is this that is mystical" (*TLP* 6.45).[5] Wittgenstein uses the term *sub specie aeternitatis* as synonymous with transcendental. It emphasizes the two different ways of accessing reality—the saying and the showing. The form of showing is the sub specie aeternitatis (transcendental) observation, which has the world as its backdrop. It is the domain of ethics and aesthetics:

> The work of art is the object seen *sub specie aeternitatis*, and the good life is the world seen *sub specie aeternitatis*. This is the connection between art and ethics.
> The usual way of looking at things sees objects as it were from the midst of them, the view *sub specie aeternitatis* from outside. (*TB* 7.10.16)

The aesthetic attitude, as well as ethical experience, belongs to the sphere of transcendental showing. The aesthetic experience is the observation of the world as a limited whole from the "outside" by means of a complete single object: the artwork. To understand the artwork we must first separate it from its environment. Whoever listens to music in a concert hall, at home or using a digital mobile device must first isolate the music from the ambient noise. After that, the world becomes the world of music, the ambient noise disappears, and the music takes up all the space. The music becomes the world. It is this ability of artwork to see the world as a whole through a limited space of facts—the artwork—that creates the experience of *surprise*. The artwork is true regardless of its relation to the world. It conveys, at the same time, an experience of logic, ethics and aesthetics. In his *Lecture on Ethics* (*LE*), Wittgenstein links ethics to the existential experience of surprise. This same observation appears in the *Notebooks*:

> Aesthetically, the miracle is that the art world exists. That there is what there is.
> Is it the essence of the artistic way of looking at things, that it looks at the world with a happy eye? (*NB* 4.11.16)

The key to understanding the "mysticism" of Wittgenstein's philosophy lies in the attitude toward the world: "Not how the world is, is the mystical, but that it is" (*TLP* 6.44). Aesthetic contemplation can serve as a logical interpretation of the world, i.e., can help you see the world correctly, and can simultaneously evoke a mystical experience. It helps us to be happy, to live in harmony with the world. But it is also clear that there is unhappiness in the world and that is why art can serve as a remedy, as a therapy to find a good and happy life. When life itself becomes art, then humans live happily. A happy life, which according to Wittgenstein is the purpose of existence, is expressed through artwork. Art is an expression and artwork is the complete expression. The artwork both says about itself and shows itself: "The work of art does not seek to convey *something else*, just itself" (*CV* 58; 67). Art has a "mystical" mission, especially music. It has to express what ordinary language cannot express, i.e., the unsayable, according to the last paragraph of the *Tractatus*.

1.2 Philosophy as therapy: understanding the melody

The second philosophy presented in *Philosophical Investigations* is a collection of fragments, notes, aphorisms and reflections that covers the period 1930-1948. The focus of these reflections makes the shift from logic to grammar. *Philosophical Investigations* is an incomplete book, as it wants to show the impossibility of giving a description of the world as a whole. Wittgenstein develops a completely new style, very different from the *Tractatus*; no more logical propositions but a disconnected discourse focused on ordinary language and operating with comparisons and analogies. Wittgenstein explores the complex nature of the mind, the restlessness of simultaneous thoughts that characterizes our experience. He proposes a therapeutic exercise of reflection for releasing us from the compulsivity of language; he points to the obsessions and traps of our language, as if language would conspire against us: "Philosophy is a battle against the bewitchment of our intelligence by means of our language" (*PI* §109). Language produces illusions that are deeply rooted in us because of the limitations of our language. Wittgenstein wants to point to these illusions, which are the source of our misunderstanding. This is what philosophy has to do: "Philosophy simply puts everything before us, and neither explains nor deduces anything.—Since everything lies open to view there is nothing to explain. For what is hidden, for example, is of no interest to us" (*PI* §126).

For Wittgenstein, "The problems of life are insoluble on the surface and can only be solved in depth. In surface dimensions they are insoluble" (*CV* 74; 84). Music shows that we have to dive into the depths, beyond the surface of the sounds, to understand its complexity:

> Music, with its few notes and rhythms, seems to some people
> a primitive art. But only its surface is simple, while the body
> which makes possible the interpretation of this manifest content
> has all the infinite complexity that is suggested in the external
> forms of other arts and which music conceals. In a certain sense
> it is the most sophisticated art of all. (*CV* 8; 11)

Music is the most refined of all art because it hides its complexity in a simple
surface. The surface of music gives access to a complexity that we try to
understand by using language. Wittgenstein's ideas on music influence the way
he reflects on language. He explores the connections that may exist between
the linguistic phrase and the musical phrase. What does it mean to understand
a spoken phrase? What does it mean to understand a melody? Wittgenstein
articulates these thoughts in the *Brown Book*, a series of lectures dictated in
1934-1935, which is considered a preparatory work for the *Philosophical
Investigations*. He observes the strange illusion that possesses us when, by
"repeating a melody to ourselves and letting it make its full impression on us,
we say 'This melody says *something*,' and it is as though I had to find *what* it
says" (*BrB* II §17). And yet Wittgenstein claims that the melody doesn't say
anything that we can express in words or pictures. And, if we recognize that,
we should say that "It just expresses a musical thought," which means that the
melody just *expresses itself*. In other words, he emphasizes the idea of melody
as a tautology, a phrase that expresses itself and nothing more. Wittgenstein
is not concerned with providing a subjective explanation of music. Rather,
he puts himself in the position of a musician, reflecting on the different ways
to play a melody: "But surely when you play it you don't play it *anyhow*, you
play it in this particular way, making a crescendo here, a diminuendo there,
a caesura in this place, etc." (*BrB* II §17). How do we justify playing the
melody in this manner and not differently? He says that we can explain the
specific performance by comparing the melody to a phrase: "At this point of
the theme, there is, as it were, a colon", etc. (*BrB* II §17). He considers the
"right" tempo of the melody. As we know, playing a melody in a different
tempo can create a completely new meaning. He asks:

> "What it is like to know the tempo in which a piece of music
> should be played?" And the idea suggests itself that there *must* be
> a paradigm somewhere in our mind, and that we have adjusted
> the tempo to conform to that paradigm. But in most cases if
> someone asks me, "How do you think this melody should be

played?," I will, as an answer, just whistle it in a particular way, and nothing will have been present to my mind but the tune *actually whistled* (not an image of *that*). (*BrB* II §17)

There are two interesting things to observe here: First, the idea that there is a paradigm in our mind telling us how to play the melody, what is the correct tempo, the dynamics, the punctuations, etc. Second, the idea that I can represent the melody through something; for example I can whistle the melody to show someone the correct tempo of the melody. But then, when I do that, what is present in my mind is the whistled melody and nothing else. Wittgenstein does not deny that understanding a musical theme may consist in finding a form of verbal expression that is though of as equivalent to the theme. The same applies for the understanding of a facial expression: We can say, "Now I understand the expression of this face" (*BrB* II §17), and what happened is that we found a word that conveys the expression of this face. However, the verbal expression we associate with the musical theme or the words we use to describe the face are not the understanding itself.

Wittgenstein says: "Consider also this expression: "Tell yourself that it's a *waltz*, and you will play it correctly" " (*BrB* II §17). Here, the word "correct" indicates that the musician knows what a "waltz" is, because he has learned the "rules" for a successful performance (see below on rules) and the verbal image of the word "waltz" may be just a hint that triggers this implicit knowledge. Wittgenstein invokes the understanding of a musical phrase as an analogy of understanding language because he wants to say that, in music, understanding comes from within, from doing the performance, and not from a reference to something outside projected onto it:

> What we call "understanding a sentence" has, in many cases, a much greater similarity to understanding a musical theme than we are inclined to think. But I don't mean that understanding a musical theme is more like the picture one tends to make oneself of understanding a sentence; but rather that this picture is wrong, and that understanding a sentence is much more like what really happens when we understand a melody than at first sight appears. For understanding a sentence, we say, point to a reality outside the sentence. Whereas one might say "Understanding a sentence means getting hold of its content; and the content of the sentence is *in* the sentence". (*BrB* II §17)

The concept of philosophy as a therapy (PI §254) conveys the idea that our concern with building models of elucidation is an obstacle to our progress, something that holds us and binds us, preventing us from continuing. The goal is not to produce new stable conclusions, but lead us to change our way of thinking or of approaching problems. His philosophical method, as McGuinn suggests, "aims to engage the reader in an active process of working on himself; it also underlines the fact that the reader's acknowledgment of Wittgenstein's diagnoses of philosophical error is a vital part of his method" (McGuinn, 1996, p. 22). Wittgenstein's therapeutic approach is essentially a slow process: "My sentences are all to be read *slowly*" (*CV* 57; 65); the patient is gradually led to a new understanding of the nature of the problems that were disturbing him; this understanding allows him to recognize that he was seeking pleasure in the wrong way, and this should bring him peace.

Wittgenstein's writing style is complex and distinctive. He shapes the philosophical process as an internal dialog using the voice of an interlocutor. The voice is introduced either indirectly through observations or directly through the use of quotation marks. The dialog presents the situation in which someone succumbs to the traps of our language while the therapeutic voice examines concrete examples as a way to get a new view of things, seeking clarity and understanding. Due to these multiple voices, his style has often been compared to music and particularly to polyphony. We can say that the different voices with their specific timbres play individual roles in the thematic development; they appear and disappear, join other voices in new contexts and connections.

Wittgenstein introduces the concept of *Übersicht* [survey, overview], which is translated in English as "perspicuity", to define this philosophical attitude that seeks to understand things by making visible their connections. This is a significant difference from an understanding produced by a theory of explanation, which is the common case in metaphysics and science. An *Übersicht* is the kind of understanding produced, for instance, by a work of music, a poem, or a work of art. Our language lacks *Übersicht*, because of the grammar, which obscures our capacity to see the connections between things:

> A main source of our failure to understand is that we do not *command a clear view* of the use of our words.—Our grammar is lacking in this sort of perspicuity. A perspicuous representation produces just that understanding which consists in "seeing connections". Here the importance of finding and inventing *intermediate cases*.

> The concept of a perspicuous representation is of fundamental significance for us. It earmarks the form of account we give, the way we look at things. (Is this a "Weltanschauung"?). (*PI* §122)

Polyphony is but one of the many musical metaphors that have been proposed for interpreting Wittgenstein. Eggers, for example, analyzes Wittgenstein's method as a "musical" elaboration of material that can be viewed in different ways. Wittgenstein operates with figures emerging from an unspeakable background; he develops a technique of changing points of view [*Blickwechsel*], moving from one figure to another or detaching figures from a noisy, unutterable background (cf. Egger, 2011, p. 232). This unspeakable background is what allows music to develop audible meanings. When we listen to a musical work, we are necessarily recognizing figures that are formed on a background, which, at the same time, is not openly manifest. In a musical work one cannot simultaneously realize all layers of expression. There is no fixed point functioning as a stable state of affairs for interpreting music. In the field of music there are states of affairs, but these are intentional, i.e., they are objectifications of subjects. The listener is an integral part of the process of musical hermeneutics.

For Wittgenstein, there is no prototype of understanding. We apply the word "understand" in very different situations. It is the use we give to the word that defines its meaning. The aesthetic understanding, especially the musical understanding, is a paradigm of the hermeneutic understanding of language. Through the musical analogy Wittgenstein guides us through the labyrinths of understanding: "Language is a labyrinth of paths. You approach from *one* side and know your way about; you approach the same place from another side and no longer know your way about" (*PI* §203). Music has a more transparent grammar and therefore can help to elucidate the grammar of language, which is more opaque.

Nevertheless, Wittgenstein does not transform the musical phrase into a paradigm of understanding; he is not concerned with developing a general model of comprehension based on musical understanding. For Chauviré (1986), Wittgenstein uses the analogy between the melody and the phrase in order to achieve an *Übersicht* [overview] of the different applications the word "understanding" can have. He uses the analogy as a bilateral tool, never as a unilateral one, going back and forth between music, language, and other kinds of representation such as pictures, faces, gestures, etc. The analogy creates a reciprocal relationship that serves to illuminate both terms of the comparison. Wittgenstein doesn't want us to think that music is the model of understanding; he rather suggests exploring some internal similarities that may exist between relative cases that can explain themselves reciprocally. The analogy points to the similarities but also to the differences between different cases of understanding. Wittgenstein believes that, instead of paradigms to explain everything, philosophy has to operate with partial models that are instruments of making analogies. He calls these instruments *objects of comparison* [*Vergleichsobjekte*]. According to Chauviré, Wittgenstein rejects the dogmatic—even perverse—use of paradigms in all research including philosophy, psychoanalysis (Freud), ethnology, physics, mathematics, etc. (cf. Chauviré, 1986, p. 1161).

2. Language games: musical understanding

Wittgenstein's theory of language games, as Sloterdijk observes, became one of the most powerful arguments of modern and postmodern pluralism (Sloterdijk, 2011, p. 128). What is a language game? It is an object of comparison for exploring similarities and differences that help to clarify some aspects of the language:

> Our clear and simple language-games are not preparatory studies for a future regimentation of language—as it were first approximations, ignoring friction and air-resistance. The language-games are rather set up as *objects of comparison* which are meant to throw light on the facts of our language by way not only of similarities, but also of dissimilarities. (*PI* §130)

The analogy between the melody and the sentence is an example of a language game. Chauviré distinguishes some strategic functions of this specific language game: (1) there is a similarity of family between the musical phrase and the verbal phrase; (2) there is no prototype of understanding; (3) musical understanding emphasizes important aspects of understanding. What is the understanding of a musical theme? In the *Philosophical Investigations* Wittgenstein reflects on this topic; similarly, as he wrote in the *Brown Book*, he asks himself how we can say that we understand a melody:

> Understanding a sentence is much more akin to understanding a theme in music than one may think. What I mean is that understanding a sentence lies nearer than one thinks to what is ordinarily called understanding a musical theme. Why is just *this* the pattern of variation in loudness and tempo: One would

like to say "Because I know what it's all about." But what is it all about? I should not be able to say. In order to "explain" I could only compare it with something else which has the same rhythm (I mean the same pattern). (One says "Don't you see, this is as if a conclusion were being drawn" or "This is as if it were a parenthesis" etc. How does one justify such comparisons?—There are very different kinds of justification here.) (*PI* §527)

By saying that music conveys nothing but itself Wittgenstein rejects the causal approach according to which music has the essential function of producing affects and emotions, the meaning of which is intentionally incorporated into musical signs. The belief that music expresses nothing but itself is in line with the idea of musical autonomy. Wittgenstein writes in the *Brown Book*:

> It has sometimes being said that what music conveys to us are feelings of joyfulness, melancholy, triumph, etc. etc. and what repels us in this account is that it seems to say that music is an instrument for producing in us sequences of feelings. And from this one might gather that any other means of producing such feeling would do for us instead of music.—To such an account we are tempted to reply "Music conveys to us *itself*!" (*BrB* II §22)

This idea of musical autonomy can be easily mistaken for self-sufficiency, as if music had the capability to speak about itself. Wittgenstein's thesis is that music is self-contained in the sense that it doesn't need to express something exterior because it is complete in itself. This crucial idea is that the understanding of music cannot be explained *causally*. Although, if there could be something through which we could express our understanding of music—such as a word we utter, or a facial expression, or a gesture we make with the hand or the head— these expressions can demonstrate understanding, they say nothing about the essence of the understanding. The understanding is embedded in music, in a melody, a phrase, a theme, etc. Wittgenstein asks how one can recognize that another person understands a musical thought. He makes an analogy between someone listening to music, or drawing a face, or playing an instrument with understanding; he asks how this understanding is to be communicated:

> What does it consist in: following a musical phrase with understanding? Observing a face with a feeling for its expression? Drinking in the expression on the face?

Think of the demeanor of someone who draws the face with understanding for its expression. Think of the sketcher's face, his movements;—what shows that every stroke he makes is dictated by the face, that nothing in his sketch is arbitrary, that he is a *delicate* instrument?

Is that really an *experience*? I mean: can we say that this expresses an experience?

Once again: what does it consist in, following a musical phrase with understanding, or, playing it with understanding? Don't look inside yourself. Ask yourself rather, what makes you say that's what someone else is doing. And *what* prompts you to say that *he* has a particular experience? Indeed, do we ever actually say that? Wouldn't I be more likely to say of *someone else* that he's having a whole host of experiences?

I would perhaps say, "He is experiencing the theme intensely"; but ask yourself, what is the expression of this? (*CV* 51; 58)

What emerges here is the issue of internal experience, which is recurrent in Wittgenstein's philosophy. Understanding is not caused by an external factor, but is internal. The understanding of a musical phrase (or a work of music) is like the sudden emergence of an acoustic configuration for which we give an interpretation. We understand music like we recognize the expression of a face or a drawing. Understanding arises out of an impulse; it happens like a "click" in our mind (Chauviré 1986, p. 1165), an explosion of meaning that leads us to connect things and through which we experience the unity: "I want to remember a melody and it escapes me; suddenly I say "Now I know it" and I sing it. What was it like to suddenly know it? Surely it can't have occurred to me *in its entirety* in that moment!" (*PI* §184)

Wittgenstein refers frequently to *gesticulations* [*Gebärde*] and *gestures* [*Geste*] to illustrate the problem of understanding. The metaphor of gestures is a recurrent one in *Culture and Value* and *Philosophical Investigations*:

This musical phrase is a gesture for me. It creeps into my life. I make it my own (*CV* 73; 83).

I should like to say: "These notes say something glorious, but I do not know what." "These notes are a powerful gesture, but I cannot put anything side by side with it that will serve as an explanation." (*PI* §610)

Wittgenstein emphasizes that musical understanding does not consist in the gestures and movements you can make while listening to music. Gesture is only a reaction in line with the sensations we may have, the movement we may make, or even the words that can accompany our understanding. Wittgenstein disassociates everything exterior that points to the understanding from the understanding itself:

> Understanding & explaining a musical phrase.—The simplest explanation is sometimes a gesture; another might be a dance step, or words describing a dance.—But isn't our understanding of the phrase an experience we have while hearing it? & what function, in that case, has the explanation? Are we supposed to think of *it* while we hear the music? Are we supposed to imagine the dance, or whatever it may be, as we listen? And supposing we do,—why should *that* be called hearing the music with understanding?? If seeing the dance is what matters, it would be better *that*, rather than the music, were performed. But that is all a misunderstanding. (*CV* 69; 79)

> Understanding of music is expressed in a certain way, both in the course of hearing and playing and at other times too. This *expression* sometimes includes movements, but sometimes only the way the one who understands plays, or hums, occasionally too parallels he draws and images, which, at it were, illustrate the music. Someone who understands music will listen differently (with a different facial expression, e.g.), play differently, hum differently, talk differently about the piece that someone who does not understand. His appreciation of a theme will not however be shown only in phenomena that accompany the hearing of playing of the theme, but also in an understanding of music in general. (*CV* 70; 80)

Gestures and gesticulations appear as primitive language games with aesthetic value. Although gestures are not articulated like language, they say more than 1,000 words compared to traditional aesthetic discourse. The gesture as the first and last image of a silent understanding appears as a primitive and ultimate manifestation of an esthetic appreciation, which it is impossible to formulate orally with accuracy. The gesture may be considered an index of a specific understanding that shows itself by the gesture. But understanding is internal. If it were external there would be a rule whereby a certain gesture would be correlated with a certain understanding. Gestures do not belong to listening with understanding, but are part of the music in the same way that music can trigger emotions and emotions can be associated with the way we listen to music. For Wittgenstein, the gesture realizes the impossibility of describing what we feel, shows the impossibility of developing a scientific aesthetics to clarify music from the logical, causal standpoint.

3. Conclusion

Wittgenstein formulated with intensity and precision a close relationship between ethics and aesthetics—"(Ethics and aesthetics are one and the same.)" (*TLP* 6.421). Both are part of the ineffable; the ethical and aesthetical attitude towards the world is the one that shows the "good life". The artist's attitudes and decisions are a matter of both ethics and aesthetics. It doesn't matter how the world is, how much misery there is in the world, the work of art has to show the possibility of seeing the world as it is, as something transcendental. The idea that we are not able to explain the world in a logical sense, together with the attitude of acceptance, leads to a "mystical" view: "There are, indeed, things that cannot be put into words. They *make themselves manifest*. They are what is mystical" (*PI* §6.53).

Wittgenstein's philosophy is not focused on culture but on language and thinking. He uses the analogy between music and language as a tool for reflecting on different issues of understanding. Music brings clarity; it has a more transparent "grammar" than language and therefore can make thing appear that are hidden by language. Wittgenstein emphasizes the autonomy of music: music doesn't say anything but itself. On the other hand, he recognizes that aesthetic understanding is only possible within a culture through the contextual references to the *forms of life*. To describe an ensemble of aesthetic rules means to describe a specific culture. Musical understanding cannot be reduced to the mechanical application of explicit rules; the expressive game of musical rules obeys a tradition that is mostly implicit, which determines the choices. The rules allow us to recognize the full expression of music.

Wittgenstein's reflection on music is focused on the music of the 19th century that belonged to his particular cultural context. He gave no thoughts to the music of his own time, for example the atonal and serial music of Arnold Schoenberg, with whom he shares similar points of view.[6] This leads us to the question if Wittgenstein's ideas on music apply only to the music he reflects on or to other kinds of music. Are his thoughts useful but limited to the music of the past? Or can he help us understand music no longer rooted in the European tradition or music that seeks formal models outside melodic and harmonic structures of tonality, such as atonal music, electroacoustic music, or digital music? On the other hand, should we consider the possibility that a shift has occurred in which music became a different kind of language with a different grammar? Or even that music lost its language?

I believe that Wittgenstein's philosophical method opens new perspectives for understanding music in a broad sense, including listening, composing, performing, analyzing and teaching. Wittgenstein develops a concept of "grammar" that is not focused on language considered as a system of signs, but on the *practice of using language*. This concept invokes the idea that language is a spatial and temporal phenomenon (*PI* §108) that has to be understood as a *language-in-use* with its distinctive patterns of use that constitute what he calls the "grammar of our concepts" (cf. McGinn 1996, p. 13). Wittgenstein's therapeutic voice tells us to look carefully into the detailed structure of our practice of using language in order to cure ourselves of the temptations of misunderstanding.

For Wittgenstein, to understand is not a process of going inwards but of looking at the surface of our practice, which is connected to a complexity of patterns that characterize our form of life. Music—similar to language—is not an abstract system of signs conveying some kind of meaning, but a particular form of life that displays structures that are constituted by the activity of making music. Wittgenstein invites us to look at the way we determine musical concepts, how in our musical practice we constitute regular patterns by following rules, how we choose to follow some rules and dismiss others, how we apply words like "correct" or "incorrect" to make aesthetic judgments about music and in general, and so on.

Wittgenstein's philosophy shows us that everything we need to know is there in front of our eyes. We don't have to look for obscure meanings that are not expressed on the surface of life, which don't help us to understand our activity of using words or making music. Wittgenstein confronts us with the roots of our confusion, which lies in the "misunderstanding of the logic of language" (*PI* § 93). As he says: "We are struggling with language. We are engaged in a struggle with language" (*CV* 11; 13). What we need to do is not to elaborate theories or empirical constructions for discovering things, but to recognize that "Since everything lies open to view there is nothing to explain" (*PI* §126).

Notes

1. The view of Wittgenstein as an *intellectual myth* was suggested by Sloterdijk (2009, pp. 125-29).
2. A review of the bibliography on Wittgenstein is beyond the scope of this essay.
3. For an overview of the efforts to make available the sources on Wittgenstein see The Wittgenstein Archives at the University of Bergen (WAB), http://wab.uib.no [accessed on August 1, 2013].
4. The works by Wittgenstein are cited according to the usual abbreviations; for *Culture and Value* (*CV*) I include the pages of both the first and the second English editions (1980; 1998). For the citations from Wittgenstein I use basically the English translations, which I changed—sometimes significantly—when I considered that the translation did not convey correctly the meaning of Wittgenstein's German text. All emphases are in the original.
5. For an account of Wittgenstein's conception of ethics in relation to Schopenhauer, see Griffiths (1974).
6. For a comparison between Wittgenstein and Schoenberg, see Eggers (2011).

References

The works by Wittgenstein are cited according to the usual abbreviations:

BrB: Wittgenstein, L. (1978). *The blue and brown book* (2nd ed.). R. Rhees (Ed.). Oxford: Basil Blackwell. Wittgenstein, L. (1980). *Das Blaue Buch: Eine Philosophische Betrachtung (Das Braune Buch)*. R. Rhees (Ed.). (P. von Morstein, Trans.). Suhrkamp: Frankfurt am Main.

CV: Wittgenstein, L. (1980). *Culture and value* (2nd ed.). G. H. von Wright & H. Nyman (Eds.). (P. Winch, Trans.). Chicago: University of Chicago Press. Wittgenstein, L. (1998). *Culture and value* (revised 2nd ed.). G. H. von Wright & H. Nyman (Eds.). A. Pichler (revised ed. of the text). (P. Winch, Trans.). Oxford: Basil Blackwell. Wittgenstein, L. (1984). *Bemerkungen über die Farben. Über Gewißheit. Zettel. Vermischte Bemerkungen.* Werkausgabe Bd. 8. G. E. M. Anscombe (Ed.). Suhrkamp: Frankfurt am Main.

LE: Wittgenstein, L. (1965). A Lecture on Ethics. *Philosophical Review, 74* (1), 3-12.

NB: Wittgenstein, L. (1979). *Notebooks 1914-1916* (2nd ed.). (G. H. von Wright and G. E. M Anscombe (Eds.). (G.E.M. Anscombe, Trans.). Oxford: Basil Blackwell.

PI: Wittgenstein, L. (2001). *Philosophical investigations [Philosophische Untersuchungen]*. The German text with a revised English translation, (3rd ed.). (G. E. M.Anscombe, Trans.). Oxford: Blackwell Publishing.

TLP: Wittgenstein, L. (1974). *Tractatus Logico-Philosophicus*. (D. F. Pears and B. F. McGuiness, Trans.). London; New York: Routledge. Wittgenstein, L. (1984). *Tractatus logico-philosophicus. Tagebücher 1914-16. Philosophische Untersuchungen.* Werkausgabe Bd. 1. Suhrkamp: Frankfurt am Main.

Chauviré, C. (1986). Comprendre la musique chez Wittgenstein. *Critique* 42, 1159-1181.

Crary, A., & Read, R. (Eds.). (2000). *The new Wittgenstein*. London: Routledge.

Diamond, C. (1991). *The realistic spirit*. Cambridge, MA: The MIT Press.

Eggers, K. (2011). *Ludwig Wittgenstein als Musikphilosoph*. Freiburg; Munich: Karl Alber.

Gmür, F. (2000). *Ästhetik bei Wittgenstein: über Sagen und Zeigen*. Freiburg; Munich: Karl Alber.

Griffiths, A. P. (1974). Wittgenstein, Schopenhauer, and Ethics. In *Understanding Wittgenstein*. Royal Institute of Philosophy Lectures (vol. 7, pp. 96-116). London: Macmillan.

McGinn, M. (1996). *Routledge philosophy guidebook to Wittgenstein and the Philosophical Investigations*. London; New York: Routledge.

Monk, R. (1990). *Ludwig Wittgenstein. The duty of genius*. New York: Penguin Books.

Rhees, R. (1981). *Ludwig Wittgenstein: Personal recollections*. Totowa, NJ: Rowman and Littlefield.

Schoenberg, A. (1975). *Style and idea*. L. Stein (Ed.). London: Faber and Faber.

Sloterdijk, P. (2009). *Philosophische Temperamente: Von Plat*

Where to Draw the Line? Representation in Intermedial Song Analysis

Lea Maria Lucas Wierød

Aarhus University

1. An intermedial approach to song analysis

Musicology has always been puzzled with semantic questions: does music have meaning? The difficulty lies in music's inability to function referentially. One might say that literature suffers from the opposite problem: verbal texts contain a centrifugal tendency to direct the recipient's attention away from their artwork character (form) in favor of their referential message (content) (Kyndrup, 2011, p. 87). However, the specific case of poetry (as opposed to prose) often displays a certain quality that maneuvers attention toward the form of the message itself; a move notably termed *the poetic function* by Jakobson (1987, p. 69). This can be understood as a shift from a semantic ("what does it mean") to a semiotic ("how does it mean") point of view, which entails a similitude between the perception of music and poetry.

The premise of this article is that the investigation of songs can benefit from focusing on the modalities that poetry and music have in common. However, due to disciplinary borders, songs are mostly split into melody and text in analysis. Wolf (2002) notes that " [...] a song is, of course, more than a mere juxtaposition of words and music," suggesting that songs convey a semiosis that reaches beyond the mere sum total of components. Taking as a starting point the proliferation of interdisciplinary theories within the field of aesthetics, chiefly intermediality studies, this article seeks to describe this deeper layer of song by pointing to the possibility of (re)uniting the analytical fields. Thus, it is a contribution to the special branch of intermediality studies that can be referred to as melopoetics.

135

Lea Maria Lucas Wierød

I suggest that rhythm is the most palpably shared component of words and music in performed songs. I regard song as a single (mixed) medium combining several modalities, of which the ephemeral and sequential quality of rhythm is the most significant. In this article, I will examine a number of ways in which poetic analysis of rhythm can be applied to music. The opposite approach—the application of musical notation to poetry—has, as I will show, been taken some times before. My reverse approach, which also builds on previous similar undertakings, is motivated by two assumptions. Firstly, since the notational practice in poetic analysis is governed less by conformity than musical notation, it provides a freer and more variable pool to choose from. In its uncontested supremacy, western musical notation would arguably be more liable to freeze the analysis in a potentially inadequate way. Secondly, the historical origin of several of the symbols used in poetic rhythm analysis testifies to the common offspring of poetic and musical notation, making my approach rather a reversion to former practices than an entirely new endeavor.

After a brief outline of the paper's theoretical background, I proceed to discussing some different approaches to song analysis while arguing that songs as multimodal objects can best be analyzed without the limitations of western musical notation symbols. Lastly, I employ an example in order to depict some possible principles of multimodal analysis of songs.

2. Theoretical background

The notion of *song* as a specific category in everyday language seems unproblematic. There is a broad consensus on what kind of thing one is referring to when talking about a song. However, the word is too broad to denote a genre in the traditional sense.[1] It rather functions as a trans-generic umbrella term covering several divergent musical genres (from a *lied* to a *rap song* etc.) as well as different types of literary text (lyrics). This is probably because the components that constitute the song are media-specific rather than genre-specific: a combination of words and organized sound is all that is required to make up a song. Genre lines are drawn on a different level. They are the result of aesthetic evaluation and historically determined institutionalizations. Regarding song as an entity thus means focusing on media-specific rather than genre-specific features. Such an approach seems to be productive with respect to interdisciplinary analysis. Moser (2007) observed a difference in the perception of reading a poem versus listening to songs and thus made the point that songs cannot be studied while focusing only on one of the modes involved, e.g. the semantic content of the text. The

136

study of songs must therefore, in this view, entail the pragmatic endeavor of describing what affect the media-specific components, for instance sound and sequentiality, have on the reception of the song.

This broad definition of the song puts strong limits on the possibility of establishing an analytical terminology that applies to all songs. Toward its end, this article uses as an example a church hymn. As a consequence, the reflections will be targeted primarily at homophonic songs designed for community singing. It is my assumption that such songs, when put into function (i.e. when they are sung) represent an inseparable unity of words and melody. Rather than two distinct items aligned and merged, I regard songs as a congenial entity.

Such a perception of song, which really amounts to a return to ancient practices of regarding all recitation as a kind of sung words, is, admittedly, in danger of imposing an anachronistic method on the object of analysis. Since the Middle Ages and the Latin adaptation of the word melodia, we have come to connect melody with distinctly musical features, as opposed to the ancient view of song as merely recited words and as a natural part of human and cosmological existence (Ringer, 2013). Kramer, in his book *Music and Poetry*, draws attention to the omnipresent tendency among poets to say: "in the beginning was the song," thus conforming to the cosmic view on words and melody as a unity (1984, p. 1). He subsequently adds his own observation of what the consequences are of the two main constituents of song (words and music) being separated. He goes on to describe how the two art forms have ever since their separation taken turns in aspiring to the condition of the other in a kind of shifting ideological hierarchy.

From the point of view of biography or authorial intention, an endeavor to amalgamate the description of words and melody is in danger of neglecting the artistic expression in one of the components. It is hard to overlook the fact that a song in our day is mostly the result of at least two poetic wills: the one of the author and the one of the composer.

However, in this investigation of songs, I wish to focus on the state of the song in its situation of performance. This choice of viewpoint subsumes the separability of the artistic intentions of the creators into the inseparability of the experience of the recipient. When songs become embedded in performative context, they can no longer be meaningfully segregated into *text* and *melody*. In performance, the song becomes one medium. Following the line of Elleström (2010) one might say that, during performance, song is one medium consisting of several modalities (whenever I apply the notion of *multimodality*, I am referring to Elleström's definition of modality—in short, Elleström detects a combination of four modalities at play in every medium:

the material, the sensory, the spatiotemporal and the semiotic). When a song hits the sensory body, it is not perceived as *text* and *melody*, but as a single sounding substance. It is this uniform phenomenon that I want to subject to investigation.

The first question which then poses itself is: what are the medial modalities most obviously shared by words and melody in a song? Several authors think that it is the way in which both words and melody make tangible the otherwise unconscious flow of time by structuring it in rhythm. Symptomatically, Kramer's ambition is to focus on structural rhythm as the shared property of music and poetry: "The overdetermined play of poetic connotation and musical combination would therefore cohere through the rhythm by which both turn time into form" (Kramer, 1984, p. 10). Similarly, Bernhart (2007, p. 88) states, when listing the ways in which words and music resemble each other, that "An important dimension of contact in songs between the words and the music is the rhythmical structure, which implies segmentation, accentuation and duration." Rhythm analysis is equally an issue for the study of poetry and music. In either case, a persistent query is the relation between rhythm and meter. I follow the tradition, explicated by for example Justin London (2004), of regarding rhythm as something emergent or phenomenally present, and meter as a cognitive scheme.[2]

It is near at hand, in turn, when dealing with the intricate rhythm-meter distinction, to touch upon the relationship between orality and literacy. Taruskin (2005, p. 1) notes, while describing the beginning of western music history, that the invention of musical notation did not coincide with the invention of music. This is one argument for the rejection of the idea that musical notation is in any way a part of music itself on an ontological level; however, the existence of oral, non-written poetry before the development of writing would then also have to reject the notion of the written words as part of the poem. This is a more dubious claim. Kjørup (2003, p. 189) launched the term *etymological fallacy* about the idea among some theorists of metrics that the oral connotation of the word *lyrics* points to the ontologically oral status of poetry. The broad range of versification mechanisms that seem to show only in writing contradicts the idea of poetry being primarily oral. Etymologically, the word for verse itself refers to the turning of the written line (Jakobson, 1987, p. 145). It seems more acceptable to regard the auditory side of music as the "real" music and hence the score as a representation waiting to be actualized.

The hegemony of "visual culture" has been criticized a number of times in recent decades, perhaps most prominently by Mitchell (2005) with the dictum that "There Are No Visual Media". Nielsen (1996) has advocated a heightened analytical attention to the fact that music is primarily auditory. He evokes dissociation from the false assumption that a musical score represents the "actual" music in a more objective way than listening. He ascribes this tendency to the idea that vision, by placing a distance between object and observer, is a more consistent and verifiable sense than hearing, and he explains how this emphasis in analysis on music's written representation is an obstacle to understanding music as chiefly an interaction with a listener. Similarly, Honing (2002, p. 227) notes about the field of empirical musicology that: "Existing theories of rhythmic structure are often restricted to music as it is notated in a score, and as a result are bound to refrain from making statements about music as it is perceived and appreciated by listeners." I wish to focus on the auditorily rhythmic material of songs, as this seems to be the meeting point par excellence for the shared modalities of words and melody.[3] Scholars concerned with the cross-field of words and music have discussed the question of how to represent such an auditory analysis in writing for a long time. I wish to compare and discuss some of these theoretical and analytical approaches and thus contribute to the ongoing debate on this intricate topic.

2.1 Analysing words like music or music like words

Brown (1970) and Bernhart (2007) have given historical outlines of the scholarly approaches to the interrelation of words and music. They both mention the 18th century author John Steele, who makes a thorough attempt at developing a detailed system to depict the prosody of speech using modified musical symbols (Steele, 1969). Although he is concerned with speech in general, his errand is still overlapping with mine, since poetry is predominantly built of the material of natural language. In a nutshell, Steele's wish is to provide notational equipment that will enable us to preserve not only the meaning, but also the sound of language. In this sense, his work represents a desire to hold on to the ephemeral passing of time, which is more evidently presented by sound as opposed to writing. See fig. 1 for an example of Steele's prosodic notational system (1969, p. 13).

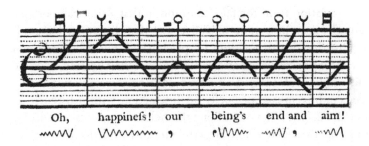

FIGURE 1. Example of Steele's prosodic notational system

The tails at the top correspond to the heads in normal musical notation, namely representation of quantity in time. The heads at the bottom designate accent, which is here understood as a moving or sliding of the voice. The form of the head, in an iconical way, shows which way the intonation is to slide. One can observe, then, that these heads bear a resemblance to the diacritical accent signs in for example ancient Greek writing. Interestingly, Steele notes this himself, stating that he did not intend this resemblance, but that the coincidence supports the usefulness of his system. He gives hints to the original meaning of the accent symbols, which today, when used in metric analysis, mean strong and weak rhythmic accents, but originally (also) designated movement of tonal pitch.[4] Steele's system then amounts to a formalization or specification of the diacritical marks in that they are regulated in quantity and pitch, which renders their denotational quality no longer relative but absolute.

Other approaches to setting musical notation to speech have been made. In the tradition of bar metrics[5] represented chiefly by Lanier (1911) and Heusler (1925-29), this particular method is important, since their approach to metrics is based on the idea that rhythm in poetry can be organized in bars like music. Recently, Fanany (2008) has shown an attempt at roughly the same thing. In her article, an example of the analytical approach, which is a musical notation applied to a text sample from Shakespeare's *Hamlet*, looks like this:

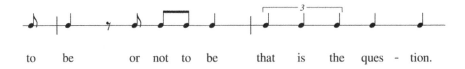

FIGURE 2. Fanany's notation (slightly adapted)

The tendency toward extensive formalization in these examples is often anticipated by the authors who employ it. Steele (1969, p. 14) warns that this "reducing of common speech to notes" should not be expected to be extremely accurate. Fanany (2008, p. 5) brings the cautionary remark that her notational system can and will vary in performance.

Patel and Daniele (2002) made similar cautionary remarks in an empirical study of the relation between rhythm in language and music. They looked at rhythmic patterns in music to see if musical compositions reflected phonetic inclinations in the composer's native language. Their method was to measure prosodic elements of language in terms of musical notation, and in doing so they noted (2003, p. 40): "However, measurement of actual musical performances raises a number of questions without simple answers. Most notably, which performance of the piece is to be measured, and how is this choice to be defended against all other recorded performances, each of which will differ in the precise timing of notes?" This reservation similarly points to the instability of the relationship between the very precise indications in musical notation and the actual freedom of articulation in performed music as well as in spoken language, especially since musical notation in our time has become much more specified and loaded with information than earlier. In Patel and Daniele this might be less of a problem, though, because they limit their study to music composed after 1800. Musical notation has since this time generally had a greater degree of correspondence between written score and performance, for example with regard to tone duration.[6] Huron and Ollen (2003) represent a more precarious case in that they reiterate the study of Patel and Daniele (2003) while expanding the empirical range of samples to also include music reaching as far back as the 16th century. This, in my view, is problematic since musical scores from before circa 1800 cannot be expected to represent performance with the accuracy to which we are accustomed today. Houle (1987) points out that musicians of today often find it challenging to read musical scores from before circa 1800, because notes—while visually still appearing the same—simply did not denote the same things back then. One of the pivotal differences is that older scores presuppose a rhythmic freedom in performance that is actually comparable to the notation of popular songs. As such, it seems very questionable to base an assessment of rhythmic variability on scores of this age. While this is a historical argument, it still points to the problems adhering to the highly stringent modern musical notation.

The study of poetic language has an analytical symbol system of its own that might be applied to music. Actually, it has several systems: the written representation of rhythm and meter in poetic language has had a turbulent history with many divergent contributions and proposals. Küper (1989)

Lea Maria Lucas Wierød

speaks of a veritable *Methodenwirrwarr* in the field of poetic metrics because of this state of unresolved authority in terminology. Cureton (1992, p. 7) notes about the traditions of rhythmical analysis that: "historically, each of these analytical systems has been developed in relative isolation from each other [...]. The result has been a huge body of writing, often useful in its particulars but lacking in coherence and consensus on just those issues that should constitute its most fundamental concerns." My assumption is that this circumstance can be turned into an advantage for the purpose of multimodal song analysis.[7] Musical notation offers only one representational system, but poetic theory of meter offers several, which makes it possible to select and/or assemble the most adequate. Furthermore, some of the symbols used in literary analysis of poetic meter today are so old that they transgress the time of the foundation of the institutional borders that led to the division of the fields of poetry and music—the division that made poetry and music "nostalgic for each other", in Kramer's words (1984, p. 3). It is the same division that made it meaningful, in the first place, to talk about the combination of words and music as an intermedial phenomenon, as indeed it makes no sense to connect songs with the notion of inter-mediality if one regards them as one coherent medium, as I have argued one should.[8]

3. Whether to draw the bar line

I put my focus in multimodal song analysis particularly on rhythm partly because, as mentioned, it makes up the focal point of the interrelation of words and music, but another reason is that it is arguably the one inherent musical feature that is most closely linked to performance. Compared to rhythmical variability, changes in harmony and melody seem to have a more radical impact on musical integrity.[9]

From the point of view of rhythmic scansion and analysis in its written representation (whether the object be words or music), the crucial point seems to be the bar line. The bar line represents the notion of arranging free flowing rhythm in metrical units. This is perhaps most obvious in musical notation, but it also shows when applied to poetic rhythm. The concept of bars can be thought of as the ultimate restriction on rhythmical freedom, as is illustrated by the fact that they are often metaphorically compared to a prison. This is for example the case in Gould's vast book on the history of musical notation, for which she chose the homonymic wordplay title *Behind Bars* (2011).

142

The existence of bar lines implies the existence of anacrusis,[10] which in turn, strictly speaking, excludes the idea of the metrical foot,[11] since if one accepts the notion of bar lines, there can be only falling feet (with or without anacrusis). In poetic metrics, the division of poetry into bars is no longer common (Getty & Brogan, 1993, p. 68), but in musical notation, the bar has been going strong since the Renaissance (Hiley, 2013).

My assumption is that a downplaying of symbols that restrict performative freedom (by being too absolute, such as the bar line or the exact length of musical note and rest values etc.) would be beneficial for representational faithfulness regarding performance of songs. This observation amounts to a curious paradox in that it states that the degree of representational information is inversely proportional with faithfulness: musical notation is at the same time too sensitive and not sensitive enough.

Concludingly, I wish to concretize my above discussion by employing as an example the church hymn *Nun komm der Heyden Heyland*, which is Luther's reworking from 1524 of the Gregorian hymn *Veni Redemptor Gentius* (the German text and the musical notes are reprinted as facsimile in Luther (2011, p. 21), of which the following score example is a transcription).

FIGURE 3

The melody is a choralized reproduction of a Gregorian chant. My choice of this example is partly motivated by the intertextual flexibility of the melody. In Denmark, it became associated with a hymn text by N. F. S. Grundtvig, *Op dog, Zion, ser du ej* (Nørfelt, 1983, p. 149).[12] This text has a radically different metrical structure. However, the melody seems to merge smoothly with both texts. This phenomenon can best be described by looking at the interplay of each of the texts with the melody.

The German text scans fairly uncontroversially as four iambs, in terms of verse feet (´ and ` denote strong and weak accent, respectively):

` ´   ´   ´

Nu kom der Heyden heyland

◡ – ◡ – ◡ – ◡

FIGURE 4

One could argue that the deictic quality of the first syllable is inclined to give the beginning of the line a spondaic character. This, then, poses the question of how the words correspond to the beginning of the melody in terms of accent: if the melody has an upbeat, this would put a damper on the recipient's disposition to interpret the first words as spondaic. The original notation of the melody, according to its historical context, does not employ bar lines, and therefore it does not inform about circumstances of upbeat. This is, then, laid out to the interpreter; and the performative result, I would suggest, is likely to stem from a fusion of wordly and melodic rhythmical gestalt. But perhaps the overall iambic contour of the words would tend to imprint a feeling of upbeat on the melody.

The hymn text by Grundtvig falls in regular trochees:

´ `    ´ `   ´   ´

Op dog, Zion! Ser du ej

– ◡   –◡   –   ◡ –

FIGURE 5

When merged with the same melody, the words tend to pull the rhythmical structure of the tones toward its own trochaic regularity. Not even the strongly iamb-reminiscent upward leap of a fourth from note 3 to 4 in the melody seems to be able to contradict this. In the melody book from 1954, linking this melody with the Grundtvig text, the musical score is provided with bar lines and no upbeat, advancing the impression that the melody should be interpreted as trochaic (Larsen & Wöldike, 1954, p. 228).

The interaction of words and music in these two songs is likely to make the performative realizations of them quite different. If so, we then have a case of one melody being, in a very formal sense, turned into two different ones by alignment with words. Thus, I find that this song displays what the empirical musicologist Repp (2007) has termed *metrical multistability*, which is the capacity of some pieces of music to be equally open to more than one metrical interpretation without any one of them being "correct", much like the mechanism in ambiguous optical illusions. The observations made here could not have been derived from musical or textual analysis alone; they only show in a melopoetic analysis that regards song as multimodal.

Notes

1. Genre has, since Aristotle, been viewed primarily as formalistic categories, although the last few decades have directed the notion of genre toward a more pragmatic definition, as, for example, Devitt (2000) sums up.

2. London's distinction is reminiscent of the distinction between phenomenal and metrical accent in Lerdahl and Jackendoff (1983, p. 17), while they also add a third category, the structural accent. Lerdahl and Jackendoff have, moreover, been of (interdisciplinary) inspiration to the theory of Richard Cureton (1992), who joins the tradition of viewing poetic rhythm in light of the temporal properties of music.

3. However, Lilja and Hopsch (2007, p. 361) argue that "tactility probably is the main perception type, speaking of rhythm." While both the ear and the eye are involved in rhythm perception, the importance of the experiencing body cannot be ignored. Interestingly, this might apply especially to church hymns, the genre exemplified in this paper, because of the identical nature of the performer and recipient.

4. This is evident also in the etymology of the word "accent" = "song added to speech" (Brogan, 1993, p. 3).

5. This is what Küper (1996, p. 393) terms this tradition.

6. Perhaps the most significant proof of this is the discovery about a century ago that a great deal of music composed approximately between 1600 and 1800 was by convention expected to alternate between long and shorter tones even in passages written with equal note values in scores (the so-called *inégalité*, similar to the concept of swing in jazz). A lot of scholarship testifies to this; important examples include Donington (1974) and Houle (1987).

7. Küper (1996, p. 6) himself also later welcomes the possibilities presented by this methodological multitude.

8. Bruhn (2010) has in observance of the specificity, and therefore limited application of the term *intermediality*, coined the term *heteromediality* as an overall term pointing to the mixed quality of all media, such as, in this case, songs.

9. This is maybe why such changes seldomly occur in the performance of western "classical" music.

10. The position of the bar metrists, in this article represented by Steele, Lanier and Heusler, amounts to a position in favor of the anacrusis, since their symbol system regards the first accentuated syllable as the starting point of meter, and any preceding unaccentuated syllables as, in a sense, lying outside or before meter.

11. The measuring in feet was common in both words and music in ancient Greek and Roman theories and thus makes up one of these originally multimodal systems for which this article advocates, as explained by Brogan (1993, p. 416).

12. The text is cited as it appears in the musical score from the appertaining melody book (Larsen & Wöldike, 1954, p. 228).

145

Lea Maria Lucas Wierød

References

Bernhart, W. (2007). Words and music as partners in song: 'perfect marriage' – 'uneasy flirtation' – 'coercive tension' – 'shared indifference' – 'total destruction'. In J. Arvidson, M. Askander, J. Bruhn, & H. Führer (Eds.), *Changing borders. Contemporary positions in intermediality* (pp. 85-95). Lund: Intermedia Studies Press.

Brogan, T. V. F. (1993). Foot. In A. Preminger, T. V. F. Brogan, F. J. Warnke (Eds.), *The new Princeton encyclopedia of poetry and poetics* (pp. 416-420). Princeton, NJ: Princeton University Press.

Brown, C. S. (1970). The relations between music and literature as a field of study. *Comparative Literature*, 22 (2), pp. 97–107.

Bruhn, J. (2010). Heteromediality. In L. Elleström (Ed), *Media borders, multimodality and intermediality* (pp. 225-236). New York, NY: Palgrave Macmillan.

Cureton, R. (1992). *Rhythmic phrasing in english verse*. New York: Longman.

Devitt, A. J. (2000). Integrating rhetorical and literary theories of genre. *College English*, *62*(6), 696-718.

Donington, R. (1974). *The interpretation of early music*. New York: St. Martin's Press.

Elleström, L. (2010). The modalities of media: a model for understanding intermedial relations. In L. Elleström (Ed.), *Media borders, multimodality and intermediality* (pp. 11-48). New York, NY: Palgrave Macmillan.

Fanany, R. (2008). The musicality of language: an application of musical analysis to speech and writing. *Journal of Music and Meaning*, 7. Retrieved September 1, 2013, from http://www.musicandmeaning.net/issues/showArticle.php?artID=7.4

Getty, R. J., & Brogan, T. V.F. (1993). Anacrusis. In A. Preminger, T. V. F. Brogan, F. J. Warnke (Eds.), *The new Princeton Encyclopedia of poetry and poetics* (pp. 68-69). Princeton, NJ: Princeton University Press.

Gould, E. (2011). *Behind bars: the definitive guide to music notation*. London: Faber Music.

Heusler, A. (1925-29). *Deutsche Versgeschichte*. Berlin: Walter de Gruyter & Co.

Hiley, D. (2013). Bar. *Grove Music Online*. Oxford University Press. Retrieved September 3, 2013, from http://www.oxfordmusiconline.com/subscriber/article/grove/music/01972.

Honing, H. (2002). Structure and interpretation of rhythm and timing. *Machine Learning* *3*(3), 227-232

Houle, G. (1987). *Meter in music 1600-1800*. Bloomington: Indiana University Press.

Huron, D., & Ollen, J. (2003). Agogic contrast in French and English themes: further support for Patel and Daniele. *Music Perception*, *21*(2), 267–271.

Jakobson, R. (1987). *Language in Literature*. Cambridge, Mass.: The Belknap Press of Harvard University Press.

Kjørup, F. (2003). *Sprog versus sprog*. København: Museum Tusculanums Forlag

Kramer, L. (1984). *Music and poetry. The nineteenth century and after*. London: University of California Press.

Küper, C. (1989). Metrik und Linguistik - einige grundsätzliche Überlegungen zu einem klassischen Methodenwirrwarr. In N.Reiter (Ed.). *Sprechen und Hören. Akten des 23. Linguistischen Kolloquiums Berlin 1988* (pp. 629-641). Tübingen: Niemeyer.

Küper, C. (1996). Metrics Today II. *Poetics today, 17*(1), 1-7.

Kyndrup, M. (2011). Mediality and literature: literature versus literature. In H. S. Nielsen and R. Kraglund (Eds.), *Why study literature* (pp. 85-96). Aarhus: Aarhus University Press.

Lanier, S. (1911). *The science of English verse.* New York, NY: Charles Scribner's Sons. (Original work published 1880).

Larsen, J. P., & Wöldike, M. (1954). *Den danske koralbog.* København, Frankfurt: Wilhelm Hansen.

Lerdahl, F., & Jackendoff, R. (1983). *A generative theory of tonal music.* London: The MIT Press.

Lilja, E., & Hopsch, L. (2007). Principles of rhythm: temporal and spatial aspects. In J. Arvidson, M. Askander, J. Bruhn & H. Führer (Eds.), *Changing borders. Contemporary positions in intermediality* (pp. 361-375). Lund: Intermedia Studies Press

London, J. (2004). *Hearing in time: Psychological aspects of musical meter.* New York: Oxford University Press.

Luther, M. (2011). *Ein Enchiridion oder Handbüchlein geistlicher Gesänge und Psalmen.* (C. Brodersen & K. Brodersen, Eds.). Speyer: Kartoffeldruck-Verlag. (Original work published 1524).

Mitchell, W. J. T. (2005). There are no visual media. *Journal of Visual Culture, 4*(2), 257-266.

Moser, S. (2007). Media modes of poetic reception: reading lyrics versus listening to songs. *Poetics, 35*, 277-300

Nielsen, S. K. (1996). Øje for øre. In M. Kyndrup (Ed.) *Formelle Rum, Æstetikstudier III,* Cambridge: Cambridge University Press.

Nørfelt, H. F. (1983). *En ny sang i Danas mund: en registrering og vurdering af melodivalget før og nu til N.F.S. Grundtvigs a-salmer i Den danske Salmebog.* København: Haase.

Patel, A. D., &. Daniele J. R. (2002). An empirical comparison of rhythm in language and music. *Cognition, 87*, B35-45.

Repp, B. H. (2007). Hearing a melody in different ways: Multistability of metrical interpretation, reflected in rate limits of sensorimotor synchronization. *Cognition, 102*, 434-454.

Ringer, A. L. (2013). Melody. *Grove Music Online.* Retrieved September 1, 2013, from http://www.oxfordmusiconline.com.ez.statsbiblioteket.dk:2048/subscriber/article/grove/music/18357?q=melody&search=quick&pos=1&_start=1#firsthit

Steele, J. (1969). *An essay towards establishing the melody and measure of speech* (R. C. Alston, Ed.). Menston: The Scolar Press Ltd. (Original work published 1775).

Taruskin, R. (2005). *The Oxford History of Western Music.* Vol 1. Oxford: Oxford University Press.

Wolf, W. (2002). Intermediality revisited: Reflections on word and music relations in the context of a general typology of intermediality. In S. M. Lodato, S. Aspden, & W. Bernhart (Eds.), *Word and music studies: essays in honor of Steven Paul Scher and on cultural identity and the musical stage* (pp. 13-34). Amsterdam/New York, NY: Rodopi.

PART THREE

Experience, Cognition, and Affect

T he next three contributions explore the biological and ethological sources of musical meaning and affect. They deal with aspects of musical experience and interpretation by going beyond a mere acoustic description of the sound. Music-as-heard calls forth expressive interpretations and emotions. This is the case for the recognition of tonality and tonal melodies, which are not merely sequences or successions of pitches. Being rooted in biological evolution, they can be linked to the transmission of meaning by establishing a kind of specific connection between perception of sounds, memory function and emotional assessment. The biological foundation of tonality can be related to animal communication and ethology. The study of the latter, especially, returns insights back to humanities and provides a novel approach to the understanding of music-related emotions. Besides these ethological claims, there are studies on analogical reference as well, which state that there are sonic analogs for dynamic processes, which could be defined as a coherent sequence of phenomena that are distributed over time and typified by parametric modulation or change. Musical materials, therefore, can represent emotions, gestures, and the patterned movements of dance by simulating the properties of what they refer to. Such analogical reference operates across the range of human expression, but it is uniquely exploited in music, where it serves as the basis for musical communication.

The first contribution by Podlipniak explores the origin and nature of tonality, not as an acoustic or perceptual trait of the sound, but as a cognitive characteristic, based on a hierarchical, schematic structure of pitches. Starting from a nativist point of view, he argues for a broad conception of tonality as an evolutionary adaptive function, which is connected to the transmission of meaning and to evoking emotions by means of tonal pitch order.

Zbikowski investigates the relationship between musical semiotics and analogical reference, especially the ability to refer to something outside of the realm of music by drawing on recent work in cognitive science on analogical processes. Music can represent phenomena that are not predominantly sonic through the resources offered by analogical reference. Relying on Peirce's study of signs as an exploration of the origins and nature of thoughts that are connected with various aspects of the experience, and the forms the sign could take as an icon, index or symbol, he elaborates on the concept of the iconic sign, which mainly represents by similarity. He therefore explores the cognitive bases for analogy to lay the groundwork for an explanation of how music can summon phenomena which are not themselves sonic, and to provide an empirical basis for Peirce's notion of the icon. He argues, further, that the range of dynamic processes for which music can offer sonic analogs extends far beyond occasional bits of text-painting. Sonic analogs of music can refer to dynamic processes, which could be defined as a coherent sequence of phenomena that is distributed over time and typified by parametric modulation or change.

Huron's contribution, finally, deals with how music induces affect. Starting from Peircean semiotics and its influence on ethology, he explores the basic concepts of animal communication, namely signals and cues, and proposes an acoustic ethological model that distinguishes four acoustical conditions that add intensity to pitch. Ethological research, in particular, has added the concept of *signaling* to the main mechanisms for affect induction and raises serious objections to the dominating model of psychological thinking with regard to emotions.

The Ability of Tonality Recognition as One of Human-Specific Adaptations

Piotr Podlipniak

Department of Musicology,
Adam Mickiewicz University, Poznań, Poland

Introduction

Tonality is understood by musicologists and musicians in many different, often mutually exclusive senses. Sometimes it is regarded as a distinctive characteristic of solely Western music (e.g. Dahlhaus, 1988), but sometimes this understanding is applied to the features of non-Western music too (e.g. Krumhansl, 1990). Even as a term restricted to the features of Western music it is assigned a variety of meanings such as an aspect of melodic relations (Thomson, 1999) or an exclusive trait of harmonic organization (Lowinsky, 1990). Also in the psychological sense, *tonality* is defined by scholars both as the hierarchical arrangements of pitch phenomena in Western music with functional harmony (e.g. Bigand & Poulin-Charronnat, 2009, p. 60) and as any arrangement of pitches in which some pitches are more important than others (e.g. Snyder, 2000). There are, however, some common denominators of almost all of these understandings. First of all, every definition of tonality involves the emphasis on the relations between the arrangements of pitches or chords. In all these arrangements one pitch or chord gains the most important function, in which case it is called *tonic*. Secondly, every tonal function depends on musical context. In other words, whether the note C is a tonic or not is established by means of cognitive assessment of its place among its neighboring notes. Thus, the tonal function is neither an acoustic nor a perceptual trait of sound. In fact, it is a cognitive characteristic (Huron, 2006), which is accompanied by specific emotional reactions (Steinbeis et al., 2006).

1. Theories of the origin and nature of tonality

The many various theoretical explanations of the origin and nature of tonality have been proposed in musicology. The theories of the origin of tonality could be divided into three categories: *physicalistic*, *historicistic* and *nativistic*. The advocates of the first stance claim that tonality has its roots in acoustic characteristics of sounds (e.g. Helmholz, 1954). Scholars who consider historicism as the most convincing explanation of the origin of tonality persuade that it is only the historical and cultural circumstances which determine both the tonal order of music and perception of tonality (e.g. Lowinsky, 1961). Nativists explain the basis of tonality as a result of inborn capacities responsible for the existence of both tonal organization in music and the common cognitive strategies of the perception of tonality (e.g. Lerdahl & Jackendoff, 1983). Of course, the contemporary nativist points of view emphasize the importance of cultural factors in establishing the tonal organization of a particular musical idiom. The physicalistic stance seems to be nowadays untenable. Nevertheless, there is an agreement that overtone series can have some influence on some tonal hierarchies. The historicistic attitude is based on behaviorism, which is also unconvincing today.

Although the understanding of the nature of tonality proposed in this paper represents a nativist point of view, it differs in some details from positions which have been presented so far. First of all, tonality is understood here in its broad sense, i.e. as "the arrangement of pitches in a piece of music so that one pitch predominates, usually accomplished by repeating the pitch and placing it in important locations" (Snyder, 2000) for example in the downbeat of the metrical cycle in isometric music. However, the temporal position of a particular pitch class does not influence its tonal stability (Prince et al., 2009). Secondly, the capacity of tonality processing is explained exclusively as a kind of specific connection between perception of sounds, memory function and emotional assessment. Thus, the supposed *innateness of tonality* is neither a set of specific rules which govern human cognition (Lerdahl & Jackendoff, 1983, p. 280) nor the products of solely "fundamental psychological principles shared by other domains of perception and cognition" (Krumhansl & Cuddy, 2010, p. 51). Finally, it is suggested that all these cognitive ingredients evolved separately as non-music abilities but their coupling, which is necessary to perceive tonality, should be understood as a music-specific adaptation of *Homo sapiens*.

2. The specificity of tonality

Human perception of tonality seems to be something special and bizarre at the same time. The perception of tonality consists in people unconsciously segregating pitches depending on their occurrence in the context of other pitches and building some expectations about which pitch will be next. Additionally, this gives listeners pleasure which makes them continue the process of perception. This process is in some sense incomparable to other ways of perceiving the external world. Although expectation is the universal rule of perception, the tonal expectations seem to be exceptional in comparison to other sound anticipations which occur when people hear surrounding noises, isolated pitches, and even the order of timbre in music. Only perception of the tonal and rhythmical organization of music and of phonological features of speech enables them to easily and unconsciously build noticeable generative systems. However, in the case of tonality the fulfilling of a particular expectation evokes specific emotional reactions, whereas in the speech perception the same process is at least less impressive. Some scholars suggest that feelings of tensions and relaxations which accompany perception of tonality are learned in the process of socialization (Meyer, 1956). In fact, it is very difficult to explain these emotional associations solely by means of social learning.

The most important factor which affects our perception of tonality is the order in which particular pitches are presented (Butler & Brown, 1994, pp. 198–208). But there is nothing special in the frequency of pitch occurrence that allows the forging of links between the hearing of *tonic* and the feeling of relaxation. Additionally, the ability of tonal recognition is learned implicitly (Cuddy, 1993, p. 24; Krumhansl, 1990, pp. 18–25; Tillmann et al., 2000), which means that interpreting pitches does not require any awareness. Of course, some positive emotional assessment accompanies almost all fulfilled expectations, but tonal relief seems to be incomparable with emotions evoked by finishing a speech or even a single sentence.

Apart from that, it seems as if tonality activates some additional memory resources. Tonal tunes are better memorized than atonal melodies both by professional musicians and non-professional listeners. Another process which tonality improves is the remembering of lyrics. While there is nothing special in improving memory by means of cross-modal associations, as in tonal-lyrics connections, the ability to facilitate sound retention is really exceptional. From this perspective tonality could be understood as some "inborn" mnemonics. The mnemonic power of tonality is based on a hierarchical, schematic structure of pitches. It contributes redundancy that is useful for memory (Snyder, 2000,

p. 149). Such an intuitively learned mnemonic tool has not been observed in other than audible modalities. For example, in the visual perception of the sequences of colors a higher frequency with which some of them occur does not improve the remembering of the whole sequences. Some effects of memory improvement achieved by the means of sound characteristics are present in speech prosody (e.g. rhymes, assonance etc.), but these methods never depend on the occurrence of a particular pitch.

So far, there has been no evidence of anything at least resembling the tonality order in speech prosody (Patel, 2008) or in any other human sound expressions. This suggests that the memory effect of tonality is domain-specific. Moreover, tonality understood in a broad sense predominates in all musical cultures (Castellano et al., 1984; Kessler et al., 1984; Ambrazevičius & Wiśniewska, 2009; Bannan, 2012). It is the only way in which pitches are organized in music except for the 20th century's atonal music. Apart from that, tonal music readily receives widespread recognition and is cultivated by all social groups (Dutton, 2009). Interestingly, people can identify the central pitch of a passage of tonal music even if the music represents a different culture (Castellano et al., 1984). All these observations provoke one to ask some vital questions: Why is the frequency of pitches important in sound perception of humans? Why do the expectations concerning tonal order evoke intensive feelings of tensions and relaxations whereas speech or other abstract sound anticipations do it less intensively? Why is it easier for people to memorize tonal melodies than non-tonal pitch sequences? Why are various kinds of tonal music so popular among people in different cultures? I think that in answering all these questions the supposition of *tonality instinct* could be helpful.

3. Tonality as the evolutionary innovation of vocal communication

One of the important questions concerning human vocal communication is the problem of which of the abilities used to communicate vocally people share with other animals and which are unique to *Homo sapiens*. This question is strictly connected with the debate about the continuity and discontinuity between human language and other primate communication systems (Fitch & Zuberbühler, 2013), as well as human music and these systems (cf. e.g. Fitch, 2006) because both language and music seem to be human specific behavioral traits. However, language and the majority of music are complex phenomena which involve numerous separate mental mechanisms among which only some are novelties and many are homologs shared with various mammalian taxa. What differentiates speech and music from other vocal communication systems of animals is syntax. The three key properties of the syntactic structure of music and language are: generativity (which allows the creation of an infinite number of expressions from discrete elements), hierarchy (which facilitates the composing of multileveled structures) and abstract structural relations (which make particular structural functions dependent on the context in which a given feature occurs) (Patel, 2013). Indeed, there are examples of songbirds' songs which exhibit meaningful combinatorial organization whose changes are recognizable by the conspecifics (Gentner et al., 2006; Woolley & Doupe, 2008; Soard & Ritchison, 2009). Yet, both the language and the music syntaxes are more complex than any so far known rules of sound organization used by songbirds and all other animals (Fitch & Zuberbühler, 2013). This suggests that the language and the music syntaxes are human specific traits of vocal communication.

The specificity implies, in consequence, the existence of the evolutionarily novel mental mechanisms. Even though there is a lively debate whether or not the language syntax is processed by means of the same mental mechanisms as the music syntax (Rogalsky et al., 2011; Patel, 2012; Koelsch, 2012b; Grahn, 2012; London, 2012), there is no doubt that every musical syntactic structure is based on different acoustic features than that of every speech. Similarly, the function of syntax in language is completely different than in music. While in language syntax is strictly connected with semantics (Dor, 2000; Bickerton, 2009), there is no similar connection in music. Even if one supposes that musical syntax resembles the syntax of phonology in language (morphosyntax) rather than lingual grammar (Lerdahl, 2013, p. 260), the elements of morphosyntax in language are meaningful too (Ladd, 2013, p. 286). In other words, morphemes and words in language have propositional meanings which are combined according to some rules in order to create a new meaning. This characteristic, referred to as *compositionality* (Mithen, 2006; Patel, 2013, p. 334) or *combinability* (Bickerton, 2009, pp. 41-43), is absent in all music (Patel, 2013, p. 334). Rather than being connected with a conceptual meaning, the musical syntax enhances and influences the induction of emotions in listeners. One of the important ingredients of musical syntactic organization which influences the emotional assessment of music is pitch order (Lerdahl & Jackendoff, 1983; Lerdahl, 2013). The emotional assessment of music is hence dependent not only on suprasegmental features that music shares with speech but also on music-specific segmental organization among which the arrangement of pitches is one of the most important. What is more, the emotional assessment of pitches dependent on the frequency of their occurrence has not yet been identified among animals. This ability, therefore, seems to be innovative (Podlipniak, 2015).

4. What mental abilities are necessary in the perception of tonal organization?

In order to perceive tonal organization of music every human being needs to be able to discriminate a sound frequency. Of course, this ability, ubiquitous among animals, is not enough even to realize tonality. Apart from that, perceived sounds have to be categorized in more or less broad and stable units of pitch (Rakowski, 1997). The next important ability is relative pitch. This ability enables the recognition and remembering of pitch sequences patterns which are independent of the absolute frequency level (Patel, 2013). However, many observations indicate that this ability is not music-specific. Relative pitch conditions not only the recognition of the same melody sung or played in different registers—in the very same way it conditions the recognition of speech intonation patterns spoken by a child, a woman or a man. In fact, amusics have been found to have difficulty in the perception of speech intonation (Liu et al., 2010), which suggests that relative pitch is processed in the brain network which is used during both music and speech perception (Patel, 2008, pp. 233-238). Apart from that, although this ability is not universal among vertebrates (McDermott & Hauser, 2005), it is present in some nonhuman mammalian species including primates (e.g. Wright et al., 2000; Yin et al., 2010), which is another piece of evidence that relative pitch is not music-specific. After all, humans are the only primates who produce music, and nonhuman primates even dislike human music (McDermott & Hauser, 2007).

Another important ability necessary in the perception of tonality is the principle of octave equivalence—a perceptive phenomenon which allows the considering of two pitches separated by one or more octaves as similar. Although this phenomenon was observed also in rhesus monkeys (Wright et al., 2000) it seems to be particularly developed in humans. While rhesus monkeys show complete octave generalization only to tonal melodies, humans are equally skillful also in the generalization of individual notes and atonal tunes. Interestingly, the privileged position of tonal melodies in monkeys' perception suggests that tonal organization of pitches gives some perceptive indications which make the categorization of pitches easier even for our animal relatives. Therefore, apart from relative pitch the perception of tonality has to consist in some additional mental abilities.

Furthermore, the perception and the recognition of tonality necessitate the specific coupling of other abilities. These are definitely the implicit recognition of statistical pitch occurrence and some memory functions which facilitate suspension of more frequently occurring pitches in the working memory. Additionally, emotional processing certainly plays an important role in this facilitation. The perception of tonality also includes a syntactic analysis which probably uses the long-term memory resources of structural characteristics specific to native music (Koelsch, 2012). These resources are acquired implicitly by listening to the music which prevails in the cultural environment of a listener. However, it seems that this implicit knowledge is not necessary to recognize some elements of tonal order in music because people are able to identify *tonic* in music pieces which did not originate in their native culture (Castellano et al. 1984). Thus, the analysis of statistical distribution of pitches seems to be the basic mental strategy employed by people in order to establish tonal relations (cf. Cross, 2005, pp. 32-33).

5. The adaptive function of tonality

Every evolutionary explanation demands to point out an adaptive function of the evolved trait. Because tonality is a structural feature of music, whose oldest primordial kind was probably singing (Bannan, 2012), the search for the adaptive function of tonality should be focused in the first place on human vocal communication. Both speech and singing are culturally transmitted vocal expressions of humans. This transmission requires a capacity for complex vocal learning (Fitch & Jarvis, 2013). The capacity of complex vocal learning is present also in some lineages of birds and mammals. However, because there are many other closely related species of birds and mammals without this capacity (including all nonhuman primates (Fitch & Zuberbühler, 2013)), this trait can be considered as a result of convergent evolution rather than as an inheritance from a common ancestor (Fitch & Jarvis, 2013). Thus, it may be helpful to analyze the functional and structural specificity of expressions by nonhuman complex vocal learners in order to find the potential analogies with human singing. The animals' vocal expressions which are most often indicated as analogous to human singing are songs of songbirds (Darwin 1871; Fitch & Jarvis, 2013; Cross et al., 2013).

Indeed, there are many similarities between songbirds' songs and human singing. Many of songbirds' songs are structurally complex, communicate different types of meanings, they are transmitted culturally from generation to generation, as well as undergo the process of spontaneous elaboration which leads to differentiation into local dialects (Slater, 2000). As complex patterns of sound sequences, songbirds' songs are ritualized displays which communicate information from sender to receiver about the sender's conditions, intentions and motivations by impacting the autonomic, endocrine and behavioral responses of the receiver (Alcorta et al., 2008). The information is often encoded in the structure of discrete sound categories. For example, it has been observed that songbirds are able to communicate information about the size of a predator (the level of a perceived threat) by means of sound patterns (Templeton et al., 2005; Soard & Ritchison, 2009). One of the structural features which is used by birds to convey information about the level of threat is the number of sound categories (Templeton et al., 2005). This indicates that songbirds are able to create at least elements of syntax. Moreover, vocal-learning birds use songs to communicate primarily the information about mate attractiveness or territorial possession, which is often concerned as affective meaning (cf. Fitch & Jarvis, 2013, p. 502). In this respect, the quasi-syntax of songbirds' songs represents something like an aesthetic display which resembles musical syntax rather than language syntax (Cross et al., 2013, p. 542). Based on that, the emotional assessment of the abstract musical sound sequence by humans is not exceptional in the animal world.

Since both the combinatorial sequencing of discrete sound categories and emotional communication by means of sound structures evolved at least in some species of birds it is probable that the same happened convergently among human ancestors. The emotions which accompany listening to tonal music seem to have no pragmatic reason and they are, thus, often even named *aesthetic emotions* (Scherer, 2013, p. 129), which do not have implications for survival (Juslin & Västfjäll, 2008). However, because the basic biological function of emotion is to assess and control the survival value of the organism's interactions with the environment (Panksepp 1998, p. 48), an emotional reaction always indicates that the ultimate cause of the reaction is important for survival. In fact, people are usually unaware of the ultimate causes of their emotional reactions to stimuli (Alcorta et al., 2008). What is then the function of tonality? What needs to be addressed to answer this question is the specific function of pitch order in human vocal expression or, in other words, the relationship between tonal structure and some adaptive function. By analogy, the examples of restricted syntax in songbirds' songs show that the adaptive function of syntactic organization of human vocal expressions may be connected with the transmission of meaning. It seems to be true in the case of language grammar whose most probable and obvious adaptive function is the aforementioned communication of a particular constrained subset of linguistic meaning (Dor & Jablonka, 2001).

But in music pitch order has nothing to do with the propositional meaning. The only meaning which seems to be transmitted by pitch order is related to the listeners' affective response. However, the expression of human emotional states is not restricted solely to music. People express their emotions also during laughing, crying, speaking and making other vocal gestures. But only music and speech are the media which are composed of discrete elements juxtaposed by means of syntactic rules. Language syntax does not seem to be involved in the transmission of information about the emotional state of communicating people. Similarly, even though language vocabulary provides many words which describe emotions, it is poor in transmitting this kind of information. Every verbal description of emotions is imprecise and ineffective. The language-based expression of emotions is rather a domain of indiscrete acoustic features of suprasegmental organization of speech phonology. These features, however, are not specific solely to language. Continuous variables which are specific to prosody (e.g. modulation of tempo and dynamics) are also present in music (Scherer & Zenter, 2001) and are evolutionarily older than discrete communicative ingredients of speech and music such as phonemes and pitches (Reybrouck, 2015). Although some discrete prosodic features (e.g. tone, stress and accent) can play particular grammatical and semantic functions in speech (cf. Ladd, 2013, p. 278), in that case their ability to convey emotional meaning is reduced. Hence, it is reasonable to assume that emotional expression in speech is mainly a domain of prosody.

Meanwhile, the evoking of emotions by means of tonal pitch order is unlike eliciting emotions by means of indiscrete elements of suprasegmental organization of speech and music. The feelings of tension and relaxation elicited by tonal recognition result from predictions which concern discrete elements—pitches. Unlike in language, discrete structural ingredients act in music as an additional evolutionarily young tool designed to elicit emotions. However, there are some similarities between tonality and language grammar as regards their inherent characteristics. Similarly to linguistic grammar in which particular semantic categories determine some universal aspects of grammar (Dor, 2000), specific emotions correlate with some aspects of pitch order in music (Podlipniak, 2013). For example, the feeling of relaxation which is induced in the listener by the appearance of *tonic* is irreplaceable with the contrasting feeling of tension. Similarly to native language users who (if they are not linguists) are completely unaware of dependencies between grammar and semantics (Dor & Jablonka, 2001, p. 38), music listeners (with the exception of some musicologists and music psychologists) do not know why certain feelings are dependent on pitch order. In this respect the relationship between semantic categorization and grammatical rules is similar to the relationship between emotional assessment and tonal organization. Moreover, in both cases people implicitly learn syntactical rules specific to their culture. In the same way grammar in language cooperates with different structural features so as to transmit propositional meanings, tonality in music is only one of many other tools which act together to elicit emotions. Also similarly to universal aspects of linguistic grammar which possess fixed meanings, a particular emotion elicited by tonality prediction is not arbitrarily chosen by culture because the feeling of relaxation is unchangeably attributed to the most frequent pitch. What is, then, the adaptive function of this specific emotional communication?

From a historical and cross-cultural perspective music seems to be in the first place a communal rather than an individual activity (Cross, 2012). Because tonality is a feature of music activity which is an inseparable part of communal performances, the probable biological function of tonality might be related to some social conditions of human existence. It can be suspected that the function of tonality is to enhance the sense of belonging to a community by providing information about social acceptance and support. This function is easily achieved by eliciting similar emotions among members of the group. The feelings of relaxation which are elicited by pitch centricity act as an unconscious signal of social acceptance and support (Podlipniak, 2015). On the other hand, the feeling of uncertainty which accompanies the appearance of the out-of-key tone suggests unconsciously lack of knowledge about social acceptance. However, once this knowledge is gained by establishing the tonal center it results in relaxation. This emotional underpinning of the exchange of mutual acceptance certainly facilitates group cohesion which is adaptive. Thus, it seems that the emotional assessment of tonal music resembles the confirmation of mutual faithfulness without words. This is possible thanks to the fact that tonal order is one of the features which enable communal singing. The implicit memory of *tonic* allows performers to intuitively orientate in the pitch space. Tonal predictions also belong to important indications of musical closures. Therefore, without a sustained memory of *tonic*, the consolidating power of music would be definitely less impressive.

6. The evolutionary scenario of the origin of tonality

One of the ingredients of the social life of apes is culture. In fact, many cultural traditions have been observed in primates (Laland & Bennett, 2009). These traditions often undergo some variations and are transmitted from generation to generation. Thus, it is reasonable to assume that the process of cultural evolution has also taken place among our direct ancestors. It is also tenable that the cultural evolution of our predecessors was cumulative and led to the elaboration of cultural practices (Tomasello, 1999). If so, culture became an inseparable part of our environment (Reybrouck, 2013). It is probable too that in the evolution of *Homo sapiens* cultural environment started to play an important selective role (Jablonka & Lamb, 2005). Hence, cultural factors cannot be omitted in any scenarios of music evolution.

Cultural changes are possible thanks to the plasticity of the brain which enables lifelong social learning. But some elements of human faculties are learned faster and more easily than others, which suggests that people are endowed with some hereditary predispositions of learning (Gazzaniga, 2008). It is especially evident in the case of language acquisition in which, despite the cultural diversity, some abilities are learned implicitly. But some scholars suggest that before certain abilities became instinctive, they were first achieved through explicit learning. Because they proved adaptive, the fastest learners of these abilities were favored in the pressure of selection. In these circumstances the genetic predisposition for implicit learning will emerge sooner or later. Because the usefulness of these abilities often depends on cultural conditions, it has been claimed that in the process of language evolution the interaction between cultural and genetic evolution has occurred (Dor & Jablonka, 2001). In this process cultural factors have played a major selective role.

Because some of the abilities used in music processing are present also in language processing, it is reasonable to suppose that music evolution has consisted in the same kind of process. At some point in the past in this process a social group preferred certain aspects of music which previously were learned as strenuously as some elements of virtuosity today. It is proposed here that one of them was a tonal organization. Before tonal organization had emerged, our ancestors were endowed with some communicative abilities which probably included social-emotional vocalizations (Merker, 2003). Because rhesus monkeys are able to categorize pitches it is reasonable to assume that hominines possessed this ability too. They also were smarter than apes thanks to the increased role of social learning in the cultural evolution (Wilson, 2012). Because none of living primates apart from humans are able to learn complex vocal expressions (Fitch & Zuberbühler, 2013), it is reasonable to suppose that this ability has evolved only in human evolutionary lineage. What is more, this ability allowed human ancestors to imitate and memorize the sequences of pitches sung by other members of their social groups. It is possible that pitch sequences became a part of some social and religious rituals.

At the beginning of the history of tonality the organization of pitches in which some pitches were preferred was an invention. It is possible that the sensation of sensory consonance and dissonance could have played a certain role in this process. Nonetheless, people had to learn the new roles of pitch organization by means of strenuous repetitions similar to the contemporary learning of writing. At the same time, the recognition of this new pitch order during communal singing became a tool of social consolidation. Instead of monotonous singing or chaotic pitch expressions people used the most frequent pitches as a reference point for mutual consolidation. The feelings of safety and relaxation which usually accompany the awareness of being a part of a well-consolidated group were easily associated with the appearance of *tonic*. Because the well-consolidated groups gain advantage over the less consolidated ones, the ability to consolidate is a very important adaptive trait of every social animal. In this case an emotional motivation works additionally as a tool which forces individuals to consolidate with other individuals in a particular group. Thus, the additional emotional reaction to chanting *tonic* facilitated group consolidation.

It is probable that such a culturally transmitted misattribution of a positive emotional reaction to pitch transformed into the hereditary trait of an individual. She or he started to intuitively assess the most frequent pitch as emotionally positive. Because of that she or he did not have to waste time in learning of the aforementioned association, which improved their social adjustment. Because the evolutionary forces favored well-consolidated individuals, these individuals who reacted to *tonic* faster and more intensely became more socially successful. It is possible that sexual selection could have played some role in this process too. After all, social acceptance and position usually increase sexual attraction (Miller, 2001), thus the "easy-consolidators" could have had more offspring. Having even a few more offspring than competitors every year in the long run gives the quantitative dominance in the whole population. Additionally, at some point of our prehistory there emerged the differences in the speed of tonal pitch sequence. Namely, some people learned faster than others thanks to a better memory of the most frequent pitch. Some of this variability was a result of the variability in people's genetic make-up which influenced working memory preferences for the memory of the most frequent pitch. In this scenario the fastest learners adapted the most successfully. In the course of time, within perhaps several thousand years, the ability of tonal pitch recognition became quick and spontaneous in one of the learners. She or he was more successful than others and her or his genes overwhelmed the whole human population. What was formerly achieved by means of many repetitions suddenly became an instinctive response to music stimuli. What was actually genetically assimilated was the specific coupling of pitch recognition, pitch memory and emotional assessment (Podlipniak, 2015). The feeling of relaxation which accompanies the perception of *tonic* is, therefore, a result of this tonal instinct.

References

Alcorta, C. S., Sosis, R., & Finkel, D. (2008). Ritual harmony: Toward an evolutionary theory of music. *Behavioral and Brain Sciences, 31*(05).

Bannan, N. (2012). Harmony and its role in human evolution. In N. Bannan (Ed.), *Music, language, and human evolution* (pp. 288–339). Oxford: Oxford University Press.

Bickerton, D. (2009). *Adam's tongue: How humans made language, how language made humans* (1st ed.). New York: Hill and Wang.

Bigand, E., & Poulin-Charronnat, B. (2009). Tonal cognition. In S. Hallam, I. Cross, & M. H. Thaut (Eds.), *The Oxford handbook of music psychology* (pp. 59–71). Oxford, New York: Oxford University Press.

Butler, D., & Brown, H. (1994). Describing the mental representation of tonality in music. In R. Aiello & J. A. Sloboda (Eds.). (1994). *Musical perceptions* (pp. 191–212). New York: Oxford University Press.

Castellano, M. A., Bharucha, J. J., & Krumhansl, C. L. (1984). Tonal hierarchies in the music of north India. *Journal of experimental psychology, 113*(3), 394–412.

Cross, I. (2005). Music and meaning, ambiguity and evolution. In D. Miell, R. A. R. MacDonald & D. Hargreaves (Eds.), *Musical communication* (pp. 27–43). Oxford, New York: Oxford University Press.

Cross, I. (2012). Music as a social and cognitive process. In P. Rebuschat, M. Rohmeier, J. A. Hawkins, & I. Cross (Eds.), *Language and music as cognitive systems* (pp. 315–328). Oxford: Oxford University Press.

Cross, I., Fitch, W. T., Aboitiz, F., Iriki, A., Jarvis, E. D., Lewis, J., Liebal, K., Merker, B., Stout, D., Trehub, S. E. (2013). Culture and Evolution. In M. A. Arbib (Ed.). *Strüngmann Forum Reports. Language, music, and the brain: A mysterious relationship* (pp. 541–562). Cambridge, Massachusetts: The MIT Press.

Dahlhaus, C. (1988). *Untersuchungen über die Entstehung der harmonischen Tonalität* (2nd ed.). Kassel, New York: Bärenreiter (Original work published 1967).

Darwin, C. R. (1871). *The descent of man and selection in relation to sex*. London: John Murray.

Dor, D. (2000). From the autonomy of syntax to the autonomy of linguistic semantics: Notes on the correspondence between the transparency problem and the relationship problem. *Pragmatics & Cognition, 8*(2), 325–356.

Dor, D., & Jablonka, E. (2001). How language changed the genes: Towards an explicit account of the evolution of language. In J. Trabant & S. Ward (Eds.), New essays on the origin of language (pp. 149–178). Berlin - Hawthorne, N.Y: Mouton de Gruyter.

Dutton, D. (2009). *The art instinct: Beauty, pleasure, & human evolution* (1ˢᵗ ed.). New York: Bloomsbury Press.

Fitch, W. T. (2006). The biology and evolution of music: A comparative perspective. *Cognition, 100*(1), 173–215.

Fitch, W. T., & Jarvis, E. D. (2013). Birdsong and other animal models for human speech, song, and vocal learning. In M. A. Arbib (Ed.). *Strüngmann Forum Reports. Language, music, and the brain: A mysterious relationship* (pp. 499–539). Cambridge, Massachusetts: The MIT Press.

Fitch, W. T., & Zuberbühler, K. (2013). Primate precursors to human language: beyond discontinuity. In E. Altenmüller, S. Schmidt & E. Zimmermann (Eds.). *Series in affective science. Evolution of emotional communication: From sounds in nonhuman mammals to speech and music in man* (1ˢᵗ ed.) (pp. 26–48). Oxford: Oxford University Press.

Gazzaniga, M. S. (2008). *Human: The science behind what makes us unique* (1ˢᵗ ed.). New York: Ecco.

Helmholtz, H. v. (1954). *On the sensations of tone as a physiological basis for the theory of music: Transl., thoroughly revised and corrected, with numerous additional notes and a new additional appendix by Alexander J. Ellis. With a new introd. by Henry Margenau* (2ⁿᵈ ed.). New York: Dover Publications.

Huron, D. B. (2006). *Sweet anticipation: Music and the psychology of expectation* (1ˢᵗ ed.). Cambridge, Mass. and London: MIT.

Jablonka, E., & Lamb, M. J. (2005). *Evolution in four dimensions: Genetic, epigenetic, behavioral, and symbolic variation in the history of life.* Cambridge, Mass: MIT Press.

Juslin, P. N., & Västfjäll, D. (2008). Emotional responses to music: The need to consider underlying mechanisms. *Behavioral and Brain Sciences, 31*(05), 600-621.

Koelsch, S. (2012). *Brain and music.* Chichester, West Sussex; Hoboken, NJ: Wiley-Blackwell.

Krumhansl, C. L. (1990). *Cognitive foundations of musical pitch.* New York: Oxford University Press.

Krumhansl, C. L., & Cuddy, L. L. (2010). A theory of tonal hierarchies in music. In M. Riess Jones, R. R. Fay, & A. N. Popper (Eds.). *Music Perception* (pp. 51–87)/ New York, NY: Springer Science+Business Media, LLC.

Ladd, D. R. (2013). An integrated view of phonetics, phonology, and prosody. In M. A. Arbib (Ed.). *Strüngmann Forum Reports. Language, music, and the brain: A mysterious relationship* (pp. 273–287). Cambridge, Massachusetts: The MIT Press.

Lerdahl, F. (2013). Musical syntax and its relation to linguistic syntax. In M. A. Arbib (Ed.). *Strüngmann Forum Reports. Language, music, and the brain: A mysterious relationship* (pp. 257–272). Cambridge, Massachusetts: The MIT Press.

Lerdahl, F., & Jackendoff, R. (1983). *A generative theory of tonal music*. Cambridge, Mass: MIT Press.

Lewis, J. (2013). A cross-cultural perspective on the significance of music and dance to culture and society. In M. A. Arbib (Ed.). *Strüngmann Forum Reports. Language, music, and the brain: A mysterious relationship* (pp. 45–65). Cambridge, Massachusetts: The MIT Press.

Liu, F., Patel, A. D., Fourcin, A., & Stewart, L. (2010). Intonation processing in congenital amusia: discrimination, identification and imitation. *Brain, 133*(6), 1682–1693.

Lowinsky, E. E. (1990). *Tonality and atonality in sixteenth-century music*. New York: Da Capo Press (Original work published 1961).

McDermott, J., & Hauser, M. D. (2005). The Origins of Music: Innateness, Uniqueness, and Evolution. *Music Perception: An Interdisciplinary Journal, 23*(1), 29–59.

McDermott, J., and Hauser, M. D. (2007). Nonhuman primates prefer slow tempos but dislike music overall. *Cognition, 104*(3), 654–668.

Merker, B. (2003). Is there a biology of music, and why does it matter? In R. Kopiez (Ed.), *Proceedings of the 5th triennial conference of the European Society for the Cognitive Sciences of Music (ESCOM). Hanover University of Music and Drama, September 8 - 13, 2003* (pp. 402–405). Hanover: Institute for Research in Music Education.

Meyer, L. B. (1956). *Emotion and meaning in music*. Chicago: University of Chicago Press.

Miller, G. (2001). *The mating mind: How sexual choice shaped the evolution of human nature* (1st ed.). New York: Anchor Books.

Mortillaro, M., & Mehu, M. S. K. R. (2013). The evolutionary origin of multimodal synchronization and emotional expression. In E. Altenmüller, S. Schmidt, & E. Zimmermann (Eds.). *Series in affective science. Evolution of emotional communication: From sounds in non-human mammals to speech and music in man* (1st ed.) (pp. 3–25). Oxford: Oxford University Press.

Panksepp, J. (1998). *Affective neuroscience: The foundations of human and animal emotions. Series in affective science*. New York: Oxford University Press.

Patel, A. D. (2008). *Music, language, and the brain*. Oxford and New York: Oxford University Press.

Patel, A. D. (2013). Sharing and nonsharing of brain resources for language and music. In M. A. Arbib (Ed.). *Strüngmann Forum Reports. Language, music, and the brain: A mysterious relationship* (pp. 329-355). Cambridge, Massachusetts: The MIT Press.

Podlipniak, P. (2013). Specific emotional reactions to tonal music - indication of the adaptive character of tonality recognition. In G. Luck, & O. Brabant (Eds.), *Proceedings of the 3rd International Conference on Music & Emotion (ICME3)*, Jyväskylä, Finland, 11th - 15th June 2013.

Podlipniak, P. (2015). The evolutionary origin of pitch centre recognition. *Psychology of Music*, OnlineFirst 0305735615577249, first published on April 16, 2015 doi:10.1177/0305735615577249.

Prince, J. B., Thompson, W. F., & Schmuckler, M. A. (2009). Pitch and time, tonality and meter: how do musical dimensions combine? *Journal of Experimental Psychology: Human Perception and Performance, 35*(5), 1598–1617.

Rakowski, A. (1997). The phonological system of musical language in the domain of pitch. *Interdisciplinary Studies in Musicology*, *4*, 211–221.

Reybrouck, M. (2013). From sound to music: an evolutionary approach to musical semantics. *Biosemiotics*, *6*, 585–606.

Reybrouck, M. (2015). Music as Environment: An Ecological and Biosemiotic Approach. *Behavioral Sciences*, *5*, 1–26.

Rebuschat, P., Rohrmeier, M., Hawkins, J. A., & Cross, I. (Eds.). (2012). *Language and music as cognitive systems*. Oxford: Oxford University Press.

Scherer, K. R. (2013). Emotion in action, interaction, music and speech. In M. A. Arbib (Ed.). *Strüngmann Forum Reports. Language, music, and the brain: A mysterious relationship* (pp. 107-139). Cambridge, Massachusetts: The MIT Press.

Scherer, K. R., & Zentner, M. R. (2001). Emotional effects of music: Production rules. In P. Juslin & J. Sloboda (Eds.), *Music and emotion: Theory and research* (pp. 361–392). Oxford, New York: Oxford University Press.

Schulze, K., Dowling, W. J., & Tillmann, B. (2012). Working memory for tonal and atonal sequences during a forward and a backward recognition task. *Music Perception: An Interdisciplinary Journal*, *29*(3), 255–267.

Slater, P. J. B. (2000). Birdsong repertoires: Their origins and use. In N. Wallin, B. Merker, & S. Brown (Eds.), *The Origins of Music* (pp. 49–63). Cambridge, MA - London: The MIT Press.

Snyder, B. (2000). *Music and memory: An introduction*. Cambridge, Mass: MIT Press.

Soard, C. M., & Ritchison, G. (2009). 'Chick-a-dee' calls of Carolina chickadees convey information about degree of threat posed by avian predators. *Animal Behaviour*, *78*(6), 1447–1453.

Steinbeis, N., Koelsch, S., & Sloboda, J. A. (2006). The role of harmonic expectancy violations in musical emotions: evidence from subjective, physiological, and neural responses. *Journal of cognitive neuroscience*, *18*(8), 1380–1393.

Templeton, C. N., Greene, E., & Davis, K. (2005). Allometry of alarm calls: black-capped chickadees encode information about predator size. *Science*, *308*(5730), 1934–1937.

Thomson, W. (1999). *Tonality in music: A general theory*. San Marino, CA: Everett Books.

Tillmann, B., Bharucha, J. J., & Bigand, E. (2000). Implicit learning of tonality: a self-organizing approach. *Psychological review*, *107*(4), 885–913.

Tomasello, M. (1999). *The cultural origins of human cognition*. Cambridge, Mass: Harvard University Press.

Wilson, E. O. (2012). *The social conquest of earth*. New York, London: Liveright.

Wright, A. A., Rivera, J. J., Hulse, S. H., Shyan, M., & Neiworth, J. J. (2000). Music perception and octave generalization in rhesus monkeys. *Journal of experimental psychology*, *129*(3), 291–307.

Musical Semiotics
and Analogical Reference

Lawrence M. Zbikowski

University of Chicago, Department of Music

I should like to begin my consideration of the relationship between musical semiotics and analogical reference with a musical example drawn from Joseph Haydn's oratorio *The Creation*, which had its premiere in April of 1798. The text for the oratorio comes from one reportedly assembled for but never used by Georg Friedrich Handel, and which was translated and abridged for Haydn's use by Baron Gottfried van Swieten. The text is a compilation of familiar quotations from the books of Genesis and Psalms with lines reworked from Milton's *Paradise Lost*, and offers any number of opportunities for pictorial representation. The instance of pictorial representation with which I shall be concerned occurs in Part 1 of the oratorio, just after God has created the division between day and night, and summons that moment in creation when the sun rose for the first time; the score is shown in fig. 1a and 1b.

As can quickly be seen, some of the ways Haydn uses music to depict the rising of the sun are strikingly obvious, and include the steady, measured ascent of the flutes and first violins through more than an octave (bars 1–10); the gradual increase of musical forces through the first nine bars; and the increase in volume, with the flutes and strings beginning *pianissimo* and all instruments sounding *fortissimo* for the arrival on D major in bar 10. Haydn also uses more subtle means to capture images of expansion and growth: the moving lines in the strings and then the winds start gradually and then pile up upon one another as the introduction proceeds; the contrabasses and cellos gradually and then more aggressively expand the register downwards; and the timbre of the ensemble as a whole becomes more brilliant with the entry of the oboes and bassoons (bar 5), and then the horns and trumpets (bar 8). And in what might be counted as a mixture of the obvious and subtle, with the arrival on D major in bar 10 Haydn introduces dotted rhythms, first in the strings and then extending to the trumpets and bassoons (in bar 12), culminating in a grand arrival on A major in bar 14 with the entire orchestra. Although dotted rhythms have a long association with grandeur, during the reign of Louis XIV they became

Lawrence M. Zbikowski

associated more specifically with the entrance of the king into the *Opéra*—that is, stately dotted rhythms signaled the entrance of the Sun King.

This is, I think, a lovely and compelling depiction of a sunrise, but what I will be concerned with in what follows is why it works: that is, how can *sounds* make reference to a process that is exclusively *visual*? I shall argue that the answer to this question can be found in C.S. Peirce's notion of an icon, which together with the index and symbol constituted the basic elements of his semiotic system. My argument will draw on recent work in cognitive science on analogical processes, and will attempt to show how music exploits such processes. This will lead to an expanded notion of the icon—at least as it applies to music—and to a fuller understanding of the role of analogical reference in musical semiotics. In the final section I would like to explore some of the different ways music can represent, through the resources offered by analogical reference, phenomena that are not predominantly sonic. My example here will be the choreography Mark Morris created for the lament with which Henry Purcell's *Dido and Aeneas* reaches its conclusion.

FIGURE 1A. Franz Josef Haydn, *The Creation*, Part I, No. 12 (recitative), "In vollem Glanze steiget jetzt die Sonne," bars 1-15

FIGURE 1B. Continued

1. Peirce's notion of the icon

One way to think of Peirce's study of signs is as an exploration of the origin and nature of the thoughts that are connected with various aspects of experience. Peirce described this connection through a set of nested triadic relationships, which begin with an object (the relevant aspect of experience), a sign which stands for this object, and the thought-structure created in someone's mind by this sign. Here is one of Peirce's formulations of these relationships, together with more formal terms for the elements involved: "A sign, or *representamen*, is something which stands to somebody for something in some respect or capacity. It addresses somebody, that is, creates in the mind of that person an equivalent sign, or perhaps a more developed sign. That sign which it creates I call the *interpretant* of the first sign. The sign stands for something, its *object*. It stands for that object, not in all respects, but in reference to a sort of idea, which I have sometimes called the *ground* of the representamen." (Peirce, 1955, p. 99) My reading of Peirce is informed by the biologist Terry Deacon's work on language evolution. This is especially so in the case of Peirce's second set of triadic relationships, which concerned the forms the sign could take: as *icon, index,* or *symbol.* Deacon notes that what was important for Peirce was the relationship between the characteristics of the sign token and those of the

Lawrence M. Zbikowski

physical object that it represented. Deacon summarized these relationships in this way: "icons are mediated by a similarity between sign and object, indices are mediated by some physical or temporal connection between sign and object, and symbols are mediated by some formal or merely agreed-upon link irrespective of any physical characteristics of either sign or object" (Deacon, 1997, p. 70).

It should be emphasized that what I have just offered is a summary of basic distinctions Peirce made rather than a comprehensive account of his theory. In his characterization of the icon, for instance, Peirce emphasized its almost purely phenomenological status: "An *Icon* is a Representamen whose Representative Quality is a Firstness of it as a First. That is, a quality that it has *qua* thing renders it fit to be a representamen" (Peirce, 1960, vol. 2, p. 276). (Peirce described a first as "that whose being is simply in itself, not referring to anything nor lying behind anything" (Peirce, 1960, vol. 1, p. 356). *Firstness* is the essential quality of a first.) Peirce then offered a way to ground this elusive concept: "a sign may be *iconic*, that is, may represent its object mainly by its similarity, no matter what its mode of being. If a substantive is wanted, an iconic representamen may be termed a *hypoicon*. Any material image, as a painting, is largely conventional in its mode of representation; but in itself, without legend or label it may be called a *hypoicon*" (Peirce, 1960, vol. 1, p. 276). In brief, then, what we typically call an icon is what Peirce termed a hypoicon; the means through which the hypoicon represented the icon— keeping in mind that the true icon has an almost purely phenomenological status—was through being similar to it.

Peirce distinguished between three different forms the relationship between hypoicon and icon could take, based on the degree of similarity between the representamen and the object: "Those [hypoicons] which partake of simple qualities, or First Firstnesses, are *images*; those which represent the relations, mainly dyadic, or so regarded, of the parts of one thing by analogous relations in their own parts, are *diagrams*; those which represent the representative character of a representamen by representing a parallelism in something else, are *metaphors*" (Peirce, 1960, vol. 1, p. 277). Peirce did not elaborate this division further, but based on his overall approach it seems fair to say that the image was, in its essential respects, indistinguishable from its object. In contrast, diagrams preserve structural relationships with their objects (but not, perhaps, their surface features), where metaphors offer a looser but still discernible connection between the icon and its object.

Although similarity was clearly important for Peirce's notion of the hypoicon (and thus for the semiotic potential of iconicity) he offered no further analysis of the basis or mechanism of similarity. There is a hint, however, in his description of the diagram, and in particular on the need for analogous relations between the hypoicon and that which it would represent. In what follows, I would like to explore briefly the cognitive bases for analogy with two aims. The first is to lay the groundwork for an explanation of how music can summon phenomena which are not themselves sonic; the second is to provide an empirical basis for Peirce's notion of the icon.

2. Analogy

As Dedre Gentner and her colleagues noted some years ago, the capacity to draw similarities between two situations or things is not unrelated to the capacity to make analogies (Gentner & Markman, 1997). Where analogy is different that it is concerned not simply with correlating elements from one domain with elements in another domain, but with mapping relationships between these domains. It is thus often described as concerned with relations among relations (or "second-order" relations).

Making analogies is something that is virtually effortless for humans. Motivated by this fact, Douglas Hofstadter argued that analogy, as the means by which concepts are assembled and connected to one another, is at the very core of human cognition (Hofstadter, 2001). At the very least, there is considerable overlap between judgments of similarity, making analogies, and processes of categorization, all of which contribute to the distinctiveness of human intelligence (Medin, Goldstone, & Gentner 1993; Glucksberg & Keysar, 1990). Perhaps more striking is that the capacity for analogy is apparently unique to our species. I say "apparently" because, at this point, we simply don't know as much as we might about the analogical capacities of other species. There is, for instance, research suggesting that chimpanzees can understand the second-order relations basic to analogy (especially for spatial reasoning). There is also evidence that dolphins have the capacity to perform analogical mappings of the sort that are necessary for complex motor mimicry (Herman, 2002, p. 278). This evidence notwithstanding, at present it appears that no other species comes close to making or using analogies with the facility and speed of humans (Call & Tomasello, 2005; Gentner, 2003; Holyoak & Thagard, 1995, pp. 39-73; Oden, Thompson, & Premack, 2001). And this capacity is available from a very early age: children as young as ten months are able to solve problems by analogy (Chen, Sanchez, & Campbell, 1997), and by the age of three years analogical abilities are quite robust (Goswami, 1992; Goswami, 2001).

Lawrence M. Zbikowski

The ability to map systematic structural relationships between disparate domains bears witness to a capacity for abstract thought—for thinking about relations between relations—of enormous flexibility and wide application. Analogy has been recognized as a key factor in human creativity (Hofstadter, & the Fluid Analogies Research Group, 1995; Fauconnier & Turner, 2002, pp. 3-16), and has been linked to the conceptual flights of fancy and processes of meaning construction created through metaphor and metonymy (Gentner, Bowdle, Wolff, & Boronat, 2001; Glucksberg et al. 1990; Glucksberg, McGlone, & Manfredi 1997; Holyoak et al. 1995, chap. 9; Holyoak, 2005). For my part, I have argued that the conceptual domains involved in such mappings need not be restricted to those involving language, an argument supported by the capacity for analogy demonstrated by primates, dolphins, and pre-linguistic children (Zbikowski, 2002, chap. 2).

Indeed, analogical mappings are often most noticeable when we are engaged with situations which exceed—or at the very least, tax to the utmost—the resources of language. The image of the sun rising over the earth for the first time is one example; another is provided by the opening of a short composition for guitar by the Argentinian teacher and performer Julio Salvador Sagreras; the score for which is given in figure 2.

FIGURE 2. Bars 1–18 of a short composition for guitar solo by Julio S. Sagreras

There are any number of odd things about this composition—the obsessive focus on repeated notes, the sudden shifts of the left hand (as in bars 1 and 3, where the guitarist is asked to play an ascending fourth on the same string), and its somewhat fragmented compositional style—but all of them start to make sense once we know the title of the work: *El Colibri*, or *The Hummingbird*. The subtitle of the work, in translation, is *Imitation of the flight of the hummingbird*. Given this, those same odd features quickly organize themselves into a coherent image. The rapid repeated notes, beginning in a low register, evoke the surprisingly visceral sound the hummingbird makes in flight; the sudden shifts along the length of the string summon the darting movements of the bird; successions of larger blocks of musical material (such as bars 1 through 3, bars 4 through 7, bars 8 through 12, and bars 13 through 16) map out the path of the bird among the different flowers it visits; and the accented non-chord tones of bars 9 through 12 capture the small motions it makes as it dips to drink. What Sagreras has given us, then, is a rather detailed sonic analog for a group of conjoined and highly dynamic processes associated with the flight of the hummingbird. The questions this raises, however, is the same as that raised by Haydn's musical depiction of a sunrise in *The Creation*: why should these *sounds* serve as analogs for processes that are, for the most part, *visual?*

To answer this question, I would like to turn to a theoretical model developed by the cognitive psychologist Lawrence Barsalou. Barsalou's theory developed out of his research on processes of categorization, and offered a way to explain how perceptual information shapes the cognitive representations that occupy our conscious thought. The theory builds on work done in the neurosciences over the past twenty years, which has shown that the perception of a physical entity engages a number of coordinated feature detectors in sensorimotor areas that are relevant to a given perceptual mode (Barsalou, 2005, p. 398). During the visual processing of a hummingbird, for instance (a process diagrammed in Figure 3a), some neurons will fire for the edges of the bird's figure, others for the surfaces of its body, color, orientation, and direction of movement. Similar distributions of activation would occur in other modalities, and would be represented in feature maps specific to those modalities. These might represent the sound of the bird, the way it feels in the hand (both in terms of the touch of its feathers and its near weightlessness), and introspective states summoned on encountering the bird (such as the thrill of discovering it or trepidation at the sight of its sharp bill). Once a pattern becomes active in a feature map conjunctive neurons in an association area capture the pattern's features for later use (Barsalou, 2005, p. 399). This aspect of Barsalou's account of the processing of perceptual information adopts the theory of convergence zones proposed by Antonio Damasio in the late 1980s. For Damasio, as for Barsalou, perceptual information is first recorded in a fragmentary fashion. The neural records of these fragments are then brought together through the distributed neural structure of the convergence zone, which Damasio describes as "an amodal record of the combinatorial arrangements that bound the fragment records as they occurred in experience. There are convergence zones of different orders; for example, those that bind features into entities, and those that bind entities into events or sets of events, but all register combinations of components in terms of coincidence or sequence, in space and time." (Damasio, 1989, p. 26) Although convergence zones are not linked to any specific modality, their basic components consist in all cases of information gathered from perception.

According to Barsalou's theory, the conjunctive neurons in the association area also support a sensory-motor reenactment of the original activation pattern. Barsalou sketches the process (diagrammed in Figure 3b) as follows: "Once a set of conjunctive neurons in a convergence zone captures an activation pattern in a feature map, the conjunctive neurons can later reactivate the pattern in the absence of bottom-up sensory stimulation. While remembering a perceived object, for example, conjunctive neurons reenact the sensorimotor states that were active while encoding it." (Barsalou, 2005, p. 399) That is, conjunctive neurons in the association area fire to partially *reactivate* the pattern of sensory stimulation, and then neurons in feature maps fire to *reenact* the earlier sensory representation. Such reenactments are, of necessity, only partial, and will be tailored to the agent's current context of action (Barsalou, 2003).

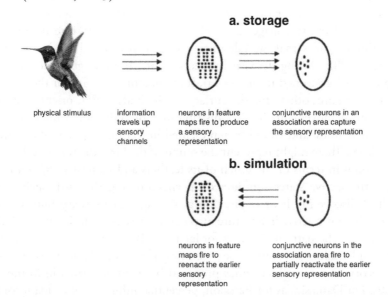

a. storage

| physical stimulus | information travels up sensory channels | neurons in feature maps fire to produce a sensory representation | conjunctive neurons in an association area capture the sensory representation |

b. simulation

neurons in feature maps fire to reenact the earlier sensory representation

conjunctive neurons in the association area fire to partially reactivate the earlier sensory representation

FIGURE 3. Illustration of the storage (a) and simulation (b) of sensorimotor information (adapted from Barsalou, 2005, Figure 15.1)

Barsalou called the fragmentary records of neural activation captured in a feature map *perceptual symbols*, and proposed that cognitive operations that make use of perceptual symbols could represent types and tokens, produce categorical inferences, combine the symbols to produce hierarchical propositions, and yield abstract concepts (Barsalou, 1999). The key to this productivity was a cognitively distributed system that Barsalou called a *simulator*. Through the neural reenactment of sensorimotor states associated with a given phenomenon, this system makes possible the simulation of the phenomenon even in its absence. According to the theory, to think of a hummingbird is to reactivate the sensorimotor states associated with your experience of hummingbirds and to thus create a mental simulation of the bird.

One aspect of Barsalou's theory that is especially important for the account of analogy I want to develop here is that the configuration of properties and relations encapsulated by the simulator for a given phenomenon may, under certain circumstances, be applied to a different phenomenon, giving rise to analogy (Barsalou, 2005, p. 422). In this way the configuration of properties and relations associated with the flight of a hummingbird could be applied to the conjoined musical events that make up Sagreras's *El Colibri*. And, *mutatis mutandis*, the same could be said were the terms of the analogy reversed: listening to Sagreras's *El Colibri* has the potential to prompt a simulation of the properties and relations associated with the flight of a hummingbird.

Let me pause for a moment to note an important aspect of analogical reference. The numerous correlations between the musical materials of Sagreras's little piece and the characteristic features of the hummingbird's flight, together with the natural propensity that humans have for analogical thought, suggest that drawing an analogy between the two is thoroughly natural. Yet it is by no means certain that a listener, without being prompted by Sagreras's title and subtitle, would make an immediate connection between the piece and the flight of the bird. What is needed is knowledge of the relational frame basic to the analogy. For example, a listener who is familiar with the conventions of programmatic musical works (such as that exemplified by Haydn's *The Creation*) will know that musical events that are exceptional or remarkable often correlate with some sort of extra-musical narrative. Confronted with the concatentation of unusual features that make up Sagreras's piece, this same listener would most likely be predisposed to look for some sort of extra-musical phenomena with which these features might be correlated. But without knowledge about programmatic music, or prompts from other domains (such as visual images of a hummingbird in flight), Sagreras's analogy in sound will most likely fail. Analogies involving sound always function within some larger context, which provides the relational frame for connecting sounds with concepts from other domains.

Let me now draw some of these ideas together and outline their importance for the notion of analogical representation that I would like to develop. Sagreras's *El Colibri* is a practical demonstration of how music can represent through patterned sound a phenomenon which is primarily visual: the flight of a hummingbird. According to Barsalou's perceptual symbol systems theory, Sagreras's musical depiction is effective because listening to the piece reactivates some of the same neural structure associated with actually seeing (or imagining, or remembering) a hummingbird in flight, giving rise to an imperfect but still vivid simulation of that event. It bears mention that what would be activated would not simply be a static picture but would instead be a highly dynamic image organized around the central features associated with the phenomenon of the bird's flight. Indeed, it is invariably the case that musical representations involve not static images but dynamic processes: we are concerned not with a bird or a horse or the sun as a celestial body but with a bird *in flight*, a horse *at full gallop*, or the sun *rising over the earth*. I should also want to note that Sagreras's depiction could summon other highly dynamic images: one friend of mine, innocent of the title of the work, suggested the image of a Greek waiter rushing to serve tables; another that of a wasp trapped in a glass jar. Any specification of the dynamic image offered by the music must be accomplished through context. That said, images that are more compelling are those that embrace more of the features and details of a sequence of musical materials: they represent a more efficient mapping between sound and image.

3. Extensions of Peirce's notion of the icon

All told, Peirce's remarks on iconicity are relatively brief, and made chiefly within the context of setting out his overall system of signs. Not so for Umberto Eco, who devoted over seventy pages of his *A Theory of Semiotics* to the phenomenon of iconism. It is apparent from Eco's analysis and critique that the icon is not nearly as simple as portrayed by Peirce, and that developing a fuller account of the way iconic signs are produced is central to understanding the function of signs as a whole. In the course of his analysis Eco dismisses analogy as a way to account for iconism, for he understands it to be little more than a formal procedure through which the transformation of object into icon can be effected (Eco, 1976, pp. 200-201). Empirical research over the past thirty years has demonstrated that there is much more to analogy than a formal procedure effecting the transformation of object into icon; brought to bear on the varieties of iconicity discussed by Eco, this research can do much to explain iconism and the species of reference it makes possible.

As a further point, analogical reference as realized through music suggests two ways Peirce's notion of an icon could be expanded. First, although Peirce appears to have been concerned almost exclusively with objects, the sonic analogs for dynamic processes offered by music reinterpret the "object" of an icon: rather than a static structure, it is a dynamic process. Second, although Peirce appeared to regard the iconic image, diagram, and metaphor as discrete categories, the examples provided by music indicate that it would be better to think of these as situated along a continuum of signs that range from those with a great deal of fidelity to the object to those that preserve only a few selected features of the object. Sound effects that aim to represent with as much fidelity as possible some actual sonic event (such as the sound of a helicopter) seem close to what Peirce would call an image. Indeed, particularly effective examples (among which I would include the imitation of bird song) might deceive a listener into thinking that the sound was produced not by a human but by its typical source (be that a helicopter or a bird). Sound symbols, which include onomatopoeic words and ad hoc sound effects interjected into the stream of speech, fall between the image and the diagram. Just where they would fall will depend in part on the extent to which they replicate the essential features of some target sound event, and in part on whether the dynamic event they aim to represent carries with it any sound at all. The sonic analogs of music seem closest to Peirce's diagram or metaphor: although they may have correlations with a real or imagined sonic event (such as a bird call or a sudden loud sound), they more typically analogize dynamic processes whose attributes are predominantly non-sonic.

4. Sonic analogs for dynamic processes in Dido's lament

It bears mention that the musical examples with which I have been concerned thus far come from a tradition of musical depiction roundly disparaged by music critics and others for the past two hundred years. Indeed, Haydn himself, commenting on a passage imitating the sound of frogs in his later oratorio *The Seasons*, characterized this sort of writing as "Frenchified trash" (Haydn, 1959, p. 197). And if it were the case that novelties such as these were the only manifestation of analogical reference through music we might well relegate music's sonic analogs to the status of mere curiosities. I would like, however, to argue that the range of dynamic processes for which music can offer sonic analogs extends far beyond the occasional bit of text-painting and into the very core of human expression. More specifically, the sonic analogs of music can be used to refer to dynamic processes associated with the emotions, the patterned movements of dance, and to the spontaneous gestures that accompany, and serve as a supplement, to speech.

FIGURE 4. Henry Purcell, *Dido and Aeneas*, Act III, Scene 2 (aria) "When I am laid in earth," bars 1–16

To support my argument I would like to consider one further example, the concluding aria of Henry Purcell's 1689 opera *Dido and Aeneas*, commonly known as Dido's lament. The score for the opening of the lament is shown in figure 4. Let me start my discussion with the emotional domain summoned by the lament. With its slow tempo, minor mode, and descending bass line, this is music that is easily understood as "sad". And yet the specificity of the music belies such a simplistic assessment: while there is no doubt that the musical materials summon an emotional domain with a negative valence, this domain is one that pushes beyond simple notions of sadness and into the realm of tragedy. One of the principal means through which Purcell accomplishes this is the ground bass which runs through the whole. The ground begins with a minor-mode descending tetrachord that, as Ellen Rosand noted, often formed the basis of ostinato patterns around which laments were organized during the seventeenth century. Speaking of the specific case of the ostinato Claudio Monteverdi used for his *Lament of the Nymph*, Rosand observed, "in its unremitting descent, its gravity, the pattern offers an analogue of obsession, perceptible as an expression of hopeless suffering." (Rosand, 1979, p. 150) Such patterns were often embellished through chromaticism, such as that used in a lament from Francesco Cavalli's opera *Egisto* from 1643 where the chromatic pitches occupy the first two-thirds of each bar. This is, of course, the same version of the descending tetrachord with which Purcell's ground begins, and in it the non-diatonic pitches acquire an agogic accent that brings them into prominence. The result is an analog for a relentless descent, one in which there is a sense of being pulled with an almost palpable effort, moving by uneasy stages toward some terrible goal. In Dido's lament the eleven repetitions of this ground summon a relentless and inevitable process through which the final tragedy of the opera will be realized.

The view of the relationship between music and affectual states that I have just sketched is one that bears a strong resemblance to that set out by Susanne Langer. Indeed, Jay Dowling and Dane Harwood, in the discussion of emotion and meaning they undertook in their 1986 *Music Cognition*, described Langer's treatment of music and emotion as one that relied on a form of Peircean iconicity. As they saw it, " […] the musical icon does not represent specific, verbalizable emotions, such as pity or fear. Music represents the dynamic form of emotion, not the specific content […]" (Dowling & Harwood, 1986, p. 206) This formulation is one with which Langer would likely be sympathetic—as Robert Innis observed, Langer saw her account of symbolization as building on that of Peirce (Innis, 2009, pp. 2-4). For my part, although I have found Langer's account of the relationship between music and the emotions promising—not least because of its emphasis on musical structure as a rich resource for the portrayal of emotions—I have found it wanting in its lack of a specific means through which the dynamic form of an emotional response is correlated with the dynamic form created by successions of musical materials; in my own work I have drawn on analogy (using an approach similar to that presented here) to explain this correlation (Zbikowski, 2011). In the case of Dido's lament, then, I would propose that the analogical resources offered by Purcell's music provide the basis for a simulation—in the sense developed by Barsalou—of an emotional state befitting profound tragedy.

Let me now turn to correlations between music and dynamic processes related to dance and gesture, making reference here to Mark Morris's choreography of the opera from the late 1980s. In his setting of the opera Morris banished singers and musicians from the stage and had the roles taken over by dancers; perhaps most controversially, Morris danced the roles of Dido and the Sorceress himself (Jordan, 2011b). There is much that can be said about Morris's choreography and its relationship to both the story of the opera and Purcell's music, but I shall want to focus on two brief features: the dance chorus's movements to the pattern of the ground, and the gesture by Morris that is correlated with Dido's plaintive *Remember me*.

In Morris's choreography for the very opening of the lament he has his chorus of dancers move forward with each chromatic pitch of the descending ground bass, and then momentarily pull back with each diatonic one. Here the dynamic aspect of Purcell's ground bass is readily apparent both in the sense it gives of moving toward a goal, and in the uneven steps with which it does so. On the one hand, I believe Morris's choreography heightens the richness of the emotional domain summoned by Purcell's music. On the other hand, the choreography also offers a visual manifestation of the dynamic process enacted by the ground bass, suggesting a correlation between the patterned movements of dance and successions of musical materials. Building on this and similar insights, in recent work I have proposed that music (especially that for social dances such as the polka or waltz) offers sonic analogs for the steps of the dance (Zbikowski, 2012). In instances such as this music makes reference not to dynamic visual images or emotion processes but to patterned bodily movement.

Morris's choreography also demonstrates how musical materials can be correlated with gestures. As part of his choreography of Dido's plea *Remember me* (the score for which is shown in figure 5) Morris performs a drawing motion (shown in figure 6) that seems to pull his chorus of dancers from the sides of the stage even as it threatens to throw him completely off balance. The gesture seems perfectly fit to the music, but note that one of the usual patterns of thought we use to organize correlations between music and movement, which maps ascending pitches with rising movements, here finds no support: although Morris's gesture describes an arcing motion that rises and falls, the singer's voice remains on the same pitch for the whole of "Remember me." Indeed, one could hear the singer's repeated D5s as providing a momentary contrast to the relentless pull of the ground bass, and thus offering an analog for the process of resisting the inevitability of fate. This seems to have been Morris's interpretation as well, for his drawing gesture derives from the American Sign Language word for "learning", as though "taking information from a book". (Jordan, 2011a, p. 27) For but a brief moment, then, the emphasis in the lament is not on death but on a kind of immortality brought about through lesson and memory.

Figure 5. Henry Purcell, *Dido and Aeneas*, Act III, Scene 2 (aria) "When I am laid in earth," bars 25–28

Figure 6. The drawing gesture made by Mark Morris (as Dido) in his choreography for Purcell's *Dido and Aeneas*

In sum, then, the dynamic processes to which the sonic analogs of music may make reference include emotion processes, the patterned movements of dance, and expressive gestures of the sort that often—and spontaneously—accompany speech. That music might be correlated with phenomena from these domains is hardly surprising, for the expressive resources associated with each contribute much to the distinctive character of human cultures.

181

Lawrence M. Zbikowski

Conclusions

The success many composers have found in summoning a wide range of vivid images—from sunrises to thunderstorms to galloping horses to spinning wheels, and of course the flight of a hummingbird—provides clear evidence for the resources music offers for iconic representation. I have argued, however, that in each case the image summoned by music is not a static picture but a dynamic process, which I would define as a coherent sequence of phenomena that is distributed over time and typified by parametric modulation or change. More importantly, musical materials can also represent emotions, gestures, and the patterned movements of dance, all of which are implicated in the construction of culture, especially through ritual. I have proposed that the key to understanding iconicity—whether it involves a static object or a dynamic process—is humans' capacity for analogy. It bears emphasis that Barsalou's theory of perceptual symbol systems suggests that analogical reference is successful because the analogical token activates a simulation of the properties of the thing to which it makes reference. Such simulations are always partial, but in the case of music a skillful composer can make them deeply compelling. Analogical reference can be seen to operate across the range of human expression but I would like to propose that it is uniquely exploited in music, where it serves as the basis for musical communication. This is not to exclude other forms of the sign from musical semiotics, but only to suggest that analogical reference, and the sonic analogs for dynamic processes that are its product, are of central importance for musical expression.

References

Barsalou, L. W. (1999). Perceptual symbol systems. *Behavioral and Brain Sciences, 22*, 577–660.
Barsalou, L. W. (2003). Situated simulation in the human conceptual system. *Language and cognitive processes, 18* (5/6), 513–562.
Barsalou, L. W. (2005). Abstraction as dynamic interpretation in perceptual symbol systems. In L. Gershkoff-Stowe & D. H. Rakison (Eds.), *Building object categories in developmental time* (pp. 389–431). Carnegie Mellon Symposium Series on Cognition. Mahwah, New Jersey: Lawrence Erlbaum Associates, Publishers.
Call, J., & Tomasello, M. (2005). Reasoning and thinking in nonhuman primates. In K. Holyoak & R. G. Morrison (Eds.), *The Cambridge handbook on thinking and reasoning* (pp. 607–632). Cambridge: Cambridge University Press.

Chen, Z., Sanchez, R. P., & Campbell, T. (1997). From beyond to within their grasp: The rudiments of analogical problem solving in 10- and 13-month-olds. *Developmental Psychology, 33*(5), 790–801.

Damasio, A. R. (1989). Time-locked multiregional retroactivation: A systems-level proposal for the neural substrates of recall and recognition. *Cognition, 33*(1–2), 25–62.

Deacon, T. W. (1997). *The symbolic species: The Co-evolution of language and the brain*. New York: W.W. Norton & Company.

Dowling, W. J., & Harwood, D. L. (1986). *Music cognition*. Academic Press series in cognition and perception. Orlando, Florida: Academic Press.

Eco, U. (1976). *A theory of semiotics*. Advances in Semiotics. Bloomington, Indiana: Indiana University Press.

Fauconnier, G., & Turner, M. (2002). *The way we think: Conceptual blending and the mind's hidden complexities*. New York: Basic Books.

Gentner, D., Bowdle, B. F., Wolff, P., & Boronat, C. (2001). Metaphor is like analogy. In D. Gentner, K. J. Holyoak, & B. N. Kokinov (Eds.), *The analogical mind: Perspectives from cognitive science* (pp. 199–253). Cambridge, Massachusetts: MIT Press.

Gentner, D., & Markman, A. B. (1997, January). Structure mapping in analogy and similarity. *American Psychologist, 52*(1), 45–56.

Gentner, D. (2003). Why we're so smart. In D. Gentner & S. Goldin-Meadow (Eds.), *Language in mind: Advances in the study of language and thought* (pp. 195–235). Cambridge, Massachusetts: MIT Press.

Glucksberg, S., & Keysar, B. (1990, January). Understanding metaphorical comparisons: Beyond similarity. *Psychological Review, 97*(1), 3–18.

Glucksberg, S., McGlone, M. S., & Manfredi, D. (1997). Property attribution in metaphor comprehension. *Journal of Memory and Language, 36,* 50–67.

Goswami, U. (1992). *Analogical reasoning in children*. Essays in developmental psychology. Hillsdale, New Jersey: Lawrence Erlbaum Associates.

Goswami, U. (2001). Analogical reasoning in children. In D. Gentner, K. J. Holyoak & B. N. Kokinov (Eds.), *The analogical mind: Perspectives from cognitive science* (pp. 437–470). Cambridge, Massachusetts: MIT Press.

Haydn, J. (1959). *The collected correspondence and London notebooks of Joseph Haydn* (H. R. Landon, Ed.). London: Barrie and Rockliff.

Herman, L. M. (2002). Exploring the cognitive world of the bottlenosed dolphin. In M. Bekoff, C. Allen, & G. M. Burghardt (Eds.), *The cognitive animal: Empirical and theoretical perspectives on animal cognition* (pp. 275–283). Cambridge, Massachusetts: MIT Press.

Hofstadter, D. R., & the Fluid Analogies Research Group. (1995). *Fluid concepts and creative analogies: Computer models of the fundamental mechanisms of thought*. New York: Basic Books.

Hofstadter, D. R. (2001). Epilogue: Analogy as the core of cognition. In D. Gentner, K. J. Holyoak, & B. N. Kokinov (Eds.), *The analogical mind: Perspectives from cognitive science* (pp. 499–538). Cambridge, Massachusetts: MIT Press.

Holyoak, K. J., & Thagard, P. (1995). *Mental leaps: Analogy in creative thought.* Cambridge, Massachusetts: MIT Press.

Holyoak, K. J. (2005). Analogy. In K. Holyoak & R. G. Morrison (Eds.), *The Cambridge handbook of thinking and reasoning* (pp. 117–142). Cambridge: Cambridge University Press.

Innis, R. E. (2009). *Susanne Langer in focus: The symbolic mind.* American philosophy. Bloomington: Indiana University Press.

Jordan, S. (2011a). Choreomusical conversations: Facing a double challenge. *Dance Research Journal, 43*(1), 43–64.

Jordan, S. (2011b). Mark Morris marks Purcell: *Dido and Aeneas* as danced opera. *Dance Research, 29*(2), 167-213.

Medin, D. L., Goldstone, R. L., & Gentner, D. (1993). Respects for similarity. *Psychological Review, 100*(2), 254–278.

Oden, D. L., Thompson, R. K. R., & Premack, D. (2001). Can an ape reason analogically?: Comprehension and production of analogical problems by Sarah, a chimpanzee (*Pan troglodytes*). In D. Gentner, K. J. Holyoak & B. N. Kokinov (Eds.), *The analogical mind: Perspectives from cognitive science* (pp. 471–497). Cambridge, Massachusetts: MIT Press.

Peirce, C. S. (1955). *Philosophical writings of Peirce* (J. Buchler, Ed.). New York: Dover.

Peirce, C. S. (1960). *Collected papers of Charles Sanders Peirce* (C. Hartshorne & P. Weiss, Eds.). Cambridge, Massachusetts: The Belknap Press of Harvard University Press.

Rosand, E. (1979, July). The descending tetrachord: An emblem of lament. *The Musical Quarterly, 65*(3), 346–359.

Zbikowski, L. M. (2002). *Conceptualizing music: Cognitive structure, theory, and analysis.* New York: Oxford University Press.

Zbikowski, L. M. (2011). Music, emotion, analysis. *Music Analysis, 29*(i-ii-iii), 1–25.

Zbikowski, L. M. (2012). Music, dance, and meaning in the early nineteenth century. *Journal of Musicological Research, 31*(2–3), 147–165.

The Other Semiotic Legacy of Charles Sanders Peirce: Ethology and Music-Related Emotion

David Huron

School of Music, Ohio State University

Charles Sanders Peirce was a remarkable scholar with broad ranging interests in many areas of philosophy, logic, and metaphysics. The influence of Peirce's ideas in the modern field of semiotics is well known. Less well known is the influence Peirce had on another discipline, the field of ethology (the study of animal behavior). Largely a European undertaking, the founders of ethology—notably Konrad Lorenz and Nico Tinbergen—were influenced by semiotic concepts in their studies of animal displays and calls. This presentation pays tribute to the achievements of ethology by returning insights from animal behavior back to the humanities and perhaps philosophy. Ethological concepts are used to provide a novel approach to understanding music-related emotion.

1. Signals and cues

Inspired by his reading of Peirce, Konrad Lorenz distinguished between two kinds of animal communications: signals and cues (Lorenz, 1939; 1970). This distinction remains a foundational concept in modern ethology (e.g., Smith and Harper, 2003). As defined by Lorenz, a signal is an evolved purposeful communicative behavior, such as evident in a rattlesnake's rattle. The rattle makes use of a purpose-evolved anatomical device to communicate a specific message to the observer. A cue is a non-purposeful artefact that is nevertheless informative, such as the buzzing sound produced by a mosquito suggesting imminent attack. Both the rattling of the rattlesnake's rattle and the buzzing of the mosquito presage the possibility of an attack. However, in the former case the communication is intentional whereas in the latter case it is an unintended consequence of the need for the insect to flap its wings. Signals involve innate behavioral and physiological mechanisms, whereas cues are commonly learned artefactual behaviors.

2. Size matters

When two animals interact, many behaviors can be classified as either agonistic (e.g., aggression), or affinitive (e.g., submission, greeting, sharing). In general, when animals create threatening displays they behave in ways that tend to make them appear larger. This includes raised hair, ruffled feathers, standing upright, arching of the back, looming, and other behaviors that make the animal seem bigger. Conversely, when animals create submissive or friendly displays, they typically behave in ways that tend to make them appear smaller, such as bowing, squatting, sitting, head-lowering, limb-withdrawing, etc.

These visual behaviors have acoustic parallels. One of the best generalizations one can make about acoustics is that large masses or large volumes tend to produce low frequencies of vibration whereas small masses and small resonant cavities tend to produce higher frequencies. The ethologist Eugene Morton (1977) carried out a seminal comparative study of vocalizations in 28 avian and 28 mammalian species. Morton found that high pitch is associated with submissive and affinitive behaviors whereas low pitch is associated with threatening and aggressive behaviors.

Bolinger (1978) observed the same relationship in a cross-cultural sample of human speech intonation. In general, high vocal pitch is associated with appeasement, deference or politeness. Conversely, low pitch is associated with aggression or seriousness. This same pattern can be observed using musical stimuli. For example, Huron, Kinney and Precoda (2006) played unfamiliar Western folksongs to listeners and had them judge the melodies according to such criterion as politeness, heaviness, and aggressiveness. Unknown to the participants, each melody appeared in three different transpositions spanning two octaves. Consistent with ethological observations, it was found that transposing a melody to a higher pitch causes the melody to be judged more polite and more submissive (see also Morton, 2006).

In another study, Huron and Shanahan (2004) coded the degree of sociability for three hundred characters in randomly selected opera scenarios. Friendly and altruistic characters were rated as exhibiting high sociability whereas self-centred or aggressive characters were rated as exhibiting low sociability. Not surprisingly, there is a significant association between the tessitura of the voice and the character's sociability: heroes are mainly tenors and sopranos, whereas villains are mainly basses and contraltos.

As with many mammals, the human voice can be broadly characterized as have two acoustical components: a source (vocal folds) and a filter (vocal tract). The frequency of the vocal folds is mainly determined by their mass and tension. The resonant frequency of the vocal tract is determined by the length and volume of the air cavity. In humans, the frequencies of the source and filter are under independent voluntary control. For example, we can produce a low pitch and low resonance when we utter a low vowel (e.g., [a]) with a low pitch. Speaking a high vowel (e.g., [i]) with elevated pitch produces a high pitch and a high resonance. However, we can also produce mixtures, such as speaking [i] with a low voice (low pitch + high resonance) or speaking [a] with a high intonation (high pitch + low resonance).

2.1 The smile

The linguist John Ohala extended Morton's observations regarding sound-size symbolism to include the vocal filter (resonant frequency) as well as the vocal source (pitch). As with pitch, resonant frequency arising from body cavities is also correlated with body size (Ohala, 1980; 1982; 1983; 1984).

Ohala argued that sound-size symbolism can be used to account for the human smile (Ohala, 1982; 1994). For over a century, scholars have pondered the apparent enigma of the smile: why would showing one's teeth (commonly associated with aggression) be construed as a sign of friendliness? Ohala drew attention to the fact that one can hear a smile (see also Tartter, 1980). Without seeing a person smiling, the smile is nonetheless evident in the sound of the voice. Flexing the zygomatic muscles characteristic of smiling causes the flesh of the lips to be drawn tight against the teeth. This effectively shortens the length of the vocal tract and so shifts the resonance of the voice upward. In short, the sound of the smile is the sound of a smaller resonant cavity. The upward shift of the spectral centroid is consistent with sound-size symbolism, which, throughout the animal kingdom, is a ubiquitous way of conveying friendly or non-aggressive intent. Accordingly, Ohala suggested that the smile originated as an acoustical display that later became generalized to include the visual component. Ohala proposed that the evolutionary origin of the smile is auditory, not visual.

2.2 The pout

Ohala extended his observations regarding the smile in the opposite direction. Instead of retracting the lips against the teeth, one can thrust the lips forward away from the teeth—lengthening the vocal tract with a characteristic drop

David Huron

in the first formant frequency. Ohala refers to this as the "o-face". An example is evident in the human "pout". According to sound-size symbolism, this lowering of the frequency should be associated with anti-social rather than pro-social behavior. Indeed, the classic "brutish" or "loutish" voice involves extending the lips away from the teeth. The cliché sound of the aggressive hooligan offers a polar contrast with the sound of smiling—consistent with sound-size symbolism.

3. Multimodal signals

Are displays such as smiling or frowning ethological signals or ethological cues? Ethologists have identified a number of ways in which signals can be distinguished from cues. One property of signals is that they tend to exhibit *redundancy* where the signal is repeated or sustained over time and over multiple sensory channels (Wiley, 1983; Johnstone, 1997; Partan & Marler, 1999). Since signals are intended to be communicated, a "subtle" signal is unlikely to have the intended effect. Employing more than one sensory modality makes the signal more conspicuous. For example, in the case of the rattlesnake's rattle, there is both a distinctive acoustical component (the sound of the rattle) as well as a distinctive visual component (the raised shaking tail). Ostensibly, even if an observer is only able to hear, or just see the snake, the signal could nevertheless be successful communicated. By contrast, many (though not all) cues do not exhibit multimodal features. This simply reflects the fact that cues are behavioral artefacts (like the buzzing of a mosquito's wings), and not explicitly intended to be communicative. We have already seen an example of the tendency for multimodal displays in the case of the smile: Ohala's main claim is that it would be wrong to regard the smile as solely a visual display.

In the past, emotion researchers have tended to focus on the visual aspects of facial expressions without considering other sensory modes. From an ethological perspective, we would expect many facial expressions to qualify as *signals*— and therefore tend to be accompanied by distinctive acoustical features, not just visual features. Facial expressions that are not accompanied by distinctive acoustical features are more likely to be artefactual cues rather than signals.

Notice that the smile and the pout displays involve only one frequency-related component of the voice—namely the filter or vocal-cavity component. Recall that we can independently manipulate the source or pitch of the voice. Once again, high pitch is associated with pro-social intent whereas low pitch is generally associated with anti-social or aggressive intent. In light

188

of the multimodal tendency of signals, if the pitch of the voice represents an authentic signal, then we ought to see a distinctive visual element that accompanies the higher/lower vocal pitch. Two studies are pertinent. The first study was carried out by Huron, Dahl and Johnson (2009; see also commentary by Ohala, 2009). We asked forty-four non-musician participants to sing neutral, high and low pitches while their faces were photographed. The high and low photographs were paired together and independent judges were asked to identify which face is friendlier. Photographs of high-pitch faces were easily perceived as friendlier than the low-pitch faces. A careful examination of the photographs revealed that, when singing a low pitch, participants tend to drop the chin, frown, and lower their eyebrows. Conversely, when singing a high pitch, participants tend to raise the chin, smile, and raise the eyebrows. In a follow-up experiment, we cropped the photographs so that only the region above the nose-tip was shown. Once again, independent judges found the high-pitch faces friendlier than the low-pitch faces. The eyebrows alone appear to provide a sufficient feature for judging the friendliness.

Producing a low pitch appears to have a causal relationship with eyebrow movement. That is, when asked to sing a low pitch, people naturally tend to lower their eyebrows. What about the reverse relationship? Does moving your eyebrows cause your voice to move up or down in pitch? A second study was carried out by Huron and Shanahan (2013). Thirty-one participants were asked to read aloud short sentences placing their eyebrows in a high, low, or neutral position. Eyebrow placement was found to have a significant (though small) effect on pitch height. That is, compared with neutral and low eyebrow placement, speaking with raised eyebrows causes the pitch to rise.

This relationship is consistent with existing research concerning eyebrow placement. Cross-culturally, low eyebrow placement tends to be symptomatic of aggression whereas high eyebrow placement is indicative of friendliness. Ethologist Irenäus Eibl-Eibesfeldt (1989) has noted that the eyebrow *flash* (quick up-and-down movement) is a common greeting for humans and that analogous displays are evidence in other primates.

In summary, there is a strong relationship between pitch height and eyebrow placement that appears to be bi-causal: moving the pitch tends to cause the eyebrows to move in tandem, and moving the eyebrows tends (to a lesser extent) to cause the pitch to move in tandem. This bi-directional causality suggests a shared or common source in the motor cortex, consistent with a single unified display. Moreover, the multi-modal connection is consistent with the existence of an ethological signal.

Once again, this apparent signalling system can be observed in music. Bonfiglioli, Caterina, Incasa and Baroni (2006) carried out a qualitative study of facial expressions from video recordings of performing musicians. They found that when the musical texture involves predominantly low pitches there is a tendency for the instrumentalist to lower her/his eyebrows. Conversely, when the music involves predominantly high pitches, there is a tendency for the instrumentalist to raise his/her eyebrows.

3.1 Sarcasm

Another basic facial expression described in the literature is the so-called contempt or sneer facial expression (Ekman, 1972). The sneer is regarded as a variant of the disgust expression. Specifically, the disgust expression involves characteristic flexion of the levator labii superioris muscles that elevate the upper lip and the depressor septi muscle that constrict the nostrils. This is presumed to have originated in efforts to reduce the inhaling of offensive odours. The sneer display is essentially "one-half" of a disgust expression. That is, flexion occurs asymmetrically on one side of the face only. Unlike the disgust display, the sneer is regarded as a social display: As Ekman notes, the disgust response effectively says "I find this disgusting" whereas the sneer says "I find you disgusting."

Plazak (2011) carried out a seminal study in which instrumentalists were asked to play various passages in a sarcastic fashion. Through sound alone, listeners were readily able to recognize musical sarcasm compared with other affective conditions. Acoustic analyses using speech-based methods showed the sarcastic renditions exhibited elevated *nasality* measures. That is, the instrumental sounds approached the *nya nya* timbre associated with vocal taunts characteristic of the sneer or contempt. Once again, from an ethological perspective, the contempt or sneer facial expression is correlated with a distinctive auditory effect (in this case nasalization). The facial expression and sound go hand-in-hand. And once again, the same auditory features can be observed in a musical context.

3.2 Cuteness

Ethologists also make use of the Peircean concept of an index. The index conveys information by virtue of its factual connection to an object. Amphibians, such as frogs, grow continuous throughout their lives. As a consequence, the size of a frog provides a good index of its longevity, and so a reasonable index of its capacity to survive. The pitch of a frog's croak is directly related to its size, and females preferentially mate with male frogs that produce the lowest croak—that is, those male frogs who have survived the longest.

From infancy to adulthood, the human vocal tract similarly increases in length. At birth, the typical vocal tract length is roughly 8 centimetres. By adulthood, the length has doubled to roughly 16 centimetres in length (Vorperian et al., 2005).

Some years ago, we carried out an experiment where listeners judged the "cuteness" of a wide variety of sound-producing objects. Listeners are in broad agreement when judging the relative cuteness of sounds. We learned that the sound-producing objects judged "most cute" share two physical attributes. They all share a small resonant cavity activated by a small amount of energy. The dimensions of the most cute-sounding objects resemble the size of an infant's vocal tract.

Of course infants are capable of generating rather loud sounds that are manifestly not cute. However, when cooing or gurgling, the small energies activating the small cavity produce sounds that readily evoke nurturing and protective behaviors—in short, they engender parenting behaviors. Imagine the dire consequences if human parents did not find their infants cute. Without this affective response, humans would cease to survive for long.

What is interesting is that the response generalizes beyond infant sounds. What a sopranino recorder, ocarina, and music box share in common is a small resonant cavity activated by a small amount of energy. Moreover, in each case, the sounds are readily described as "cute". We hear these sounds a vulnerable, innocent and helpless.

For the first year of life, the vocal tract grows rather slowly. After 12 months, the rate of growth increases notably (Vorperian et al., 2005). It is in the first year, that the vocal tract produces the cutest sounds—a period in which the neonate is most vulnerable, and most in need of parental attention. The infantile quality of the voice is echoed in characteristic visual features, including a round (rather than long) face, large eyes (relative to the head size), small nose, and small ears. These are the classic "baby face" features.

The musical use of cuteness is apparent in the recordings of the American popular singer from the 1920s, Helen Kane (whose voice became the model for the Betty Boop cartoon character). Kane had a diminutive stature, including a small head, and correspondingly short vocal tract. Her singing style is quintessentially "cute" sounding. Unlike the intentional lowering of vocal pitch, or the voluntary smiling resonance, the bulk of the vocal tract length is fixed by anatomy—and therefore a true index of infantile vulnerability in both the Peircean and ethological senses.

4. Faces and voices

Let's pause and summarize. We have seen some evidence consistent with the multimodal tendencies of ethological signals. Specifically, we have observed that smiling exhibits both characteristic visual and characteristic auditory features, and that the auditory component is consistent with sound-size symbolism. We have also observed that pouting exhibits both characteristic visual and characteristic auditory features, and that the auditory component is consistent with sound-size symbolism.

We have also observed a close relationship between vocal pitch height and eyebrow position. Specifically, voluntary efforts to raise or lower the pitch of the voice produce involuntary tendencies to move the eyebrows in a parallel fashion. At the same time, voluntary efforts to raise or lower the eyebrows produce involuntary tendencies to move the pitch of the voice in a parallel fashion. This bi-causal relationship is consistent with multimodal redundancy whose purpose is to increase the conspicuousness of signals. Moreover, the auditory component of this display is consistent with the sound-size symbolism.

We have further observed an association between the sneer/contempt expression, where flexing the nose causes a distinctive visual expression accompanied by audible nasalization of the voice—consistent with the multimodal tendency of ethological signals. Finally, we have seen an example of an index in the form of auditory cuteness—with the acoustical characteristics of a short vocal tract linked with characteristic baby-face visual features. In each case, all of the acoustic-related features (with their corresponding affects) can be observed in musical contexts.

5. Sadness and grief

Charles Darwin (1872) made an important distinction between *sadness* and *sorrow*. Here we propose to use the terms *sadness* and *grief* instead. Sadness is an affective state characterized by low physiological arousal. When sad, a person typically exhibits slow heart rate, shallow respiration, slumped posture, loss of appetite, sleep, reduced engagement with the world, a tendency to avoid conversation (i.e., mute), and contemplation/reflection (thinking sad thoughts). Grief, by contrast, is an affective state characterized by high physiological arousal. When in a state of grief, a person typically exhibits fast heart rate, erratic respiration, flushed face, tears, nasal congestion, pharyngeal constriction, vocalizing (anything from quiet sobbing to loud wailing), and ingressive vocalizing (sound production while inhaling). Sadness and grief are often interleaved together; that is, periods of psychic pain commonly involve alternating periods of (quiet) sadness and (louder) grief.

Both sadness and grief are associated with distinctive sounds. People who are sad or depressed typically speak with a (1) quieter voice, (2) slower speaking rate, (3) low pitch, (4) small pitch movement, (5) poor articulation, and (6) dark timbre (Kraepelin, 1899). These same features have been observed in nominally sad music. For example, music in the minor mode is quieter in dynamic level (Turner & Huron, 2008), exhibits a slower tempo (Post & Huron, 2009), is slightly lower in overall pitch (Huron, 2008), employs smaller average melodic intervals (Huron, 2008), involves more mumbled articulation, and makes use of darker timbres (Schutz, Huron, Keeton, & Loewer, 2008).

People who experience grief also exhibit characteristic vocalizations. Grief vocalizations can range from quiet moaning to loud wailing. The vocalizations are commonly high in pitch, exhibit gliding (often descending) pitch contours, sniffling, ingressive phonation (vocalizing while inhaling), punctuated exhaling, and involve pharyngealized voice (due to the constricted pharynx) (e.g. Fox, 2004). The constricted pharynx introduces vocal instability—producing distinctive alternation between modal and falsetto phonation (commonly called "cracking" or "breaking" voice). Breaking voice is perhaps the most telltale sound associated with grief.

Paul and Huron (2010) studied the role of "breaking" voice in music. Country music fans were recruited; they identified 31 instances of cracking or breaking voice in their record collections. Each identified song was paired with a matched (control) song from the same album sung by the same singer--a song that did not contain any instance of breaking voice. Lyrics were assembled for both the target and control songs. Without hearing the music, independent judges rated the lyrics for grief-related content. Breaking voice was found to correlate positively with grief-related lexical content in the lyrics.

Why, we might ask do voices break? In general, grief exhibits a highly distinctive set of physiological characteristics, including watery eyes, nasal congestion, constriction of the throat, and erratic breathing. When crying for an extended period, the face tends to become "puffy" with notable inflammation around the eyes. Oddly, researchers on crying have failed to notice that, in isolation, any medical doctor would diagnosis these symptoms as characteristic of a systemic allergic response. Moreover, inflammation—such as that seen in the face after a long bout of crying—is caused by histamines. These are the same histamines that cause an allergy sufferer to reach for a bottle of antihistamines.

Notice that the allergic response leads to characteristic visual (facial) features, and also leads to distinctive vocalizations through the accompanying pharyngeal constriction. In short, crying appears to borrow the systemic allergic response, leading to characteristic visual and auditory features consistent with an ethological signal. This sort of physiological "borrowing" is known as an *exaptation* (Gould & Vrba, 1982).

The features of crying are not limited to the effects of an allergic response. For example, allergy sufferers are not compelled to vocalize. In the case of crying, however, the tendency to vocalize is so strong that the vocal cords remain engaged even when inhaling. The ingressive phonation characteristic of crying is consistent with an innate compulsion to make a sound.

Notice that crying bears all the hallmarks of an ethological signal. Crying appears to commandeer the allergic response as an exaptation that produces both distinctive visual features as well as distinctive acoustical features. That is, grief entails multimodal elements congruent with the goal of conspicuousness.

If crying is a signal, what does it signal? Limitations of space preclude any detailed exposition here. Jeffrey Kottler has proposed that weeping is the human "surrender" signal (Kottler 1996; Kottler & Montgomery, 2001). Kottler has documented how weeping "turns off" aggression or argument and leads to sympathetic altruistic behaviors directed toward the person crying. For the person crying, assistance is purchase at the cost of a loss of social status. That is, crying parallels the submission/surrender displays found in many other social animals. Support for Kottler's theory comes from the work of Gelstein et al. (2011) on the olfactory effects of tears. Tears were collected from women volunteers who had been induced to weep by watching a sad scene from a movie. For comparison purposes they also collected saline solution that was trickled down the women's cheeks. Men were then asked to smell both the real and imitation tears. They couldn't tell the difference: neither had any noticeable odour. Nevertheless, the real psychic tears produced a marked physiological effect: testosterone levels dropped significantly when the men were exposed to the real tears. In addition, other measures showed that sniffing the tears significantly impeded sexual arousal. The results of this study suggest that psychic tears contain a chemical pheromone—an odourless air-borne hormone that influences the behavior of others.

6. Sadness as cue

Recall that sad speech is associated with six acoustic features: quieter, slower, lower in pitch, more monotone, mumbling, and dark timbre. What, we might ask, do all six features share in common? It turns out that all six features can be plausibly attributed to low physiological arousal. Low energy is associated with low epinephrine levels and low acetylcholine levels. Acetylcholine has a marked impact on muscle tone and reactivity. Specifically, low acetylcholine leads to weakness (flaccid muscle tone) and sluggishness (slow muscular reactivity). Slow muscle movement causes sluggish movement of the lips, tongue and chin. That is, the articulatory muscles move slower producing a slower rate of speaking as well as a more mumbled articulation. When the pulmonary muscles (involved in breathing) are relaxed, the subglottal air pressure drops, producing a quieter sound. Similarly less tense vocal folds result in a lower overall pitch. Slow movement of the cricothyroid muscle results in less responsive pitch movements, leading to smaller pitch intervals or a more monotone pitch inflection. Finally, the relaxed facial musculature includes weak zygomatic activity; there is no active smile, so the lips tend to pull away from the teeth resulting in a longer vocal tract, and consequently a darker timbre. In short, all of the features of "sad voice" can be plausibly regarded as artefacts of low physiological arousal.

An important observation to be made about sad voice is that people tend to be mute when sad: sad people don't vocalize much. This contrasts with grief. Although crying can be done quietly, there is a strong compulsion to vocalize when crying. As we have seen, the compulsion to vocalize is so strong that weeping tends to engage the vocal folds even when inhaling—a rare phenomenon.

In continuing research we have been looking at the uniqueness of nominally sad facial expression and vocalization. Although the research is not complete, it appears that there is no distinctive or unique "sad" facial expression. A presumed "sad" face appears to be indistinguishable from a "sleepy" or "relaxed" face. The "glum" faces commonly observed on a public bus or train are often deemed sad. However, people thought to appear sad are often simply relaxed. We are currently carrying out an experiment to test whether listeners can distinguish between "sad" voice and "sleepy" voice. We predict that it is difficult or impossible for listeners to distinguish sadness from sleepiness.

Summarizing, we might contrast sadness with grief as follows:
1. Unlike grief, sadness is not associated with a compulsion to vocalize.
2. Unlike grief, sadness does not appear to exhibit a clearly unique facial expression.
3. All of the characteristics of sad speech can be attributed to low physiological arousal—that is, they are artefacts of low energy.

David Huron

4. Sad voice may not be distinguishable from sleepy voice (Shanahan and Huron, in progress).

In short, sadness looks like an ethological cue whereas grief looks like an ethological signal.

7. Acoustic ethological model

With this background, we might now address the question: How do we reconcile the seemingly contradiction claims that low pitch is associated with aggression and that low pitch is also associated with sadness? We have claimed that sadness is a covert affect. As a cue, sadness entails no overt expression. Nevertheless, observers learn to infer sadness through its association with low physiological arousal. Moreover, the low pitch is linked to other features arising from low physiological arousal, notably quiet voice. That is, the combination of low pitch and low intensity are likely to be interpreted by experienced listeners as indicative of sadness. Notice, however, that the acoustic features linked to sadness are the same as those associated with other states of low physiological arousal—including sleepiness and relaxation. This suggests that sleepiness, relaxation, and sadness share the same acoustic features, and should be easily confused with one another.

Aggression, by contrast, taps into the sound-size symbolism evident in calls throughout the animal kingdom. Accordingly, the association between low pitch and aggression or seriousness is likely to be a true ethological signal. If this is the case, then the link between low pitch and aggression ought to be biologically prepared—in contrast with sadness. Similarly, high pitch is also likely to be interpreted according to sound-size symbolism, and also likely to be an ethological signal.

Table 1 provides a summary of the theory presented here. We might refer to this as the Acoustic Ethological Model (AEM). This model can be regarded as a refinement of the model proposed by Morton (1977). Specifically, the AEM introduces a second dimension: adding intensity to pitch. Accordingly, the model distinguishes four acoustical conditions: (1) high pitch and high intensity is associated with fear or alarm, (2) high pitch and low intensity is associated with appeasement or friendliness, (3) low pitch and high intensity is associated with aggression or seriousness, and (4) low pitch and low intensity is associated with sadness, sleepiness, and relaxation. Three of the four conditions are candidate ethological signals, with one quadrant regarded as a candidate ethological cue.

	Quiet	Loud
High pitch	appeasement, friendliness	fear, alarm
Low pitch	sad, relaxed, sleepy	aggression, seriousness

TABLE I. Acoustic Ethological Model

8. To signal or not to signal

In ethology, the purpose of a signal is to change the behavior of the observer (Bradbury & Vehrenkamp, 1998). For example, when being attacked, a wolf can signal its submission to a conspecific aggressor by rolling over on its back, exposing its belly and whimpering. The immediate effect of this behavior is to terminate the aggression of the dominant animal. The surrender display signals to the dominant animal that it has won the altercation. The remarkable part of this interaction is how the signal transforms the behavior of the observing animal: the angry aggressive attack immediately dissolves.

From an evolutionary perspective, one needs to ask the question "Why would any animal make a signal?" Evolutionary logic compels us to the conclusion that a signal will be made only if it is to the benefit of the signalling animal. If a signal reduces the fitness of the signalling animal, then the signalling behavior would be selected against.

Notice that there are plenty of affective states that should remain covert—that is, not communicated to others. Suppose for example, that you have stolen my food. I might be angry with you, but if you are clearly more powerful than me, it would be foolhardy for me to express anger in your presence. A better strategy would be to mask my feelings, and wait for an appropriate opportunity (such as assembling an alliance) that could ultimately prevail over you. Conversely, if I am the more powerful individual, there might be value in my overtly expressing anger—even if I do not actually feel anger. An expression of anger might make you respond in a deferential way—for example, abandoning your food so that I can take it. In short, in some cases an expression of anger can have a beneficial effect, even in the absence of any matching feeling. In other cases, no expression of anger should take place, even if one feels angry.

Here we see compelling reasons for separating affect from expression. For example, there are good reasons to distinguish two forms of anger: hot anger (anger that is displayed) and cold anger (anger that is felt but not displayed). Whether anger is expressed depends on whether the signal is beneficial to the signalling animal.

Notice that this logic is incompatible with the most popular understanding of emotional display — what might be called the Emotion Communication Model (ECM). This model might be described as follows: A person feels an emotion (such as happiness), and this causes them to generate an appropriate display (such as smiling). An observer perceives (recognizes) the display and infers that the individual feels happy. In the ECM model, it is assumed that the purpose of an emotional display is to communicate the affective state of the individual making the display. However, this assumption makes no biological sense. Instead, an expression should be viewed as *other*-directed: the expression is intended to change the behavior of the observer to the benefit of the signaller (Bradbury & Vehrenkamp 1998). Expressions of anger, sadness, happiness, etc. may certainly be regarded as communicative acts, but it is wrong to assume that they are intended to convey one's affective state.

Of course there are many variations to the basic ECM paradigm. An individual might engage in some deception—such as displaying an emotion that is not truly felt. Or an individual might attempt to mask or hide an otherwise spontaneous expression, such as turning away from an observer so they cannot see one's tears.

Several emotional displays are thought to be cross-culture universals (e.g., Ekman, 1972). At the same time, Ekman has suggested that purported universal expressions are often modified by local "display rules"—shaping various aspects of the display in culturally unique ways. Some evidence suggests that certain emotions may be culture-specific (e.g., Lutz, 1988).

Ethologists offer a very different perspective concerning the nature and function of displays, such as smiling or frowning. As we have seen, ethological research raises serious objections to the ECM model just described.

Tomkins (1980) has characterized emotions as motivational amplifiers— internal feeling states that encourage or compel an individual to behave in particular ways. Understood as motivational states, there are good reasons why some emotions would be experienced without any accompanying expression. Many affective states can exercise a transforming effect on behavior without being communicated: e.g., jealousy, love, hunger, disappointment, suspicion, pride, curiosity, etc. Of course, some affective states may indeed be recognizable even though they are not expressive signals (e.g., sleepiness, pain, etc.). But these states are recognized because of the spill-over of physiological concomitants that observers learn to decipher through past experience. The observed features for these states are artefacts rather than intentional communications; that is to say, they are ethological cues rather than signals.

In the past, some psychologists have tended to reify emotions as their expressions. In Ekman's work, for example, there is a clear tendency to equate emotions with distinctive (facial) expressions. Any feeling-state that has no expression is deemed not to be an emotion. From an evolutionary and ethological perspective, these views are clearly problematic.

With this background, we can return to consider the contrast between sadness and grief.

9. Depressive realism

If sadness and grief are different affective states, we might ask what purpose they serve, and why they tend to co-occur.

Consider the etiology or causes of sadness. "Clueless Carl" is eager to date beautiful women. He approaches several beautiful women, each of whom declines his invitation for a date. After a series of such failures, Carl experiences feelings of sadness. Research indicates that sadness leads to reflection and reconsideration of life strategies (Nesse, 1991). Carl is likely to consider his own assets and liabilities, and recognize that he is not an especially handsome or accomplished man. He might consider other women he knows who are less physically beautiful but have other attractive qualities. In short, a bout of sadness is likely to cause Carl to reevaluate his romantic strategy, and to encourage him to set more realistic goals.

In general, people tend to hold overly optimistic self-appraisals (Ross & Nisbett, 1991). People tend to think they are more attractive, more intelligent, and more interesting than others judge them to be. We tend to look at the world through rose-tinted lenses. One might expect that when we are sad, we become pessimistic, underestimating ourselves. Instead, when sad, we are more realistic in our self-appraisals. This phenomenon is referred to as depressive realism (Alloy & Abrahamson, 1979). Compared with happiness, sadness encourages more detail-oriented thinking, less judgment bias, less reliance on stereotypes (Clore & Huntsinger, 2007) and greater memory accuracy (Storbeck & Clore, 2005). Listening to nominally sad music is known to induce depressive realism (Brown & Mankowski, 1993).

10. Mourning

When bad things happen in people's lives, they often experience alternating periods of active grieving (crying) and quiescent sadness. We might refer to this oscillating pattern as mourning. Recall that sadness induces depressive realism and is typically accompanied by periods of reflection. Sadness causes us to think of how we might adapt to problematic circumstances (Nesse, 1991).

As we have seen, crying exhibits all of the hallmarks of an ethological signal. Recall that signals are intended to change the behavior of the observer. And indeed, crying does have a profound affect on others. In particular, crying leads to affiliative, supportive, and compassionate behaviors.

When bad things happen in our lives, there are two kinds of resources one may call upon to mount an effective response. One resource is our friends and family: people around us can come to our assistance. The second resource is ourselves. By thinking-through the situation, we can formulate strategies that help us cope with the difficulty.

My claim is that crying and sadness are different emotions that serve different (yet complimentary) purposes. Sadness is intended to change my behavior: reflection causes me to lower my expectations and contemplate different strategies that are better adapted to the environment. My crying is intended to change your behavior: crying encourages observers to become more altruistic. Said another way, sadness is an personal/covert emotion, whereas grief is a social/overt emotion. When we experience difficulties in life, we adapt through a combination of our own resources (sadness) plus help from others (solicited through crying).

Notice that this theory explains why crying would be an ethological signal whereas sadness would be an ethological cue. Sadness is simply not designed to be communicative. This does not necessarily mean that sensitive observers cannot recognize sadness in others, although it does suggest that sadness can be mistakenly attributed to another person, whereas assessments of grief are likely to be accurate.

11. Honest signalling

If crying is a signal—intended to influence the behavior of observers—then why do we often cry in private? Moreover, why do we often try to mask or hide the fact that we are crying?

To the extent that observers respond to signals in a biologically prepared manner, signals can be used deceptively (Smith & Harper, 2003; Zahavi, 1977). Observers need reassurance that a signal is authentic rather than deceptive. Considerable research has been carried out regarding mechanisms intended to ensure the honesty of signals (Pentland, 2008). Several mechanisms have been proposed.

One approach is to make a signal involuntary. Unlike the social (voluntary) smile, the genuine or "Duchenne" smile, for example, is difficult or impossible to "fake" (Freitas-Magalhães, 2006). Similarly, blushing is a response not under voluntary control. People who blush easily usually dislike this, however, observers are usually delighted by people who blush easily. These attitudes can be traced to honest signalling: we appreciate honesty in others, but feel vulnerable when our own signals are beyond our control. If crying is to remain an effective social signal, this can be best assured by making the response involuntary. As an involuntary response, we can expect it to arise even in non-social settings. People cry alone, not because crying is not intended to be observed, but because crying is an honest signal. Finally, the phenomenal experience of someone crying is hardly that of a person engaged in a Machiavellian trick to con bystanders—even if the evolved purpose of crying is to solicit help from others. The unconscious mind knows when to appeal for help, even if the conscious mind is an unwilling participant.

Another approach to honest signalling is the handicap principle, where making a signal must be "costly" for the individual making the signal (Zahavi & Zahavi, 1997). Like all appeasement displays, crying incurs the cost of the loss of social status. If an individual does not want to pay this cost, then they should attempt to hide or suppress their crying.

12. Affect induction

A core question in music-related affect is how music might lead listeners to experience some emotion: How does affect induction take place? Several plausible mechanisms have already been identified, including associative, empathetic, and cognitive emotional generators (Huron, 2002; Tuuri & Eerola, 2012). To these sources of emotion, ethological research suggests adding yet another—what might be called signalling. First, let us review three commonly identified emotional generators.

A first mechanism is simple association. As in the case of a conditioned response, certain sounds or sound patterns may become associated with past emotional experiences. The associations may be entirely arbitrary, as when a nominally sad passage reminds a listener of a past happy event such as winning the lottery.

A second mechanism is empathetic. In this case, a listener recognizes acoustic features associated with particular emotions. Mirror neurons (for example) might induce an observer to vicariously experience feelings akin to those being displayed. For example, a listener might hear acoustic features associated with sadness, and consequently be induced to feel sad through some sort of mirror process.

A third mechanism is cognitive. Conscious thoughts can lead a listener to a particular experience. For example, when listening to Beethoven's fifth symphony, a listener might be reminded of Susan McClary's discussion of Beethoven's work as a depiction of rape, and by interpreting the sounds in light of McClary's suggestion, experience discomfort or alarm while listening to the work.

Signalling theory offers a fourth mechanisms for affect induction. Recall that the purpose of a signal is to change the behavior of the observer. For example, witnessing the submission display of a conspecific, the aggressor animal stops behaving aggressively. That is, the signal changes the behavior of the observer in a way that suggests feelings of anger are replaced by affiliative, playful, or altruistic feelings.

If crying is an ethological signal, then the purpose of crying cannot be to make the observer also experience grief. Instead, crying is effective when it transforms the observer's state to affiliative, sympathetic and compassionate feelings. Notice that ethologists make the strong claim that the evoked behaviors in the observer are biologically innate. Signals are evolved behaviors whose effectiveness depends on stereotypic patterns of response. Accordingly, exposure to acoustic features of "grief" in music would be expected to induce affiliative, sympathetic, peaceful, altruistic or compassionate feelings, not grief.

Notice that since all four of these purported generative mechanisms are presumed to operate concurrently, one could well imagine more than one affect being induced in response to the same stimulus. For example, upon hearing a "lament", a listener could well experience sadness/grief (through mirror-neuron-mediated empathetic responses) as well as compassionate feelings due to a biologically prepared response to signal features.

13. Musical repercussions

Ethology offers a number of useful insights for research in music-related affect. First, ethologists argue that displays must confer a fitness benefit for the displaying animal, otherwise the display would be selected against. This insight raises grave difficulties for the Emotion Communication Model described earlier. We should be wary of the idea that feelings are indiscriminately echoed in vocalizations or facial expressions. Only some feeling states ought to be overtly expressed; that is, as behavioral motivators, some emotions should be overt while others remain hidden. Whether an emotion is overtly expressed or covertly masked will depend on the benefit to the signaller. Overt expressions (signals) are intended to change the behavior of the observer, not to induce an emotion similar to that of the signaller. One should not view a display as symptomatic of the signaller's affective state; instead it should be regarded as an effort to induce in the observer an affective state that is beneficial to the signaller.

In order for signals to be communicated, they should be conspicuous. Accordingly, signals tend to be multimodal. The most likely candidates for signals are those that exhibit both distinctive visual and distinctive acoustical features. In other words, any sound property that originates as a signal is likely to be accompanied by distinctive visible behaviors, such as characteristic facial expressions. Examples of candidate signals including smiling, sneering, and crying. As we have seen, each of these expressions involves distinctive multimodal features.

Some covert affective states can occasionally be inferred by an astute observer. Such covert displays (cues) are unintentionally informative. Signals primarily enhance the fitness of the signaller; cues enhance only the fitness of the observer.

Signals and cues might be regarded as "push" and "pull" forms of information. Signals "push" information into the environment—whether they are observed or not. Cues "pull" information from the environment, even though the information was not intentionally placed in the environment. Once again, through experience, the buzzing of a mosquito can be heard as presaging the possibility of attack, even though the sound is an artefact of rapidly moving wings.

The acoustical features associated with grief—wailing, moaning, sniffling, punctuated exhaling, ingressive phonation, pharyngealized voice, and cracking or breaking voice—are linked to distinctive visual features and exhibit the hallmarks of an ethological signal. By contrast, the acoustical features associated with sadness—quiet dynamic, slow tempo, low pitch, monotone pitch contour, mumbled articulation, and dark timbre—appear to be simple artefacts of low physiological arousal. Listeners may infer that these features indicate sadness, but these same features will be evident in other states, such as sleepiness and relaxation.

We would therefore expect laments, cry songs, funerary wailing, and other "grieving" expressions to be highly communicative, and cross-cultural in their meaning. By comparison, we might predict that musics associated with low physiological arousal—such as meditative music, New Age music, devotional music, relaxing/easy listening, and lullabies/cradle songs—would be easily confused with sad music. Nominally sad music would therefore exhibit greater cultural confusion than "grief" or "lament" music.

In light of their differences, I have proposed that sadness is a personal/covert emotion whereas grief is a social/overt emotion. Nevertheless, sadness and grief tend to co-occur because they represent complementary strategies for dealing with personal difficulty.

Finally, with regard to affect induction, the concept of an ethological signal provides a previously overlooked mechanism for generating affect in observers. If ethologists are right, these behavioral changes are automatic and species-wide. Although the emotional experience of music is strongly shaped by cultural milieu and individual experience and association, research on signals suggests that signal-features should exhibit a high degree of cross-cultural agreement. Like Ekman's display rules, the experience of signals might be expected to be modified by local cultural interpretation. However, if ethologists are right, signals should exhibit a common affective core deserving of the adjective "universal".

14. Coda

Scholars have long been interested in the function, evolution, etiology, ontology, behavior, and phenomenology of emotion (Cornelius, 1996). There are different approaches to the study of emotion however. The Emotion Communication Model has dominated emotion research for several generations. Yet modern ethology suggests that the ECM model is biologically implausible. Displays don't evolve unless they they tend to benefit the displaying individual.

A key insight from ethology has been to distinguish how information benefits actors differently. Displaying and observing animals come to the information transaction with different — sometimes converging, often diverging — aims. Inspired by Peirce's ideas, early ethologists took concepts such as signal, cue, and index, and applied these to the analysis of animal interactions. After more than half a century, the results are worthy of the attention of semioticians, including those who have traditionally worked outside of the domain of biology.

In particular, ethology offers considerable insights for those interested in the study of music and emotion. For example, ethology provides a straightforward explanation for why grief displays are more likely to evoke compassion in an observer rather than empathetic grief. Such conceptual tools appear to provide useful methods for handling some of the thorniest problems in music-related emotion, including the difficult problem of distinguishing represented emotion from evoked emotion.*

* N.B. This paper is an expanded version of Huron (2012).

References

Alloy, L. B., & Abramson, L. Y. (1988). Depressive realism: Four theoretical perspectives. In L. B. Alloy (Ed.), *Cognitive processes in depression* (pp. 223-265). New York: Guilford.

Bauer, H.R. (1987). Frequency code: Orofacial correlates of fundamental frequency. *Phonetica, 44*, 173-191.

Bolinger, D. L. (1964). Intonation across languages. In J. H. Greenberg, C. A. Ferguson & E. A. Moravcsik (Eds.), *Universals of human language, Vol. 2: Phonology* (pp. 471-524). Stanford, CA: Stanford University Press.

Bonfiglioli, L., Caterina, R., Incasa, I., and Baroni, M. (2006). Facial expression and piano performance. In M. Baroni, A. R. Addessi, R. Caterina, M. Costa (Eds.), *Proceedings of the 9th International Conference on Music Perception and Cognition* (pp. 1355-1360).

Bradbury, J. W., & Vehrenkamp, S. L. (1998). *Principles of animal communication*. Sunderland, MA: Sinauer.

Brown, J. D., & Mankowski, T. (1993). Self-esteem, mood, and self-evaluation: Changes in mood and the way you see you. *Journal of Personality and Social Psychology, 64*, 421-30.

Calhoun, C., & Solomon, R. C. (1984). *What is an emotion? Classic readings in philosophical psychology*. Oxford: Oxford University Press.

Clore, G. L., & Huntsinger, J. R. (2007). How emotions inform judgment and regulate thought. *Trends in Cognitive Science, 11*, 393–399.

Cornelius, R. R. (1996). *The science of emotion: Research and tradition in the psychology of emotion*. Upper Saddle River, New Jersey: Prentice-Hall.

Cruttenden, A. (1981). Falls and rises: meanings and universals. *Journal of Linguistics, 17*, 77-91.

Darwin, C. (1872). *The expression of the emotions in man and animals*. London: John Murray.

Eggebrecht, H. H. (1955). Das Ausdrucks-Prinzip im musikalischen Sturm und Drang, *Deutsche Vierteljahrsschrift für Literaturwissenschaft und Geistesgeschichte, 29*, 323-349.

David Huron

Eibl-Eibesfeldt, I. (1989). *The biology of peace and war: Men, animals, and aggression*. New York: Viking.

Ekman, P. (1972). *Emotion in the human face: Guide-lines for research and an integration of findings*. New York: Pergamon Press.

Fairbanks, G., & Pronovost, W. (1939). An experimental study of the pitch characteristics of the voice during the expression of emotion. *Speech Monographs, 6*, 87-104.

Fox, A. A. (2004). *Real country: Music and language in working-class culture*. Durham, NC: Duke University Press.

Freitas-Magalhães, A. (2006). *The psychology of human smile*. Oporto: University Fernando Pessoa Press.

Frey II, W.H. (1985). *Crying: The mystery of tears*. Minneapolis: Winston Press.

Frijda, N. (1986). *The emotions: Studies in emotion and social interaction*. Cambridge: Cambridge University Press.

Gelstein, S., Yeshurun, Y., Rozenkrantz, L., Shushan, S.,Frumin, I., Roth Y., & Sobel, N. (2011). Human tears contain a chemosignal. *Science, 331*, 226-230.

Gould, S.J., & Vrba, E.S. (1982). Exaptation – a missing term in the science of form. *Paleobiology, 8*, 4-15.

Heinlein, C. P. (1928). The affective characteristics of the major and minor modes in music. *Journal of Comparative Psychology, 8*, 101-142.

Hevner, K. (1935). The affective character of the major and minor modes in music. *American Journal of Psychology, 47*, 103–118.

Huron, D. (2002). A six-component theory of auditory-evoked emotion. *Proceedings of the 7th International Conference on Music Perception and Cognition*. Sydney, Australia.

Huron, D. (2008). A comparison of average pitch height and interval size in major-and minor-key themes: Evidence consistent with affect-related pitch prosody. *Empirical Musicology Review, 3*, 59-63.

Huron, D. (2012). Understanding music-related emotion: Lessons from ethology. In E. Cambouropoulos, C. Tsougras, P. Mavromatis and K. Pastiadis (Eds.), *Proceedings of the 12th International Conference on Music Perception and Cognition. Thessaloniki* (pp. 473-481). Greece: ESCOM.

Huron, D., Dahl, S., & Johnson, R. (2009). Facial expression and vocal pitch height: Evidence of an intermodal association. *Empirical Musicology Review, 4*, 93-100.

Huron, D., Kinney, D., & Precoda, K. (2006). Influence of pitch height on the perception of submissiveness and threat in musical passages. *Empirical Musicology Review, 1*, 170-177.

Huron, D., & Shanahan, D. (2013). Eyebrow movements and vocal pitch height: Evidence consistent with an ethological signal. *Journal of the Acoustical Society of America, 133*(5), 2947-2952.

Huron, D., Yim, G., & Chordia, P. (2010). The effect of pitch exposure on sadness judgments: An association between sadness and lower than normal pitch. In S. M. Demorest, S. J. Morrison, P. S. Campbell (Eds.), *Proceedings of the 11th International Conference on Music Perception and Cognition* (pp. 63-66). Seattle, Washington: Causal Productions.

Johnstone, R. A. (1997). The evolution of animal signals. In J. R. Krebs and N. B. Davies (Eds.), *Behavioural Ecology* (pp. 155-178). Oxford: Oxford University Press.

Kottler, J. A., & Montgomery, M. J. (2001). Theories of crying. In A. Vingerhoets & R. R. Cornelius (Eds.), *Adult crying: A biopsychosocial approach*. Hove, East Sussex, UK: Brunner-Routledge.

Kraepelin, E. (1899). *Psychiatrie. Ein Lehrbuch für Studierende und Ärzte, Klinische Psychiatrie. II*. Leipzig: Johann Ambrosius Barth, 1899. Trans. by R. M. Barclay as *Manic-depressive insanity and paranoia*. (Original work published Edinburgh: E. & S. Livingstone, 1921).

Ladinig, O., & Huron, D. (2010). Dynamic levels in Classical and Romantic keyboard music: Effect of musical mode. *Empirical Musicology Review, 5*, 51-56.

Lorenz, K. (1939). Vergleichende Verhaltensforschung. *Zoologische Anzeiger*, Supplement, *12*, 69-102.

Lorenz, K. (1970). *Studies in animal and human behaviour, Vol. 1*. London: Methuen.

Lutz, C. A. (1988). *Unnatural emotions: Everyday sentiments on a Micronesian atoll and their challenge to Western theory*. Chicago: University of Chicago Press.

Morton, E. S. (1977). On the occurrence and significance of motivation-structural rules in some bird and mammal sounds. *American Naturalist, 111*, 855-869.

Morton, E. (1994). Sound symbolism and its role in non-human vertebrate communication. In L. Hinton, J. Nichols, & J. Ohala (Eds.), *Sound symbolism* (pp. 348-365). Cambridge: Cambridge University Press.

Morton, E. (2006). Commentary on 'The influence of pitch height on the perception of submissiveness and threat in musical passages' by David Huron, Daryl Kinney, and Kristin Precoda. *Empirical Musicology Review, 1*, 178-179.

Nesse, R. (1991). What good is feeling bad? The evolutionary benefits of psychic pain. *The Sciences, 31*, 30-37.

Ohala, J. (1980). The acoustic origin of the smile. *Journal of the Acoustical Society of America, 68*, S33.

Ohala, J. (1982). The voice of dominance. *Journal of the Acoustical Society of America, 72*, S66.

Ohala, J. (1983). Cross-language use of pitch: an ethological view. *Phonetica, 40*, 1-18.

Ohala, J. (1984). An ethological perspective on common cross-language utilization of F0 in voice. *Phonetica, 41*, 1-16.

Ohala, J. (1994). The frequency code underlies the sound-symbolic use of voice pitch. In L. Hinton, J. Nichols, & J. Ohala (Eds.), *Sound symbolism* (pp. 325-347). Cambridge: Cambridge University Press.

Ohala, J. (2009a). Signaling with the eyebrows - Commentary on Huron, Dahl, and Johnson. *Empirical Musicology Review, 4*, 101-102.

Ohala, J. (2009b). The ethological basis of certain signals of affect and emotion. In S. Hancil (Ed.), *The role of prosody in affective speech* (pp. 17-30). Bern: Peter Lang.

Partan, S., & Marler, P. (1999). Communication goes multimodal. *Science, 283*, 1272-1273.

Paul, B., & Huron, D. (2010). An association between breaking voice and grief-related lyrics in Country music. *Empirical Musicology Review, 5*, 27-35.

Pentland, A. (2008). *Honest signals: How they shape our world*. Cambridge, MA: MIT Press.

Plazak, J. (2011). *Instrumental irony and the perception of musical sarcasm*. PhD dissertation. School of Music, Ohio State University.

David Huron

Post, O., & Huron, D. (2009). Music in minor modes is slower (except in the Romantic period). *Empirical Musicology Review*, *4*(1), 1-9.

Scherer, K. R. (2004). Which emotions can be induced by music? *Journal of New Music Research*, *33*, 239–251.

Scherer, K., London, H., & Wolf, J. J. (1973). The voice of confidence: Paralinguistic cues and audience evaluation. *Journal of Research in Personality, 7*, 31-44.

Schutz, M., Huron, D., Keeton, K., & Loewer, G. (2008). The happy xylophone: Acoustic affordances restrict an emotional palate. *Empirical Musicology Review*, *3*, 126-135.

Shanahan, D., & Huron, D. (2014). Heroes and villains: he relationship between pitch tessitura and sociability of operatic characters. *Empirical Musicology Review, 9*(2), 141-153.

Smith, J. M., & Harper, D. (2003). *Animal signals*. Oxford: Oxford University Press.

Storbeck, J., & Clore, G. L. (2005). With sadness comes accuracy; With happiness, false memory: Mood and the false memory effect. *Psychological Science, 16*, 785-791.

Tartter, V.C. (1980). Happy talk: Perceptual and acoustic effects of smiling on speech. *Perception and Psychophysics, 27*, 24-27.

Tinbergen, N. (1951). *The study of instinct*. Oxford: Clarendon Press.

Tomkins, S. S. (1980). Affect as amplification: some modifications in theory. In R. Plutchik & H. Kellerman (Eds.), *Emotion: Theory, research and experience* (pp. 141-164). New York: Academic Press.

Turner, B., & Huron, D. (2008). A comparison of dynamics in major- and minor-key works. *Empirical Musicology Review, 3*, 64-68.

Tuuri, K., & Eerola, T. (2012). Formulating a revised taxonomy for modes of listening. *Journal of New Music Research, 41*(1), 1-16.

Vorperian, H., Kent, R., Lindstrom, J., Kalina, C. Gentry, L., & Yandell, B. (2005). Development of vocal tract length during early childhood: A magnetic resonance imaging study. *Journal of the Acoustical Society of America, 117*(1), 338-350.

Wiley, R. H. (1983). The evolution of communication: information and manipulation. In T. R. Halliday & P. J. B. Slater (Eds.), *Communication* (pp. 82-113). Oxford: Blackwell.

Williams, C. E., & Stevens, K. N. (1972). Emotions and speech: Some acoustical correlates. *Journal of the Acoustical Society of America, 52*, 1238-1250.

Zahavi, A. (1977). Reliability in communication systems and the evolution of altruism. In B. Stonehouse & C. M. Perrins (Eds.), *Evolutionary ecology* (pp. 253-259). London: Macmillan.

Zahavi, A., & Zahavi, A. (1997). *The handicap principle: A missing piece of Darwin's puzzle*. New York: Oxford University Press.

Zentner, M., Grandjean, D., & Scherer, K. R. (2008). Emotions evoked by the sound of music: Characterization, classification, and measurement. *Emotion, 8*, 494-521.

Part Four

Intermediality and Transdisciplinarity

Intermedial and transdisciplinary investigations are of the utmost importance in contemporary research on theoretical musicology. The next four contributions are illustrative of these developments. They deal with the analysis of *medial* properties in terms of perception and analyze the borders between media and possibilities of "intermedial" referencing. This is especially true for musical performance and movie productions, which need a theoretical framework for a complex analysis that takes into account elements from the fields of the visual, advertising and web semiotics. The broadening of the field and scope of musicology by including music, pop culture, gender issues, rhetoric, advertisement and ideology has given art music the ability to free itself from standard aesthetics. Having been first explored in popular music, it has now also major impact on the study of art song and opera productions. The complex interaction of the voice, gestures, instruments, lighting and scenery as part of the multimedia text, as well as the economic framework that underpins a production, are major components of music, music making and music understanding.

Nellestijn's contribution deals with the restaging of an opera for the TV screen. Starting from the idea that media are not given facts but cultural constructions that are determined by predominant aesthetic conventions, he examines medial properties in terms of perception, and provides a model of intermedial analysis, exploring the possibilities of media transposition, media combination and intermedial referencing.

Pádua explores the semiotic perception of art songs of a Brazilian composer as the result of a particular observation. Relying on a transdisciplinary methodology she conceives the performance of art song as a multimedia text that juxtaposes literary and musical text, as well as voice, gestures, instruments, lighting and scenery. Using the concept of image as a transversal concept that pervades both disciplines, she tries to establish connections between the artwork and external elements, distinguishing perceptive from evoked images, relying on the Peircean notions of image, hypoicon, image, diagram, and metaphor.

Marino's contribution, finally, explores the intermedial ambiguities of the notion of musical genre. Using the concept of intermediality as a form of mediation between different levels of signification, he explores the ability of music to make music out of the nonmusical. He claims that the intermedial, translating capability of music is exemplified convincingly by the problematic notion of genre, particularly in Pop Music. After a broad theoretical framing of the notion of musical genre, relying on Hjelmslev's strata of signs, he displays an explorative lexical-semantic analysis of a corpus of nearly 100 genre names in popular music with the aim of building a name-based typology of genres and understanding the logic that underlies this typology.

The Death of Klinghoffer: From Stage to Screen

Maarten Nellestijn
Utrecht University

The opera *The Death of Klinghoffer*, by composer John Adams, librettist Alice Goodman, and director Peter Sellars, from the moment of its US première in 1991 in the Brooklyn Academy of Music on, has led to an intensive debate in both the newspapers and the scholarly domain. Central to these debates are its supposed merits and shortcomings regarding its representation of sensitive political issues. This precariousness was heightened after 9/11, shortly after which a performance of the two opening choruses was canceled in an act of self-censorship at the hand of the Boston Symphony Orchestra. It is not unthinkable that the increased difficulties of getting the work staged after 9/11 were a factor leading to the 2003 TV adaptation by Penny Woolcock, which premièred on the British network *Channel 4*, and subsequently released on DVD that same year. In an article published in 2009 in the *Journal of the Society for American Music*, Ruth Sara Longobardi (2009) discussed this restaging of *Klinghoffer* for the TV screen in relation to a change in the depiction of racial identities in the post-9/11 United States. In this article, Longobardi shows that while the 1991 production avoided the depiction of race in connection with terrorism, the TV production makes this aspect explicit. Further, she argues that the gaze of the camera and the narrative it enforces relegate the music to the background, as if it were nothing more than a soundtrack. According to her, the narrative component—not present in the 1991 production—is resonant with a change in the discourse on terrorism in the media and public domain. The infamous War on Terror inscribed a melodramatic teleology into the news and discussion of the events after 9/11. The TV production, Longobardi argues, deals with historical events with a certain factuality, as if it were a news item or documentary.

Here I want to offer a counter-argument to Longobardi's article. First of all, I think that her arguments directed against the camera and the narrative it shapes do more than just offer a critique on post-9/11 ideology. It is an aesthetic argument as well, and I am of the opinion that it is a conservative one, that a priori elevates staged opera to a higher status, and sees filmed opera as an inferior derivation. Further, I will argue that the TV production offers an alternative interpretation that to some extent resists the narrative tendencies in depictions of terrorism attributed to post-9/11 media from within. The documentary-like quality in Woolcock's production can be seen as having a sense of irony, whether this was intended by Woolcock or not. The translation from stage to television offers the opportunity of doing cultural work on a larger scale, but it does this work in the context of television's, or perhaps rather cinema's, aesthetic code. To support my argument, I will offer an outline of the differences between the 1991 production and the 2003 TV production, for which I will use a model for intermedial analysis by Lars Elleström (2010). This model makes possible the analysis of medial properties in terms of perception, and allows for the idea that media are not given facts, but cultural constructs with certain aesthetic conventions specific to that medium. I will also discuss Irina Rajewsky's (2010) ideas on media borders. She argues that intermedial artworks can be divided into roughly three categories: *media transposition*, *media combination* and *intermedial referencing*. Also, I will explain why I think that the production allows for, and invites, a critical reading of its own narrative (and, consequently, narrative in the news) by referring to genre conventions in cinema. It has some qualities in common with the action film genre, and I think that these qualities can make one conscious of the good-evil binary and teleological resolution of violence with violence inherent in this genre.

1. From opera to soundtrack: the camera and narrative

Longobardi argues that the TV production of *Klinghoffer* imposes a narrative—in the sense of a clearly identifiable plot, where cause leads to effect, and the audience's attention is guided by such a structural framework—on the opera through the visual domain. In the 1991 production, narrative was largely absent, and there were no visual references to the hijacking. The set was comprised of "a cage of steel bars [...] that evokes an abstract space" (p. 283). Similarly, each singer played multiple roles, both of Arab and Western characters. These means served to "obfuscate any sense of narrative or historical specificity [...] and to interrogate dichotomy" (p. 283). Instead, in the TV production the singers and actors are cast to visually confirm this racial dichotomy. "Woolcock begins with the Arab body, emphasizing its visual difference as a locus of significance and as an anchor for the opera's historical trajectory" (p. 295). Similarly, it was filmed on an actual cruise ship. Longobardi connects this tendency towards realism and specificity to documentary, stating that "authenticity in this film is also signaled by documentary-like conventions: handheld cameras, real audio, dates and places at the bottom of the screen all suggest objectivity and accuracy" (p. 304). To strengthen her arguments she invokes a theory on narrative in documentary by film theorist Bill Nichols to explain the production's cultural work. The imposition of a narrative, she argues, precludes the possibility of a plurality of interpretations. Thereby, it mutes discourse on the subject discussed, and imposes a strict moral hierarchy. According to her, this reflects changes in discourse on terrorism in the post-9/11 United States, thus effectively doubling the media's tendency towards melodrama. Longobardi diagnoses that this narrative is not present in the music or libretto, but that it is imposed by the camera. The camera not only imposes a moral order, but also demotes the opera's music to a mere soundtrack. Television and cinema are visual media, and the role of sound as a background element seems to come naturally to it. If the diminution of the importance of opera's music in a filmed production makes that production derivative and untrue to "the original", as Longobardi seems to argue, it becomes hard to think of filmed opera as an acceptable practice at all.

Longobardi also states that due to the nature of staged opera, the collaboration between the artists involved in the original production led to conflict, and because of this hodgepodge fabric of competing artistic efforts, to the possibility of a multiplicity of interpretations. According to her, Woolcock's film denies exactly this possibility. Moreover, Longobardi idealizes operatic production and the ideals of people involved in this process. "[O]pera is not necessarily (and I would argue rarely) produced by a like-minded community, but more often by a fiercely interactive and dialogic, sometimes even antagonistic (perhaps anarchic) body of citizens" (p. 307). Of course, she talks about the conflicts between different artists expressing themselves in different media that together form an operatic whole, and these artists' converging opinions leading to conflict in the production process itself. However, she also seems to imply that artists in opera are more free-spirited than, for instance, television- or filmmakers, which would be nothing more than an ill-founded generalization. Since film and television similarly are collaborative efforts (albeit hidden behind a screen), I do not see why the collaboration argument would not apply to them. Longobardi seems to prefer stage opera aesthetics, and although she argues that in her analysis *Klinghoffer* "is not treated as a single work, but as a number of independent works that signify separately and uniquely" (p. 279), she does not seem to allow for a difference between opera and television or film due to their differing aesthetic confines and technical possibilities. Moreover, she considers the TV production inferior because it upsets the hierarchy between image and music of the "original"; she foregrounds the moral objections to this change in hierarchy, connects this aesthetic argument to the ethics of representation: "The camera [...] positions race as a defining element of the opera; and race, as a text that depends on the visual, has the potential to quiet other, more unwieldy characteristics of identity, and of the musical score" (p. 296). Silencing the music is equated with silencing moral reflection. While I do not want to deny that the aesthetic and political domain overlap, nor want to argue that her political argument is invalid because it conflates aesthetics and politics, one needs to ask: "Is Longobardi's reading confined by her aesthetic views on opera, leading to a blind spot for resistive qualities that reside in things specific to the televisual or cinematic domain?"

2. Intermedial analysis

To illustrate why the TV production has to be judged by a different aesthetic standard, Lars Elleström's (2010) model for intermedial analysis proves a valuable tool. This model comprises two components: one that explains the medium as an object in a socio-historical context, and another that explains the perception of such an object. Elleström accounts for the idea that every medium is a construct formed in a specific historical context. When discussing media as objects, he distinguishes between *basic, technical* and *qualified media*. These are abstract categories, and a medium can contain aspects of all three of them. Basic media are components that cannot be reduced to smaller parts. For instance, a theatre performance can be divided into speech, music and moving bodies. However, writing, for example, cannot be divided into separate components by this means. Technical media are the material components to realize a specific medium, such as a screen or a piece of paper. That of the qualified medium is a key concept in Elleström's model, because artworks generally cannot be reduced to either technical or basic media. Qualified media are shaped by both a technical aspects and qualifying aspects. These qualifying aspects refer to the cultural side of a medium, and can be divided into the *contextual qualifying aspect*—essentially historical, cultural and social circumstances—and the *operational qualifying aspect*. This second aspect largely refers to the aesthetics associated with a certain medium. It can be explained as a set of rules that determines how to communicate within that medium. The perception of media is explained with the concept of modalities. Elleström distinguishes between four modalities: the material, sensorial, spatiotemporal and semiotic modalities. These modalities are not strictly separable and more often than not overlap. The *material modality* is the perceptible interface of a certain medium, such as a screen, sound waves or human bodies. The *sensorial modality* comprises the manifestation of sensations, such as seeing and hearing. The *spatiotemporal modality* explains how a certain medium is experienced in time and space. A photo, for instance, has fixed dimensions, a flat surface and does not change over time. The *semiotic modality* explains how a medium constructs meaning. I have mapped both the 1991 stage production[1] and the 2003 TV production in terms of these modalities in table 1. The properties mentioned have aspects that can be linked to a multiple of these modalities, but I have chosen to place them in the category that seemed most suitable. As will become obvious, it is impossible to discuss the items in this list without considering what Elleström would call their technical and qualifying aspects.

Modality	1991 stage production	2003 TV production
Material	Human bodies, live produced sound, opera house	TV screen, speakers with flattened sound, living room
Sensorial	Hearing, seeing	Seeing, hearing
Spatiotemporal	Three-dimensional, ambiguity between non-diegetic and diegetic space, non-fluidity of refracted time, partially fixed sequentiality, spectator controls perspective	Two-dimensional, no ambiguity between non-diegetic and diegetic space, fluidity of refracted time, fixed sequentiality, gaze dictated by the camera
Semiotic	Language, musical structure, symbolic representation of locations and people	Language, musical structure, actual locations and people

TABLE 1. Comparison in terms of Elleström's four modalities

In the material modality, the physical presence of actors on the one side, and the flat screen on the other needs no explanation. A conspicuous feature is that in the TV production the music sound is flattened. This is not only due to technical properties of the television set, but also a consequence of the manner in which the sound was recorded. In fact, the sound quality is conspicuously bad for a filmed opera production, which I will get back to later on. In such a case it is equivocal whether this perceptive quality belongs to the material or sensorial modality. Another difference is that there is generally less (or even no) ambiguity between the diegetic and nondiegetic space in cinema or television. On the stage, the actor and his character appear before the spectator at the same time, but in cinema the actor and character are perceived as one. It is possible to make a distinction between television programs that address the viewer directly, and do not represent but document—such as live transmissions of sports events, game shows, reality TV and the news—those that do not directly address and represent a fictional space—this is the case for most television films and series. Television series—and especially modern television series—have become more and more similar to cinema in terms of aesthetics. But a common point between reality TV and fictional TV is that the television screen conveys something of a factual quality: "what you see is what you get", the idea that there is no actor or reality under the surface of the representation. Christian Metz (1974) speaks of "the impression of reality experienced by the spectator" (p. 4). André Bazin (2005) argues that cinema came into being due to man's need for the preservation of images, and drew the conclusion that "[p]hotography and the cinema [...] are discoveries that satisfy [...] our obsession with realism" (p. 12). Actors are not seen as actors representing characters, but usually seen as reduced to their characters. Similarly, it would be strange to represent the performance space as a stage in cinema or cinematic television, because this would challenge the reality effect that is central to cinema. The 2003 production of *Klinghoffer* seems to align more with cinematic conventions in terms of diegesis, and this is also reflected sonically, as every sound effect in Woolcock's production is put into the service of realism. All sound effects in this production are connected to the diegetic situation through association and synchronization. Nonmusical sounds in Woolcock's production, such as gunshots and footsteps, are presumably all diegetic, again because of the assumption of the reality of the representation. The diegetic status of sound is less obvious in theater. Consider the sound of footsteps heard during a performance. It would be leap of faith to assume that such a sound is meant to be part of the fictional representation and, even if so, it would sound absurdly exaggerated due to the acoustic nature of the proscenium. Thus, its diegetic status would be ambiguous.

Due to the possibility of montage in television (*refracted time* in my schema), it is possible to shift the representation from one scenic space or perspective to another without a noticeable transition. In the case of theater, this would lead to short breaks during which it would become obvious that the scenery is being changed. This is a technical aspect that differentiates between potentialities of creating a narrative in theatre, cinema and television. It is easier in television and cinema to hide the technical apparatus and maintain an illusion, and the prevailing practice in these media is indeed to exercise this possibility.[2] In theater, a spectator has control over the direction of her gaze. Even though a director is able to guide the spectator's perspective to a certain extent, the spectator can choose to avert her eyes from the action to observe other aspects of the performance. In cinema and television, the gaze is directly controlled by the camera. Because of this, the camera offers more control over the flow of the narrative. The lack of detail offered by especially a television set's low-resolution screen even requires such visual focusing, because the spectator would otherwise be unable to distinguish details in a complete wide-angle shot. Perhaps a narrative based on cause and effect is inherent to cinema's and especially television's technical aspects, even though one can distinguish different conventions regarding such practices in different styles of filmmaking.

Above I have already touched upon differences in technical and qualifying aspects of the staged and television productions. It would be beyond the scope of this chapter to make an in-depth comparison of the contextual qualifying aspect, the histories of stage opera and televised opera in this paper. However, there are two interesting points about filmed opera worth mentioning. Firstly, historically it is possible to distinguish between opera for television and opera for cinema, as argued by Marcia Citron (2000). The first category consists of mainly registrations of live performances. Here, the camera is usually aimed in a fixed position at the proscenium, and montage occurs mainly to transgress the delay between different acts. The second category comprises cinematic translations of opera productions that are especially created for the white screen, where no audience was present during filming. Montage is much more common, as are changing camera perspectives and close-ups. Many in-between forms exist. For example, Peter Sellars has made studio productions based on his stage versions of three Da Ponte operas. These productions take on a mixture of aesthetics of film, television and theater. Woolcock's production clearly shows more resemblance to the second category of cinematic productions than to the first of television relays, although it was meant to be disseminated primarily via television's infrastructure. Secondly, most film translations of operas are lip-synched, due to the technical difficulties of recording singing voices on the set—the voices need to sound synchronous to the accompanying orchestra, which out of practical considerations is usually recorded separately—and capturing the singers/actors with the camera simultaneously (Citron, 2000). While Woolcock's production shows more similarities with filmic opera than with the television relay, the production is not lip-synched; the production team had to go through painstaking efforts in order to realize this, and this process led to a reduced sound quality that is surely noticeable. Woolcock's production largely adheres to cinematic aesthetic conventions. These are partly based on the potentiality of television as medium, but are not fixed. This means that it was certainly possible to make a different kind of TV production, one more in line with the original production, but this would probably have led to an end result in which the medium's possibilities were not used to a satisfactory extent.

Rajewsky (2005) discusses to what extent media borders are pre-determined. While media-specific conventions such as cinema aesthetics are not fixed, they are based on technical aspects—*medial difference*, in her words—specific to the medium (Rajewsky, 2005). Because of this difference in technical aspects, a distinction can be made between genre and medium, intertextuality—or intramediality—and intermedial referencing. She also differentiates three categories of intermedial artworks. *Media transposition* is the translation of artworks to a different medium; a film based on a novel would be an example. *Media combination* is the stacking of different media that can normally be considered to be independent, together forming a single artwork. Rajewsky offers opera and film as examples of this category of artworks. The third type makes use of *intermedial references*, which are references across media borders, similar to intertextual references. These can point to certain aesthetic conventions of media foreign to them, or to the contents of a specific artwork in another medium. While both productions of *Klinghoffer* can be seen as media combinations—actors/singers, music, stage/scene, and words can be seen as separate media—it is possible to see Woolcock's production as an instance of media transposition. There are definitely technical differences between the two versions. These differences had to some extent an effect on the contents of the work, although these changes were also affected by aesthetic conventions that could have been ignored. But because of these medial differences, judging the film from the perspective of opera aesthetics—with which I especially mean the elevated status awarded to music, but also a broader frame of reference—potentially limits the interpretation.

3. Special effects and ironic representation

Because Woolcock's production has aspects that are familiar from television and cinema, it can be more easily perceived as referring to genres pertaining to these media. Longobardi has stressed the documentary-like aspects of the production, but it might be useful to place it into a cinematic context. The production was released on DVD in the year of its television première, and the DVD's sleeve offers a good starting point for discussing a series of qualities of the film that align it with the action film genre. Film posters and DVD sleeves are important marketing tools for filmmakers, and must make clear what type of film they advertise in just a short moment of exposure. A pose in which a character holds a gun in her hand is typically used as a signifier for films that belong to the action film genre, as is the case with, for example, *Die Hard* (1987, directed by John McTiernan), *Lethal Weapon* (1987, directed by Richard Donner), and *The Peacemaker* (1997, directed by Mimi Leder). The DVD sleeve of Woolcock's *Klinghoffer* shows the murder scene from the film: lead hijacker Molqi aims a pistol prominently placed in his hand at the head of Leon Klinghoffer. When comparing this DVD sleeve with that of one of the films mentioned above, the similarity becomes obvious. A *Klinghoffer* viewer familiar with the action film genre is invited to don her action film goggles, and perceive a particular set of signifiers as action-film-like.

What becomes clear from the documentary *Filming "The Death of Klinghoffer"* is that the production team had to reinvent the process of sound recording during filming. As I mentioned before, cinematic opera is usually lip-synched, due to the difficulty of filming simultaneously with recording the singers and the orchestra. In this case, a separate recording of the orchestra was made in advance. During the shooting, a conductor was equipped with a mobile device holding the operatic score and a video feed of John Adams conducting the recording session with the London Symphony Orchestra, with which he directed the singers on site by proxy. The recording of the LSO was playing in the background during shooting, barely audible, in order for the singers to orient themselves musically. Due to this unique approach, the singing voices sound rather flat when compared with the orchestral sound due to the differing acoustic properties of the set and the studio. The reduction in sound quality is not intentional, but reveals that there is something artificial going on, even while the singers' lips are moving in-sync with the music. Here again, a fixation on visual realism becomes apparent. But this obsession with verisimilitude and special effects is also notoriously prominent in the action film genre. In both, this applies to sound as well as the image: the dominance of sounds of gunshots and panicking people in the diegetic sound space feature prominently, perhaps exaggeratedly, in both action films and Woolcock's production. Longobardi complains that the music functions more as a soundtrack than as operatic music. Aside from the question whether this debases Adams's opera (to which I personally would answer: "No"), it has the effect of making the film cinematic rather than documentary-like. Documentaries generally contain music, but this music tends to be less prominent or melodramatic. At the start of the hijacking in the film, the music starkly resembles stock film music. The violin section plays dissonant figures, while the rest of the orchestra plays in a sweeping upward motion. Rather surprisingly, electronic drum rolls punctuate this texture. During the murder scene, the strings play a high sustained and dissonant tone, while the brass section lets sound a dramatic and dissonant downward figure followed by a drum roll on acoustic timpani. The choice of music for these scenes—with features resembling Hollywood film music—seems to underscore the idea that it is exactly this: a fictional and dramatic representation. It is no surprise that many action films use these Hollywood tropes of dramatic orchestral music; *The Peacemaker* and *Die Hard* would be good examples of this scoring strategy. But the prominence of electronic drums—also when Molqi announces that the terrorists will start killing hostages if their demands are not met—provides a link more specifically with action films from the 1980s. Examples of such films are *Red Heat* (1988, directed by Walter Hill) and *The Terminator* (1984, directed by James Cameron). But here also the television series *Miami Vice* (1984-1990, created by Anthony Yerkovich) comes to mind. Thus, the original production of *Klinghoffer* already had musical properties—intermedial references to cinema, in Rajewsky's terms—that link the opera to action films. Woolcock's film makes use of these musical properties by aligning her added visual narrative with these dramatic moments and, in doing so, makes these references to action films strongly explicit. While these references were intermedial references in the original production, they came back home to film in Woolcock's production in the form of intramedial references—if you consider cinematic opera as an instance of cinema—and become more obviously meaningful.

While it is not possible to pursue a full analysis of representational strategies in the action film genre here, one might argue that many of these films refer to contemporary fears concerning crime and terrorism, and offer a fantasy of a violent upholding of the law and/or political status quo. Often, but not always, the terrorists and criminals in these films are of foreign origin—such as a Bosnian terrorist in *The Peacemaker*, or German criminals in *Die Hard*. Typically, these films offer an explicitly teleological narrative in which a violent conflict is resolved by using justified violence. This use of action film references might be worrying because it aligns Woolcock's production with these arguably conservative, stereotyping and pro-violence narratives, but this aspect of the *Klinghoffer* film can also be read as ironic. Opera and action film, originating from hardly compatible cultural spheres, seem absurdly juxtaposed, and this potentially has the effect of distancing the viewer. To illustrate my point: the media figure prominently in Woolcock's production. For example, consider the ample presence of the press complete with a battery of photographers during scenes in which the ship's passengers are interviewed about the hijacking. Maybe this suggests that we should ask ourselves: "Is the dramatic narrative resulting from the media a polarized, teleological narrative, similar to these of action films?" Longobardi raises more or less the same question about Woolcock's *Klinghoffer*, but her interpretation is that the film tries to make us believe that the narrative offered is natural, and that we should not question it; that it conceals this narrative quality through its immanent reality effect and the camera's focused gaze. She expresses distrust for the camera and the mode of narrative that is connected to it. When following Longobardi's aesthetic argument to the letter, one might wonder whether these media are at all capable of responsible and/or progressive depictions of politically sensitive subjects because such a form of narrative is closely connected to technical aspects of cinema and television. Contrary to this, I think that the odd juxtaposition of opera and action film in the context of documentary-like features reveals narrative as a construct. And to understand this, one has to see the film not as a mere rendition of an opera, but at least in part as cinema.

Elleström's model for intermedial analysis offers a good starting point for mapping the medial properties of a certain artwork. His model gives space for discussing the technical borders of media, but also their culturally constructed aspects. As Elleström himself admits, these aspects of media cannot be unequivocally categorized within this model. There is overlap between the different modalities, but it is also impossible to speak of the modalities and qualifying aspects separately. This suggests that an analysis using this model can lead to different outcomes in different hands (but does this not hold true for all analytical models?). This makes one realize that the choice of technical materials is also a subjective matter; in the case of opera, cinema and television, there is a certain infrastructure, but due to these media's composite natures, they leave a lot of room to play with different materials and aesthetics. Woolcock could have chosen another form for her film, perhaps similar to the original theatrical production, even though she used television's infrastructure. While Elleström shows us that it is difficult, or even impossible, to make definite conclusions as to where media borders lie, Rajewsky's distinction between the intramedial and intermedial needs these borders—and a differentiation on a material basis—in order to function. In the case of opera and film, due to their combinative nature, making these distinctions becomes difficult. I have based my choices regarding the use of the categories of transposition, combination and referencing on what I perceive to be the conventions associated with cinema and opera. While this reveals my argument for medial difference to be a matter of perspective, this also holds true for Longobardi's argument. Even so, it cannot be denied that the stage and television set, with their own technical aspects, have influence on the modes of representation associated with them. While viewing media as inherently different and unchangeable, defined only by their technical properties seems to miss the mark, inverting this relationship and arguing that media are nothing more than a set of conventions proves equally unsatisfactory.

While many aspects of action films can be seen in Woolcock's film, it remains unclear whether these were intentional or the result of coincidence. However, because film similarly is a collaborative effort, meaning can arise out of conflict between differing artistic efforts, just as with opera. Even if Woolcock had no intention of showing action film aesthetics, the music and DVD sleeve add this potential meaning. While the documentary aspects Longobardi mentions are certainly present in Woolcock's film, and while it is certainly maintainable that the film resembles post-9/11 media and their penchant for narrative concerning the discourse on terrorism, a resistant reading, too, is possible. Perhaps it is true that the film offers less potential for competing interpretations than the 1991 BAM production, but stating that the film infallibly steers one to a single stereotyping interpretation is a misconception.

Notes

1   Here I base my observations on Longobardi's description of the 1991 performance.
2   This convention is subverted in for example Lars von Trier's film *Dogville* (2003); such an approach is highly marked and becomes an expressional device in itself.

References

Bazin, A. (2005). The ontology of the photographic image. In H. Gray (Trans.), *What is Cinema?* (Vol. 1, pp. 9–16). Berkeley: University of California Press.
Citron, M. (2000). *Opera on screen*. New Haven: Yale University Press.

Elleström, L. (2010). The modalities of media: a model for understanding intermedial relations. In L. Elleström (Ed.), *Media borders, multimodality and intermediality* (pp. 11–48). Hampshire: Palgrave MacMillan.

Longobardi, R. S. (2009). Re-producing Klinghoffer: Opera and Arab identity before and after 9/11. *Journal of the Society for American Music, 3*(3), 273–310.

Metz, C. (1974). On the impression of reality in the cinema. (M. Taylor, Trans.) In C. Metz, *Film language: a semiotics of the cinema.* New York: Oxford University Press.

Rajewsky, I. O. (2005). Intermediality, intertextuality, and remediation: a literary perspective on intermediality. *Intermedialités, 6,* 43–64.

Rajewsky, I. O. (2010). Border talks: the problematic status of media borders in the current debate about intermediality. In L. Elleström (Ed.), *The Modalities of Media: A Model for Understanding Intermedial Relations* (pp. 51–68). Hampshire: Palgrave MacMillan.

The Perception of Art Songs Through Image: A Semiotic Approach

Mônica Pedrosa de Pádua

Federal University of Minas Gerais (UFMG)

Introduction

In the current panorama of music research, the researcher/interpreter is faced with the need to develop tools to understand, appreciate and take ownership of the repertoire. It is his or her responsibility to create his or her own reading mechanisms for the production of meaning, and, ultimately, the production of knowledge.

Thus, in this paper, I present a proposal of a transdisciplinary methodology for studying Art Song, which consists in the integrated study of music and literature, using image as the transversal concept that pervades both disciplines. This proposal can be considered transdisciplinary inasmuch as it articulates analytic tools of thinking and of discourse with creative intuition, and organizes knowledge according to network models, in which every point, directly or indirectly, connects to every other.[1]

My interest originated from the need to understand the object song and develop means to perceive it. I think of the Art Song as a multimedia text, in which the literary and musical texts appear juxtaposed, in a synchronous way and in a complementary relationship. The entire structure of performance— voice, gestures, instruments and even lighting or scenery—can be, eventually, also part of the multimedia text. In order to unite the heterogeneous elements of poetry and music in a whole that constitutes the song, I suggest a model of synthesis that uses, as a common parameter, image in its multiple forms.

In this paper, I intend to show that the perception of images created by songs is a semiotic task. Thus, I use the semiology of music to establish connections between the work and external elements, which we may call extrinsic references.[2] The tripartite theory of Jean Molino and J. J. Nattiez (1990, 2002)[3] brought rigor to the process of creating interpretants for the various elements of the song. The corpus chosen for this work consists of some songs by Brazilian Nationalistic composer Oscar Lorenzo Fernandez (1897-1948).

1. Perceiving image

As we approach images in a song, we firstly must ask ourselves how we could define them. At first, we may think that images usually connect themselves to visuality. Christin (2004, p. 284) defines the image as "a presence, that is, a visual data that preexists to the subject that perceives it, an "always-already-there-before" which evidence and which enigma are imposed to the look in an imperious way, whether it is a dream or a framework."

By referring to a "dream" or to a "framework", we observe that Christin approaches both the material and mental aspects of the visual image. Lucia Santaella (2001, pp. 15-32) also divides the world of images into two domains. The first one is the domain of images as visual representations, such as, for example, cinematographic images or drawings. The second one is the immaterial domain of images in our minds, in which images appear as "visions, fantasies, imaginations, plans or, in general, as mental representations."

According to Mitchell (1987, p. 13), mental images do not seem to be stable and permanent; they also vary from one person to the next and do not seem to be exclusively visual in the way real pictures are, but involve all the senses. Furthermore, the author tries to show that even images "proper" are not either stable, static or permanent, since they are not perceived in the same way by viewers and they are not exclusively visual, but involve multisensory apprehension and interpretation.

Mental images are a subject of research on the field of neurosciences. On this domain, besides visual images, other modalities of mental images are also objects of study, such as, for example, sound image or movement image. Some kinds of mental images can evoke or include information from multiple modalities and experiential domains, as proposed by studies on multisensory imagery (Hubbard, 2013).[4] Multisensory imagery, nevertheless, "gives access not to something like the real complexity of experience but to aspects of the ways our minds internally represent experiences and objects" (Starr, 2010, p. 288).

Recent neurophysiological and psychological research has come to the conclusion that all perception has image characteristics (Reybrouck, 2001, p. 123). For neuroscientist Damásio (2002a, p. 123), the factual knowledge is acquired through images. By looking at a landscape, by listening to a song or by reading a book, an individual forms mental images from various sensorial modalities. Images thus formed are called perceptive images, in opposition to evoked images, which come from locals of storage in the mind. Evoked images of things or events that took place in the past or we imagine can happen in the future are momentary and imprecise constructions, attempts to replicate patterns that have already been experienced. They happen side by side with the vivid images formed by stimuli that come from the exterior and stay in the conscience in a brief and incomplete way (Damásio, 2002a, pp. 128 and 136). Moreover, Damásio (2002a, p. 175; 2002b, pp. 74 and 357) proposes that feelings are, in their essence, corporal images perceived by the senses, juxtaposed to the images that we see, hear or touch, for instance. When those images are accompanied, an instant later, by a *sense of the self* in the act of knowledge, they became conscious (Damásio, 2006, p. 357).

Listening to a song involves, at the same time, perception and evocation of images. Perception happens in the tiny, brief instant of the present, in the moment we get in touch with the song's sonority. Evocation comes through the memory's work that builds images from other images, in an apparently never ending semiosis. Perception and evocation happen during the moment the song unfolds in time (Pádua, 2009).

In a song, the images created by the poem interact with the images created by the music. What differentiates the *given* image—the one that does not depend on our will to be received—from the *constructed* image itself is that the last one presupposes acts of perception (Bosi, 2004, p. 22) that are aimed at its exploration, its comprehension, its dominance.

Bosi's ideas find resonance in Paillard's (1994) concepts of representational and dispositional memory. The former allows cognitive control as opposed to the latter, related to a quasi-automatic body's reaction to a stimulus.

In an analogous way, Reybrouck (2001, p. 123) states that "dealing with music, in fact, is an experiential as well as a conceptual affair" and that "it implies time-bound reactivity (a kind of wired-in reactions to standardized stimuli) as well as higher level cognitive processes that are the outcome of mediation between stimulus and reaction."

In this work, I will consider image as a conceptual operator, a theoretical operation, a transversal way to explore, in a song, the relations between music and literature. It is, therefore, a reading operation through which we can "read" a song (Pádua, 2009).

In order to build a strategy for the perception of images, I set off from the concepts of mosaic and network. I conceive the song as being a mosaic of images of various sensorial characteristics. I compare the mosaic, which juxtaposes fragments of images, to the network models, which also connect heterogeneous elements.[5] The connections come from a creative process. The overall image of a song, like a mosaic, is the result of the reunion, the juxtaposition of various types of images created by their literary and musical elements. I then deal with the ideas of simultaneity, density and saturation. The final image, juxtaposing many images, fragmented, dynamic, constantly changing, is created through relationships.

2. A semiotic perception of musical structures: the image as a sign

Under the Peircean point of view, images as mental representations are interpretants. According to Peirce (2005, p. 269), "every time we think, we have the presence of some feeling, image, conception or some other representation that works as a sign in our conscience." The language can be seen as a translation of the images that occur in the mind. In the same way, we translate musical structures into images.

In a poem, images are formed from figures of speech constructed by words and syntactical structures in a game of reiterations. Poetic language also possesses a sound materiality, constituted by the sonority of words, rhymes, alliterations and assonances, by the metric, the accentuation of syllables and their articulation in rhythmic sequences that may be regular or not. Poetry and music have in common a sound materiality. The emphasis in this materiality allows us to cross-read the song as musical and poetic form.

The musical structures and the expressive sounds of a poem do not allude only to our hearing experience. They relate to various sensorial categories from which we build images—perceived or evoked—that can be spatial, temporal, of movement and of feeling and emotions. The process of evoking unveils universes of senses which relate music to colors, different planes in space, as well as texture, harshness, liquidity, hardness, and so on. Terms utilized to characterize sounds include: sweet, velvety, shining, hard, warm, cold. All of which are intimately connected to images which are captured by sight, touch, smell, taste.

I deal with the symbolical associations related to the senses, and by these I mean not only the five senses that are usually classified. In fact, we possess various systems of monitoring. We can feel differences of temperature and pressure, the position of the articulations (proprioception), the corporal movement (kinesthetics), and the internal sensations of our body, the sum of multiple stimulations derived from the various parts of the organism and that result in our emotions (cenesthesia). The complexity of human senses is, naturally, beyond the scope of this paper. What matters for us are our active mechanisms of perception involved in the processes of semiotic construction of images.[6]

Let us see, then, how the symbolical perception of musical structures may occur, so that next we are able to verify from which sound elements from music and poetry in a song one may perceive visual, spatial, plastic and movement images, temporal images and, finally, feelings as images. In order to do that, I shall make use of the concepts of Peirce (2005), adapting them for the musical domain.

As we know, Peirce distinguishes three categories of sign: the icon, the index and the symbol. To characterize a musical structure as a symbol, there must be a convention, established a priori, that dictates its meaning. Certain meaning attributions given to musical structures, in a considerable part of our occidental musical culture from the last three centuries, could be called symbolic, because we became acculturated to certain associations, such as, for instance, the associations between high and low pitches with their spatial counterparts. However, I think that, since those are not organized systematizations, such as, for example, the verbal language, the musical sign fits in the category of icon.

On the level of iconicity, Peirce distinguishes the hypoicons, ruled by similarity and by relations of comparison. Those are divided into three sublevels: images,[7] diagrams and metaphors. Images represent their objects because they present similarity in appearance. Diagrams present similarity in the relations. Metaphors present similarity in meaning.

In music, chords played in tremolo (rapidly alternating) in the low region of the piano may be classified as image, inasmuch as they might represent, for example, the sound of thunder. The schematic representation of a musical form may correspond to diagram. The innumerous relations established between sound and, for instance, elements connected to other sensorial categories, such as sight or touch, correspond to metaphor. They may result in expressions like a bright sound or a harsh sound.

Let us consider some image categories we can perceive in song and verify, in the songs of Lorenzo Fernandez, some examples of how this process of perception of images happens.

Elements connected primarily to sight construct what we can call visual images in music, but they are, in short, metaphorical perceptions of the sound qualities. Thus, the shining, the light, the color of a chord, of a harmony or of a vowel fall into this metaphorical iconic relationship.

We shall now look at the poem by Brazilian symbolist poet Luís Carlos da Fonseca (1880-1932), upon which the song *A saudade* was composed:

A saudade	**Longing**
A saudade a dor mais pura,	Longing, the purest pain,
Tão pura fica ao chorar,	So pure stays when crying,
Que seu pranto transfigura	That it's weeping transfigures
A morte, que é noite escura,	Death, a dark night,
Numa noite de luar.	Into a moonlight night.

From this poem we can perceive images of the transformation of a dark night into a moonlit night, brought by the feeling of longing. On the music of the song *A saudade*, we can also perceive a transformation (figure 1). Let us see the perfect chord of F# major on the word "luar" (moonlight). Notice the open sound of the vowel in that word. The chord concluding the suspended harmony section is an unexpected resolution that gives a sudden clarity to the song. The chord refers to the visualization of light. It is relative to sight. The sign is metaphor. The chord is a sign of light.

As part of the plasticity of a musical form, we can find elements that take part in the construction of space. We can get a sense of spatiality depending upon the localization of sound sources in relation to a listener. On the other hand, we can notice the musical space created by sound settings that result from the organization of musical parameters, particularly pitch and intensity. I understand that this kind of spatiality, in terms of semiotics, is real. We have measures of spatiality that can be more symbolic or more iconic, which depend on our conventions and on the symbolic universe that we built from our musical learning and cultural experiences.

The succession of notes, the chord progressions, the scales ascending or descending, intervallic leaps, the succession of syllables and words create images of motion. We can relate movements of music and poetry to rhythms and modalities of motion found in nature, as well as to gestural forms and patterns of movement experienced by the body, thus generating a symbolic process of great expressive power.

FIGURE 1. A saudade, ms. 17-24

The song *Berceuse da onda que leva o pequenino náufrago* (Lullaby of the wave that carries the little castaway) excels for its plasticity. It pictures a scene in the middle of the ocean and the encounter between the child and Yemanja, a deity from Afro-Brazilian religion. In figure 2, we see how the magnitude of musical space is enlarged by increasing the distance between the lowest and the highest notes of the tessitura, resulting in a range of six octaves. The voices in the piano line, which at the beginning of the song were closer, are more clearly separated as the song progresses. The space widens even more because the pedal note is now at a much lower register. The movement created by the music builds the enormous and agitated volume of the sea, in which the deity Yemanja seems to be evoked with great drama.

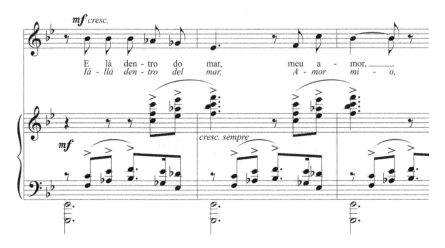

FIGURE 2. Berceuse da onda que leva o pequenino náufrago, ms. 38-40

Music is sound movement that unfolds in time. The experience of time occurs immediately, since music is a succession of sound and silence. The experienced time, the living time can, however, be different from the time of memory. For Bachelard (1988, p. 39), memory is full of gaps, discontinuous and made of fragments. Continuity is a human construction, an act of will that tries to put together present, past or future events that we plan or expect to happen. If a performance of a song or a reading of a poem lasts two minutes, we deal with time measured conventionally. The time of memory, the evoked time, different from the clock time, perceived by means of different processes is an iconic time.

Let us now turn our attention to the song *Vesperal*, a setting of a poem by Brazilian Modernist poet Ronald de Carvalho (1893-1935):

Vesperal	**Vesperal**
O céu parece que adormece,	The sky seems to be asleep,
O céu profundo	The deep sky
Paira no ar um longo beijo doloroso,	A long, painful kiss floats in the air
Caricioso…	Caressing…
A tarde cai.	The afternoon falls.
A sombra desce sobre o mundo	The shadow descends upon the world
A sombra é um lábio silencioso…	The shadow is a silent lip…

In this poem the memory of a kiss floats together with images of the sky in the dusk. We can also perceive dark images from the closed sonority of the vowels. The irregularity of the rhythm of the verses and the silences caused by suspension points create slow images.

In the song *Vesperal*, the fragmentation of the melodic lines, the irregular time signatures, the variations on the repetitions, the silences, the suspended cadences and the evoked and the perceptive images of landscape seen in the poem suggest a discontinuous, nonlinear narrative that plays with the images of memory (figure 3).

FIGURE 3. *Vesperal*, ms. 6-12

Finally, as we saw, the feelings are also images, signs that we perceive in a symbolic process that starts from cenesthesia. Associations of musical structures with images of emotions such as joy, sadness, anger or fear are one of the most effective expressive powers of the musical language.

In *Canção do Mar* (Song of the sea), the moment of invocation of the estrela d'alva (morning star) gives voice to a character who suffers in dramatic melodic inflections. The strikingly sustained high note is an iconic sign, the image of a scream ripped off the throat (figure 4).

FIGURE 4. *Canção do mar*, ms. 30-38

3. Final considerations

A song is not just a whole composed of poetry and music, but also the result of our own particular observation. This observation depends on texts and contexts—ours and the authors'—we are familiar with. In Art Songs, we perceive images that are translated in terms of our own experience. We expand the content of a score for a before and an after, through the images of our memory, triggering a large collection of texts, among them our own personal and intimate history.

I believe this work may open new perspectives for the interpretation of Art Song. It also proposes an original way to approach significance in music and poetry through images, providing thereby a different way of perceiving and experiencing the elements of song. I believe this proposal could provide material for the investigations that have as their object music, literature and other media, among them, opera, theater, film and dance.

Notes

[1] For a deeper understanding of the characteristics of transdisciplinary approaches, I refer the reader to Domingues (2004, pp.17-40).

[2] Intrinsic references are those that relate musical elements to each other, and extrinsic references are responsible for creating a multitude of interpretants that relate music to aspects of human life and of the reality that surrounds us. In this regard, I refer the reader to Nattiez (1990).

[3] The tripartite model of Molino and. Nattiez establishes three levels of symbolic object: poietic, immanent and aesthesic (1990, 2002, 2005). The immanent level corresponds to observation, as much as possible, of the configuration of the musical structures of the work. The poietic level concerns the compositional strategies of the author. The aesthesic level concerns the construction of significance performed by the receiver of the work (Nattiez, 2002, pp.7-39).

[4] For studies about connections between auditory and visual imagery I refer the reader to Zatorre et al., 2005; Halpern et al, 2004. For relations between kinesthetic and auditory imagery: Reybrouck, 2001; Proffitt, D.R., 2006; Hommel et al., 2001.

[5] Examples of network models are Deleuze's concept of *rhizome* (1995) or Levy's *hypertext* metaphor (2006). The network configuration is a way to produce, store or disseminate information and can be modified each time a new reading takes place. Some of its properties are the capacity to connect heterogeneous elements and interconnectivity, in which every point can be connected to another in a way in which sense cannot be determined or be placed in a hierarchy by a regulatory center.

[6] The number of senses considered varies in different scientific and philosophical approaches, sometimes exceeding 20. For example, the Spanish philosopher Zubiri (1898-1983) in *Inteligencia Sentiente: Inteligencia y Realidad* provides us with a list of 11 senses: sight, hearing, smell, touch, taste—the five traditional—vestibular and labyrinthic sensitivity, heat, cold, pain, kinesthesia and cenesthesia (1998).

[7] Specific terminology created by Peirce to distinguish sublevels of iconicity. Not to be confused, thus, with *image* in the sense of any sign.

References

Bachelard, G. (1988). *A dialética da duração*. São Paulo: Ática.

Bosi, A. (2004). *O ser e o tempo da poesia*. São Paulo: Companhia das Letras.

Christin, A.-M. (2004). Da imagem à escrita. In: Süssekind, F and Dias, T. (Eds.). *Historiografia literária e as técnicas de escrita: do manuscrito ao hipertexto* (pp. 279-292). Rio de Janeiro: Edições Casa de Rui Barbosa: Vieira & Lent.

Damasio, A. (2002a). *O erro de Descartes: emoção, razão e o cérebro humano (Descartes' error: emotion, reason and the human brain)*. São Paulo: Companhia das Letras.

Damasio, A. (2002b). *O mistério da consciência: do corpo e das emoções ao conhecimento de si (The feeling of what happens)*. São Paulo: Editora Schwarcz.

Deleuze, G. & Guattari, F. (1995). *Mil platôs: capitalismo e esquizofrenia*. V.1. São Paulo: Editora 34.

Domingues, I. (2004). Em busca do método. In: Domingues, I. (Ed.) *Conhecimento e transdisciplinaridade II: aspectos metodológicos* (pp. 17-40). Belo Horizonte: Editora UFMG.

Fernandez, O. L. (1930). *Berceuse da onda que leva o pequenino náufrago*. Milano: G. Ricordi.

Fernandez, O. L. (1961). *A saudade*. São Paulo: Irmãos Vitale.

Fernandez, O. L. (1971). *Canção do mar*. Rio de Janeiro: Arthur Napoleão.

Fernandez, O. L. (1946). *Vesperal*. São Paulo: Irmãos Vitale.

Halpern, A. R., Zatorre, R. J., Bouffard, M., & Johnson, J. A. (2004). Behavioral and neural correlates of perceived and imagined musical timbre. *Neuropsychologia, 42*, 1281–1292.

Hommel, B., Müsseler, J., Aschersleben, G., & Prinz, W. (2001). The theory of event coding (TEC): a framework for perception and action planning. *Behavioral and Brain Sciences, 24*, 849–937.

Hubbard, T. L. (2013). Auditory imagery contains more than audition. In S. Lacey & R. Lawson (Eds.). *Multisensory imagery* (LLC, 221-247). Springer Science+Business Media.

Lévy, P. (2006). *As tecnologias da inteligência: o futuro do pensamento na era da informática*. São Paulo: Editora 34.

Mitchell, W. J. T. (1987). *Iconology: image, text, ideology*. Chicago, London: The University of Chicago Press.

Nattiez, J.-J. (2002). O modelo tripartite de semiologia musical: o exemplo de La Cathédrale Engloutie de Debussy. Tradução de Luiz Paulo Sampaio. In: *Debates*, V.6 (pp. 7-39). Rio de Janeiro: Centro de Letras e Artes da UNIRIO.

Nattiez, J.-J. (1990). *Music and Discourse: Toward a semiology of music*. Princeton: Princeton University Press.

Nattiez, J.-J. (2005). *O Combate entre Cronos e Orfeu: ensaios de semiologia musical aplicada*. São Paulo: Via Lettera Editora.

Pádua, M. P. de (2009). *Imagens de brasilidade nas canções de câmara de Lorenzo Fernandez: uma abordagem semiológica das articulações entre música e poesia (Images of Brazilianness in Lorenzo Fernandez's Art Songs: a semiological approach of the articulations between music and poetry)*. Belo Horizonte: Faculdade de Letras da UFMG. (Doctoral Thesis)

Paillard, J. (1994). L'intégration sensori-motrice et idéo-motrice. In M. Richelle, J. Requin, M. Robert (Eds.), *Traité de psychologie expérimentale*. 1 (pp. 925-961). Paris: Presses Universitaires de France.

Peirce, C. S. (2005). *Semiótica*. (Coelho, José Teixeira. Trans.) São Paulo: Perspectiva.

Proffitt, D.R. (2006). Embodied perception and the economy of action. *Perspectives of Psychological Science. 1*, 10–122.

Reybrouck, M. (2001). Musical Imagery between Sensory Processing and Ideomotor Simulation. In R. I. Godøy, & H. Jörgensen (Eds.). *Musical Imagery* (pp. 117 – 132). Lisse: Swets & Zeitlinger.

Santaella, L. & Nöth, W. (2001). *Imagem: cognição, semiótica, mídia*. São Paulo: Iluminuras.

Starr, G. G. (2010). Multisensory imagery. In L. Zunshine (Ed.). *Introduction to cognitive cultural studies* (pp. 275-291). Baltimore: Johns Hopkins.

Zatorre, R. J., & Halpern, A. R. (2005). Mental concerts: musical imagery and the auditory cortex. *Neuron, 47*, 9–12.

Zubiri, X. (1998). *Inteligencia Sentiente: Inteligencia y Realidad*. Madrid: Alianza.

"What Kind of Genre Do You Think We Are?" Genre Theories, Genre Names and Classes within Music Intermedial Ecology

Gabriele Marino

University of Turin, Italy

1. Genre as intermediality

While single genre histories have been quite explored (e.g., Charlton, 1994; Borthwick & Moy, 2004; F. Fabbri, 2008), the notion of *musical genre* is not very much studied in itself, as a theoretical entity (cf. F. Fabbri, 1982, 2012; Hamm, 1994; Moore, 2001; Marx, 2008). This is not that surprising, as it is a crucial notion (possibly, the highest level of abstraction we can deal with as we talk about music), but, at the same time, a very ambiguous one.[1]

In this paper, the notion of *intermediality* is employed in a broad and non-plurimedial (Wolf, 2002) sense. Intermediality is here considered as "in-betweenness"; namely, as a form of mediation between different levels of signification. In particular, we address the capability of music to make music out of the "nonmusical" (or, in other words, to "translate" things into music, by using musical-specific means).[2] The notion of in-betweenness is well summarized and visualized in Crapoulet's study on the musical artwork as a performance (2008, p. 127); the diagram she displays, in order to depict the musical piece as an intermedial node, is—enlighteningly—not so different from Tagg's graphic explanation of his semiotic analysis method.[3]

In short, the idea proposed in this paper is that the intermedial, translating capability of music is well exemplified by the functioning of the musical genres, as we can deduce it by the names of the genres themselves. After a general theoretic framing of the notion of musical genre, the result of an explorative lexical-semantic analysis of a corpus of genre names is displayed; the aim is to build up a name-based typology of genres (a meta-typology, as genres are already a way by which we classify music) and to understand the possible basic values underlying this typology.

2. A spatial and intermedial conception of music

Our starting point is reconsidering common sense representations of music as a "combination of different kinds of music" and academic theorizations developing the very same idea in the light of Lotman's linguistically-modeled notion of *semiosphere* (1985; though Lotman was never particularly interested in music, cf. Tarasti, 2002, p. 4).

Many of the visual representations of music that it is possible to find on the Internet are centered on the notion of *genre*, as they depict music as an assemblage of genres.[4] These representations can work by (i) affinity (e.g., the ones based on users' activities on social networks such as Last.fm, or on collaborative resources such as Wikipedia) or genealogy (that is, by following a historical-evolutionary development); they can be (ii) synchronic or diachronic; they can be (iii) graphic, logical (e.g., flowcharts), topographic (e.g., maps, 3D sets) or geographic (i.e., they place music in geographic maps). This spatial conception of music, seen as an assemblage of different types of music, finds an illustrious ancestor in the "clouds simile" proposed by Xenakis (1979) and recovered by F. Fabbri (2002, 2005, 2008).

Furthermore, it is possible to imagine music as a four-dimensional macro-generic semiosphere that takes into account the three spatial-topologic dimensions as well as the diachronic variable. It would be a transtextual and trans-medial, ecological (i.e., in a dynamic biologic-like equilibrium) set, which includes a variety of elements: (i) real and possible, (ii) material (people, devices, places, etc.) and nonmaterial (knowledge, values, stories, relationships, etc.), (iii) musical (music itself) and nonmusical (pieces of the world, discourses music translates into music, discourses about music etc.).

Within this ecological system, nonmusical elements are *musicified*; that is, are incorporated in the musical semiosphere, through a process of *semiotic translation* (*intersemiotic translation* or *transmutation*; according to Jakobson, 1959) we might precisely call *musicification*.[5]

3. Definitions of genre and the dynamics of genres relations

Here is a quick review of the main studies dedicated to musical genre concerning popular music. While the works of F. Fabbri have a prominent theoretic purpose, the others are sociological studies based on empirical researches, which theoretical remarks are mainly based on case studies (cf. F. Fabbri, 2012, p. 180, note 5).

Musical genre is a key interest in F. Fabbri's scholarly production (1982, 1999, 2002, 2005, 2012). To sum up, he defines genre as "a set of musical events (real or possible) whose course is governed by a definite set of socially accepted rules" (1982, p. 52) and lists the following five types of rules: (i) formal and technical; (ii) semiotic (that is, related to Jakobson's communicative functions and to enunciation strategies); (iii) behavioral; (iv) social and ideological; (v) economical and juridical. F. Fabbri (2012) stresses the importance of considering his typology (and, more generally, musical genre theorizations and musical theorizations coming from a semiotic standpoint) as dynamic and capable of dealing with the diachronicity of musical genres, rather than static grids focused on the synchronic dimension only (as the "conventions accepted by a community"—i.e., the aforementioned "socially accepted rules"—that determine them and the prototypes chosen to epitomize them are historically motivated).

For Holt (2003, 2007; cf. Marx, 2008), a musical genre is a "set of symbolic codes that are organized and constituted ['codified'] in a social network at particular moments in history, whose boundaries are negotiated in multilayered ontologies between different interpretative contexts [within which a genre is 're-codified']" (2003, pp. 92-93). Holt distinguishes between (i) *historical genres* and *abstract genres* of a higher taxonomic order (e.g., "vocal", "sacred" music etc.); between (ii) "marketing categories and labels" (e.g., "chill out") and proper genres; between (iii) "core-boundary genres" (e.g., country and jazz vs. rock; i.e., genres that define themselves in opposition to other genres) and "in-between genres" or "decentered models" (e.g., "Latin-pop", "zydeco", "Mexican American popular music"; i.e., syncretic genres). It has been noticed that the latter type, and the notion of in-betweenness in particular, might be an unclear, controversial category; as contamination should be rather considered a structural component of the genre constitution itself (Marx, *op. cit.*).

Lena (2012) identifies four dominant forms ("Avant-garde", "Scene-based", "Industry-based" and "Traditionalist") and two main flow trajectories from one form to the others (AgSIT vs. IST; namely, from Avant-garde, to Scene-based, to Industry-Based, to Traditionalist, and from Industry-based, to Scene-based, to Traditionalist), in order to describe how American pop music develops, "how genres cohere"; that is, "how styles, conventions and goals are crystallized so as to define musical communities" (p. 23). Outside the USA, Lena finds also a fifth form: the "Government-purposed genre" (e.g., in China, Serbia, Nigeria, Chile). Lena lists 12 dimensions through which the four dominant forms are articulated; they include organizational, economic, interpersonal and aesthetic features. She lastly suggests that three causes can block the emergence of genre forms: "(1) the absorption of particular musical styles into proximal styles and streams, (2) aesthetic and social factors that prevent the expansion of the musical scene to new audiences and performers, and (3) racist exclusion" (p. 109).

Negus (1999) and Brackett (2002) stress the marketing and commercial value of musical genres (cf. also Holt, 2007, pp. 3, 18). For Negus, besides, genres become more than a mirror of society and a model for society itself. As an example, he reports that departments within major record companies have shaped their structure and functioning on the model of the socio-cultural system implied by the musical genre they deal with and try to sell (e.g., hip hop).

4. Genre and style as two forms

Great is the confusion under the sky of terminology, as Berruto (2011) points out. That of "genre vs. style", the latter being the other big umbrella term for musical categorizations, is quite an issue, and perhaps a Gordian knot or an *aporia*. While musicologists rather prefer *style*, and socio-cultural scholars prefer *genre*, in common use the two terms are employed indiscriminately, as synonyms of *type* or *kind* of music.

In the terms of a possible subordination of one to the other, the *querelle* between F. Fabbri and Tagg, in one corner (backing the pre-eminence of genre), and Moore, in the other (backing that of style), is really interesting and meaningful (cf. Moore, 2001). Berruto (2011) seems to back a similar position to Fabbri and Tagg's; for him, genre is something defined in "cultural, social, ethnographic and multimodal terms" (p. 30; my trans.), it is a hypernym of *register*, and the latter is a close notion to *style*. While genre has a functional value, style has an aesthetic one.

We can try to sum up by starting back with Dahlhaus. "Before the nineteenth century, Dahlhaus contends, genres were born from the blending of social function (e.g., the liturgy, a festival, or a dance) and compositional norm, of extramusical purpose and the musical means available to fulfill [*sic*] it" (Kallberg, 1988, p. 239). We might add that those means are available because they were specifically designed and/or chosen—in the set of the possible ones—and conventionally employed for that purpose. Therefore, from this perspective, a musical genre can be defined as a socio-culturally connoted and a functionally justified musical style (the "compositional norm"). Obviously, we have to suppose the entire musical spectrum as condensed in the word "style" (meaning a "recognizable musical form") in order to make this definition work.

After the Baroque epoch, music gradually lost its nature of an exclusively functional practice (up to the late Romantic and Wagnerian conception of "absolute music"); so that, according to Dahlhaus, the social value of musical genres had been fading more and more, increasingly in the 20th century, making room to the individuality of the great composers. In fact, *The New Grove Dictionary of Music and Musicians* assigns two different domains to genre and style: "Genres speak of the men who created them and the people who readily received them, and a personal style speaks of the artist's view of life" (Pascall, 2001); "Indeed a genre, working for stability, control and finality of meaning, might be said to oppose the idiomatic diversity and evolutionary tendencies characteristic of both form and style" (Samson, 2001). In these terms, genre is the domain of the "collective", style of the "individual".

Genre and style are clearly closely related, but their overlap is still partial (we will see how stylistic features, and musical features in general, are just a part of the elements contributing to the definition of a musical genre). Genre includes style (it is a component of genre), but does not overtake it (style is not reducible to a component of genre). Style, indeed, is a cross-generic notion and, more generally, a transversal notion. The style of a single musician can be highly recognizable in spite of the different types of music—i.e., genres—he has been confronting with. Musicians "belonging" to different genres can share similarities that lead us to include them in the same "stylistic area" (e.g., "hardcore" is a transversal stylistic connotation, employed to define genres such as "hardcore techno", "hardcore punk" and "hardcore hip hop"; and we might also imagine a "hardcore reggae" or a "hardcore folk"). We can make a genre out of a style (it is what happened to most of the sedimented musical forms we can now call genre within popular music) and make a style out of a genre (doing the opposite operation). The latter case happens when we say, for instance, a piece of music is in a "hardcore" (as we have just seen), "black metal", "punk" or "funk" style; in such cases, we are referring only to certain formal features. It happens the same when we turn a genre into an adjective; stating music is a "funky jazz" does not mean we are placing it within that genre ("funk") or, in other words, *culture*, but that it employs, incorporates or imitates certain stylistic features (for a socio-culturally connoted notion of "style", cf. Hebdige, 1979; cf. also the notion of *habitus*—though, with differences—in the works of Charles Sanders Peirce and Pierre Bourdieu). It happens the same, also, when we turn an author into an adjective; when we say, for instance, a piece of music is "zappesque", "zappian" or "Zappa-like" (from Frank Zappa).

While both imply—or rather, consist of—rules, style is something that has to do with music, with its forms, its codes (from the Latin *stilus*, the stylus stick used by Romans to write upon wax tablets). Genre is something musical that involves the "outside world," that makes reference to social and cultural forms and codes (from the Greek γένος, "descent", "race").

In conclusion, a—simplifying indeed, though operative—"atomic definition" of musical genre is here proposed, linking together the two different forms and the two different levels of signification we have been dealing with (i.e., "genre" and "style"). A "musical genre" is a linguistic label (a name) assigned to a set of recognizable musical features (a musical form; or, in other words, a "musical style", reflecting and proposing a musical aesthetics), carrying socio-cultural connotations (a "socio-cultural style", reflecting and proposing a system of values).

5. Corollaria and further remarks

The idea of genre and style as two normative forms, two structures, respectively dealing with the musical matter and the socio-cultural value assigned to it, cannot fail to think of Hjelmslev's *strata of sign*; therefore, genre can be described as the "form of content", and style as the "form of expression".[6] It has to be observed that statements such as these are obviously simplifying the issue; style cannot be meant as a "pure musical form", external to any socio-cultural connotation. A "primary level" of meaning (and subsequent socio-cultural connotations), concerning the musical matter, comes from its very syntactic structure (Middleton, 2001, pp. 301-310); cf. also the "doctrine of the affections" that, from Ancient Greece up to the Baroque era, linked certain musical figures to certain emotions.

There is a strong connection, and maybe an almost complete overlap, between the notion of genre, considered as an architextual basin (Genette, 1982), and the notion of "imaginary"; namely, the set of actual and virtual musical circumstances that circulate in social discourses and let listeners put a single piece of music in a coherent whole. As for imaginary, genre precedes and follows the individual texts: "Each text proposes a sense and, at the same time, proposes the rules by which it is built and it should be experienced. Genre, in short, is constructed as something given, it is the final datum that is set as the initial one, it is the effect of its continuous regeneration" (Marrone, 2001, p. 83; my trans.). At first, a genre "coheres", is codified, by induction. Then, it works by deduction—and works as a binding, normative and even racist (Sorce Keller, 2012a; Lena, 2012, pp. 98-109) Destinant: "It is a fundamental structuring force in musical life. It has implications for how, where and with whom people make and experience music" (Holt, 2007, p. 2). The dialectics between the imaginary and the functioning of musical genres is interesting and needs further investigation.

Toynbee (2000, pp. 102-129) points out that even the so-called "free improvisation", a type of radical, "nonidiomatic" (namely, that does not want to refer to any musical idiom) musical form, developed by musicians such as Derek Bailey since the 1950s, had to bend its ideological principles to the logic of the musical genre, in order to survive; becoming, *de facto*, a genre like the others, with its own formal, technical, semiotic, behavioral, social and economical rules. Genre is such a strong entity that even when we try to imagine or daydream music, we cannot get out of its domain. As an extreme example, it is possible to refer to the reviews of imaginary records in rock journalism (Marino, 2011). The reviewed records are imaginary, indeed they do not physically exist, while the described music cannot be nothing but a combinatory of actually existing music and musical genres; to describe Frankenstein-like patchworks such as these, Agostini (2002) used the image of "chimera music".

All these remarks lead us to the notion of a "generic contract" between "the musical genre" and the listener (Kallber, 1988). And to the notion of a *model listener* (cf. Eco's *model reader*, 1990), as it is designed by the musical text itself, equipped with a set of given competences (Stefani, 1982) and experiencing the musical text through a set of given expectations (Barbieri, 2004).

6. Genre names and labels

It seems Adorno had formed his idea of "jazz" music mostly by listening to German "jazz" orchestras which music was a mere imitation of the great American jazz of the time (from Duke Ellington to Miles Davis; whom Adorno probably was not aware of). He believed that music was "jazz" and built his famous—negative and influential—speculations upon "jazz" on the basis of that (Robinson, 1993, qtd. in F. Fabbri, 1997, p. 4). Labels are important, and effective.

Names are important, and ambiguous. They are boxes that need to be filled with something, and if there is no agreement about this "something", they may become *mysterious boxes*. Going back to the competences of the listener, musical genre names are written in quite an esoteric language; they incorporate existing slangs (nowadays, particularly from youth, urban and Internet cultures), but they also create a new slang of their own. They are always elliptical, they always leave something hidden, implied, yet crucial in order to de-codify what they are referring to; something the listener has to know and has to add to the genre name, which actually works like a *key word*. There is a gap between the meaning of the genre as a word belonging to the common lexicon and what it is actually pointing to and out, as a mechanism of musical signification.

This is particularly clear in what might be called "nontransparent labels", such as "trap" music. The literal meaning of "trap" is obviously "a contrivance used for catching game or other animals, as a mechanical device that springs shut suddenly"; while its musical meaning refers to "a music genre that originated in the early 2000s from Southern hip hop and crunk in the Southern United States. It is typified by its lyrical content and trademark sound, which incorporates 808 sub-bass kick drums, sped-up hi-hats, layered synthesizers, and "cinematic" strings. ... The term "trap" was literally used to refer to the place where drug deals are made. Fans and critics started to refer to rappers whose primary lyrical topic was drug dealing, as 'trap rappers'."[7]

A lot of musical genre names are nontransparent labels just like "trap" and have actually nothing to do with music; the elements which participate in the naming of the genre say nothing about the musical features, but maybe say *everything* about the pragmatics of the music.

A bibliographic review of the genre theory literature provided just two genre typologies with a focus on genre names and their meaning. The one are the "film roundups" proposed by Bordwell (1989) and Stam (2000), quoted in Chandler (2000, p. 1). The other is the attempt at a musical translation of Borges' parody of the "animal genres" (already referenced in Hamm, 1994) proposed by Dawes (2006). Dawes'—half-joking—proposal is interesting, but it displays two key issues (leaving out the fact that he calls Borges "Borge", putting the missing "s" only in the Saxon genitive): (i) he is not systematic in his taxonomy and (ii) his remarks are affected by highly arguable opinions (e.g., "slide", "house" and "math (rock)" are considered "arbitrary titles"; "skiffle" and "hip-hop" "nonsensical names").

An interesting—and systematic, indeed—example of name classification is provided by the *Grand taxonomy of rap names*, an infographics realized by "Pop Chart Lab" in 2010. As is clear, it does not deal with musical genres, but with rappers' names, displaying "266 sobriquets from the world of rap music, arranged according to semantics".[8] The rappers' names included are organized in six macro-classes: (i) Physical or metaphysical attributes; (ii) Animal, vegetable, mineral; (iii) Wordplay; (iv) Alphanumeric; (v) Crime; (vi) Titles and honorifics.

In this respect, two fertile and growing fields are the study of "folksonomies" ("folk taxonomies"; Vander Wal, 2007) and the "music ontology". Analytical findings in researches addressing the social tagging of musical genres get close to the ones here proposed (cf. the "Tag Type" in Lamere, 2008, p. 103, Table 2; the *semantic facets* identified in Sordo et al., 2013, p. 349, Table 1; p. 352, Table 2; p. 354, Table 5); our classification is more reductionist, as the classes are fewer in number and more inclusive in capacity.

In the following section, the result of an explorative analysis of genre names is proposed; namely, a typology of homogeneous classes regarding "what element may become a genre name". Not every one of the following is a proper musical genre, although they are all used as genre labels. Some of them may rather be called, more generically, *music definers* or *music categories*; that means they are words we do use to describe and classify music, which is a wider and—at the same time—an Ur-categorization in comparison with the notion of genre. Focusing on the notion of musical genre, we can therefore imagine a scale of hypernymity-hyponymity, from the broader "definer" to the narrower "genre" and then "style" (as we said, style is an internal component of genre; and, as we will see, style represents just one of the possible sources of a genre name).

The classification, far from being definitive and complete, cannot take into consideration all the classes' overlaps, which are organic, for it is not possible to make clear and unique distinctions and assignations; e.g., "riot grrrl" is, at the same time, (i) an onomatopoeia; (ii) a connotation, implying a judgement, suggesting how to classify a person; and (iii) it refers to an attitude or a behavior. It is not important that one agrees with every single choice (i.e., in which class each individual genre or label is actually put); the typology to be able to enlighten an interesting topic and suggest a method for further research would be preferred. In these terms, hopefully, the present paper would meet the type of Internet corpora-based studies upon musical genre (like the ones upon folksonomies and Carson & Zimmer, 2012a and 2012b) suggested and wished for by F. Fabbri (2012, pp. 188-190).

Due to space restrictions, it is possible here to engage neither in a genre by genre analysis, nor in a class by class explanation. The second step of the analysis is directly displayed; i.e., the "genre definers" classes, exemplified by some significant cases. The corpus of the reviewed genre names (approximately 200) consists of (i) the main historical genre names (with particular regard to popular music), (ii) the genre tags list the author had defined for the new database of the Italian music magazine *sentireascoltare.com* (2012) and (iii) the genre neologisms analyzed by Carson and Zimmer (2012a, 2012b).

7. What genre names are about: genre definers' classes

So, *what kind of genres* can we find circulating in the social discourse? What can genre names refer to, showing the very different elements which may become candidates for a genre name? Six macro-classes and as many corresponding value dimensions (or, in other words, *functions*) are found: (i) Music (descriptive), (ii) Aim (prescriptive), (iii) Lyrics (thematic), (iv) Culture (aggregative), (v) Geography (locative), (vi) Totem (i.e., object; symbolic). Each class is articulated into sub-classes, identifying a continuum of musical/ nonmusical elements and features.

7.1 Music. Descriptive

(i) Onomatopoeia / plastic rhyme / scat: skweee, riot grrrl, swing, reggae, ska, bebop, hip hop. *(ii) Sound / mimicry / synaesthesia*: bassline, bass (music), drone, noise, hard (rock), heavy (metal), thrash (metal), black (metal), soft (metal), sludge, grind, industrial, filthstep, acid (techno), acid (jazz), hot (jazz), cool (jazz), jungle, chillwave. *(iii) Synaesthesia / metaphor / connotation*: blues, reggae, punk, doom (metal), Paisley Underground. *(iv) Connotation / atmosphere / ambience / setting*: "canzone d'autore" (auteur song), progressive (rock), progressive (house), Madchester, riot grrrl, intelligent (techno), intelligent dance music (IDM), hipster (house), free (jazz), free (improvization), Grebo, folk, popular (music), classical (music), art (music), serious (music), soul, hardcore, emo, dark, gothic, industrial, desert (rock), country, urban, epic/power/folk/medieval (metal), technical (death metal), brutal (death metal), space (music), exotica. *(v) Technical / stylistic / compositional elements*: crooning, rap, screamo, glitch, chiptune, minimalism, minimal (techno), microhouse, isolationism, electronic (music), techno, fusion, drum and bass. *(v, bis) Rhythm*: jungle, downtempo, big beat, wonky, 2-step, math (rock), halfstep, slowcore. *(vi) Performance features*: glam, shoegaze, crab core.

7.2 Aim. Prescriptive

(i) Function / purpose: ambient, chill out, easy listening. *(ii) Situation / ideal setting for listening*: disco, lounge, cocktail, country, college (pop), pub (rock), exotica. *(iii) Market category*: alternative, indie, mainstream, Muzak, pop, adult oriented rock (AOR), FM (rock). *(iv) Phenomenology / affects-effects / agogicity*: dance, hip hop, trip hop, 2-step, footwork, rock and roll, psychedelic (rock), crunk, rave, trance, hypnagogic, isolationism, improvization, swing, dream (pop), funk, jazz.

7.3 Lyrics. Thematic

Love song, Christmas carol, porn (metal), pornogrind, Christian (rock), Christian / death / black / epic / folk / medieval (metal).

7.4 Culture. Aggregative

(i) Attitude / behavior: riot grrrl, gangsta (rap), crunk, brostep. *(ii) Socio-cultural connotation / (sub)culture*: New Age, punk, Grebo, emo, dark, rave. *(iii) Antonomasia / producer or originator / pioneering artist, album or song*: singer-songwriter (*cantautore* in Italian), Tin Pan Alley, Muzak, garage (rock), black (metal), death (metal), crust, bluegrass. *(iv) Time / diachronic variable*: Space Age pop, Eighties, new-, neo-, nu-, post-.

7.5 Geography. Locative

(i) Place: Charleston, house, garage (house), Goa, Madchester. *(ii) Country*: Brit pop, j-pop, k-pop, "canzone napoletana" ("Neapolitan song"), UK garage. *(iii) Ethnicity*: Latin pop, Latin hip hop, Latin jazz.

7.6. Totem. Symbolic

Funk, jazz, baggy, crunk, Paisley Underground, hair (metal), trap, PBR&B.

8. Sur-categorizations and derivative forms

As we said, we have to reckon the existence of broader music definers and classifiers, identifying neither proper genres, nor styles, but, more generally, "types" or "areas" of music. Shuker (2005, pp. 120-123) calls them "metagenres" (e.g., "Christian rock", "world music", "alternative rock"); Holt (2007), as we have seen, calls them "abstract genres" (e.g., "vocal" or "sacred music"; to which we might add "avant-garde", "experimental", "abstract", "improvization" etc.); F. Fabbri (2012, p. 180, note 4) calls them "superordinate categories" (e.g., "popular music").

On the other hand, we face the "genrefication"; namely, the overgrowth of genre labels neologisms, due to which "there are so many subgenres and factions" (Bruce Springsteen, quoted in Carson & Zimmer, 2012a, p. 190) segmenting and narrowing the musical matter more and more, especially within popular music. Zwicky (2010) coined the term "libfix" to define those word parts that become highly productive free combining forms in the field of neologisms; examples of musical libfixes are "core", "tronica", "step", "fi", "ton", "hop", "tech", "psych". Along with other affixes and suffixes (e.g., "pop", "rock", "jazz", "metal", "electro", "synth", "house", "techno", "beat", "post", "new", "neo", or "nu"), these combining forms are employed to make sub-genre distinctions or, in other words, to create derivative or compound genres (Bakhtin had already proposed the distinction between primary and secondary—i.e., compound—literary genres [cf. Bakhtin, 1986]). The result of the combinations spread by these musical "-fixes" are second generation terms such as these (some of them are portmanteau words): electro-pop, synthpop, garage-rock, psych blues, post-rock, post-metal, metalcore, nu-rave, nu-soul, ragga-core, Nintendo-core, jazzcore, Moombahton, folk-tronica, live-tronica, brostep, halfstep, tech-house, tech-step, clown-step, lo-fi, glo-fi etc.

9. Underlying dichotomies

A sur-categorization (which actually attempts to be an Ur-categorization), showing the eight basic dimensions and value dichotomies lying beneath the six genre definers' macro-classes (and that, by crossing each other, actually build the definers' classes up) is here proposed: (i) Musical (stylistic features) vs. nonmusical (socio-cultural references); (ii) Denotation (musical description) vs. connotation (socio-cultural implication); (iii) Technique (process) vs. aesthetics (product, result); (iv) Syntax (grammar) vs. semantics (lexicon);[9] (v) Conceptual-ideological (exclusive) vs. nonideological (inclusive); (vi) Autonomous vs. confronting or synchronic vs. diachronic; (vii) Transparent vs. nontransparent; (viii) Emic (community insider) vs. etic (community outsider).

Due to space restrictions, it is not possible to explain in detail each dichotomy and the relations between the definer classes and the dichotomies; most of all, further study is needed upon this last point.

10. Conclusion

The process of giving music a name, a necessary practice which is actually impossible to get out of (natural language is the chief meta-language, according to Benveniste; it is a "fascist" system, according to Barthes; for the importance of the "semiotic act of naming", cf. F. Fabbri, 2012, pp. 180, 187), that becomes a true obsession for anyone handling music (musicians, listeners, critics and scholars), implies a specific meta-knowledge (namely, a knowledge focused not on music itself, but on discourses about music), representing a precious key to understanding how communities understand and appropriate music, what they consider meaningful in it. Something (musical or nonmusical, concrete or abstract, real or possible) which is so meaningful that it may become—amongst the others—the unique element capable of synthesizing the identity of that particular music; i.e., the genre name itself.

With the act of naming—never a neutral, always a strongly meaningful and ideological act—we can still believe we have the power to create something new. As Eco reminds us in the *exitus* of *The Name of the Rose* ("*Stat rosa pristina nomine, nomina nuda tenemus*"), names seem to stand as the only thing we have left. Yet, never totally mastering them.

Notes

[1] The author would like to thank Franco Fabbri and Jacopo Tomatis, from the University of Turin, Italy, for their useful remarks and their kind feedbacks.

[2] *Extra-musicality* is a notion that pertains to the level of the *extroversive analysis* (cf. Monelle, 1992) and is quite an issue (cf. Sorce Keller, 2012b). Hence, Tagg & Clarida (2003, p. 271) propose to employ the term *paramusicality*.

[3] Cf. *tagg.org*, bit.ly/1h2NmVG. Web pages last access: April 6, 2015; all the URLs are shortened via "bit.ly".

[4] Cf. *pearltrees.com*, bit.ly/1dlK5BP.

[5] For instance, William Basinksi's *The Disintegration Loops* ("2062", 2002) and Bruce Springsteen's *The Rising* ("Columbia", 2002) represent two very different ways of "musically handling" the very same *piece of the world*: the September 11, 2001 attacks. For the word *musification*, cf. Edlung (2004); for *musicalization*, cf. Lesure (1984), Costa (1999, p. 136), Wolf (1999).

Gabriele Marino

[6] A naïve but effective look at such a proposal can be taken by reading how a popular Internet joke synoptically translates some musical genres into verbal language, in order to show the "Differences between music genres"; cf. *pbs.twimg.com*, bit.ly/1mKkzwg.

[7] Cf. *wikipedia.org*, en.wikipedia.org/wiki/Trap_(music_genre).

[8] Cf. *popchartlab.com*, bit.ly/1fshrhS.

[9] Frye (1957) seems to back the hypothesis of a syntax-based genre definition.

References

Agostini, R. (2002). Chimere. Note su alcune musiche (im)popolari contemporanee. In F. D'Amato, (Ed.). *Sound Tracks* (pp. 97-125). Roma: Meltemi.

Bakhtin, M. M. (1986). *Speech genres and other late essays* (1st ed.). Austin: University of Texas Press.

Barbieri, D. (2004). *Nel corso del testo*. Milano: Bompiani.

Berruto, G. (2011). Registri, generi, stili: alcune considerazioni su categorie mal definite. In M. Cerruti, E. Corino, & C. Onesti (Eds.). *Formale e informale* (pp. 15-33). Roma: Carocci.

Borthwick, S., & Moy, R. (2004). *Popular music genres*. Edinburgh: Edinburgh University Press.

Brackett, D. (2002). (In search of) musical meaning: genres, categories and crossover. In D. Hesmondhalgh & K. Negus (Eds.). *Popular music studies* (pp. 65-83). London: Arnold.

Carson, C. E., & Zimmer, B. (2012a). Among the new words. *American Speech, 87*(2), 190-207.

Carson, C. E., & Zimmer, B. (2012b). Among the new words. *American Speech, 87*(3), 350-368.

Chandler, D. (2000). *An introduction to genre theory*. 2nd ed. Retrieved April 6, 2015, from *aber.ac.uk*, bit.ly/1jXEBjj.

Charlton, K. (1994). *Rock music styles*. Madison, WI: Brown & Benchmark.

Costa, M. (1999). *Estetica dei media*. Roma: Castelvecchi.

Crapoulet, E. (2008). From intermedial music to interactive multimedia event: the performance of Ravel's miroirs. Culture, language and representation, vol. vi. *Cultural Studies Journal Of Universitat Jaume I*, 121-136.

Dawes, C. (2006). *Imploding musical genre*. MA Thesis available at Open Access Dissertations and Theses. Paper 6539. Retrieved April 5, 2015, from *orgalt.com*, bit.ly/1qamtds

Eco, U. (1990). *I limiti dell'interpretazione*. Milano: Bompiani.

Edlund, J. (2004). *The virtues of the musifier*. Retrieved April 5, 2015, from *musifier.com*, bit.ly/1EISUb5

Fabbri, F. (1982). A theory of musical genres. In D. Horn & P. Tagg (Eds.). *Popular Music Perspectives* (pp. 52-81), Göteborg and Exeter: International Association for the Study of Popular Music.

Fabbri, F. (1997). Il Compositore e il Rock. *Musica/Realtà, 53*, 30-36.

Fabbri, F. (1999). Browsing music spaces. Paper delivered at IASPM (UK) conference. Retrieved April 5, 2015, from *tagg.org*, bit.ly/1h2AVZW.

Fabbri, F. (2002). *Il suono in cui viviamo*. 2ⁿᵈ ed. Roma: Arcana.

Fabbri, F. (2005). Ricostruire una storia della popular music e dei suoi generi. In A. Rigolli (Ed.). *La divulgazione musicale in Italia oggi* (pp. 41-50). Torino: EDT.

Fabbri, F. (2008). *Around the clock*. Torino: Utet.

Fabbri, F. (2012). How Genres are Born, Change, Die: Conventions, Communities and Diachronic Processes. In S. Hawkins (Ed.). *Critical Musicological Reflections* (pp. 179-191). Aldershot: Ashgate.

Frye, N. (1957). *Anatomy of criticism*. Princeton: Princeton University Press.

Genette, G. (1982). *Palimpsestes*. Paris: Editions du Seuil.

Hamm, C. (1994). Genre, performance and ideology in the early songs of Irving Berlin. *Popular Music, 13*(2) 143-150.

Hebdige, D. (1979). *Subculture*. London-New York: Routledge.

Holt, F. (2003). Genre formation in popular music. *Musik & Forskning*, No 28. Department of Musicology, University Of Copenhagen.

Holt, F. (2007). *Genre in popular music*. Chicago: University of Chicago Press.

Jakobson, R. (1959). On linguistic aspects of translation. In R. A. Brower (Ed.). *On Translation* (pp. 232-239). Cambridge, MA: Harvard University Press.

Kallberg, J. (1988). The rhetoric of genre: Chopin's nocturne in G minor. *19ᵗʰ-Century Music, 11*(3), 238-261.

Lamere, P. (2008). Social tagging and music information retrieval. *Journal of New Music Research, 37*(2), 101-114.

Lena, J. C. (2012). *Banding together*. Princeton: Princeton University Press.

Lesure, F. (1984). Introduzione. In G. Cogeval & F. Lesure. *Debussy e il simbolismo* (pp. 25-40). Roma: Fratelli Palombi.

Lotman, J. (1985). *La semiosfera*. Venezia: Marsilio.

Marino, G. (2011). *Britney canta Manson e altri capolavori*. Falconara Marittima (AN, Italy): Crac Edizioni.

Marrone, G. (2001). Premessa. In P. Fabbri & G. Marrone (Eds.), *Semiotica in nuce, Vol. II* (pp. 80-85). Roma: Meltemi.

Marx, W. (2008). Review of F. Holt, "Genre in Popular Music". Chicago: University of Chicago Press, 2007. *Journal of the Society for Musicology in Ireland, 4*(9), 27-34.

Middleton, R. (2001). *Studiare la popular music*. 2ⁿᵈ ed. Trans. by Melinda Mele. Milano: Feltrinelli.

Monelle, R. (1992). *Linguistics and semiotics in music*. New Jersey: Harwood Academic Publishers.

Moore, A. F. (2001). Categorical conventions in music discourse: style and genre. *Music & Letters, 82*(3), 432-442.

Negus, K. (1999). *Music genres and corporate cultures*. New York: Routledge.

Pascall, R. (2001). Style. In S. Sadie, J. Tyrell, & L. Macy (Eds.). *The New Grove Dictionary of Music and Musicians*. 2ⁿᵈ ed. London: MacMillan Publishers-Grove Music Online.

Gabriele Marino

Samsom, J. (2001). Genre. In S. Sadie, J. Tyrell, & L. Macy (Eds.). *The New Grove Dictionary of Music and Musicians*. 2nd ed. London: MacMillan Publishers-Grove Music Online.

Shuker, R. (2005). *Popular music*. 2nd ed. London-New York: Routledge.

Sorce Keller, M. (2012a). Generi musicali. *MSK. About Music*. Retrieved April 5, 2015, from bit.ly/1h2B5R8.

Sorce Keller, M. (2012b). How very "musical" is the "extra-musical". *MSK. About Music*. . Retrieved April 5, 2015, from bit.ly/1eZsP84.

Sordo, M., Gouyon, F., Sarmento, L., Celma, Ò., & Serra, X. (2013). Inferring semantic facets of a music folksonomy with wikipedia. *Journal of New Music Research*, *42*(4), 346-363.

Stefani, G. (1982). *La competenza musicale*. Bologna: Clueb.

Tagg, P., & Clarida, B. (2003). *Ten little title tunes*. New York and Montreal: The Mass Media Music Scholars' Press.

Tarasti, E. (2002). *Signs of music*. Berlin: Walter de Gruyter.

Toynbee, J. (2000). *Making popular music*. London: Arnold.

Vander Wal, T. (2007). Folksonomy coinage and definition. Retrieved April 5, 2015 from *vanderwal.net*. bit.ly/1mawMIq.

Wolf, W. (1999). *The Musicalization of Fiction*. Amsterdam-Atlanta, GA: Rodopi.

Wolf, W. (2002). Intermediality Revisited. In S. M. Lodato, S. Aspden, & W. Bernhart (Eds.). *Word and Music Studies, Vol. 4* (pp. 13-34). Amsterdam-Atlanta: Rodopi.

Xenakis, I. (1979). *Arts/Sciences. Alliages*. Tournai: Casterman.

Zwicky, A. (2010). Libfixes. *Arnold Zwicky's Blog*. Retrieved April 5, 2015, from bit.ly/P8OGjQ.

PART FIVE

Analysis and Beyond

The interaction between analysis and extramusical interpretation brings together five contributions by Pawłowska, Martinelli, Liddle, Hatten, and Thumpston, which explore aspects of musical experience and interpretation by transcending a mere acoustic description of the sound. They all combine theoretical groundings with musical analyses, proposing a type of hermeneutics that relies on the concepts of musical topic, musical allusions and anthropomorphic conceptions of music in terms of musical agency and narrativity.

Małgorzata Pawłowska discusses the concept of narrative in an opera by Dusapin. Starting from the current disbelief in narrativity she discusses transformations of the concept. She elaborates on the distinction between story and discourse and argues then for new ways of musical narratives with the music work exploiting the capacities of discourse, language and the relation between text and music.

Martinelli provides a semiotic approach to Lennon's and McCartney's strategies for lyrics composition. He stresses some important oppositions in the narrative dimensions of their songwriting strategies (e.g. being versus doing, personal versus impersonal, etc.), in their different authorial (and sometimes cultural) ideologies (evident in nearly all cases in which the two authors would work separately on the same stylistic type of song: a love song, an autobiographical one, etc.) and the continuity (or lack thereof) between technical and personal resources as well as actual songwriting choices.

Liddle's contribution explores the relationship between music and the sublime in pre-Romantic aesthetics, relying on the conceptions of the sublime by Burke and Kant. The Burkean sublime involves a certain aestheticizing contemplation of the *great* and *terrible* with the locus of the sublime residing in the conception of the observer; the Kantian sublime, on the contrary, resides in an object that exceeds our powers of perception. It reveals the transcendental dimension of experience but separate from the phenomenal world. This disjunction resulted in an infinite longing as the essence of Romanticism for which a solution was found in the arts with music as their fullest exponent. The sublime as such became a musical topic, exemplified in this contribution by the analysis of some of Beethoven's late piano sonatas.

Hatten's contribution on agential energies puts the focus on melodic forces, evolving around Larson's analogs to physical forces such as gravity, magnetism, and inertia. A melody is experienced as an emergent quality associated with the musical discourse of a virtual human agent. As a coherent unfolding and shaping through time, the most basic cognition of a melody as an energetic shaping has deep biological rootedness, which makes it possible to attribute organic urgings to gestures in a tonal melody, experienced as a virtual body in a virtual environment. Musical analyses and interpretations of Beethoven, Bach, Haydn and Chopin exemplify this clearly.

Thumpston's anthropomorphic conception of music, finally, explores the same concept of musical agency. Starting from music's absence of semantic specificity, she argues that the detection of a sense of yearning or striving in music implies the presence of some form of persona or agent in the musical discourse. This attribution of a musical persona is elaborated on the basis of a tripartite theory of musical agency with a distribution of musical signifiers from low to high level.

A Story or Not a Story?
Pascal Dusapin's Opera *Roméo & Juliette* and New Ways of Musical Narratives

Małgorzata Pawłowska

Academy of Music in Krakow

1. Time of change for the concept of a narrative

There is no doubt that a narrative has been subject to transformation throughout the history of literature and art. In 1979 Jean-François Lyotard claimed that people no longer believed in the so-called *grand narratives* (Lyotard, 1979). In the 1980s, Paul Ricœur asked himself a question, whether the narrative function as such was going to die. Eventually he hoped it was not when he wrote:

> Perhaps we are witnesses […] of death of a certain kind […] It cannot be ruled out that metamorphosis of the plot will approach a barrier beyond which it will not be possible to recognize a formal principle of temporal construction that would make the story told uniform and complete. But still…still… Perhaps one should *in spite of everything* put trust in the requirement of inner coherence that today gives structure to the reader's expectation as well as one should believe that new narrative forms that we are still unable to name, and which are now being born, will testify that narrative function might change but cannot die (Ricœur, 1983, p. 50).

Pascal Dusapin's opera *Roméo & Juliette* was written in 1988. At that time, great European myths—those of Orpheus and Eurydice, Faust, Don Juan or just Romeo and Juliet—were in music more and more frequently subject to deconstruction and a platform for playing with various musical conventions.

This is the case of the works alluding to the theme of Romeo and Juliet by Boris Blacher (1950), Bernadetta Matuszczak (1970) and Pascal Dusapin (1985-1988). Another symptomatic element of musical interpretations of Romeo and Juliet's story of the period is multiplication of the main protagonists. In Matuszczak's work there are three Romeos and three Juliets, in Dusapin's opera the lovers are doubled, and in Grisey's *Chants de l'amour* from 1984 in which the names Romeo and Juliet appear, the duet of two lovers is multiplied as if in a fit of madness. Therefore, in the second half of the 20th century, we can observe a radical change in approaching the subject of Romeo and Juliet, exploited to a great extent in the earlier history of music (to mention but the most important works by Benda Bellini, Berlioz, Gounod, Tchaikovsky, Prokofiev). In musical works written in the period from the 18th to the mid-19th century and alluding to Shakespeare's drama, we could always recognize the story of Romeo and Juliet, whereas in the works of Blacher, Matuszczak, Grisey and Dusapin there are references to the archetype rather than the story itself.

Paradoxically, whereas new works in literature and art (including music) provoked the question of whether narrative function as such was not going to die, narratology as a research perspective flourished. In the 1980s and 1990s a narrative turn took place, as a result of which the concept of a narrative was transferred from the theory of literature to many other fields, such as history, philosophy, sociology, ethnology, laws, art sciences, pedagogy, psychology, medicine and even natural sciences. Postclassical, transdisciplinary narratological approach (after narrative turn) is a result of a common belief, that narrative is a primary act of mind, transferred from life to art and all human artifacts, and not just as a kind of structure of literary texts. Mark Turner (1998, p. 4) observed, that "narrative imagining—story—is the central instrument of the thought."

As Barbara Hardy (1968, p. 5) claimed,

> Narrative [...] is not to be regarded as an aesthetic invention used by artists to control, manipulate and order experience, but as a primary act of mind [...]. The novel merely heightens, isolates and analyzes the narrative motions of human consciousness. [...] For we dream in narrative, anticipate, hope, despair, believe, doubt, plan, revise, criticize, construct, gossip, learn, hate and love by narrative. In order really to live, we make up stories about ourselves and others, about the personal as well as the social past and future.

A historian and cultural critic, Hayden White explained the penetration of the narration concept into his field:

> Narrative might well be considered a solution to a problem of general human concern, namely, the problem of how to translate knowing into telling, the problem of fashioning human experience into a form assimilable to structures of meaning that are generally human (Micznik, 2001, p. 194).

On the global, interdisciplinary plane the importance of narration started to be perceived as the means of bringing order to and bestowing significance on chaotic, dispersed elements.

The concept of narrative identity appeared. It allowed one to capture that which is processual; in that approach the past is of an open nature—its interpretation depends on the future.

In contemporary narratology one of the primary paradigms is cognitive narratology (Herman, 1990), which focuses on perceiving, viewing and processing narration by man. It was already St. Augustine who emphasized the significance of an active, attentive mind in deliberations regarding time, related to perceiving narration. The philosopher quotes an example of reciting poetry:

> A man's alert attention being in the presence, leads future into the past: future continues to diminish, while the past grows and finally—after the future is completely consumed—all becomes nothing but the past[1] (Ricœur, 1983, vol. 1, p. 37).

Without "a mind that accomplishes these things" according to St. Augustine, there would be neither diminishing future nor growing past (Ricœur, 1983, vol. 1, p. 37).

Cognitivists claim that narration is born in nothing less than a process of reception, viewing; while perceiving phenomena of a temporal nature we create narration out of these phenomena by combining facts with one another, complementing underspecified places, ordering into thought patterns we know. In turn, narration authors may "play" with a recipient's expectations, confirming them in the process of narration or surprising the recipient.[2] However, many of the narrative aspects have to be encoded in the work itself, in its form and structure. Today when transdisciplinary narratology becomes more and more popular and musical narratology is in the phase of a dynamic development, we can ask how this narrative function changes in music.

2. Dusapin's Roméo et Juliette and narratological interpretation?

Dusapin (1988) emphasized more than once that his opera was not designed to be a story, and it certainly was not supposed to present the story of Romeo and Juliet. He wrote in a preface to his score: "This is more than a story, this is an archetype [...] To have a story that is not a story theatrical elements must be minimal." On the other hand, the composer (1990) uses the word "story" or "tale" in reference to this work in the following meaning: "*Roméo & Juliette* is the story of a Project: how to sing together with a single voice, how to come together, how to become a true duo [...] The overall formation was the tale of the techniques involved." What is obvious is that the composer's and librettist's intention was to ignore the linearity of a literary program and avoid clearly defined semantics. However I would like to make an attempt to have a look at this opera from the narratological perspective in order to check what is going on with narrativity here. Even if the opera steers clear of repeating the story of Romeo and Juliet, it does not mean that it cannot construct some other narrative.

In the course of my interpretation, I will use the terms *story* and *discourse* from the point of view of the traditional narratological distinction between two levels of narration (Shen, 2005). As Gerald Prince writes in *Dictionary of Narratology*, story is the *what* of a narrative, and discourse is its *how*; story is *the narrated* as opposed to the discourse, which is *the narrating* (1987). In musical analysis, as proposed by Vera Micznik in 2001 and appropriated by Byron Almén in 2008, the description of the story level concerns the identification of coherent music units (thematic material, musical events, musical actants) as a kind of a static structure, whereas the description of the discourse level is connected with meanings resulting from syntagmatic, relational aspects of how the musical events are linked together and how the musical material is transformed.

3. The work

Pascal Dusapin today is an author of 100 works representing various genres, from solo pieces for different instruments, through chamber, orchestral, vocal and choral music, to opera. Initially—in the 1970s and 1980s—he concentrated on instrumental works, where he explored unique trajectories of musical narratives that were supposed to develop in an unexpected and unconventional way.

Roméo & Juliette (1985-1988)—the first of six operas by Dusapin—is without doubt a key work in his artistic development. On the one hand, it has been perceived as a turning point for the transformation of his style (simplification), while on the other hand as a synthesis of his previous achievements. One of the composer's leading aims from 1977 was an attempt to "deal with" a then problematic relation between the vocal part and instruments, between text and music. The issue, which had previously been raised in a number of smaller vocal-instrumental and vocal works, such as *Igitur* (1977), *To God* (1985), *Mimi* (1986), *Il-li-ko* (1987) and *Anacoluthe* (1987), culminated in this first opera by Dusapin, where it became one of the work's major themes. The author also used fragments of those earlier works in the opera (the last two of them in particular), inserting their reconstructed versions in a new context. Therefore, it can be said that they are in fact sketches for *Roméo & Juliette*, while at the same time they remain autonomous works. The situation should not seem surprising when we realize that those works were mostly written alongside the opera—the very first notes were composed in 1985, while the entire opera was finished three years later.

The work was commissioned by French Institutes in Bremen and Bonn as well as by a foundation, Louis Vuitton for Opera and Music. In connection with the 200th anniversary of the French Revolution, the theme of revolution (here treated metaphorically) became one of the opera's motifs. Dusapin wrote a dedication: *for Alice (Juliette) & Théo (Roméo) Dusapin*. Deciphering of this dedication leads to the twins—Dusapin's children born on March 22, 1989. However the score was finished on August 8, 1988 and published in the same year. It means that the children received the dedication before they were born, while their symbolic identification with Romeo and Juliet does not indicate a couple, but archetypal "any Juliet" and "any Romeo", which tells us a lot about the way the composer approached the subject.

The central (fifth) part of the opera (*La Révolution*) was dedicated to the memory of Giacinto Scelsi. The score was finished one day before the Italian composer died.

The libretto was written by Dusapin's friend, a poet Olivier Cadiot, who had previously collaborated with him on the occasions of the already mentioned works-satellites of the opera.

It is the only opera by Dusapin in French (however, he incorporated other languages as well). Similarly to other works by the composer, a clarinet solo has a very significant part. It is most likely a result of a long-term cooperation between Dusapin and an excellent clarinetist Armand Angster.

The piece consists of nine parts with the entirely instrumental central part entitled Revolution, which clearly marks the division between what occurs *before* and *after* (table 1).

Movements / duration	1. 14' *Prologue*	2. 11' *Le début*	3. 5' *Le matin*	4. 16' *Avant*	5. 8' *La révolution*	6. 9' *Après*	7. 15' *Le soir*	8. 6' *La fin*	9. 1' *Épilogue*
Isotopies	I. Lack & Deficiency			II. Change	III. Revolution	IV. The New World		V. Disillusionment, Disorientation	
Narrative scheme	I. The initial order				II. Disturbance of the initial order	III. New order		IV. Disturbance of the new order	

TABLE I

In this opera Dusapin takes advantage of a whole arsenal of contemporary means using those taken from diverse conventions known from musical tradition at the same time. Numerous references to tradition are present in the form of quotations (textual as well as musical) and musical topics such as military march, revolution hymn, love poetry, Renaissance madrigals. Differentiation of musical language and material is located in between two pairs of extremes: 1) intimacy of chamber ensemble and fullness of vocal-orchestral sound; 2) complex sound material with microtones, clusters, numerous glissandi and, on the other hand, simplified, diatonic, *quasi*-modal material. It was the composer's intention to reduce stage effects to a minimum: it is music that is to be *visible* here, it should be *the sounds staged*.

The story level in Dusapin's opera is in itself multilayered. The literary text is poetic and enigmatic. We can say it is a polyphonic story, because there are three coexisting plots intertwined together. Therefore we can distinguish here:
- The story of *love*
- The story of *revolution*
- and the most intriguing one in the light of a narrative theory, the story of a *discourse*.

The first one, the story of love, shows a couple (later reinforced by characters' doubles) setting off on a metaphorical journey. Love is here connected with the idea of revolution and courage in love with that of introducing changes. At a certain moment Julia says:

> tout va mal
> ici de A à Z
> tout à recommencer
> courir de nouveau

The composer (1988) writes in a commentary to the score: "No attempt was made to interpret revolution, but rather to make use of it, to use everything that shows any ambition to introduce new language and new song." Therefore the subplot of revolution is associated with the very story of discourse. New language, exploring various means of speaking and singing, seeking possibilities in vocal duet, reflecting upon creation of opera—in other words: metaopera.

Of course, all of these concern not only the libretto, but at the same time the musical material. Stories of love and revolution manifest themselves through topics of love lyric or military march, whereas the story of a discourse manifests itself by means of meaningful use of musical material.

Now I would like to provide some examples from the opera. First of all, we will take a look at *Part 2* entitled *Le début - The Beginning*.

We read in synopsis: The two heroes meet in a garden. They recognize each other, fall in love and take their first singing lessons with Bill, the master singer...

In this part musical-verbal images of childhood, morning and springing love are presented. At first, a vocal quartet a cappella is singing about the sun which has not risen yet but slowly appears on the horizon—polyphonic texture with elements of the hocket technique, narrow-range melodic patterns and quasimodal harmony can be found here. All unaccompanied voices constitute a delicate introduction which makes up a light and fresh aura stressed by the use of the expressive term très doux later in that part. Moreover a murmurando choir joins in, the clarinet plays a melody imitating bird song (the expressive term comme un chant d'oiseau), in vocal parts whispers, whistled notes and loud breaths appear.

The gentleness, freshness and carefreeness of *The Beginning* is enhanced by quoting nursery rhymes later on in the part, for instance *Who Killed Cock Robin*.

Romeo and Juliet are depicted as children playing a game: a secret password is being mentioned after which the nursery rhyme begins, interrupted with exclamations of "once again, once again" and singing "tralalala". After that Julia begins to sing as if examining the language itself and possibilities of exchanging the pronoun I for we, you for I:

> I (we) shall have
> You (I) will have ...
> o let us have / have / let them have

The musical-verbal reaction to these words is very strong: the choir and vocal quartet begin a sung/spoken unsynchronized stuttering as if in disarray (the expressive term: *comme en "bégayant"*); then the wind instruments join in— the forever-accompanying clarinet and the wind instruments' choir which bursts in *ff* with hoquetus-like sequences imitating phonemes of language, so difficult to pronounce.

Romeo and the choir assume that Julia has lost her mind and that "it is insane what people can think up"; together with the words *C'est fou ce...* in Romeo's part a *glissando* from d to gis[1] in the falsetto register and then backwards to even lower unpitched sounds occurs.

After around 30 measures in which the disease and frenzy of language are presented, a love duet by Romeo and Juliet appears, commented upon by Bill who moderates this "singing lesson". Here we clearly have a reference to love lyric tradition in both text and music: the expressive term *très très doux*, gentle melodious *legato*, *quasi*-consonances, though filled with microtones.

The simultaneous singing of the lovers could be referred to as *quasi*-unisono singing because, for instance, when the two voices meet on the same word "love", instead of an octave we have a microtonal interval between the major and minor sevenths. Apart from that, harmonic thirds and seconds are frequent, which in the context of the whole piece points to outright consonant harmony.

After nine bars of an intimate polyphonic duet with a short ecstatic culmination the choir joins in while Romeo and Juliet sing a waltz (the expressive term *comme une valse*) in *nota contra notam* counterpoint texture made of parallel tritones (!) [see figure 1]. It is interesting that microtonality disappears here altogether and all the musical features suggest the lovers' symbiosis, except for the perverse use of tritone.

These are the words of the duet which point to waiting for the lover rather than love being fulfilled:

o april night how fair and bright
my love-my-love-come not
come-not-again

FIGURE 1. A fragment of the love duet – waltz, part 2 *Le début*, Édition Salabert 1998, p. 44

After that love lyric topic a culmination in *tutti* follows, featuring the choir singing fragments of a poem by the Victorian author Alfred Lord Tennyson, *Blow Bugle Blow*.

Now let us move to *Part 4*, titled *Avant (Before)*.
We read in a synopsis: They have grown considerably and the time has come to take on responsibilities. And as absolutely everything is going badly, they decide to have a Revolution… They sing hymns with their doubles, Romeo 2 and Juliet 2, who have by now become aware of their voices, make speeches and take up arms. The orchestra and the choir begin to form a single nation and play at making war, Romeo takes himself for Saint-Just and they are all leading lights in the revolution. Everything is ready for the great evening. The Revolution in song.

265

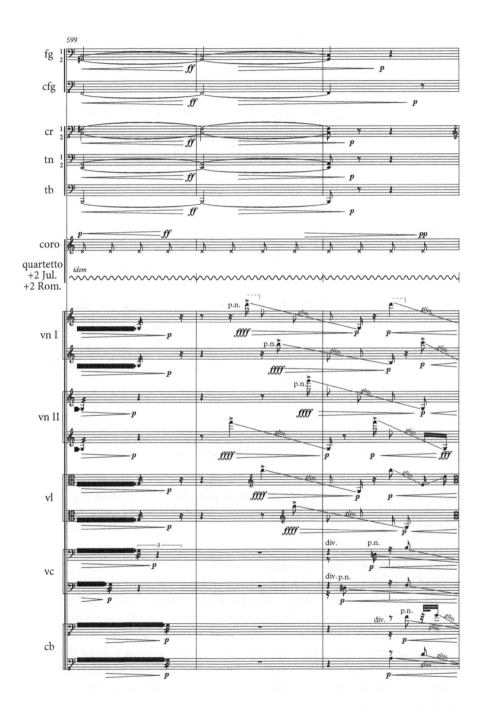

FIGURE 2. Onomatopoeic war sounds, part 4 *Avant*, Édition Salabert 1998, p. 101

This is the turning point in the opera's narration. What has been anticipated and looked for so far now takes on distinctive shapes.

In this part the elements characteristic of revolution appear: musical topics of military march and revolution hymn (anticipated in *Prologue*), quotations from *The Song of Marseille* and *A Long Way to Tipperary* (known as a popular soldiers' song from World War I), onomatopoeic war sounds like for instance the strings' *glissandi "comme une bombe qui siffle"*, sudden appearances of low wind instruments *fff "comme une bombe qui explose"*, rapid repetitions in trumpets "*comme une mitraillette*", choristers' thumping, and many others (figure 2).

The whole fragment starts from a gentle pedal note *cis* in the lower register of the strings and the choir which, together with an added second *dis*, constitutes the sounding center of the first few dozen measures. Building up a whole volume of sound happens gradually up to Bill's recitation of the words "*long time ago there was a monster, long time ago, long time ago*" and his illustration of the monster's roar. At the same time, the vocal quartet sings the subsequent letters of alphabet and articulates the concepts: *A Abstraction …, Activité …, Aliénation …, Animal, Appropriation, Argent….* Rudimentary issues are considered here.

After around 60 measures the narrative pacing is interrupted—the orchestra falls silent for several seconds. Only Bill utters revolutionary watchwords. Then Romeo 1 and Juliet sing light-hearted melodies with the words: "matin léger marchons léger allons avant."

The polyphony of different musical actions and topics piles up while the sounding center is secured by a march-like ostinato in low-register instruments (sometimes also in solo instruments) $f - c$. After that, from measure 100 of that part occurs a 20-measure-long fragment of a contrasting character: it is devoid of text (vocalizes in the choir's part), set in *piano* dynamics and in a slow half note motion; next both couples begin to sing together for the first time—*a cappella*, in a *quasi*-hocket technique (the *f-c* ostinato is still present here), [figure 3].

Then—again by contrast—comes a group of war sounds and diverse sonoristic effects in tutti together with the choral chant "Vive à jamais la liberté!" That uproar is decisively disrupted by Bill's exclamation:

stop! stop! stop!
je connais la fin de cette histoire…
l'ordre du présent est le désordre du futur…

Figure 3. Both couples sing together for the first time, part 4 *Avant*, Édition Salabert 1998, p. 97

That moment of extradiegetic narration informs the viewer that we are dealing with "fiction aware of its own fictionality" here. The last 30 measures are a subtle fading out within the topic of madrigal in which most voices (the choir, the vocal quartet, Romeo and Juliet), woodwinds and strings—*legato* vocalizes in *piano* dynamics with gentle melodic lines and close to modal harmony—take part. The vocal quartet sings:

> c'est magnifique c'est ça
> le thème l'idée…
> et l'ordre du présent est le désordre…
> ce héros vole au combat cette femme est belle
> cet homme est léger à la course

The last words before "the Revolution" are those of Romeo (a cappella):

> j'y vais j'y vais là
> enfin comme promis oui…
> je pense à votre projet au futur oui

An example from *Part 6 (After)* is also worth quoting due to the reference to Native American chants of ritualistic origin which appears there.

The technique close to hoquetus is used here, which in fact was characteristic of Native Americans' music making. The composer wrote in a note to vocalists included in the score:

> Il est recommandé de chanter avec une voix très âpre, *ethnique* et sans vibrato intempestif… Mais il faut beaucoup s'amuser avec ces *Indiens*…

In this part of the piece three languages appear simultaneously: Native American, French and English, for instance the following words:

> it's right here…
> the land
> we were given…
> home…

A short quotation from the previous love duet *O April Night* is used here, which highlights the archetype of return present here. At the end of this part the choir depicts "sounds of the wind and leaves" and woodwinds "birds singing".

4. Narrative in Dusapin's Roméo & Juliette? New ways of musical narratives

Only three fragments of the opera have been described above. Now we shall have a look at the whole narration. As I have already mentioned, the *story* of *discourse* is amongst the themes of the opera. The protagonists are to perform an opera, they learn to sing. Hence the work exploits the capacities of discourse, language as well as the relation between text and music, which is the reason we observe a whole range of means of expression here. The central part titled *Revolution* is written only for instrumental ensemble with no text or vocal parts.

The voices, present in the rest of the parts, move along the multigrade scale between mechanistic speech and melodious singing and in particular moments also exclamations, roars, onomatopoeic sounds of nature. The very process of passing from speech to singing and *vice versa* is important here. Even though the direction of changes on a narratological trajectory is not evident, it can be simplified that the protagonists gain the ability of opera singing in parts 7 and 8 while this fact has already been anticipated in part 2 (the love duet). It seems symptomatic that a rapid exchange occurs between the two couples: Romeo and Juliet 2 who so far have only been using speech or *quasi*-speech begin to sing exactly at the moment when the first couple is suddenly going from singing to speech. Here also an opposite process of losing one's singing and speech as the protagonists start stuttering up to a state of aphasia takes place.

It may be assumed that in the case of Dusapin's postmodernist work we come across self-referential function of the classical narratological terms story and discourse. If story is the *what* of a narrative and discourse is its *how*, in this opera a certain shift in reference to the discussed layers takes place. Thus the discourse here can be interpreted on the level of both *raconté* [the *what* of narrative] and *racontant* [the *how* of narrative]. In other words: *racontant* becomes *raconté*.

This has significant consequences for musical narration. The meaning results from an accumulation of processes and the structure itself to a much greater extent than from the verbal text which is very enigmatic here.

In 20th century music an escape from well-defined semantics of stories perceived in a linear way as coherent and complete coincides with new tendencies in structuring musical pieces frequently "freed" from tonality or fully verbalized semantics. According to Victoria Adamenko in the music of the 20th century mythologism as such is being foregrounded (on the structural level) through liberation from the mediation of dominant forces preserved in traditional principles of organization, for instance in tonality. Myth is understood here as an expression of the primary and fundamental feature of human culture, as a model of intelligent activity (Adamenko 1-8; Mali 2003). The author (2007, p. XII) claims: "The void created by the disappearance of tonality was inevitably filled with those prime elementary structuring methods first used in myths." Shifts in the levels of story and discourse in Dusapin's opera seem symptomatic and can be treated as an example of changes in musical narration.

Mythologism in Dusapin's Romeo et Juliette is highlighted by symmetries and oppositions in the arrangement of parts as well as by the metaphor of getting back to the roots in part 6 *After* (*quasi*-modal fragments, ritualistic time) and lots of symbols (a knight killing the dragon, home, the promised land) and figures ("long long time ago..."). The mere names of outermost parts suggest frames of the drama or story: *Prolog* and *Epilog.* Symptomatic of a certain play with time is the fact that in the libretto of the parts before *Revolution* events from the past are focused on while after *Revolution* there is a symbolic return to the beginnings.

As presented in the chart (figure 1) in the course of narration five subsequent isotopies can be distinguished which may correspond with Vladimir Propp's (1928) narrative functions:

- Isotopy I: *Deficiency and Search*—parts 1., 2. I 3. (*Prologue, Beginning, Morning*]. Searching for language, singing, assertion about the lack of something, insufficiency.
- Isotopy II: *Change*—part 4. (*Before*). What has been anticipated, searched for, takes on distinctive shapes. The change can be seen in the transformation of Romeo who now is ready to follow Juliet's "project of the future", as well as in the appearance of the second couple of Romeo and Juliet's doubles and a full spectrum of musical means used
- Isotopy III: *Revolution*—part 5. The medium is altered; the vocals fall silent. Instrumental music occurs which develops from a single note *d* into a theme, then the texture becomes denser.
- Isotopy IV: *The New World*—part 6., 7. and around a half of part 8. The discovery of the new world, symbolic "return": musical language becomes more consonant with the use of onomatopoeic sounds of nature, while the protagonists turn into "real opera singers". All the vocal parts are all-singing. The process of synthesizing the musical material begins.
- Isotopy V: *Disillusionment, disorientation*—the second part of part 8 and part 9. At a certain point the synthesis of material and reversing former principles assumes features of a special kind of madness, becomes a self-parody and points to disillusionment with the New World, new opera and love. The protagonists begin to stutter. Bill—the narrator—utters a volley of words taken from various phrases from the opera which sound mocking now. The clash of his sarcastic part with the Latin antiphon sung by the second couple disorientates the audience. Lyricism is mixed with mechanistic utterances, melodiousness with the impossibility of presenting melodies and fluency.

Let us compare the course of narration in Dusapin's opera with the classic narrative schema. The classic narratologists, Greimas as well as Todorov, describe narration as a passage from some initial order to the final order through the proper intrigue (see Greimas, 1966; Todorov, 1990, p. 29; Braningan, 1992, p. 4; Grabocz, 1999; Prince, 2003, p. 63):

I. The initial order.
II. Disturbance of the initial order.
III. The main intrigue (a trial, or series of trials).
IV. The return of the initial order or establishing a new order.

Does *Roméo et Juliette* by Dusapin fit in this classic narrative scheme? The ending of the opera precipitates us from the classic framework. It can be claimed that we have here:

I.   The initial order (the situation of the *lack* of something, the first four parts, *tout va mal ici de A à Z, tout à recommencer*)
II. Disturbance of the initial order (*Revolution*) and the approached immediately
III. New order
IV. Disturbance of the new order

According to Byron Almén, *transvaluation* is crucial for constituting a musical narrative. Almén adopts the concept from James Jakób Liszka's *The Semiotic of Myth* (1989, p. 71), who defines transvaluation as "a rule-like semiosis which revaluates the perceived, imagined, or conceived markedness and rank relations of a referent as delimited by the rank and markedness relations of the system of its signs and the teleology of the sign user."

To Almén (2003, p. 12), "Musical narrative is the process through which the listener perceives and tracks culturally a significant transvaluation of hierarchical relationships within a temporal span."

Some hierarchies within a narrative may be violated, there might be some transgression. "The narrative then unfolds a certain, somewhat ambivalent, resolution to the crisis, depending on the pragmatics of the tale: the disrupted hierarchy is restored [...] or, on the other hand, the hierarchy is destroyed [...]" (Liszka, after: Almén, 2008, p. 73).

Consequently, according to Almén, the dynamism of musical narrative can be perceived in the light of two binary oppositions: order/transgression and victory/defeat. The most important aspect seems to be a change achieved in the narrative treated as a process.

We can say that this *transvaluation* does take place in the opera. It is reached in parts 7-8 before the disillusionment deprives us of security as for the gained values. Each part introduces something new, and Revolution is a turning point, beginning from which the musical language gets simplified. The new found modality (within the scope of sound material), the new expressive qualities as well as the whole symbolism of text and music—all this refers to the idea of coming back to the roots. The so-called "all-singing" of the voices and instruments, "liberation" of music in parts 7 and 8 suggest that a long way has been traveled from the beginning of the opera's narration.

Thus a question arises: does the final disorientation and disillusionment invalidate the reached change, processually treated *transvaluation?* Did we come back to the point of departure or did nothing happen? Or perhaps time went round in a circle?

There is no possibility that, after all that occurred on the time axis of this work, the ending of the piece could be perceived in the same manner as the opening. Narrativity was not ignored here; the process of change went too far.

It can be claimed that narrativity here is even increased as compared to a traditional opera due to the presence of the narrator located once within, and some other times beyond, the world depicted in the piece. Friction clearly appears between *diegesis* and *mimesis* (for instance in Bill's intervention: *stop! stop! stop! je connais la fin de cette histoire…*).

Even the names of the outermost parts point to the frames of a drama or a story: *Prolog* and *Epilog*. A temporal dimension got stressed by means of the titles of the rest of the parts.

Moreover, the part of the clarinet solo assumes the proportions of the actant. Its permanent presence, concluding several phrases and parts, accompanying other voices when the whole orchestra remains silent, "commenting upon" the events invest it with an integrating and controlling function for the discourse as if it were the second narrator (see Abbate, 1991). Dusapin (1988) himself writes in a note to the score: "His presence, while discrete, is of crucial importance. He attracts all sources of energy and channels them to other fields, to other musical points." The polyphony of the story and techniques and languages used, as well as shifts and changes as compared to classic schemes make the work particularly intriguing for the researcher of narration. At the same time, they open it up for multiple interpretations.

It seems that with reference to Dusapin's postmodernist opera, which bears signs of deconstruction, we can talk about narrativity. However, the recipient of such narration has a greater responsibility—or greater freedom. In all narrations, notwithstanding their time of creation or style, a recipient's active mind is necessary to combine elements into a cohesive whole, although in traditional compositions narrativity is encoded, to a large extent, in the text itself. The overall tendency shows that in recent years the focus has moved more towards the recipient.

Therefore referring finally to Ricœur's words quoted at the beginning: a narrative function in music may change in the course of history but it is difficult to imagine that it would disappear. Of course in the 20th and 21st centuries we have many examples of the works ignoring narrativity such as *Moment-form* or pieces without a clear beginning or ending or some minimal music. However Dusapin's opera seems to be an example of music which is a narrative, though constructed differently than most previous works depicting Romeo and Juliet's story in the whole history of music. The lack of a tonal syntax as well as of a coherent story with precisely determined meanings is replaced with the highlighting of other elements of narrative shaping such as meaningful operating with structures, depicting certain discursive processes, novel usage of the narrator. Above all, if music is still able to perform the process of *transvaluation*, it can still perform a story, but maybe we just do not have to put it into words.

Notes

[1] Translated from the Polish edition by Aneta Ptak.
[2] One would wish to cite St. Augustine once again: "that which the mind expects, through that which it considers, may pass into that which it remembers" (Ricœur 1983, vol. 1, p. 38). Translated from the Polish edition by Aneta Ptak.

References

Abbate, C. (1991). *Unsung voices: Opera and musical narrative in the nineteenth century*. NJ: Princeton.
Adamenko, V. (2007). *Neo-mythologism in music. From Scriabin and Schoenberg to Schnittke and Crumb*. New York: Pendragon Press.
Almén, B. (2003). Narrative archetypes: A critique, theory, and method of narrative analysis. *Journal of Music Theory, 47*(1), 1-39.

Almén, B. (2008). *A theory of musical narrative.* Bloomington & Indianapolis: Indiana University Press.

Braningan, E. (1992). *Narrative comprehension and film.* New York: Routledge.

Dusapin, P. (1990). *Synopsis of Roméo et Juliette in a booklet for the recording.* Radio-France, cond. L. Pfaff.

Dusapin, P., & Cadiot, O. (1988). *On Romeo and Juliet. Foreword to the scores of Roméo et Juliette.* Paris: Éditions Salabert.

Grabocz, M. (1999). Paul Ricœur's theories of narrative and their relevance for musical narrativity. *Indiana Theory Review, 20*(2), 19–39.

Greimas, A. J. (1966). *Sémantique structurale. Recherche de méthode.* Paris: Libraire Larousse.

Hardy, B. (1968). Towards a Poetics of Fiction. *Novel, 2.*

Herman, D. (Ed. (1999). *Narratologies: New Perspectives on Narrative Analysis.* Ohio State University Press, Columbus.

Liszka, J. J. (1989). *The semiotic of myth.* Bloomington: Indiana University Press.

Lyotard, J.-F. (1979). *The postmodern condition: A report on knowledge.* University of Minnesota Press (Original work published 1984).

Mali, J. (2003). *Mythistory: the making of a modern historiography.* Chicago: The University of Chicago Press.

Micznik, V. (2001). Music and narrative revisited: Degrees of narrativity in Beethoven and Mahler. *Journal of the Royal Music Association, 126,* 193-249.

Prince, G. (2003). *Dictionary of Narratology.* University of Nebraska Press: Lincoln & London (Original work pubished 1987).

Propp, V. (1968/1928). *Morphology of the folktale.* Austin: University of Texas Press.

Ricœur, P. (2008). *Time and narrative.* Krakow: Wydawnictwo Uniwersytetu Jagiellońskiego (Original work published 1983).

Shen, D. (2005). Story-discourse distinction. In D. Herman, M. Jahn, & M. L. Ryan (Eds.). *Encyclopedia of Narrative Theory* (pp. 556-568). London, New York: Routledge.

Todorov, T. (1990). *Genres in discourse.* Cambridge University Press.

Turner, M. (1998). *The literary mind: the origins of thought and language.* Oxford University Press.

Authorship, Narrativity and Ideology: The Case of Lennon-McCartney[1]

Dario Martinelli

Kaunas University of Technology
International Semiotics Institute

Introduction

The authorial partnership between John Lennon and Paul McCartney, during the 1960s (or afterwards, as individual songwriters), has been the subject of several forms of categorization, not rarely confining with uncritical *clichés*: some of them were based on solid grounds (e.g., Lennon gave more importance to lyrics, McCartney to music), others were facile stereotypes (e.g., Lennon was the rocker, McCartney the balladeer, an insight dismissed by several songs).

In the present essay, I intend to offer a semiotic analysis of the two songwriters' approach and strategies for lyrics composition. In doing that, I hope to fill two particular gaps left by popular music studies in assessing the famous songwriting partnership and the specific artistic differences between Lennon and McCartney, as authors (and, partly, as personalities). Firstly, methodologically speaking, an expressively semiotic approach to the topic is lacking. Secondly, contents-wise, my opinion is that some aspects of the partnership, that I consider crucial were almost entirely overlooked, namely: some important oppositions in the narrative dimensions of Lennon's and McCartney's songwriting strategies (e.g.: *being* versus *doing*, *personal* versus *impersonal*, etc.); the different authorial (and sometimes cultural) ideologies (evident in nearly all cases in which the two authors would work separately on the same *stylistic type* of song: a love song, an autobiographical one, etc.); the continuity (or lack thereof) between technical/personal resources and actual songwriting choices.

This essay is part of a larger research project analyzing Lennon-McCartney songwriting, which will include specific themes (one being already forthcoming in Martinelli, 2013) and, of course, a detailed insight into musical composition. For this reason, and not painlessly, I have decided to refrain from dealing with the most political and ideological aspects of the pair's repertoire, which I consider important enough to deserve separate, extensive treatment (currently in preparation), and which I have partly anticipated in Martinelli (2010).

A final note: the sources for the songwriting anecdotes presented in this essay are of course endless, and it would be impossible to quote them all without falling into the cliché of "postmodern citationism" so hilariously mocked by Umberto Eco (1992, pp. 105-107). I shall therefore indicate here a few of those that I consider the richest ones available: Miles (1997), Norman (1981) and MacDonald (1994) for The Beatles as a group, and Rodriguez (2010) and Badman (2001) for the so-called solo years.

1. Shaping songwriting personalities

In Martinelli (2013), I attempted to trace a little overview of the events and circumstances that, in a socio-cultural sense, might have been instrumental in the development of Lennon's and McCartney's songwriting skills, taste and choices (education, experiences, social condition...).[2] On top of everything, both Lennon and McCartney (and the other two Beatles as well) belonged to the working class of Liverpool. Such a condition certainly helped to develop a critical attitude towards the establishment and social conventions, and most of all exposed them to a certain social and cultural milieu.

When we think about the catalog of places, people and situations created by the authors in their most evocative songs, we hardly find images of aristocracy or middle class (in fact, we rather find verses like "I don't need a castle, they've got castles in Versailles", as in McCartney's *Beautiful Night*, 1997). What we find is a street with a barbershop (mind: barbershop, not beauty salon), a bus station and the "suburban skies" of *Penny Lane* (1967); a street-band used as alter ego for *Sgt. Pepper's Lonely Hearts Club Band* (as opposed to anything fancier, like an orchestra or a string quartet); songs called *Working Class Hero* (Lennon, 1970), *Power to the People* (Lennon, 1971) or *Average Person* (McCartney, 1983), etc.

To say it all, also the way the songs' characters tend to behave is very coherent with the authors' social status. There are no special people or heroes in Lennon's and McCartney's writing:[3] what they do is nothing "that can't be done" (*All You Need Is Love*, 1967). It is significant that, when McCartney, in 1989, wrote *How Many People?* about a real hero (Chico Mendes, the Brazilian environmental activist assassinated in 1988 while fighting to preserve the Amazon rainforest), he makes it clear that a most disturbing thing is that an ordinary person was killed ("How many people have died? One too many right now for me, I wanna see ordinary people living peacefully").

Also, both authors developed teenage passions for the skiffle craze, the Teddy boy fashion and finally rock'n'roll, with their generally rebellious attitude, the development of a specific youth culture and the interest for Afro-American music (with its repeated references to sex and transgression). At the same time, thanks to his father's semi-professional passion for jazz and the Tin Pan Alley tradition, McCartney was also exposed to the American classics (an element that would help to shape the more sophisticated taste that The Beatles had in comparison with other rock'n'roll bands).

If it is no surprise that Tin Pan Alley experienced lyricists could elaborate particularly refined sets of lyrics (see names like Oscar Hammerstein, Lorenz Hart or Ira Gershwin), one should not forget that also rock'n'roll (and its most important root, blues) could often take a particular care for words. Authors like Carl Perkins, Buddy Holly and Chuck Berry had shown a remarkable reluctance to repeat the simplistic straightforwardness of the "I love you, let's rock"[4] formulas of the genre, opting for a richer imagery inhabited by people who had names (Johnny B. Goode, Peggy Sue…) and features (Blue Suede Shoes, Brown-eyed Handsome Man…).

Thirdly, both attended institutes of a humanistic type, except that Lennon was in an art college and McCartney in a grammar school. It is my conviction that these choices played a role—we shall see eventually—in Lennon's inclination to a visually-descriptive approach to lyrics writing, and McCartney's preference for a narrative one.

Not incidentally, when it came to literary taste, Lennon became enamored with the visual inventiveness of writers like Lewis Carroll (paying homage to him in songs like *I Am the Walrus*, 1967, inspired by Carroll's poem *The Walrus and the Carpenter*), while McCartney fell in love with great narratives such as those of Charles Dickens (writing songs like *Jenny Wren*, 2005, based on the character from Dickens's novel *Our Mutual Friend*). We shall see later that Lennon, too, could be capable of dense narratives, so perhaps at this point it would be fair to say that, in turn, McCartney too could take a rather visual/imaginative approach (a song like *Monkberry Moon Delight*, 1971, would very clearly make the case). If anything, a subtle difference would lie in McCartney's preference for a surrealistic construction of the lyrics, rather than a visionary one.[5]

Finally, in a more advanced stage of their careers, both authors, together or separately, had the chance to expand their horizons by taking different kinds of experience. The biographers' favorite topic in this respect is of course drugs, and there is no denial here that the three main drugs of choice of the band (amphetamines, marijuana and LSD) played specific roles in their creativity: amphetamines (taken during the pre-fame days until more or less 1964) possibly had an impact on the immediate simplicity and quickness of the early songs; marijuana (which the group was famously initiated into by Bob Dylan in late 1964) was certainly responsible for the more meditative and edgy attitude displayed from 1965 onwards; and of course LSD (taken for a limited period, and in totally different proportions between Lennon and McCartney,[6] during the second half of the 1960s) had a visible influence on the most visionary and surrealistic episodes of their repertoire.

Having said that, the picture would be far from complete if we did not add other key events, namely, the personal meeting with Bob Dylan (and the repeated exposure to his albums) was not only the occasion for Lennon and McCartney to smoke their first joint, but made a significant impact on the development of their songwriting. As often reported, the Dylan–Beatles summit was a win-win trade for both sides: while Dylan was inspired to pursue a richer rock-oriented musical direction (inaugurating his electric period that possibly led to the best three albums of his career), Lennon and McCartney (the former, in particular) understood that their lyrics could not go on forever with simple, impersonal love songs like *From Me to You* or *I Want to Hold Your Hand*, and became interested in more reflective, autobiographic and inventive writing.

In addition to this, although in different moments and with different people, both Lennon and McCartney were influenced by avant-garde movements. McCartney, the only Beatle to live in the center of London, had already been in the thick of the Swinging London era since late 1964. He was dating a theatrical actress, Jane Asher; attending concerts of composers like Berio and Stockhausen; meeting people like Bertrand Russell, Michelangelo Antonioni and Rene Magritte (from whom he purchased a few paintings, including *Le jeu de mourre*, which inspired the logo for the band's

Apple company); and most of all frequenting and supporting the underground movement (he sponsored the International Times magazine and the Indica Art Gallery, among other things). To Lennon, the turning point occurred around 1968, and the key to it was his relationship with the experimental artist and Fluxus-member Yoko Ono, who managed to forge in her partner a solid interest for avant-garde, situationist art and post-modernism.

Certainly more visible in the musical production, the impact of these experiences on Lennon and McCartney was significant in the lyrics department too. Thematically, the two authors expanded their range of topics, became able to see artistic potential in a wider number of events and situations (not infrequently following Duchamp's "found object" principle), and did not mind daring to deal with less comfortable or socially acceptable issues. Formally, the poetic abilities were implemented in various ways, and again became more courageous in structure and logic (words could now be picked for sound rather than meaning, the narrative construction would become more complex and multilayered, etc.).

Third: starting from 1965, interest in the hippie culture and the acquisition of a certain (not always focused) socio-political conscience prompted the couple into dealing with themes such as pacifism (e.g., *All You Need Is Love*, 1967) and civil rights (e.g., *Blackbird*, 1968), and—during their solo careers— feminism (e.g., Lennon's *Woman Is the Nigger of the World*, 1972), animal rights (e.g., McCartney's *Looking for Changes*, 1993), the Irish question (both Lennon and McCartney had a go at commenting on the so-called *Bloody Sunday* in *Sunday Bloody Sunday* and *Give Ireland Back to the Irish* respectively, both released in 1972), and others.

Fourth: the period of meditation in India, in early 1968, helped both authors to open up new thematic venues, including spirituality (not necessarily in a religious sense, as in cases like *Across the Universe*), nature (e.g., *Mother Nature's Son*) and environmentalism/animal advocacy (e.g., *The Continuing Story of Bungalow Bill*).[7]

Finally, between the end of the 1960s and the beginning of the 1970s, Lennon and McCartney experienced two opposite, yet equally formative, changes in lifestyle. In 1972, Lennon moved from the semi-decadent life in the luxurious residential area of Weybridge (40 km from London) to the very heart of New York, diving into city-life (*New York City*, 1972) and hanging out with the local left-wing intelligentsia (*John Sinclair*, 1972, *Angela*, 1972…). McCartney, though not completing abandoning London, found himself increasingly attracted by country life (*Heart of the Country*, 1971, *Country Dreamer*, 1973…).

One more experience applies to Lennon only, and yet had a huge impact on his songwriting. The psychotherapy sessions conducted with Arthur Janov in 1970, based on the notion of the *primal scream*, turned a visionary, imaginative lyricist, as Lennon had been in the second half of the 1960s, into a straightforward, honest and occasionally brutal one. With basically the sole exception of the song *#9 Dream* (1974), Lennon's whole solo career is marked by a firm determination to be a "reporter" of his own feelings and experiences, from the most painful (e.g., *My Mummy Is Dead*, 1970) to the most ordinary ones (e.g., *Cleanup Time*, 1980).

On the other hand, even though autobiographical songs are far from rare in McCartney's repertoire, there is no doubt that the latter always found it more comfortable to remove himself, as a recognizable character, from a song's spotlight, and to convey a message from an impersonal, or straightaway fictional, perspective.

Not that this may have any statistical relevance, but it is certainly significant that, besides all the many "I's" and "Me's" that each author may have employed in their songs, McCartney never used the words "Paul" or "McCartney" in his songs, while Lennon did use his given name pretty often (*The Ballad of John and Yoko*, 1969, *Hold On*, 1970, *God*, 1970, *#9 Dream*, 1974 …).[8]

2. Lennon or McCartney

2.1 Autobiography vs. fiction

There is no doubt, thus, that Lennon's most inspired lyrics are those that contain autobiographical elements and have self-confession and honesty as central values; and that McCartney is at his best when he depicts fictional stories and uses literary and metaphorical elements to express his feelings. To an extent, a thorough analysis of Lennon's songs is more revealing of his life than any (often contradictory) interview or statement he delivered to the media: he certainly is one of the most satisfying answers to the demand for sincerity and authenticity that rock mythology has always had. Conversely, McCartney must be primarily appreciated for his storytelling qualities, and the ability to invent characters with a specific name (and often surname too) which yet are synecdoches for universal feelings and values (Jude for self-confidence, Eleanor Rigby for loneliness, the girl in *She's Leaving Home* for generational conflicts, etc.).

Having said that, and admitting that these are the respective strengths of the two authors' lyrical abilities, there is an element of unfairness in this overall judgement. In Lennon's case, one cannot obviously disregard his "psychedelic" period, between 1966 and 1969, where several fictional songs of capital importance in his songwriting appeared: *Lucy in the Sky with Diamonds*, *Being for the Benefit of Mr.Kite* and, most of all, *I Am the Walrus* (all released in 1967), to name the most famous ones, are remarkable proof that Lennon, too, was no alien to storytelling as such. If anything, it may be noted that all such cases still use personal experience as points of departure, reaffirming the centrality of the latter in the author's inspiration: to concentrate on the three songs mentioned, the first was inspired by a drawing of Lennon's first son Julian, the second was almost a

word-by-word transcription from an old Victorian circus poster that Lennon had purchased in an antique shop, and the third was based on Lewis Carroll's tale *The Walrus and the Carpenter*.

McCartney, too, could base his fictional characters on personal life's events,[9] but then again he could also make up characters without any source whatsoever (Desmond and Molly Jones from *Ob-la-di Ob-la-dà*, Maxwell Edison from *Maxwell's Silver Hammer*, Rocky Raccoon and dozens of others). Lennon seemed to need a point of departure from real life, but that does not make his fictional songs less remarkable in structure, inventiveness and narrative skills. In addition to that, Lennon was a notable craftsman of the traditionally British art of nonsense (Lear, Joyce, Carroll, etc.), and that—again—departs from the traditional idea of *authenticity* in songwriting (although, as I maintain later, I do not see the reason why imagination cannot be part of an author's autobiographical artistic paradigm).

On the other hand, McCartney's confidence with storytelling has often produced a boomerang effect on him when it comes to the critical assessment of his songwriting. Exactly because of this constant (and unmotivated, in my humble opinion) demand for honesty and egocentrism as the greatest values in rock songwriting (a demand normally inspired by such figures as Bob Dylan, Leonard Cohen, Bruce Springsteen and the same Lennon[10]) was often the driving force behind those critics who considered McCartney's lyrics "lightweight" and "meaningless". Such evaluation, however, clashes with three major facts. Firstly, McCartney *did* produce very inspired autobiographical songs, which are rightly considered among his best works (*Maybe I'm Amazed*, 1970, *Let It Be*, 1970, and *Here Today*, 1982, are three of the most cited examples of the category). Secondly, McCartney could effectively transform personal experience into semi-fictional narration, creating a pop equivalent of the rhapsody or the historical novel genres (see for instance *Penny Lane*, 1967, *Lovely Rita*, 1967, and *Mull of Kintyre*, 1977). Thirdly, only a narrow-minded conception of *autobiographical song* will maintain that imagination and storytelling are *not* parts of a person's life, and therefore do *not* reflect that person's feelings and sentiments: as we shall see, for instance, one of McCartney's most recurrent lyrical themes is loneliness, so there is no doubt about his *personal* sensibility towards it. Yet, it is intriguing that the author's favorite way to discuss the issue is to invent fictional characters and stories: *All the lonely people* in McCartney songs are partly or totally fictional, from the mentioned *Eleanor Rigby* (1966) to *The Fool on the Hill* (1967), up to more recent characters like those in *The Average Person* (1983) or *Footprints* (1986).

More than anything, however, it is always a bit disappointing to notice that, when talking about authenticity, rock critics are in fact implying a *certain* kind of it, what we may call a *maudit* version. Singers are authentic if they talk about their own dark side, fears, troubles, painful memories, unpleasant events. If they do, then they are authentic, if they do the opposite, then it does not really matter if their cheerfulness and optimism are "honest" (that is, if they reflect exactly how they feel): the critics' pick of words will now be "corny", "fruity", "lightweight", "banal". McCartney wrote and writes dozens of songs about domestic experiences, country life, family, children, monogamous love, and the joy of all these things. As his life, statements and close associates' accounts repeatedly show, he seems to be *exactly* like this, cherishing these values and thoroughly enjoying them. Therefore, when he sings "Bring a bag of bread and cheese and find a shady spot beneath the trees / Catch a breath of country air and run your pretty fingers through my hair" (*Tomorrow*, 1971) or "A love so warm and beautiful stands when time itself is falling / A love so warm and beautiful never fades away" (*Warm and Beautiful*, 1976), the unbiased rock critic should assume that he is, indeed, being very authentic and true to his feelings.

In fact, speaking of honesty, I must confess that I find it a bit pathetic that, since the mythization of Beethoven and the romantic conceptualization of the genius, so many critics and musicologists have only been keen to depict struggling, instinctive and tormented musicians as artistically valuable, and fail to consider equally important assets like rationality, balance and purposefulness, as Renaissance and Enlightenment had no significant part in music history.[11]

2.2 To be vs. to do

Another chief difference between Lennon and McCartney (with, again, some exceptions) is in the Greimasian modalities of their narration. Regardless of autobiographical or fictional elements, what is very interesting in the two authors is how effectively their songwriting personalities operate in the processes of characterization and description, within a song. To Lennon, things and people *are*, to McCartney, they *do*. What does that mean? It means, coherently with Greimas' precepts, that Lennon prefers the description of a state of being (emotions, states of mind, visual aspects, thoughts...), while

McCartney is much more keen to make things *happen* in a song (actions, physical movements, changes of space, passing of time…). A Lennon song may occupy its entire length in describing a person (probably himself) not moving a finger yet going through all kinds of feelings. One of his famous characters (indeed, a variation of himself) is the *Nowhere Man* (1965):

> He's a real nowhere man
> Sitting in his nowhere land
> Making all his nowhere plans for nobody
> Doesn't have a point of view
> Knows not where he's going to
> Isn't he a bit like you and me?
> …

The man sits down throughout the whole song, but instead we learn a great deal of what is going on in his head. On the other hand, McCartney may take another person (probably invented) and, while he qualifies her personality by using single adjectives, he may let her *do* a lot of things. That is what happens in the teenage girl who escaped from home in *She's Leaving Home* (1967):

> Wednesday morning at five o'clock as the day begins
> Silently closing her bedroom door
> Leaving the note that she hoped would say more
> She goes downstairs to the kitchen clutching her handkerchief
> Quietly turning the backdoor key
> Stepping outside she is free
> …

A lot of action takes place, here, and basically in every single line the girl is caught doing something. The room for feelings is very limited, yet McCartney is far from neglecting that part: rather, he is more interested in suggesting them in a more subtle way, and—most importantly—*through* the actions themselves. In "leaving a note that she hoped would say more" we understand the indecisiveness of the girl and a degree of fear. In "clutching her handkerchief" we realize that she is, or has been, crying. And, in later passages of the song, we also learn more (like the famous *reason* why she is leaving, through the words of the parents "We gave her everything money could buy": she received material goods, but apparently no real affection).

2.3 Subjective vs. objective

One consequence of the two previous oppositions is that Lennon takes a more diegetic position in his songs. His narration is more often than not *subjective*, and his presence and point of view in the songs is almost always tangible. Lennon is a "director" who appears in his "movies" as himself, in the style of Woody Allen, Nanni Moretti or Federico Fellini. McCartney is often *outside* the story, in a non-diegetic position and with an *objective* perspective. Whatever he has to tell the listener, he prefers to let a character say: in that sense, and keeping up with the movie game, he may remind us more of the likes of Luchino Visconti, Alfred Hitchcock or Peter Weir.

It is rather significant that, in a very interesting linguistic analysis of The Beatles' lyrics, Lennon was found using the first person singular more often than McCartney, who instead prevails in the usage of the first person plural (Petrie et al., 2008, p. 201).

To better illustrate this opposition, one can mention the various love songs written by the duo, together or separately. Love, of course, is unanimously considered the main message conveyed by The Beatles, the very thing that—according to them—"we all need". The stereotype according to which McCartney would have been the only romantic balladeer is unfair in two ways: it overlooks the many great love songs written by Lennon, and it trivializes McCartney's sensibility in exploring and refining the genre of the romantic ballad.

In both authors we find a primary tendency to treat the topic in relation to their personal experience. Leaving aside marginal relationships and one night stands (those, too, having been described in songs, as in the famous case of *Norwegian Wood*, 1965), we can safely say that the main women in the two authors' lives have been seven. In the case of Lennon: Cynthia Powell (first wife and mother of his first son Julian), Yoko Ono (second wife, artistic partner, and mother of his second son Sean) and May Pang (long-time assistant, girlfriend for over a year during the separation from Yoko Ono between 1973 and 1975). In the case of McCartney: Jane Asher (regular girlfriend for about four years, between 1963 and 1968), Linda Eastman (first wife, artistic partner and mother of his four older children), Heather Mills (second wife and mother of his youngest daughter Beatrice) and Nancy Shevell (current wife).

Naturally, Ono and Eastman (with 11 and 29 years of marriage and artistic collaboration respectively) are by far the most regular presence in the two authors' love songs. However one should not disregard the way the other partners were addressed in songs that were, in some cases, extremely popular. In chronological order:

1. The presence of Powell in Lennon's songs is a good documentation of the latter's evolution in character and attitude to women. Most of the songs about his first wife are songs of jealousy (*You Can't Do That*, 1964; *Run for Your Life*, 1965…), traditional patriarchal values (*When I Get Home*, 1964; *A Hard Day's Night*, 1964…) and even domestic abuse (the line "I used to be cruel to my woman, I beat her and kept her apart from the things that she loved", though inserted in the mostly-McCartney 1967 song *Getting Better* was actually written by Lennon). The transition from Powell to Ono was, among other things, an opportunity for Lennon to rethink his male identity and become more apologetic towards the female genre (*Jealous Guy*, 1971; *Woman*, 1980, etc.).

2. Asher is the subject of such songs as *Here, There and Everywhere* (1966) and *Good Day Sunshine* (1966), which portrays the happiest moments of the relationship, or *We Can Work It Out* (1965) and *I'm Looking through You* (1965), which instead describes the difficulties the two had in communicating.

3. Then there was May Pang, the *other* Japanese girlfriend, who had an 18-month long relationship with Lennon, between the summer of 1973 and early 1975. This period, known to Lennon fans as "The lost weekend", was at the same time a wild and productive one: in the company of such heavy-drinking buddies as Harry Nilsson, Ringo Starr and Keith Moon, Lennon nevertheless managed to finalize three albums, the most successful of which, *Walls and Bridges* (1974), contains references to the (temporary) end of his relationship with Ono (*Going Down on Love*) and to the somewhat unexpected joys of the new affair (*Surprise Surprise*).

4. In the 21st century, after the death of his first beloved wife Linda, McCartney saw the light at the end of the tunnel with Heather Mills, but the marriage—as widely reported by the gossip media—ended up in a bitter divorce, so the songs dedicated to Mills are a balanced combination of very devoted and passionate (*Your Loving Flame*, 2001; *Heather*, 2001…), and documents of the crisis and the end of the relationship (*Riding to Vanity Fair*, 2005; *Nothing Too Much Just Out of Sight*, 2008…).

5. McCartney married for the third time in 2011 the American business woman Nancy Shevell. His recording activity since that time has included only the album *Kisses from the Bottom*, which is a collection of re-arranged standards from the Tin Pan Alley era, plus two original songs written in that style. Sure enough, the two songs (*My Valentine*

and *Only Our Hearts*, the former in particular for its very open references) are about Shevell. At the time of writing this essay, there is no anticipation of McCartney's new release, but it is not difficult to predict that more songs about the new wife will appear.

At any rate, the centrality of Ono and Eastman in Lennon's and McCartney's lives is strong and undisputable. Both women were huge influences at a personal and artistic level, witnessing the difficult transition from The Beatles' experience to their solo careers, collaborating in their music in various ways (including being members of Lennon's Plastic Ono Band and McCartney's Wings, and co-writing some of their most famous hits, like *Imagine*[12] and *Live and Let Die*[13]), and of course "being family" for the longest period of the their lives. No wonder, thus, that the main subject of their love songs is these two women. Interestingly, the approach to songwriting, in this particular topic, presents at the same time moments of divergence and convergence. Indeed, if they could both be quite honest about their relationships, and make their companions rather tangible presences in the songs, Lennon was still keener than McCartney not to give the listener any other chance than to identify Yoko Ono in the song. For instance, there are no fewer than seven Lennon songs where the name "Yoko" is pronounced explicitly and repeatedly: McCartney uses the name

"Linda" only once, in *The Lovely Linda* (1970). Secondly, Lennon's love songs tend to refer to the *hic et nunc* of his relationship with Ono, so we get to know feelings, events and even places that really happened and exist (as in the faithful accounts of domestic life that appear throughout the whole 1980 *Double Fantasy* album, where even a failed transatlantic phone call gets reported—see *I'm Losing You*). McCartney, on the other hand, even in those cases where he openly refers to Linda (by his own admission, the most prominent cases are *Maybe I'm Amazed*, 1970, and *My Love*, 1973), still manages to keep a kind of impersonal tone, not calling his wife by name, and expressing feelings and values with which most listeners can identify themselves. In other words, if, in order to express the same concept ("love despite geographical distance", in my example) Lennon would use lines such as "From Liverpool to Tokyo, what a way to go" (as he writes in *You Are Here*, 1973), McCartney would opt for something like "And when I go away, I know my heart can stay with my love" (*My Love*, 1973).

Personal/Impersonal is however not the only difference in the *Subjective/Objective* macro-category of this section. One must add also the *Realist/Verisimilar* one. Indeed, if, from circa 1965 onwards, it is almost impossible to find a Lennon love song that is *not* related to a real relationship he is going through at any particular moment, in the case of McCartney we could easily say that the actual majority of his ballads are about *fictional* love stories, starting from his most celebrated song in absolute, *Yesterday* (1965): there was no "she" who "had to go" at that point of his life.[14] The list is extremely long, and it involves some of his most famous tracks: from *When I'm 64* (1967) to *Another Day* (1971), from *Oh! Darling* (1969) to *No More Lonely Nights* (1984), "nothing is real" (as another song of the duo would go): McCartney makes up his love stories in a way that is certainly verisimilar (nothing absurd happens in these songs, nobody falls in love with aliens, etc.), but it is simply *not* what is happening to him. His love songs, in most cases, are the most faithful definition of a possible world.

Occasionally, but only occasionally, Lennon might employ less personal and pinpointed tones in his love songs, but if he decides to do that, it is not to go *impersonal*, but rather to go *universal*, that is, to talk about love as *value* and *principle*. It is obviously the case of the very well-known *All You Need Is Love* (1967), but also of the lesser known but perhaps more significant *Love* (1970).

2.4 Lennon and McCartney

Given all these differences between the two authors' backgrounds and specific songwriting approaches, it is no wonder that, once the interpersonal chemistry was found between the two, the partnership proved to be very rich and complementary. Much has been said about the Lennon–McCartney *match*, although usually comments tend to focus on superficial aspects, such as "McCartney provided the tender side, and Lennon was the rocker," or "McCartney was the optimist and Lennon the realist." Again, none of these clichés are entirely false, yet all are incomplete and somehow unable to catch the complexity of the two personalities. A typical example of this superficiality is the assessment of the song *We Can Work It Out* (1965). As a track where each of the pair's contribution is very distinguished and recognizable (McCartney wrote the chorus, "Try to see it my way…", and Lennon the bridge, "Life is very short…"), scholars were rather quick in saying that the chorus is the optimistic/positive part and the bridge is the pessimistic/fatalist one, conforming to the above-mentioned protocol. As a matter of fact, knowing the background of the song (McCartney intends to address the communication problems with his then-girlfriend Jane Asher), but also by attentively reading the lyrics, it is really almost the opposite. What is at stake here, in comparing the two songwriters' contributions to the song, is two different ways of solving an interpersonal conflict. In McCartney's passage, we have:

Try to see it my way,
Do I have to keep on talking till I can't go on?
While you see it your way,
Run the risk of knowing that our love may soon be gone.
We can work it out...

Think of what you're saying,
You can get it wrong and still you think that it's alright.
Think of what I'm saying,
We can work it out and get it straight or say goodnight.
We can work it out...

So: yes, sure, "we can work it out" (and that is the optimistic part), but only on the condition that the girlfriend admits she is wrong and instead surrenders totally to her partner's opinion. It is hardly a constructive way to solve a conflict. It rather shows the male partner as pretty resentful, and determined to have it his way. Plus, he really sees that, if she does not listen to him, the relationship will end. It is, indeed, a pessimistic view.

On the contrary, Lennon suggests that

Life is very short and there's no time
For fussing and fighting, my friend.
I have always thought that it's a crime.

In this case, we have a more reasonable approach, and conflict resolution experts would certainly agree that Lennon has more chances to "work the relationship out". He suggests simply stopping fighting, regardless of who is right or wrong, because life is too short for these things. To waste one's life fighting "is a crime". Lennon's passage, thus, does not demand a *winner* in the fight but, more wisely, a ceasefire.

Given this and similar cases,[15] I prefer to focus here on a lesser known bunch of collaboration episodes, where—in my humble opinion—more interesting elements can be drawn to attention. It is for instance intriguing to analyze some of those cases where one of the songwriters intervenes on his partner's *pre-existing* set of lyrics, in order to give advice or even suggest modifications. In situations like these, it is easier to single out the creative impact that the couple had on each other. I shall select the examples on the basis of their different nature: the first one is a *replacement* of lyrics, the second is an *addition*, the third a *reinforcement* (meaning that one partner was not convinced of a given verse, and the other reassured him by pointing out a potential that the former had not considered), and the fourth one is a result of on-the-spot *improvisation*, showing the exceptional chemistry between the two.

Starting with *replacement*, in one very early collaboration, *I Saw Her Standing There* (1963), McCartney had written most of the lyrics already, yet Lennon argued that the beginning ("Well, she was just seventeen, never been a beauty queen") was far from satisfying, and suggested instead "Well, she was just seventeen, you know what I mean", encountering his partner's approval (it is indeed the recorded version). The change of a single sentence is however very revealing of the different approaches, in particular McCartney's inclination for narration and *to do* modalities, and Lennon's tendency for the *to be* and the preference for moods description. McCartney is indeed working in his Dickensian way, trying to offer us an accurate portrait of the girl. He is telling us her age (which Lennon accepts), but he also adds aesthetic and possibly social features: the girl has never been a beauty queen, that is, she is not outstandingly good-looking, but also she is a simple girl. The teenager McCartney (the song was first conceived in 1960, when McCartney was 18, and most of all not famous yet) knows his *league*, so to speak: he is a working-class young man frequenting a bar in the periphery of Liverpool. The girls he can "target" and "afford" to dance with (sorry for the chauvinistic jargon) are far from being posh and beautiful. However, and there goes the link with the following verse ("And the way she looked was way beyond compare"), that girl has something special in her looks, and that becomes the feature that makes her very charming. So, we have a working-class girl who is not beautiful but still manages to be very attractive. It could have been an unusually profound sociological statement for a rock'n'roll song, except that, indeed, that is a rock'n'roll song, and rock'n'roll is about sex and straightforwardness. That is where Lennon intervenes: by stating "you know what I mean", he achieves several purposes in one shot. First, there are no more hints at anything less than "the perfect girl": she is 17 and she looks in a way that bears no comparison, period. Basically, it is like moving from Liverpool to Hollywood: from a simple girl of the people, the protagonist has now switched to a sort of movie star. Second, Lennon cuts off the narrative aspirations of the song, and reminds the listener that this is a rock'n'roll song, where the various *A Wop Bop a Loo Bop a Lop Bam Booms* tend to replace sophisticated expressions. Third, and most importantly, now the song is clearly sexy, as the "You know what I mean" is a double-entendre that in fact is not even that "double". The Beatles were not yet ready to be more elaborate in their lyrics, but they were certainly already capable of understanding what makes a song commercial.

McCartney's literary abilities will however come to hand in later years, when indeed The Beatles take on a more challenging approach to lyric writing. Exactly in the *Rubber Soul* album, a primarily Lennon song benefited enormously from McCartney's knowledge of narrative mechanisms, providing us with an appropriate example for the category *addition*. *Norwegian Wood* is an excellent proof that Lennon was also capable of descriptive and original storytelling. The story, as widely known, gives a fictionalized account of one of Lennon's infidelities to his first wife Cynthia. The girl, probably a groupie, lives in a small apartment decorated with Norwegian wood furniture: she and the first-person narrator have a one-night stand, but apparently there is not enough room in the bed for the both of them, so he ends up sleeping in the bathtub. The following morning, as the girl had to go to work quite early, the protagonist finds himself alone. How then to conclude such a story? That is where McCartney steps in, applying the classic strategy of the Chekhov's rifle to the song. Of all the lyrics, the only part that sounds a bit *sui generis* is the very moment when the girl shows off the apartment and says: "Isn't it good? Norwegian wood!" The wood, that particular type of wood, is a charming but unnecessary (and therefore suspicious) element of the narration. It is a *rifle*, and therefore has to *fire*, sooner or later. McCartney suggests that the events take a dark turn: the protagonist had to sleep in the bathtub and woke up in solitude; therefore why not make him annoyed by the girl's behavior, so that—in a eerie *coup de théâtre*—he decides to set fire to the apartment, sadistically mocking the girl's words ("Isn't it good? Norwegian wood!") while he witnesses the house burning[16]?

The third suggestion (*confirmation*) I want to mention concerns *Hey Jude*, the 1968 single that provided the band with their longest stay at the n.1 spot of the American charts. The song was entirely written by Paul McCartney, who submitted it to Lennon's opinion in what he thought was a working version that needed improvement exactly in the lyrics department. In the first bridge, McCartney had used the verse "Don't carry the world upon your shoulders", which made perfect sense in a song that talks about facing the struggles of life and re-gaining self-confidence, using the metaphor of a difficult songwriting process (and Lennon's son Julian as the initial protagonist, as we saw in a previous note). On the second bridge, for lack of better words, McCartney temporarily writes "The movement you need is on your shoulder", with the intention of replacing the line later, perhaps with the help of his partner (reasons for this discontent were basically two: the word *shoulders* had already been employed in the above-mentioned line, sounding too particular to be repeated; and, also, McCartney felt that a movement on the shoulders was a goofy image that reminded one of a parrot—Roylance et al., 2000,

p. 297). While performing the song to Lennon, and once reaching the critical point, McCartney reassures his partner that the awkward line will be fixed later: Lennon, however, does not agree, and suggests instead leaving what he considers "the best line in the song" (Roylance et al., 2000, p. 297). Why so? First-hand sources do not elaborate on that, but one can make reasonable guesses. First, the most obvious interpretation, in the context of a song that advocates finding in one's self the strength to cope with difficult times, is that Jude will need to count on his own resources. In order to "take a sad song and make it better", Jude needs a "movement", and that was with him all along: he already has the strength within him to make a change in his own life, to take a step forward and move on—he just has to choose to use it. But, one may object, why not use the heart or the soul (or something *inside*, anyway) to picture the location of this movement, as it would sound more traditional (and perhaps, McCartney meant to end up in those whereabouts with his lyrics)? That, it is my guess, was the potential that Lennon understood in the line. By the repetition of the word "shoulder", listeners are obviously invited to relate that line with the previous "Don't carry the world upon your shoulders". In this sense, the meaning of the passage becomes more complex: not only is Jude advised not to carry an unnecessary burden upon himself as a generally-wise commonsensical way of dealing with problems (that is, not being too hard on one's self, and focusing only on the things that one has the power to change). Now, with the second appearance of Jude's shoulders/shoulder, we also learn that he does not need to do it because something is *already* on his shoulders, and that is his own strength and resources. In other words, Jude has much more potential than he thinks he has, and that is where he should start from, to make the song better. Thirdly, pushing the interpretation a bit, one may even think that the image of the shoulders, instead of a parrot, may remind one of a metaphorical backpack containing Jude's experiences and resources, like those bundles tied on a stick that fairy tales' children fill with all they need before leaving home. If the *Norwegian Wood* addition had proved McCartney's ability to understand the potentials of narration, the *Hey Jude* confirmation now proves Lennon's skills with the potentials of images.

Finally, the ultimate demonstration of Lennon–McCartney's complementarity and ability to stimulate each other goes through an instance of total *improvisation*. As George Martin, The Beatles' artistic producer, had learned from the early days, whenever a song has a coda to be faded out, it is always wise to keep the recording on when Lennon and/or McCartney are performing their vocals: there is always the possibility that they will improvise some scat-singing or vocalizations that will add character and originality to the track (the chief example being the long coda of the just-mentioned *Hey Jude*). So, in early 1968, when The Beatles are recording an upbeat rock song which indeed has a fade-out ending planned, Martin leaves the microphone on as the couple is laying down the backing vocals. The song (written by Lennon) has no title yet, but it mentions a "bull-frog" and a "sheep-dog" on the way (again, as typical of the author, more as evocative images, rather than with specific narrative purposes). As the finale arrives, McCartney—inspired by the "sheepdog" passage—launches a howl, which already energizes the song, but most of all inaugurates a chain of improvised lines. After hearing the howl, Lennon has an illumination: he combines the bull-frog and the sheep-dog and starts singing *Hey Bulldog*! (which will become the actual title of the song), soon joined by the partner. A bit later, they both start bouncing dog-related sentences and jokes. In the end, the following dialog is committed on record:

> John Lennon: Ehh.
> Paul McCartney: Awooooo!
> JL: Hey, Bulldog
> JL & PM: Hey, Bulldog
> JL & PM: Hey, Bulldog
> JL & PM: Hey, Bulldog
> JL & PM: Hey, Bulldog
> PM: Hey man!
> JL: What's that boy?
> PM: Woof!
> JL: What did you say?
> PM: I said "Woof"
> JL: D'You know any more?
> PM: Awooooo! Aaaaaaaaaah hah hah!
> JL: You got it! That's right! Yeah.
> PM: That's it man, Wooohooo, That's it, you got it!
> JL: Ah ah ah ah ah!
> PM: Don't look at me man, I only have 10 children
> JL: Yahoo! Ahaa… ha ha ha ha ha ha ha
> PM: Quiet! Quiet!

3. Conclusions

The ideal conclusion to an essay like this would be to check two separately-written songs, one per author, that deal *exactly* with the same theme, written *exactly* at the same time and place, under *exactly* the same conditions. Unfortunately, there seems not to be such a case in The Beatles' discography. Or is there? If we abandon for a second the realm of official repertoire, we find that in 1968 John Lennon wrote a song (which remains unreleased to this day) that is perfectly simmetric (in the way I mentioned) to an officially-released one by Paul McCartney. Maybe he (or they) decided not to release it, precisely because there was no point in putting out two virtually identical songs; or maybe Lennon was not particularly happy with those lyrics, because what he actually did (three years later) was to record the same melody with totally different words, and that song became the very well-known *Jealous Guy*. The song I am talking about is *Child of Nature*, while its realeased *sister song* is McCartney's *Mother Nature's Son* (which appears on the 1968 album *The Beatles*, better known by its nickname *The White Album*).

It is interesting to compare the two lyrics, because indeed they constitute a unique example of Lennon and McCartney writing at the same time two different songs on the same subject and in the same context: during their period of meditation in Rishikesh, India (in early 1968), right after a lecture given by their guru Maharishi Mahesh Yogi on the position of human beings as "sons of the mother nature", they both disappeared into their respective bungalows to write a song. *Mother Nature's Son* is of course easily available on record, but *Child of Nature* too can be found on websites like YouTube without difficulty.

By comparing the two lyrics, it is intriguing that, faced with the same subject and conditions, the two authors employed their natural inclination to songwriting, displaying at least three of their most recurrent strategies. McCartney prefers an approach that is 1) more fictional (the song is in first person, but not entirely applicable to his life: to begin with, he was not born as a poor "country" boy, but he lived in a suburban area of Liverpool), 2) general (the song does not have any specific reference to the context where it was generated) and 3) active (things "happen" in this song, even if it is a relaxed/meditative one: he sits in different places, he sings songs, he sways daisies):

> Born a poor young country boy, Mother Nature's son
> All day long I'm sitting singing songs for everyone.

> Sit beside a mountain stream, see her waters rise
> Listen to the pretty sound of music as she flies.
>
> Find me in my field of grass, Mother Nature's son
> Swaying daisies sing a lazy song beneath the sun.
> …

Lennon, in turn, is 1) autobiographical (the song is clearly about him), 2) circumstantial (Rishikesh is mentioned, so the connection with the origin of the song is made explicit) and 3) reflexive (Lennon often prefers to describe his state of mind rather than his actions—significantly, while he is "on the road to Rishikesh" he is *dreaming*, rather than walking):

> On the road to Rishikesh
> I was dreaming more or less,
> And the dream I had was true
> Yes, the dream I had was true
>
> I'm just a child of nature
> I don't need much to set me free
> I'm just child of nature
> I'm one of nature's children
>
> Sunlight shining in your eyes
> As I face the desert skies
> And my thoughts return to home
> Yes, my thoughts return to home
>
> I'm just a child of nature
> …
>
> Underneath the mountain ranges
> Where the wind that never changes
> Touch the windows of my soul
> …

To wrap the whole argument up, the following table should approximately summarize the main songwriting elements/strategies of the pair, in relation to the semantic categories analyzed here.

	John Lennon	Paul McCartney
Models (roughly, in chronological order of appearance)	Rock'n'roll, Lewis Carroll, Bob Dylan, Yoko Ono/Fluxus avant-garde.	Rock'n'roll, Tin Pan Alley, Charles Dickens, Swinging London avant-garde.
Modalities	To be	To do
Narration	Weak	Strong
Point of view	Subjective	Objective
Imagery	Visual, imaginative, realist, emotional	Dynamic, verisimilar, surrealistic, descriptive
Contents	Autobiographic	Fictional
Recurrent themes	hic et nunc, universal/ personal love, "blues"	impersonal/personal love, loneliness, hope

Notes

[1] "FAIR USE" NOTICE: This article contains copyrighted material (excerpts from song lyrics), the use of which has not been specifically authorized by the copyright owners. I am making such material available exclusively in my efforts to advance understanding of issues of scholarly significance.

[2] Additional insights on the socio-cultural aspects of The Beatles' repertoire can be found in the very interesting Womack-Davis (2006).

[3] The use of the word "hero" in Lennon's above-mentioned manifesto-song is clearly metaphorical, and used for contrastive purposes: "As soon as you're born, they make you feel small."

[4] Needless to say, the whole genre's jargon was permeated with slang words for sexual activities (to rock, to roll, to twist, to shout, to shake, to rattle… they all mean one thing, really)

[5] Similarly to that artistic movement (of which he is a declared fan), McCartney's imagery may look verisimilar in almost everything, except that, here and there, queer or dreamy elements may appear, exactly like a melting clock or a disquieting muse in a totally ordinary context. In *Rocky Raccoon* (1968), for instance, we get a very linear narration of a cowboy seeking revenge against a rival in love, getting wounded in the duel, being checked by a drunken doctor and lying in a hotel room where a copy of the Gideon bible stands by the bed. Everything looks like a typical country and western story, except that, out of the blue, we hear "And now Rocky Raccoon he fell back in his room / Only to find Gideon's bible / Gideon checked out and he left it no doubt / To help with good Rocky's revival." The Gideon's bible ceases to be the typical hotel bible published by Gideons International, and becomes a book delivered by the actual Gideon, the bible character, who apparently was occupying the room right before Rocky.

6   While Lennon and George Harrison started using LSD from 1965 and in repeated instances, McCartney reportedly surrendered to the "peer pressure" (as he stated in an interview for The Beatles Anthology documentary) only in late 1966, and took the drug only a few times.

7   For more on this subject, I of course suggest the specifically-written Martinelli (2013).

8   A datum that we shall later confirm by the repeated appearance of the word "Yoko" in Lennon's songs.

9   Jude, for instance, is a variation of Julian, Lennon's son, whom McCartney was visiting at the time of Lennon's bitter divorce with his first wife Cynthia Powell. By singing "Hey Jules, don't make it bad, etc.," McCartney was meaning to console the then-5-year-old child, with whom he had developed a close bond of the "child–favorite uncle" type.

10 And of course one cannot help noticing how all these authors managed to produce some of their very best songs by again drawing from fiction and imagination: the sole example of Dylan's *Like a Rolling Stone*, arguably his most fascinating set of lyrics, would make a perfect case for the virtues of *thematic inauthenticity* in rock.

11 I have dealt more at length with the concept of authenticity in popular music in Martinelli (2010).

12 *Imagine* is credited to Lennon only, but by his own admission Ono would have deserved co-author status for providing the inspiration for the song concept (based on Ono's poem *Cloud Piece*, written in 1964), and specific verses (Blaney, 2007, p. 51).

13 While in some cases (like the 1971 album *Ram*) the use of the "Paul and Linda McCartney" credit was quasi-fictitious (and mostly motivated by Linda's "comments" on McCartney's compositional ideas), in the James Bond theme *Live and Let Die* the co-authorship was effective and tangible. The middle reggae-like bit that goes "What does it matter to ya? Etc." is entirely Mrs. McCartney's creation.

14 To say it all, however, McCartney later admitted that, in writing those lyrics, he might have unconsciously thought about his mother, whom he had lost when he was 14—that is, in "the past", in a "yesterday".

15 To be fair, anyway, it is not like rock critics *always* get it wrong, and clichés are *always* superficial. The well-known case of *Getting Better*, with McCartney writing lines like "I have to admit, it's getting better, a little better all the time" and Lennon replying, "It couldn't get much worse", sound like the most stereotypical opposition of the partnership, yet this is exactly what is going on: McCartney is doing the "Mr. Optimism" character, and Lennon is playing the cynical one.

16 Incidentally, dark humour and political incorrectness are two additional qualities that rock critics failed to notice in McCartney's songwriting. It has always fascinated me how a song like *Maxwell's Silver Hammer* is considered a fruity comedy-song, when its lyrics are about a ruthless serial killer and the point is exactly that of creating a sarcastic contrast between the cheerful music and such naughty verses.

References

Badman, K. (2001). *The Beatles diary, vol.2: After the break-Up*. London: Omnibus Press.

Blaney, J. (2007). *Lennon and McCartney: Together Alone*. London: Jawbone Press.

Eco, U. (1992). *Il secondo diario minimo*. Milano: Bompiani.

MacDonald, I. (1994). *Revolution in the head: the Beatles' records and the sixties*. New York: Random House.

Martinelli, D. (2010). *Authenticity, performance and other double-edged words. Essays on popular music*. Helsinki/Imatra: ISI.

Martinelli, D. (2013). Fur is over, if you want it: Environmentalism and animal advocacy in The Beatles' repertoire. Paper presented at the Symposium *Music and Environment* (Technological University of Sydney, Australia, April 2, 2013)

Miles, B. (1997). *Paul McCartney, Many years from now*. London: Vintage.

Norman, P. (1981/2003). *Shout! The true story of the Beatles*. 3rd edition. London: Pan Macmillan.

Petrie, K. J., Pennebaker, J.W, & Sivertsen, B. (2008). Things we said today: a linguistic analysis of the Beatles. *Psychology of Aesthetics, Creativity, and the* Arts, *2*(4), 197–202.

Rodriguez, R. (2010). Fab four FAQ 2.0: The Beatles' solo years 1970–1980. Milwaukee: Hal Leonard.

Roylance, B. (Ed.) (2000). *The Beatles anthology*. San Francisco: Chronicle Books.

Womack, K., & Davis, T.F. (Eds.) (2006). *Reading the Beatles: Cultural studies, literary criticism and the Fab Four*. Albany, NY: State University of New York Press.

The Sublime as a Topic in Beethoven's Late Piano Sonatas

Jamie Liddle

The Open University, UK

"The moral law within us, and the starry heavens above us" Kant!!!
(Beethoven, 1972, p. 235)

1. The sublime – Burke and Kant

Over the last two decades several studies (Bonds, 1997, 2006; Brown, 1996; Sisman, 1993; Webster, 1997) have discussed the relationship between music and the sublime in pre-Romantic aesthetics, examining the evocation of the sublime in the music of the late 18th century. These writers have naturally focused on the two most influential conceptions of the sublime within that cultural context, those of Burke (*A Philosophical Enquiry into the Origin of our Ideas of the Sublime and Beautiful,* 1757) and Kant (*Critique of Judgment,* 1790). The Burkean sublime begins with "whatever is in any sort terrible, or is conversant about terrible objects, or operates in a manner analogous to terror" (Burke, 1757, p. 39). Such terrible objects produce in the observer the effects of mingled terror (or pain) and pleasure: terror arising from the apprehension of the immeasurably large and powerful; pleasure at observing this from a place of safety. A storm at sea is therefore sublime, but only if one is not actually involved with it at the time. The Burkean sublime thus involves a certain aetheticising contemplation of the great and terrible in order to produce its effect, and this implicitly suggests that the locus of the sublime does not reside in the sublime object itself, but rather in the conception of the observer; the sublime is a quality of mind, not of objects.

The Kantian sublime explicitly develops this notion. The sublime for Kant is to be found in a "formless object" (Kant and Pluhar, 1987, p. 98), an object whose form is of such magnitude that it exceeds our powers of perception. Crucially, this formlessness, which Kant terms "unboundedness", is always accompanied by a "thought of totality" (Kant and Pluhar, 1987, p. 98), that is, a conception of the mind that allows reason to understand the magnitude of the unbounded, even if the imagination cannot perceive it. Kant refines his definition by distinguishing the *mathematical* from the *dynamic* sublime. In the mathematical sublime the imagination is overwhelmed by temporal or spatial magnitude: the experience is too great to be taken in at once (it is unbounded and formless); we cannot perceive infinite size. The dynamic sublime, in contrast, is evoked by overwhelming or infinite power, in the face of which we are rendered helpless: volcanoes, hurricanes "the boundless ocean"; "compared to the might of any of these, our ability to resist becomes an insignificant trifle" (Kant and Pluhar, 1987, p. 120). We experience again the mixed pleasure and pain familiar from Burke.

In both instances though, the central point of Kant's conception is that the sublime is not a quality of the object itself; rather, it is an attribute of the reason of the observer. The sublime arises only after there is an initial check to the perceptions and imagination by the mathematical or dynamic; there is a frustration when the inability to perceive or overcome the infinite is encountered. This frustration, however, is supplanted by the sublime moment when the power of reason overcomes this: we are unable to perceive infinity, but we are able to understand it as an Idea (the *thought of totality*). The source of the sublime thus resides explicitly in the mind, rather than in objects: it is the discovery of the transcendence of reason over the inadequacy of perception and our finiteness; it is the discovery of the infinite within.

2. The post-Kantian sublime and art

The Kantian sublime was deeply problematic for the Early Romantic poets and philosophers. Kant's sublime reveals the transcendental dimensions of experience, the capacity of the individual to exceed unbounded nature, but in doing so it separates him irrevocably from the phenomenal world—he is forever removed from nature. This disjunction between the noumenal and the phenomenal within oneself inevitably results in an unending yearning for reconciliation, the "infinite longing" that Hoffmann (1810, p. 238) described as the essence of Romanticism. The solution to this problem that writers such as the Schlegel brothers, Schelling, Wackenroder and Tieck proposed was to be found in the arts: in art the Ideal and the real, the noumenal and phenomenal, the infinite and finite are reunited; in art we experience a perceptible manifestation of the Ideal. For the early Romantics the art that achieved this most fully was music. Unlike the other arts, music was considered to be "ideal in its essence" (A.W. Schlegel, qtd. in Bonds, 2006, p. 21), it was understood to be non-representational and even incorporeal, and thus uniquely placed to reunite the noumenal and phenomenal. Schelling in 1802 (1981, p. 280), for example, considered that

> Musical form is a process whereby the infinite is embodied in the finite; hence the forms of music are inevitably forms of things in themselves. In other words, they are forms of ideas exclusively under a phenomenal guise [...] music brings before us in rhythm and harmony the [platonic] form of the motions of physical bodies; it is, in other words, pure form, liberated from any object or from matter.

Since music alone could truly manifest the Ideal in the real, the result was that for the Romantics the goal of music must explicitly be to create such a perceptible manifestation of the infinite. Crucially, this emphasis on music as an intuition of the infinite inevitably aligns it with the aesthetics of the sublime; the apprehension of the infinite is at the heart of Kant's conception. The early-Romantic aesthetic of music, in other words, was that rather than being able to express the sublime, music was placed in the unenviable position of actually having to *be* sublime, to create or evoke the effect of the sublime within the listener.

3. The sublime as musical topic

The understanding of music as sublime was relatively short-lived—it is essentially an early-Romantic viewpoint—but it had a pervasive effect on aesthetics and criticism, persisting through much of the nineteenth century. However, the studies by Bonds, Brown, Sisman and Webster highlighted above have each turned to pre-Romantic aesthetics instead, drawing on writers such as Sulzer, Michaelis and Crotch in order to establish characteristics that were used to create the effect of the sublime or, in some cases, to evoke a sublime "style", largely within the music of Haydn and Mozart. Webster, for example, identifies various types of contrast that he argues Haydn uses to create sublime effects: contrasts of dynamics, register, rhythm and harmony. He adds that devices such as "gestural shocks" (sudden, unexpected contrasts), tonal or generic incongruities and certain types of musical climaxes can all be used to create the effect of the "incommensurable", which he associates with the sublime (Webster, 1997, p. 70). Through this approach, these authors gravitate more or less explicitly towards the notion of a topical signification of the sublime; their studies essentially raise the question of whether the sublime can occur as a musical topic. This represents an important change of emphasis, because the possibility of topical signification suggests, contra Romanticism, that rather than having to create the effect of the sublime—rather than aiming to *be* sublime—music may *signify* the sublime as a subject of its discourse.

Wye Jamieson Allanbrook (2010), however, has argued that the sublime cannot function as a topic in music, largely because the identification of a stable signifier is problematic; there are no conventional figures that invariably and recognisably evoke the sublime as a topic. Instead, she argues, sublimity is consistently associated with excesses of what Leonard Meyer termed *secondary parameters*—dynamics, forces, range etc. Such excess is essentially a quantitative marker, which inevitably raises the issue of how much musical excess is required to suggest the infinite, or to produce shock and awe. This is compounded by developmental issues; what might once have been considered as shocking, sudden or sublime quickly becomes normalized and therefore loses the ability to create an overpowering effect. The evocation of the musical sublime is thus frequently reduced to a question of degree, thereby becoming unquantifiable and subjective, hardly suited to topical signification.

However, whilst the objections raised by Allanbrook might be true of many instrumental genres, particularly the symphony, I would argue that the piano music of the nineteenth century does offer the potential for signifying the sublime topically. This genre forms a distinctive musical sub-culture, producing topics and signifiers that are unique to that subculture, and I will consider the manner in which one specific gesture functions, at the least, as a "prototopic" (Monelle, 2000, p. 17) of the sublime, i.e. a relatively stable, conventionalised signifier.

4. The pianistic sublime

The simultaneous (or near-simultaneous) sounding of the extreme registers of the instrument creates an emergent musical meaning that consistently signifies extremes of magnitude. This correlation is essentially based on the "high-low" associations of pitch with "up-down"; simultaneously high and low pitch will always correlate with simultaneous "up and down" i.e. with a physical space (or perhaps object) that is extremely large. This is often combined with extremes of dynamic, texture and virtuosity to produce a correlation with extreme force. Within the aesthetic context of the late eighteenth and early nineteenth centuries the emergent meaning of overwhelming size and power produced by this gesture suggests an obvious correlation with the extremes that characterize the well-established "cultural unit" (Eco, 1977) of the sublime[1]. Crucially, although these correlations depend upon the "secondary parameters" of dynamic, texture and range, the accretion of these individual parameters results in a characteristic, recognisable gesture, whose function is more-or-less invariable—a stable signifier in other words. The recurrence of this stable signifier in similar situations across numerous individual works thus suggests a process of topical semiosis, in short, a topic of the sublime[2].

Significantly, this pianistic topic of the sublime inherently highlights the limits of human perception. Playing the extreme registers of the instrument pushes towards the limits of the audible spectrum; beyond these points it becomes increasingly difficult to distinguish distinct pitches, and it is also difficult to hear individual melodies so far apart, to hold both in the mind's ear at the same time. Moreover, this gesture frequently exposes the limitations of the instrument; its use pushes towards the extremes of the possible and, in cases such as the first movement of Beethoven's *Hammerklavier* sonata, almost beyond them. Thus, the more obvious connotations of the gesture also point inextricably towards the limits of the listener, the instrument and indeed even of music itself. In doing so, this topic may also signify not simply extremes of magnitude or force, but also the boundary between the finite and the infinite that characterises sublimity.

This topic does not really arise in the earlier piano repertoire, largely because of developmental issues (it does not seem to occur in Mozart or Haydn, for example). However, it can be found in Beethoven's piano sonatas, particularly the late works, where it produces a striking and unusual effect. As the piano literature developed through the nineteenth century this topic became more common, and its basic connotations are retained even into the 20th century[3]. In the music of Chopin, Liszt and even Ravel this topic is almost invariably dysphoric in connotation, with a tendency to emphasize the marked minor mode (frequently with dissonance and chromaticism), as well as excesses of texture and virtuosity. This basic dysphoria tends to produce a correlation of this gesture with the negative extremes that characterize Burke's conception of the sublime—the mingling of terror and pleasure.

The opening of Chopin's Etude in A minor op. 25 number 11 (figure 1[4]), for example, produces a troping of this sublime topic with the topical allusions created by the slow march theme that begins the piece. This main theme, with its slow tempo and plangent semitone, evokes a funeral march on its first appearance; when it is subsequently harmonized a more elegiac variant of the topic results—a noble, military hymn. This is contrasted immediately with the gesture described above: extremes of dynamic, register and virtuosic figuration produce a sudden moment of overwhelming force, a juxtaposition that creates a gestural shock of the type suggested by Webster.

The striking appearance of this second topic creates a relatively straightforward signification of sublime force, overwhelmingly dysphoric in nature because of the unequivocal minor key. The troping of this signification with the march topic, however, produces a more complex signification that transforms the character of the theme from pathos to heroism (Samson, 1985, p. 72), the combination of the sublime and military aspects perhaps suggesting the sublimity of war, for example.[5]

FIGURE 1. Chopin Op. 25 No. 11, bars 1-8

5. Beethoven Op. 110 - Finale

In contrast to the Burkean overtones of such Romantic instances of this topic, I would suggest that earlier manifestations in the music of Beethoven centre on the Kantian sublime; they signify not the sublime terror of Burke, but the transcendental apprehension that is the locus of Kant's conception. This is seen most clearly in the finale of the Ab Piano Sonata, Op. 110[6]: as so often in Beethoven's late works it is this movement that is the longest and most significant movement, functioning as the focus of the entire piece. This movement is constructed as a clear opposition of two entirely contrasting topics, which are juxtaposed into four sections with a transformative coda. In this movement Beethoven uses topical signification in an overt way, drawing not on conventional forms, but conventional signifiers to create the movement.

The two topics that he uses could hardly be more opposed. The first part of the movement comprises an aria topic (figure 2), preceded by a recitative, both of which also evoke Ratner's *Empfindsamkeit* topic (Ratner, 1980, p. 22). After the aria has run its course it is opposed directly to a second topic, that of the learned style, which is clearly evoked through the use of fugue (figure. 3).

This opposition operates on several levels, the first of which is a basic opposition of dysphoric and euphoric significations: the aria is unremittingly tragic in its expression (it is in a minor key and comprises overwhelmingly descending lines with a strong emphasis on the descending semitone) and this is contrasted with the more positive assertion of the fugal theme (in a major key, with an ascending line that moves by ascending leaps of a fourth; even the 6/8 metre might be considered to evoke something of the pastoral).

FIGURE **2.** Beethoven Op. 110, bars 9-12

More importantly, this juxtaposition creates an explicit opposition between the significations of the topics themselves. In drawing upon the aria topic (a transcontextualisation of an inherently vocal form) Beethoven overtly invokes the individuality and expressionism of that operatic form as part of the "meaning" of the finale[7]; the pathos of the *Empfindsamkeit* style heightens the intensely emotive, individualistic quality of the section. The use of the learned style, in contrast, gestures towards compositional artifice, appealing explicitly to the intellect[8]. Indeed, this can be taken further, by suggesting that the use of strict counterpoint evokes the notion of compositional order, of complex compositional thought: the learned style signifies the reason of a compositional mind. This opposition of topics thus creates an explicit contrast between the emotions and the mind, and this fundamental dialectic produces a narrative trajectory across the movement as the topics interact and develop[9].

FIGURE 3. Beethoven Op. 110, 3rd movement, bars 26-46

The course of this narrative is important in understanding the topic of the sublime that occurs in the coda; this arrives at the climax of a long process. The learned style topic is initially presented as the antithesis of the overt emotionalism of the aria; reason is asserted strongly against tragedy and emotionalism. After the initial juxtaposition of the topics, however, an intensified version of the aria returns, its melodic line continually fragmented, punctuated by rests so frequently that it resembles a voice struggling through excess emotion (figure 4). This coincides with a harmonic disjunction as the music is wrenched into the remote key of G minor.

FIGURE 4. Beethoven Op. 110, 3rd movement, bars 116-119

This intensification of the aria transforms the subsequent return of the fugal section: the theme is inverted, removing the assertion of the original, and this is compounded by the ambiguous tonality, which, although ostensibly in G major, is inflected with the dysphoric minor throughout (figure 5). As the fugue develops this turns increasingly towards the minor, coinciding with a marked increase in contrapuntal complexity as stretto entries of the original thematic contour combine with simultaneous diminution and augmentation.

FIGURE 5. Beethoven Op. 110, 3ʳᵈ movement, bars 136-147

This process culminates in the dissolution of the fugue as the tightening entries produce rhythmic saturation: what emerges over the strong minor entry in the bass (bar 160f) is a thematic fragment, doubled in thirds and sixths, which is eventually reduced simply to alternating fourths. In this way the intensified aria seems to affect the "reason" of the learned style topic; it inverts and becomes increasingly dysphoric, before the very processes that define it—the contrapuntal techniques—all but exhaust themselves. Thus, despite the increase in rhythmic vitality (heralded in the *Nach und nach wieder auflebend* marking) there is almost a breakdown of the "reason" of the learned style topic.

The breakdown of the fugue, however, serves a transitional function: after the harmonic dislocation created by the G minor aria, the alternating fourths finally arrive back on the dominant, triggering a faster transition passage, based on a yet greater diminution of the fugal theme. Following this, the coda is announced by an emphatic restatement of the original fugal theme in the tonic, a powerful bass entry in octaves with fast, complex accompanying figuration. This return of the theme builds inexorably over 35 bars of music, continually ascending with the hands moving progressively further apart, out to the limits of the keyboard, combining the extremes of register with extremes of dynamic and texture to arrive at the final climactic passage of the entire sonata (figure 6).

FIGURE **6.** Beethoven Op. 110, 3ʳᵈ movement, bars 200-2013

It is this point in the finale that I argue gestures towards the sublime. The extremes of register, dynamic and texture create an emergent meaning that will invariably be correlated with extremes of size and power. This climax arrives at the limits of music, and in doing so it arrives at the limits of the finite, the limits of perception. At its height this gesture transgresses the beautiful completely—the sound produced is pure power, at the limits of register, dynamic and process. At this point beauty is no longer an adequate aesthetic to understand the music; we turn towards the sublime instead. (That this moment of transcendence is brief is, perhaps, indicative of its sublime nature: the sublime is always fleeting; it is the thunderbolt that overwhelms, the flash of lightning, the moment of transcendental apprehension.)

Crucially, the arrival of this sublime climax is directly connected to the assertion of the fugal theme. Although the theme is transformed at this point[10], the association with the learned style topic is still retained; it is still a recognisable fugal theme, and it carries the memory of the earlier fugal treatment. I would argue that there is therefore a troping of the "reason" of the learned style—the dominance of the mind, rather than the emotions— with this sublime topic. The transcendent moment at the climax of the whole sonata is not achieved by overt, individualized emotionalism, but rather by musical reason. Beethoven is not engaged in simple mimesis here—the representation of a sublime *object*—nor is he invoking a Burkean terror in the listener. Rather, in the troping of reason with the sublime the transformative climax of this movement is as close to a topical signification of the Kantian sublime as possible. Beethoven's music here signifies an overwhelming power than reveals the limits of the finite, gesturing towards the infinite. It presents a sophisticated symbol, not just of a sublime object, but rather of the moment of the transcendental apprehension of the sublime, the ability of reason to grasp the infinite.

Notes

1 The association of the extreme registers of the piano with the sublime is also made briefly by Hatten in his discussion of Beethoven's *Ghost* Trio, Op. 70 no. 1 (2004, p. 32). Kinderman makes a similar point concerning the "astonishing disjunction in pitch" that marks the transition from the Credo to the Benedictus in the *Missa Solemnis*: there the high registers in particular "evoke celestial regions that transcend earthly existence; their symbolic importance is unmistakable" (2009, pp. 277-278).

2 I have identified this as a topic, in preference to Monelle's "prototopic" because the association of the gesture with the sublime moves beyond iconic signification (size, power etc.) towards indexicality.

3 This gesture may be found in prominent locations within, for example, Chopin's *Etude*, Op. 25 nos. 10 and 11, Liszt's *Chasse Neige, Sposalizio* and *Après une Lecture du Dante* and Brahms' 1st and 3rd Piano Sonatas; it is even found amongst character sketches such as Burgmüller's *L'Orage*. Twentieth century works that feature this gesture include Ravel's *Ondine* from *Gaspard de la Nuit*, Prokofiev's *Suggestion diabolique* Op. 4, No 4 and the 3rd Piano Sonata and even Debussy's *Feux d'Artifice*. This represents only a very selective sampling of the significant number of works in which this gesture may be found.

4 All musical examples in this paper are reproduced by kind permission of Peters Edition Limited, London.

5 Although this brief analysis focuses on the topical allusions of the march theme in interpreting its troping with the "sublime" topic, it is worth considering the alternative imagery evoked by the title that is often appended to this piece; the "Winter Wind" is itself a source of the Burkean sublime.

6 The Ab Sonata Op. 110 forms the focus of the present analysis, but it is important to consider that the topic of the sublime suggested here also features prominently in the *Hammerklavier* sonata, Op. 106, as well as in both Op. 109 and 111. In each of these cases the troping of this gesture with other topics produces what might be considered different facets of the sublime: the occurrence of this topic in the penultimate variation of the finale of Op. 109, for example, is inherently associated with the religious connotations of the hymn-like theme, this combination of topics suggesting an epiphanic moment of quasi-spiritual transcendence.

7 Agawu discusses the use of aria as a topic, demonstrating its occurrence elsewhere in Beethoven's instrumental music, particularly the *Pathétique* Sonata and the A minor quartet Op. 132 (see Agawu (1991, pp. 28-30, 44, 114).

8 On the relationship between the learned style and the intellect see Sisman (1993, pp. 70/1).

Jamie Liddle

⁹ It is also noteworthy that, in addition to the main opposition considered here, the individuality of the vocal expression of the aria is also opposed to the plurality of voices that is inherent within a fugue. There is a sense then in which the opposition of the two topics in this movement thus functions on several levels: emotionalism vs. the intellect, individuality vs. community, the gallant style vs. the strict style etc. This plurality of oppositions indicates something of the wide range of connotations present in individual topics, highlighting the semantic richness of the universe of topical signification.

¹⁰ Hatten, for example, sees the transformation of the theme as the transcendence of "Classical lyricism and heroism" over the fugal style, its climax achieving "spiritual affirmation" (Hatten, 2004, p. 254).

References

Agawu, V. K. (1991). *Playing with signs*. Princeton, N.J.: Princeton University Press.

Allanbrook, W. J. (2010). Is the sublime a musical topos? *Eighteenth-century Music, 7*(2), 263–279.

Beethoven, L. v. (1972). *Ludwig van Beethovens Konversationshefte*. Vol. 1. K. Köhler, G. Herre and G. Brosche (Eds.). Leipzig: VEB Deutscher Verlag für Musik

Bonds, M.E. (2006). *Music as thought: listening to the symphony in the age of Beethoven*. Princeton, New Jersey: Princeton University Press.

Bonds, M.E. (1997). The symphony as pindaric ode. In E. Sisman (Ed.), *Haydn and his world* (pp. 131–153). Princeton, N. J.: Princeton University Press.

Burke, E. (1757) *A philosophical enquiry into the origin of our ideas of the sublime and beautiful*. J.T. Boulton, (Ed.) (1967) London: Routledge & Kegan Paul Ltd.

Brown, A. P. (1996) The sublime, the beautiful and the ornamental: English aesthetic currents and Haydn's London symphonies. In O. Biba, & D. Wyn Jones, (Eds.), *Studies in Music History, presented to H. C. Robbins Langdon on his seventieth birthday* (pp. 44-71). London: Thames and Hudson.

Eco, U. (1977). *A theory of semiotics*. London: Macmillan

Hatten, R. (2004). *Interpreting musical gestures, topics, and tropes*. Mozart, Beethoven, Schubert. Bloomington, Indianapolis: Indiana University Press.

Hoffmann, E. T. A. (1810, 4th and 11th July). Recension von Beethovens 5. Symphonie. *Allgemeine musikalische Zeitschrift*.

Kant, I., & Pluhar, W. S. (1987). *Critique of judgment*. Indianapolis, Ind.: Hackett Pub. Co.

Kinderman, W. (2009). *Beethoven*. 2nd ed. Oxford: Oxford University Press

Monelle, R. (2000). *The sense of music: Semiotic essays*. Princeton, N.J. & Oxford: Princeton University Press.

Ratner, L. (1980). *Classic music: Expression, form, and style*. New York: Schirmer.

Samson, J. (1985). *The music of Chopin*. London, Boston & Henley: Routledge & Kegan Paul

Schelling, F.W.J von (1981). Extracts from *Philosophie der Kunst*. In P. le Huray, & J. Day (Eds.). *Music and aesthetics in the eighteenth and early-nineteenth centuries* (pp. 274-281). Cambridge, Cambridge University Press.

Sisman, E. (1993). *Mozart: the 'Jupiter' symphony*. Cambridge: Cambridge University Press.

Webster, J. (1997). The Creation, Haydn's late vocal music, and the musical sublime. In E. Sisman (Ed.) *Haydn and his world* (pp. 131–153). Princeton, N.J.: Princeton University Press.

Melodic Forces and Agential Energies: An Integrative Approach to the Analysis and Expressive Interpretation of Tonal Melodies

Robert S. Hatten
University of Texas at Austin

1. Characterizing melody

Melody is not merely a sequence of pitches in a certain rhythm often found in the upper voice. When we hear, and follow, the melody of a tonal composition, we are experiencing an emergent quality that I call *melos*, which I define as the *foregrounded and continuous expressive focus associated with the principal musical discourse of a virtual human agent*. Following the *melos* may lead us from one voice-leading to another, and even from one line in the texture to another, regardless of register (Pierce, 2007, pp. 46-49) or even timbre (Webern's *Klangfarbenmelodie*). *Melos* may at times be enhanced or thickened or refracted by associated contrapuntal, imitative, or accompanimental lines that are derived from the primary melos and are thus highly dependent upon it.

Perceptually, a melody is a *temporal gestalt*: we hear its continuity in terms of its coherent unfolding, and we remember it as a whole because of the impelling implications of its energies—its shaping through time. Our capacity to form meaningful temporal gestalts from even isolated perceptual flashes of information is evolutionarily embedded, based on the survival value of, for example, interpreting a predator from discontinuous percepts that imply the continuous movement of an agent (e.g., a tiger stalking through tall grass). Rousseau (1781) argued that melody originated in the primal vocal gestures or utterances of primitive humans, and scientific research supports the view that an infant's innate as well as interactively developed gestural competencies underlie the subsequent development of both language and music (Trevarthen, 1986). Thus, the most basic cognition of melody as energetic shaping has a deep biological rootedness; we understand immediately the potential for an ascending contour to increase expressive tension and a descending contour to release it, as familiar to us from the vocalization of sighs and vocal gestures prior to the intonation curves of speech.

When melody evolves into patterns of discrete pitches as theorized by modal systems, it is not simply relegated to an abstract permutation of those pitches as confined by divisions of the octave into fifth and fourth.[1] Chant also draws on a concept known as *centonization*: characteristic motives that are expressive of the mode's intervallic *distinctive features*.[2] Later tonal melodies also move beyond stepwise voice-leadings to exploit leaps that feature characteristic intervals or voice-leadings in a key, such as the striking diminished fourths featured in the opening theme from the C minor slow movement of Schubert's Piano Trio in Eb major, op. 100, perhaps inspired by the motto opening of the Allegro theme in Beethoven's Piano Sonata in C minor, Op. 111. These gestures can become what Asafiev in 1947 (Asafiev & Tull, 1977) termed *intonations*, or characteristic motivic patterns that, through frequent use, carry familiar associations for a given style. Some melodic intonations may also be theorized as topical figures, such as the *pianto* or sigh (Monelle, 2000), or they may arise from the melodic expansion of ornaments—an example being the turn figure, expanded to create what Meyer (1973) terms axial melodies. The intonations of language may play a role either in terms of characteristic inflections (Beethoven's "Muss es sein? Es muss sein!") or as inspired by literal speech melodies (as in the operas of Mussorgsky, Janáček, Shostakovich, and Kurt Weill, or more recently in the works of Steve Reich).

Due to its expressive use of leaps, tonal melody may exhibit segregation into registrally discrete voice-leadings, creating what is known as compound melody. But melody may also generate its own texture polyphonically, from simple echoes to the systematically imitative procedures of the Baroque. Melody may be thickened by unsystematic heterophony, as exhibited by many native cultures when a group of men and women sing a monophonic *melos*, or by systematic *planing*, as in Debussy's chord streams of triads, sevenths, and ninth chords. Such harmonic thickening of a single line was an early discovery in the Renaissance; what we would call descending parallel 6/3 chords were described as *fauxbourdon*. Melody may be enhanced in terms of overtone resonance, as already suggested by the organ, when applying the quint or tierce (a twelfth or a seventeenth) to a single line. I have discovered examples of overtone resonance explicitly notated by Beethoven and Schubert (Hatten, 1993). And *melos* may be enhanced by the more subtle *Decktonen*, Schenker's cover tones, as found in the Haydn sonata movement discussed below.

But what gives melody its expressive force is often summarized as its *energetic shape*—as variously theorized by Kurth (1956), Toch (1948), Zuckerkandl (1956), and myself (Hatten, 2004). Such energetic shaping is often characterized by organic analogues of growth (expansion/decay) or other human gestural analogues of expressive meaning (yearning/yielding). One of the most fundamental gestural analogues is that between a melody and the breath: a prototypical tonal melody "sings" in breath groupings, and those groups wind down to closure as coordinated with the falling off suggested by the expenditure of breath. In tonal music, breath-units are formalized into phrases, and structured hierarchically into sentences or periods, articulated by not only melodic but also harmonic cadences. Tonal *melos* stitches together such phrases into a continuous thematic *discourse*, evolving through the techniques of variation, development, and developing variation (Schoenberg, Carpenter, & Neff, 2006), as seen in the Mozart sonata below. Instead of aligning its closure with harmonic closure, however, a melody may "liquidate" (Schoenberg), transforming into either closural dissolution or transitional fragmentation, or "precipitate"—my term for condensation to a fundamental motive. Along the way, the thread of *melos*, its *filo* (Allanbrook, 1992), can take on various formal functions, ranging from thematic to transitional/ developmental to closural/cadential (Caplin, 1998), and topical characters, ranging from prototypical singing style to more instrumental *Sturm und Drang* or brilliant style (Ratner, 1980; Allanbrook, 1983).

But a melody can also feature those discontinuities we associate with impassioned speech—breaks that reflect more powerful emotion (as characteristic of *empfindsamer* style), thus providing melody an expressive range from aria through arioso to lyrical or dramatic recitative. Within a lyrical theme, disruptions—what I call *rhetorical gestures* (Hatten, 2004)— may be absorbed, or themselves *thematized* as part of a dramatic discourse, thus enabling melody to extend beyond the lyric mode to imply dramatic agency. Such rhetorical gestures may even suggest what I call *shifts in level of discourse* (Hatten, 1994), enabling a melody to comment upon itself by means of a *narrative agency* (Hatten, 2004).

Of course, all of these extra resources of melody draw upon its contextual resources in harmony, counterpoint, rhythm, meter, timbre, texture, form, etc. In other words, melody's expressive force is *emergent*, not only from its own contoural, voice-leading, gestural, topical, continuous, and discontinuous properties, but from its syntheses with (or thematic opposition to) all the other aspects of the texture. With respect to thematic opposition, I have shown how a single theme (the main theme launching the finale of Beethoven's

Op. 101) can incorporate a successive opposition of topics (familiar types such as fanfare or pastoral musette), and that dialogical opposition may be developed tropologically, by combining or fusing the general expressive meanings of the topics in a way akin to metaphor (Hatten, 1994). Monelle (2000) has similarly demonstrated how the subject and countersubject in Bach's A♭ major fugue from WTC II, topically oppositional, can interact tropologically throughout the fugue. And most recently (Hatten, 2014), I have demonstrated even further tropological interaction in the famous example quoted by Ratner (1980) and Allanbrook (1983, 1992), the opening theme of Mozart's Piano Sonata in F major, K. 332. The opening theme features a troping of four topics: singing style (melody and Alberti bass), pastoral (pedal point and emphasis on the subdominant), *Ländler* (3/4 meter and dance gestures), and yodeling (alternating melodic leaps), as well as an interruption by means of a rhetorical gesture with potential *empfindsamer* character in m. 4, leading to a learned style treatment of the yodeling figure (imitation in m. 7, suspension in m. 8). *Melos* is particularly enhanced by topical flavorings in this example.

As an *unmarked* (Hatten, 1994) or general concept, melody often refers simply to the upper voice, and theorists often substitute more clinical terms such as line, voice (leading), motive, or theme (which may include harmony). Yet even the strict practices of counterpoint reference a "cantus," and the sung aspect of a "voice" is a distinctive property of melody as a marked term. Proto-typical melodic structures in instrumental music are often marked "cantabile," which implies legato execution, and their singability is based on a more vocal range (tessitura) and intervallic content (primarily stepwise, with only the oc-casional expressive leap, and with dissonances carefully resolved). By extreme contrast, an instrumental "line" comprised of isolated "points" will not be interpretable as a melody if it exceeds gestalt constraints for temporal conti-nuity; pointillism as a style is intended to achieve that negation of vocal *melos*.

Because of its vocal origins, however, most tonal melodies imply human expression—the intimacy of the voice, the breath, the bodily vibration, the intonation—as carriers of direct feeling. These aspects are modeled, with more or less intimacy, in instruments that can accurately reflect the bodily gestures of their performers as analogues to the voice, even when manipulations of motives may suggest that a melodic gesture has been sublimated from its immediacy as index into a more abstract status as symbol (Lidov, 2005, p. 157). However, the *implications* of linear and disjunct motion and patterning in a tonal field, as theorized by Meyer (1973) can actually enhance the palpability of expectations and the sense of organic urgings attributed to gestures in a tonal melody, which can be experienced as a virtual body moving in what I call a *virtual environment* (Hatten, 2004). Steve Larson (2012) offers a compelling account of tonal (and metric) analogues to physical forces such as gravity, magnetism, and inertia that constitute the *virtual environment* within which we hear a melody's own agential forces being constrained—analogous to those forces working on the body in the real world (Hatten, 2004). Example 1 shows these forces acting on pitches in a simple melodic descent: *gravity* (G) pulls 4 or 2 down to a stable platform (3 or 1), *inertia* (I) reflects the tendency of a process or pattern to continue (even past a stable platform, here, past the tonic C to B), and *magnetism* (M) reflects the tendency of a pitch to move to the closest stable pitch (hence, F is more attracted to E than to G, and B is more attracted to C than to A). My own contribution to these forces, and my complementary account of agential forces (Hatten, 2012), will inform the following analyses and expressive interpretations of tonal melodies in works from Bach to Chopin.

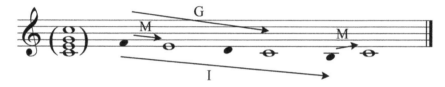

FIGURE 1. An illustration of Steve Larson's musical forces (from Hatten, 2012)

2. Analyses and interpretations

My choice of melodies to examine embraces a variety of styles (Baroque, Classical, Romantic) as exemplified by keyboard or piano works in slower tempi, where melody is most transparent and emotionally powerful:
1. Bach, Sinfonia in E minor, BWV 793
2. Haydn, Piano Sonata in A♭ major, Hob. XVI/46, C. Landon, no. 31, II. Adagio
3. Mozart, Piano Sonata in F major, K. 533, II. Andante
4. Beethoven, Piano Sonata in A♭ major, Op. 13, II. Adagio cantabile
5. Chopin, Nocturne in B major, Op. 62, no. 1

Robert S. Hatten

2.1 Beethoven, Piano Sonata in Ab major, Op. 13, II. Adagio cantabile

Beethoven's *Adagio cantabile* is well-known enough to be recognized by his tempo and character designation alone. We know from descriptions of Beethoven's playing that, in contrast to Mozart's technique, he favored an unbroken finger legato achieved in part by slightly overlapping the pitches. The designation "cantabile" may be understood to imply this rich legato, and thus Beethoven's notated slurs are free to indicate, not legato, but accentuation. In their treatises, C.P.E. Bach, Quantz, and Leopold Mozart agree that the beginning of a slur implies a slight accentuation or emphasis. Beethoven's slurs for this theme (Figure 2) do not always correspond with the downbeat (the *gravitational* platform of the meter, according to Larson); hence, his melody resists the gravitational pull of the downbeat (see mm. 2, 5, and 7), creating a physiological sense of lifting. This independence from the virtual environment of the meter and its implied weight lends individual character to the melody and contributes to our impression of a virtual agent with its own will. The concept of agency (Hatten, 2010b, 2012) is historically emergent and significant for what we think of as melody, in that the *embodiment* of tonal energy takes us far beyond the perceptual gestalt of a temporal sequence of pitches. Agency endows that temporal sequence with not only an individual identity, but also a sense of intentionality ("will"), and ultimately expressive meaning and spiritual significance.

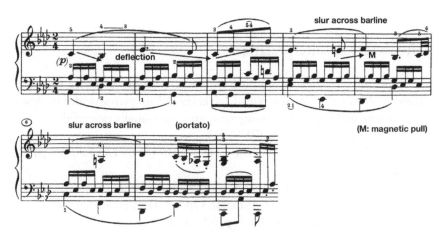

Figure 2. Beethoven, Piano Sonata in C Minor, Op. 13, second movement (Ab major), main theme, mm. 1-8. © Copyright 1952/1980 by Henle Verlag, München

Meyer's (1973) concept of melodic implication is grounded in patterns, both stylistic and strategic (or work-specific) that tend to continue in predictable ways; Larson refers to such continuational forces in the tonal field as analogous to *inertia*. I prefer the term *momentum* because agential energy is clearly required to create the initial movement, especially when it counters the pull of gravity, and to maintain movement against decay due to what I call *friction* (Hatten, 2012). Beethoven's *Adagio cantabile* melody begins with a pattern that might well have given in to the gravitational pull of the Ab tonic platform (C-Bb-Ab), but he chooses instead to leap from Bb up to Eb. This deflection (Meyer, 1973) or reversal (Narmour, 1990) requires energy, and hence implies an agent both willing and able to exert it (Hatten, 2012). Eb then yields to the gravitational pull downward toward a stable tonal platform provided by the tonic chord's scale-degree 3. Gravity is here enhanced by the magnetic pull of the half-step from Db to C. At that point, renewed agential energy is again required to ascend. The emerging pattern of tonic arpeggiation upward would imply, according to Meyer, continuation to the higher C, but Beethoven suggests a loss of energy (hence, a loss of momentum) when the inertia of continued upward motion moves past Ab merely to Bb instead of C, thus anticipating that it will give way once more to gravity, which it does by dropping to Eb. A performance can easily capture the implied agential energies of these contours, which negotiate individual agential energies in a field of virtual environmental energies.

Next, agential energy is required for the melody to urge upward from Eb to E-natural, at which point the resolution to F reflects the environmental forces of magnetism (the charged half-step ascent, drawn up by the pull of a more stable F) and inertia or momentum (the continuation of a stepwise, chromatic ascent). Once again, momentum gives way and the melody succumbs to gravity, this time dropping to Bb. A larger-scale pattern is heard to emerge from the sequential replication of ascending steps followed by a drop down by a 4th or 5th, and this patterning in turn creates a strategic (work-specific) implication for continuation (implying momentum and reflecting inertia at a higher level). Note, however, that the slurs keep the pattern from implying the *same* expressive shape each time—instead, this level of accentuation further shapes the listener's inference of an independently willing (or experiencing) agent, moving at times with and at times against the gravitational pull of the metric downbeat. Note that I have now included, as does Larson, meter as a contributor to the virtual environmental force field(s) through which we can experience melody as embodied motion, akin to the way we experience our own bodies' motion in the physical world.

Robert S. Hatten

Finally, the stepwise descent to tonic, suggesting yielding to gravity, is made expressive by means of a *portato* articulation that, by giving individual weight to each note, may imply a reluctance to yield. The inertial force of the descent bypasses the stable tonic platform, but instead of yielding to magnetism and its half-step pull of 7 directly back to 1, the implied agent gracefully evades obvious closure by a leap up to 2 before yielding, as if on its own terms, to the inevitable tonic degree. This final arrival on 1, initially implied by the opening two notes, has been successfully deferred until now, where it can serve as melodic completion of a *hierarchical implication* spanning the entire melody.

When we consider the harmonization of this melody, we discover not only an expressively appropriate "yielding" progression from V4/2 to I6, emphasizing the bass as melodic counterpart to the soprano, but also the soprano's melodic leap to E♭ as expressively countering the bass's yielding to C with an energy that, when taken together, implies a *gestural trope* (Hatten, 2004): the yielding bass descent coupled with the positively energized soprano leap upward combine their expressive senses into a merged meaning, a trope of yielding and yearning, or positively inflected resignation, that elsewhere I have termed *abnegation* (Hatten, 1994). Through the synthesis of a hopeful soprano and a resigned bass we can infer a noble spiritual acceptance on the part of a virtual agent. Thus, melody can interact with a contrapuntal line in the bass and its harmonic realization to become part of a highly nuanced expressive gesture with emergent meaning.

Beethoven was so taken with this play between soprano and bass utilizing the V4/2-I6 progression that he returned to the contrapuntal and harmonic relationship for the *Adagio molto e cantabile* opening theme from the third movement of his Ninth Symphony. The intertextual relationship may also be understood in terms of each theme's drawing on a familiar intonation for the Classical style (compare Mozart's use of this pattern for the theme found in the middle episode of the slow movement from his Piano Sonata in C Minor, K. 457).

2.2 Bach, Sinfonia in E minor, BWV 793

Bach was no stranger to *cantabile*. In the title page of his manuscript (1723), he prefaces the inventions and sinfonias with a note indicating that the pieces are meant for (1) instruction in playing cleanly in two or three obbligato parts, (2) modeling composition of inventions and their development, but (3) "*most of all to achieve a cantabile style in playing*", and (4) "to acquire a taste for the elements of composition" (my emphasis). The Sinfonia in E minor is clearly based on a two-bar melody (Figure 3) with a prototypical arch structure and a harmonic trajectory from tonic to dominant. How does counterpoint affect this melody, as subject for invention? The *stretto* imitation in the bass at first supports the agential energy of the melody's initial leap and its momentum to an initial climax on G, but the sustained G is then expressively inflected by a melodic reversal in the bass line that initiates a descent by step. Here again, we see a tropological effect as the energy of the melodic ascent, at first supported, is now drained away by the contrary motion in the bass. But the original melody persists, agentially, and even though it starts to give way to F♯ (reflecting the pull of magnetism and gravity) it finds just enough energy to defer the inevitable stepwise, inertial descent by first reaching from F♯ up to A. This leap is filled with pathos from the effort of straining against gravity, and the continuation reflects near emotional exhaustion as the melody ultimately yields, in a prolonged sigh (the stepwise descent), to the gravitational downbeat and harmonic arrival of m. 3. Note how Larson's concept of inertia accounts for the descent's continuation past the downbeat (but perhaps the rhythmic acceleration into sixteenths also expresses a sudden *frisson* in the virtual agent). The agential energy for the next full entry in the alto appears sufficient to reverse this accelerated descent and help push it back upward (cf. BaileyShea, 2012, for this kind of interaction between voices). But again, the free bass descent inflects the gesture with a kind of recognition of the energy required to rise against the descending weight of grief. Measures 3-6 double the melodic invention, first with upper thirds, then with the lower sixths of invertible counterpoint, and this thickening of the melody lends intervallic weight to the expressive contour. The *melos* is enhanced further by the descending eighths in the bass of m. 6.

FIGURE 3. Bach, Sinfonia in E Minor, BWV 793, mm. 1-22. © Copyright 1853 by Bach-Gesellschaft, Leipzig

2.3 Haydn, Piano Sonata in A♭ major, Hob. XVI/46, C. Landon no. 31, II. Adagio (D♭ major)

Haydn's early (1767 or 1768) piano sonata movement is reminiscent of the Baroque sinfonia, although its contrapuntal two-voice opening sounds at first like a compound melody (Figure 5). The lower part quickly defines itself as a functioning bass line for a periodic four-bar phrase; a third voice, added to a varied repetition of the opening phrase, serves as an enhancing countermelody rather than a competing line.

Figure 4. Haydn, Piano Sonata in A♭ Major, Hob XVI: 46; C. Landon no. 31, 2nd movement (D♭ major), mm. 1-20. © Copyright 1964-66 by Christa Landon, Vienna

The effect of compound melody, resulting from a counterpoint in which neither voice is completely independent, is a spectacular emergent effect of the upper two voices in mm. 13-20. The hocket-like, rhythmic "give-and-take" of the two voices creates the sense of one melodic braid comprised of two interlocking strands—one melody with a dialogical interior, if you will, rather than a straightforward duet. Note also that trills are used as coloristic embellishments that lack cadential fulfillment, until the very last one satisfies the conventional implication of closure.

2.4 Chopin, Nocturne in B major, Op. 62, no. 1

Chopin is also a master of melody made more intricate. The famous return of the opening melody as a continuous line of trills in mm. 68-75 is but one example.[3] The opening melody, however, is striking for another reason: it sounds like it is constantly being renewed, as the stepwise descents from B, D♯, and F♯ constantly "recycle" (Figure 5). The overlapping of cadences with continuation also supports the notion of "endless melody" (later to be associated with Wagner); note how the cadence to B in m. 10 elides with a cadential move to G♯ minor, at the same time that the melody elides from the cadential pitch B to recycle its stepwise descents, as though the melody had simply continued with a change of harmonic color.

But Chopin also enhances his melodies, along the lines discussed in the Haydn slow movement, by means of decorative counter-melodies whose effect is as though a single melodic beam were diffracted into two rays of light, as in mm. 11-14. The upper line in m. 11 (D♯-E) sounds at first like an isolated coloristic addition enhancing V7/iv to iv, but in m. 12 this simple motive expands into a line of its own, and melodic interest shifts as we follow its climactic yearning to F♯ in m. 13. If we hear a passionate duet in m. 13, by m. 14 the upper line has taken over completely and the lower part has thickened into chordal enhancement rather than independent line. Rosen (1972) notes the shifting of melodic and accompanimental roles in a single phrase as marking the new textural style of Haydn's String Quartets, Op. 33, and he demonstrates it with the opening theme from the first movement of the first quartet of that groundbreaking opus.

The constantly regenerative character of Chopin's main theme is complemented by the increasingly improvisatory character of the music beginning in m. 21. Here, above relatively static harmony, a sustained high note loses its sustaining energy and begins to fall, drifting in free figuration down an octave, an impressive yielding to gravity. The immediate repetition is marked by rhythmic irregularities that make the gesture interpretable as an improvisatory arabesque. In performance I emphasize freedom from strict rhythm and let the overall gesture guide my rubato. Chopin introduces an even freer arabesque with his improvisatory cadenza in m. 26, a rhetorical gesture that dynamically disrupts the otherwise unmarked flow of this already improvisatory section. For this gesture, agential energy is injected quite suddenly and forcefully, suggesting the independent will of a virtual agent.

FIGURE 5. Chopin, Nocturne in B Major, Op. 62, no. 1, mm. 1-14. © Copyright s.d. by Peters, Leipzig

Although the improvisatory section does not constitute a prototypical melody in the Western tradition (it sounds more like a Moorish arabesque), the gestural burden of melody is quite focused: each arabesque is one expansive gesture. And although the section does not constitute the B section of the Nocturne, where a more prototypical aria-like melody is found (mm. 37-67), the improvisatory gesture is treated to an impressive developing-variational return in the coda, which features two even more extended arabesques, and where the ethnological "otherness" of the gesture is marked by unusual chromaticism (see especially mm.85-88).

2.5 Mozart, Piano Sonata in F major, K. 533, II. Andante (B♭ major)

This late work of Mozart's is extraordinary in its thoroughgoing use of developing variation. The initial three-note melodic motive is used to launch the second theme and the development section, each time with fresh continuations that have the effect of improvisatory arabesques in their own right. Other motives are also featured in fascinating transformations, as well, but I will focus on the gestural shape of the main theme (see Hatten, 2010a, for an extended analysis of this movement, focusing on its emotional expressiveness).

Given its importance thematically for the entire movement, the initial motive is rather unmarked—merely a neighbor-note figure (Figure 6). What is marked is the catastrophic drop by a tritone in m. 2 to a diminished-seventh sonority. This surprising rhetorical gesture sets the drama, and it is not a gesture that can be explained with reference to gravity alone. Nor might we imagine a virtual agent willing such an untoward event. The very extremity of the shift suggests an encounter with an *external* agency. And that more negative external agency (whether imagined as Fate or Chance) has impacted the virtual agent's course in a way that demands a response. The response, already initiated by the third beat of m. 2, is remarkably positive: energy is invested to leap back up, all the way to C, with a celebratory turn figure that, complemented by the 4-3 suspension in the alto, suggests spiritual resilience in the face of adversity. After reveling in this expansive response, the melody accelerates a stepwise descent to close in four bars with an incomplete authentic cadence. This descent, interpreted as an expressive gesture motivated by the ongoing drama, may suggest a shiver of awed acceptance, thereby further marking the preceding shift to a positive realm as spiritually significant.

FIGURE 6. Mozart, Piano Sonata in F Major, K. 533, second movement (Bb major), main theme, mm. 1-10. © Copyright 1960/1956 by Presser

Developing variation is exemplified by the second theme's use of the opening four-note motto, with the answering cascade a diminution of that contour, leading to a hocketing imitation of the neighboring quarter notes. Mozart's counterpoint here has the effect of enhancing a single motive by dramatizing its increasingly dissonant drops as echoed within a diminutional cascade (compare the opening of the development section, which begins with the motto dropping a diminished fourth, mm. 47-48).

The closing theme accelerates this cascade, by developing the turn figure featured in m. 3. This initially rather unmarked closing theme is nevertheless expressively enhanced by its place in the dramatic trajectory. Just as the first theme recovered from its dissonant drop, by a sudden leap upward, the second theme recovers from its dissonant imbroglio by a sudden restoration of pure consonance. Thus, the closing theme, though expressively unmarked by itself, carries a special aura of relieved contentment merely by continuing in the restored major mode. But the closing theme echoes the introduction of discordant elements found in the second theme by developing its own series of increasingly dissonant leaps (d5, m7, d7) and modulatory feints toward Ab major and F minor, before ultimately cadencing in F major. We follow the changing *melos* as it leads to a climactic "arrival 5/3" in m. 42. Note that the aria-like *portamento* leap both restores consonance and avoids the perfect closure implied by the harmony. By analogy with the rhetorical arrival 6/4 (Hatten, 1994), this "arrival 5/3" rhetorically marks a breakthrough in the expressive drama of an initially unmarked closing melody that increasingly takes on agential striving and expressive individuality. *Melos* in this closing theme has become fully dramatic. Mozart achieves the agential drama by means of developing variation, enhanced by a topical transformation from simple conventional closing material through *empfindsamer* sighs to an aria-like climactic breakthrough, followed by galant decorum in the long-deferred cadence.

Notes

[1] Some composers have found abstract algorithms a useful heuristic for inventing melodies (or their harmonizations). Consider Mozart's experiments with ars combinatoria, or Gershwin's exploration of Schillinger's (1946) permutation method to derive themes for *Porgy and Bess*, or the stochastic algorithms explored by Xenakis.

[2] The inspired chants of Hildegard von Bingen already introduce levels of freedom and complexity that extended beyond the constraints of modal divisions (Gebuhr, 2012).

[3] Note how different this is from the diminutions in Beethoven's Op. 111 finale variations; these liquidate into oscillations and trills that dissolve the melody, requiring another voice to re-sound that melody, bell-like, on top (see also the last variation from the finale of Op. 109). Chopin, on the other hand, maintains the melody inside his chain of trills by implied accentuation of each tone.

References

Allanbrook, W. J. (1983). *Rhythmic gesture in Mozart: Le Nozze di Figaro and Don Giovanni*. Chicago – London: University of Chicago Press.

Allanbrook, W. J. (1992). Two threads through the labyrinth: Topic and process in the first movements of K. 332 and 333. In W. J. Allanbrook, J. M. Levy, & W. P. Mahrt (Eds.), *Convention in eighteenth- and nineteenth-century music: Essays in honor of Leonard G. Ratner* (pp. 125-171). Stuyvesant, NY: Pendragon Press.

Asafiev, B., & Tull, J. R. (1977). *B. V. Asaf'ev's Musical Form as a Process: Translation and Commentary*. PhD diss., Columbus: The Ohio State University.

Bach, J. S. (1723). Title page to *Inventions and sinfonias, Autograph of 1723*. Berlin State Library.

BaileyShea, M. (2012). Musical forces and interpretation: Some thoughts on a measure in Mahler. *Music Theory Online, 18*(3). Retrieved January 15, 2013, from http://mtosmt.org/issues/mto.12.18.3/mto.12.18.3.baileyshea.php

Caplin, W. E. (1998). *Classical form: A theory of formal functions for the instrumental music of Haydn, Mozart, and Beethoven*. New York – Oxford: Oxford University Press.

Gebuhr, A. K. (2012). *Hildegard!* Friendswood, TX: TotalRecall Publishing.

Hatten, R. S. (1994). *Musical meaning in Beethoven: Markedness, correlation, and interpretation*. Bloomington – Indianapolis: Indiana University Press.

Hatten, R. S. (1993). Schubert the progressive: The role of resonance and gesture in the Piano Sonata in A, D. 959, *Intégral* 7 (1993), 38-81. Reprinted in French in *Cahiers F. Schubert* 9 (Paris, Octobre, 1996), 9-48.

Robert S. Hatten

Hatten, R. S. (2004). *Interpreting musical gestures, topics, and tropes: Mozart, Beethoven, Schubert.* Bloomington – Indianapolis: Indiana University Press.

Hatten, R. S. (2010a). Aesthetically warranted emotion and composed expressive trajectories in music. *Music Analysis, 29*(1-3), 83-101.

Hatten, R. S. (2010b). Musical agency as implied by gesture and emotion: Its consequences for listeners' experiencing of musical emotion. In K. Haworth & L. Sbrocchi (Eds.), *Semiotics 2009: Proceedings of the annual meeting of the Semiotic Society of America* (pp. 162-69). New York: Legas Publishing.

Hatten, R. S. (2012). Musical forces and agential energies: An expansion of Steve Larson's model. *Music Theory Onlinen,* 18. Retrieved January 15, 2013, from http://mtosmt.org/issues/mto.12.18.3/mto.12.18.3.hatten.php

Hatten, R. S. (2014). The troping of topics in Mozart's instrumental works. In D. Mirka (Ed.). *The Oxford handbook of topic theory* (pp. 514-538). New York – Oxford: Oxford University Press.

Kurth, E. (1956). *Grundlagen des linearen Kontrapunkts: Bachs melodische Polyphonie.* 5th Ed. Bern: Krompholz.

Larson, S. (2012). *Musical forces: Motion, metaphor, and meaning in music.* Bloomington – Indianapolis: Indiana University Press.

Lidov, D. (2005). *Is language a music? Writings on musical form and signification.* Bloomington – Indianapolis: Indiana University Press.

Meyer, L. B. (1973). *Explaining music.* Berkeley: The University of California Press.

Monelle, R. (2000). *The sense of music: Semiotic essays.* Princeton, N.J.: Princeton University Press.

Narmour, E. (1990). *The analysis and cognition of basic melodic structures.* Chicago: The University of Chicago Press.

Pierce, A. (2007). *Deepening musical performance through movement: The theory and practice of embodied interpretation.* Bloomington – Indianapolis: Indiana University Press.

Ratner, L. G. (1980). *Classic music: Expression, form, and style.* New York: Schirmer Books.

Rosen, C. 1972. *The Classical style: Haydn, Mozart, Beethoven.* New York: W. W. Norton.

Rousseau, J.-J. (1781). *Essai sur l'origine des langues, Où il est parlé de la mélodie & de l'imitation musicale.* In *Œuvres posthumes de J. J. Rousseau,* Vol 3 (pp. 211-327). Genève: Du Peyrou.

Schillinger, J. (1946). *Schillinger system of musical composition.* 2 Vols. New York: Carl Fischer, Inc.

Schoenberg, A., Carpenter, P., & Neff, S. (2006). *The musical idea and the logic, technique and art of its presentation.* Bloomington, Ind.: Indiana University Press.

Toch, E. (1948). *The shaping forces in music: An inquiry into the nature of harmony, melody, counterpoint and form.* New York: Criterion Music Corp.

Trevarthen, C. (1986). Form, significance and psychological potential of hand gestures of infants. In J.-L. Nespoulous, P. Perron, & A. R. Lecours (Eds.), *The biological foundations of gestures: Motor and semiotic aspects* (pp. 149-202). Hillsdale, N.J.: Lawrence Erlbaum Associates.

Zuckerkandl, V. (1956). *Sound and symbol.* 2 Vols. (W. R. Trask, Trans.). New York: Pantheon Books.

The Embodiment of Yearning: Towards a Tripartite Theory of Musical Agency

Rebecca Thumpston

Keele University

"To strive, to seek, to find, and not to yield"

The closing line of Alfred, Lord Tennyson's dramatic monologue *Ulysses* is among the most famous statements of striving in English poetry (1972, p. 646). The poem ends with a heroic statement about moving forward, yet the enduring sense of the prose is one of loss. The poem speaks of Ulysses' spirit yearning and his goal "To sail beyond the sunset, and the baths/Of all the western stars" (p. 646) until he dies. A beautiful meditation on age, Tennyson's words are tinged with sadness built on the knowledge that the things for which we yearn are often not achieved: "We are not now that strength which in old days/Moved earth and heaven; that which we are, we are" (p. 646). Yearning, Tennyson seems to say, is bound with desire, but that desire may remain forever idealized. Striving, by contrast, is the means to actualize desire, an attempt to make manifest the object of desire.

Yearning and striving are human characteristics. To perceive a sense of either in music is therefore to conceive of music anthropomorphically, to attribute to the music a sense of agency. In Tennyson's prose, semantic specificity allows the yearning to "belong" to the title character. While biographical knowledge of Tennyson's life might complicate the understanding of agency (the yearning of implied author and poetic speaker might merge), the prose has a clearly-defined subject to whom the yearning is attributed. Unlike language, wordless music lacks semantic specificity: a central criticism leveled by Jean-Jacques Nattiez (1990) against music as a narrative medium is music's absence of a clearly-defined subject and predicate. However, the detection of a sense of yearning or striving in music implies the presence of some form of persona, or agent, in the musical discourse: Kendall Walton has argued that "[w]here there is behaviour there is a behaver" (1997, p. 63); and Anthony Newcomb asks, "if music is (or represents) actions and events, who is acting?" (1997, p. 131). Therefore, if music elicits a sense of yearning or striving, one must question who it is that acts in this way? Does the music have its own subjectivity? If the actions are attributed to a persona, how does this persona arise? Is the persona "in" the music, or a construct in the mind and body of the listener? Reference to Hans-Georg Gadamer and Naomi Cumming's work on subjectivities helps to solve these complex theoretical enigmas.

This paper explores how striving and yearning are manifested in Benjamin Britten's Symphony for Cello and Orchestra, Op. 68 (1963). Following an engagement with Cumming and Gadamer's thinking, I place yearning and striving within a tripartite theory of musical agency. Following Nicholas Reyland, I propose that agency can be manifested in music at three interlinked levels of signification: mandatory, virtually-mandatory, and elective. This tripartition acts as a theoretical map in the complex process of understanding how listeners posit personae in musical discourses. I place yearning and striving within this framework, questioning who it is that both yearns and strives in Britten's Cello Symphony.

Drawing on Cumming (1997, 2000), James Munk (2011) identifies a number of strategies by which agency can be cued in instrumental music, among them textural individuation (as in the concerto model), musical topics, and representations of gesture, voice, and willed action. Striving is a form of willed action. Readings of senses of agential will in music have been explored most prominently with regard to tonal and formal conventions. Cumming notes that "a tonal line may be heard as having volitional content" (1997, p. 10), a statement that builds on Eero Tarasti's (1994) concept of actorial agency: as Cumming notes, "the agent, or 'subject' of the music, is either striving toward something, being an actor, or suffering action" (1997, p. 11). Recent work by scholars including Matthew BaileyShea (2012a, 2012b) and Robert Hatten (2012) has furthered thinking in this realm. Following these authors, I argue that striving is experienced as an embodied, virtually-mandatory response to micro-level musical units in Britten's Cello Symphony. These micro-units are scalic, deriving from the horizontally-presented descending tetrachord that opens the work. In the opening movement, this scalic unit is used to generate a dialogue between gestures of energy and stasis, deriving from a binary that emerges between upward and downward gestures: energized passages exhibit upward movement and embody a sense of agential striving, which is lost in the static passages. Yearning, by contrast, is best understood as an elective response at a macro-level, understood over an extended durational span: the tonal architecture of the whole work. Yearning also plays upon the up/down binary: the work "yearns" for the move from D minor to D major that is realized at the close of the Symphony. The embodiment of striving therefore allows the listener to construct a yearning persona in the music. Striving is a second-level response to yearning. Like Ulysses, the work strives to achieve the object of desire of its yearning. Striving applies literally, therefore, in the more or less immediate present, and is extended metaphorically to longer term striving. Yearning is longer term, and achievement of the desired state of that yearning is realized via moment to moment embodied striving.

In attempting to understand the somewhat nebulous concept of musical yearning I perceive existing in the Cello Symphony, this reading focuses on a single, but nevertheless central, aspect of Britten's composition. However, my work also recognizes the fluidity of perceptions of agency and the paper therefore concludes with analysis of what I term *intra-agency*: an interpretative space which recognizes the wavering location of agency, existing in a realm between the listener, work, performer, persona and composer. This framework allows me to recognize what Fred Maus labels the pervasive indeterminacy of agency: "[t]he claim is not that different listeners may interpret the music differently (though they undoubtedly will), but rather that a single listener's experience will include a play of various schemes of individuation, none of them felt as obligatory" (1988, p. 68). Yearning and striving are therefore best understood as manifestations of intra-agency, shown diagrammatically in the paper's conclusion.

1. The attribution of a musical persona

In her celebrated article "The Subjectivities of 'Erbarme Dich'", Cumming argues that "[v]ocality, gesture and agency may be drawn together to motivate a synthesis that forms the experience of an active agent or *persona* in a musical work" (1997, p. 11). Agency, for Cumming, is linked with volition, which is inextricably bound with music's representations of gesture and the vocal grain. Referring to gesture and vocality, Cumming (1997, p. 10) suggests that: "one feature of these conventions [...] is the perception of them as sites for the unfolding of the 'will'. A tonal line may be heard as having volitional content, exercising a subliminal control that 'contains' or 'undergirds' the gestural expression even as it unfolds." Working through the lenses of two theoretical viewpoints (the hermeneutic tradition established by Gadamer, and a semiotic stance developed from the work of Charles Sanders Peirce and David Lidov), Cumming's motivation is to understand the process of identification the listener has with the various subjectivities at play in Bach's aria. Gadamer's views are of relevance here.

In *Truth and Method*, his magnum opus exploration of philosophical hermeneutics, Gadamer proposed a phenomenological account of all understanding. Two aspects of his work are pertinent here: the concept of play (*Spiel*), and the notion of historically-effected consciousness (*wirkungs-geschichtliches Bewußtsein*). Jeff Malpas (2009) comments on the former: "Gadamer takes play as the basic clue to the ontological structure of art, emphasizing the way in which play is not a form of disengaged, disinterested exercise of subjectivity, but is rather something that has its own order and structure to which one is given over."

Cumming (1997, p. 7) recognizes the applicability of Gadamer's thinking on play to music, and comments on his bid to understand "the relationship between the individual and shared strategies of expression" through comparison with children's theatrical play. As she notes (1997, p. 7): "when children 'play' at being a character, or actors assume a role, they do not simply 'express' themselves, but take on the characteristics of the persona they wish to represent, suppressing those attributes of their own subjectivity which do not support their intention." Cumming observes that, for Gadamer, works of art function in a comparable manner: they "have a similar capacity to bring a submission of the personal to their own processes" (Cumming, 1997, p. 7). As Gadamer (1989, p. 102; also quoted in Cumming, 1997, p. 7) argues: "the 'subject' of the experience of art, that which remains and endures, is not the subjectivity of the person who experiences it but the work itself. This is the point at which the mode of being of play becomes significant." From this, Cumming concludes that musical works have their own subjectivity. She suggests that the listener becomes actively engaged with this subjectivity, "not following his or her own impulses but guided by those of the work" (Cumming, 1997, p. 7). Indeed, Gadamer (1989, p. 105) argues that "the structure of play absorbs the player into itself, and thus frees him from the burden of taking the initiative."

The suggestion that a musical work has its own subjectivity has interesting implications for inquiry into musical agency. If subjectivity is inherent in a musical work, one must question how it emerges. Might it be the case that a listener is able to posit a musical persona, or agent, only when their own subjectivity is engaged by the work—a process that stems, in part, from a multifaceted and multisensory interaction with sound that arises as a consequence of performance? In other words, might the inherent subjectivity in a work cue a mandatory or virtually-mandatory subjective response in the listener that subsequently allows the listener to elect to construct a musical persona?

2. Towards a tripartite theory of musical agency

My tripartite theory of musical agency adopts Reyland's approach to the analysis of a network of signifiers and other triggers in film music.[1] Reyland argues that music's contributions to film and elsewhere should be analyzed and theorized from a range of interacting vantage points, named after the different yet interacting modes of perception they require of an audio-viewer. He calls these mandatory, virtually-mandatory, and elective. Reyland proposes the following diagram to show the distribution of signifiers (see figure 1).

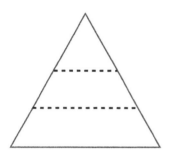

Elective, e.g., pitch organization, musical form, thematic/ motivic connections, unity.

Virtually-mandatory, e.g., learned 'Pavlovian' responses to style topics, degrees of consonance/dissonance, shifts from major to minor.

Mandatory, e.g., psychophysiological responses such as the startle reflex, sub-bass frequencies, expressive intensities, disgust mechanism.

FIGURE 1. Reyland's diagram showing distribution of signifiers

Reyland's diagram highlights a disparity in music theory that work like my research into agency seeks to counterbalance. The vast bulk of music theory and analysis deals with pitch structure, requiring elective, often highly-intellectualized, appreciation, and often an active choice from a listener to follow and interpret such elective features. Yet, as shown diagrammatically, this is the thin end of the wedge of music perception: the virtually-mandatory cues of semiotics and their affect on our bodies, and more primitive cognition systems of the mandatory effects, are arguably far more prominent. In Reyland's schema, the majority of musical signifiers belong to the lower two tiers of the pyramid: mandatory and virtually-mandatory responses. Mandatory responses, the lower tier of the triangle, are psychophysiological: cues that all listeners experience preconsciously. The middle tier represents "learned" responses, experienced by entrained listeners in a particular cultural community, while the tip of the pyramid denotes elective signifiers, arising from complex musical interactions, experienced by (or at least comprehensible to) a minority with advanced musical training. The dotted lines between the categories highlight the fluidity of perception, with many signs blending codings from all three levels.

Reyland's categorizations provide a useful, even revisionist, framework for analytical thought about musical agency. In extending this line of thinking, I amplify Reyland's contention that the majority of agential cues are culturally-conditioned, thereby changing the distribution of signifiers (see figure 2). In reaching this conclusion I draw on Gadamer's notion of historically-effected consciousness. For Gadamer, individuals are situated within a particular culture and history. Therefore, as Cumming (1997, p. 6) notes: "the individuality of an interpreting subject's experience cannot be denied, but neither is it to be dislodged from the social context of a learned tradition." Applying Gadamer's rationale to the understanding of agency, the altered diagram highlights the fact that the majority of agential cues have a historical/cultural element: one cannot, for example, interpret the willful striving of a leading tone towards tonic resolution unless one is situated in a Western musical tradition where tonal relationships are understood implicitly.

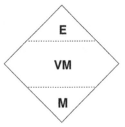

Figure 2. Diagram showing revised agency-focused schema

This tripartition helps to explain the process by which listeners can posit personae in musical discourses. Might it be the case that for a musical agent or persona to be conceived, the work must first cue some form of agential response in the listener at a lower, more primal level, i.e., a mandatory or virtually-mandatory response? Here I return to Gadamer's (1989, p. 105) argument that "the structure of play absorbs the player into itself, and thus frees him from the burden of taking the initiative", a claim that resonates with Edward Cone's (1982, p. 239) concept of *expressive potential*, which refers to the range of possible responses to, or interpretations of, any given work. This potential is not unrestricted, because "the expressive content—the human activity or state of mind adduced as an interpretation of the music—must be congruous with the structural content—the musical action itself." Added to this, I contend that each and every performance has an expressive potential, which further shapes listeners' agential responses: a listener is able to posit a persona (an elective act), only when their own subjectivity is engaged—a process that stems, in part, from a multifaceted and multisensory interaction with sound that arises as a consequence of performance. In the context of yearning and striving in Britten's Cello Symphony, might it be the case that yearning is understood only in light of the embodied (virtually-mandatory) act of striving?

3. The embodiment of striving

Striving is an example of agential will. Perceptions of will in music often evolve in response to movement. BaileyShea (2012a, p. 9) has examined striving manifested through upward movement in the Adagio of Samuel Barber's Op. 11 String Quartet: "the quartet continually creates the impression of a singular musical persona struggling—and ultimately failing—to rise up to a stable major mode". BaileyShea's (2012a, p. 13) argument examines the sense of struggle that exists in the rising melody: "the overall effect is that of an agonizing effort—an unsteady climb where the melodic agent traverses *seventeen notes* in a clear upward arc and yet only rises a single step overall." Drawing on Arnie Cox's (2006 and 2011) theory of the mimetic hypothesis, BaileyShea (2012a, p. 11) contends that the "struggle" is experienced by the listener in an embodied manner: "when I imagine what it's like to be the Adagio melody, I imagine a painful, difficult struggle to rise upward. But since I know *I'm* not ascending when I'm listening to the piece, I imagine the melody itself as the agent of the action and I empathize with its plight."

BaileyShea (2012a and 2012b) also utilizes Steve Larson's writings on musical forces. Larson (2012, p. 22) argues that "our immediate experience of musical motion is shaped primarily by our embodied intuitive understanding of physical motion—not by our intellectual understanding of physics." He argues (p. 2) that music is controlled by three primary forces: melodic gravity—"the tendency of notes above a reference platform to descend", melodic magnetism—"the tendency of unstable notes to move to the closest stable pitch", and musical inertia—"the tendency of pitches or durations, or both, to continue in the pattern perceived". BaileyShea notes an important distinction between passive and active movement. The latter, explored by Hatten (2012), is applicable to willed action:

> Larson's analyses tend to promote a fundamentally passive view […]. We get the sense that music moves without volition, un-folding as a chain reaction of physical forces like dominoes set in motion. Hatten prefers more active interpretations, with mu-

sical agents operating intentionally in an unfolding drama [...] musical motion remains unpredictable, fully dependent on an agent's actions (BaileyShea, 2012b).

The perception of a sense of striving in musical movement is imbued with a sense of willful action: the music struggles for something, driven by some form of desire. For the listener, the illusory movement is tied to the achievement of something desired: the listener enacts the role of the agent struggling to achieve a desired state. In my reading of Britten's Cello Symphony, upwards striving is embodied in a comparable manner to Barber's Adagio. An embodied response to striving on a micro-level allows the listener to engage in the elective act of positing a longer range yearning persona in the musical discourse. This is the "mind" in the music that perceives the macro-level yearning for the rise from what cellist Pieter Wispelwey (2010) describes as the "menacing darkness" of D minor to the "stark light" of D major.

4. Striving in Britten's Symphony for Cello and Orchestra

Britten's Symphony for Cello and Orchestra exhibits a dialogue of upward and downward gestures which embody, on different durational scales, senses of both yearning and striving. Unlike in the traditional concerto model, Britten does not cast the solo cellist as dramatic protagonist: within a sonata form structure, Britten shares thematic material evenly between soloist and orchestra. Agency is thus not cued by textural individuation. Peter Evans (1963) has examined the structure and motivic developments of the Symphony. His commentary is analytically rigorous, but does not examine the more sensuous properties existing in the work, such as the tension that exists between energized and static gestures. I argue that energized passages are understood via rising motion, while stasis is marked by a lack of motion. The opening movement exhibits a number of attempts to energize the musical discourse, which I suggest are perceived via a sense of willful striving embodied in rising motion. In support of this assertion I refer to Hatten's observation that "[a] basic characterization of agency for human perception and cognition is the reconstructed locus or source of a given perceived expenditure of energy" (Hatten, 2009, p. 162).

The Symphony begins with a horizontally-presented descending tetrachord in the double basses, tuba and bass drum (see figure 3—tetrachord marked a).[2] The unusually low sonority foregrounds the tetrachord, signaling its importance in the musical narrative. The sense of descent is reinforced in the solo line. In spite of the initial rising fourth, the semitone descent from D to C♯ in bar 3 is heard as the most important interval in the solo line. Note that Britten gives the instruction to perform the final chord from top to bottom, thereby emphasizing the semitonal descent. The importance of the semitone is also marked by the repeated chord preceding it: as Evans observes, the cello line "reiterates notes before emphasizing a crucial interval, here the semitone" (1963, pp. 3-4). Downward motion is therefore set up as the status quo.

FIGURE 3. Opening of Cello Symphony showing descending tetrachordal motif.
© Copyright 1963 by Boosey & Hawkes Music Publishers Ltd. Reproduced by permission of Boosey & Hawkes Music Publishers Ltd

The first attempt to energize the music is found in the build-up to the *vivo* at figure 2 (see figure 4). Here, the orchestral line descends, but the solo line strives against the descent in a willful, energized rising of pitch in the double-stopped semiquaver pairs in bars 3-4 of the example shown. However, despite the build-up of energy, the music soon wanes into a static passage in which there is little or no sense of willful intent and no rising motion. Indeed, as soon as figure 2 is reached, downward motion once again prevails. Evans (1963, p. 5) notes that "the cello's minor-third figurations elaborate a descending scale, and [the scalic tetrachord] has another, still more devious, offshoot in the angular brass octave-transposed figures." Table 1 expands on Evans' analysis of the opening movement, showing my analysis of the interaction of energized/static passages with scalic motion. The upper four rows are drawn from Evans (1963, p. 8), while the lower four rows show my analysis of the movement's more sensuous properties.

FIGURE 4. Energized build-up to vivo. © Copyright 1963 by Boosey & Hawkes Music Publishers Ltd. Reproduced by permission of Boosey & Hawkes Music Publishers Ltd

Following the period of stasis, there is a second, more concerted, attempt to energize the music (see figure 5). This second attempt is particularly prominent for two reasons. First, the striving is heralded by the beating of the timpani, the physicality of which is experienced in a highly embodied, virtually-mandatory manner. Roland Barthes' (1985, p. 299) comments on his experience of hearing Schumann's *Kreisleriana* resonate here: "I actually hear no note, no theme, no contour, no grammar, no meaning… No, what I hear are blows: I hear what beats in the body, what the body beats, or better: I hear this body that beats." Following the quite literal beating of the timpani, the opening tetrachord is inverted and later extended. The now rising tetrachord is experienced as embodied: the listener can question what it is like to be that melodic line striving upwards. The listening response is comparable to that noted by BaileyShea (2012a, p. 11) in Barber's Adagio: "when I imagine what it's like to be the [inverted tetrachord] I imagine a painful, difficult struggle to rise upward." Of course, as BaileyShea notes, the listener recognizes that the motion is not real and that the listener does not, herself, move. She thus projects her mimetic musical agency outwards: "since this agency cannot be identified directly with the actions of the performers, it remains an ideal agency that is not us. We call this agent 'the music'" (Cox, 2006, p. 53). The listener's virtually-mandatory, embodied response to striving thus acts as a catalyst for the identification of a yearning persona in the musical discourse. As detailed in the table (Table 1), there are two further attempts to energize the music, but these are short-lived and a sense of stasis pervades the remainder of the movement.

Themes	Exposition			
	A	B1	B2	C
Key centres and approx. mode	D min.	Transitional (towards A or F)		A 'maj.' (versus F Mixolydian)
Chief melodic interest	Solo	Solo	Solo + Orch.	Solo
Figure number	1	2	B. 7 of fig. 4	6
Performance direction	*Allegro maestoso*	*Vivo*		*Tranquillo*
Time signature (primary)	3 2	4 4	4 4	3 2
Energized or static?	Primordial energy followed by build-up of energy	Release of energy in lyricism	Waning of energy	Static
Predominant direction of motion	▼ then ▲	▼	▼	▼

TABLE I. Detailing structure and sensuous properties of Britten's Cello Symphony, movement I

Development			Restatement			Coda
on A and B2, with central interlude			A	B1	C	B2 and A
F / Unstable			F min.	D maj.	D 'maj' (versus B-flat Mixolydian)	D min. + D maj.
Solo & Orch. in antiphony			Orch.	Orch.	Orch., finally Solo	Solo + Orch. in counterpoint
8	11	13	17	19	21	24
Agitato	*Lusingando*	*Agitato*	*Maestoso*	*Vivo*	*Tranquillo*	*Maestoso*
4 / 4	6 / 4	4 and 3 / 4 2	3 / 2	4 / 4	3 / 2	3 / 2
Build-up of energy driven by timpani and rising pitch leading to a further release of energy in lyricism	Static	Attempt to energize: build-up of energy leading to recapitulation	Energized, but without the drive of the exposition	Release of energy in lyricism, but waning fast	Static	Static
▲	Little or no scalic movement	▼ and ▲ Sense of direction unclear	▼ then ▲	▼	▼	▼

B. & H. 19071

FIGURE 5. Inversion of tetrachord at development. © Copyright 1963 by Boosey & Hawkes Music Publishers Ltd. Reproduced by permission of Boosey & Hawkes Music Publishers Ltd

5. The embodiment of yearning

Returning to Tennyson, striving in Britten's Cello Symphony can be seen as the means to actualize the yearning's object of desire. Unlike the perception of striving, which develops in response to small, contained stepwise movement, experienced in the more or less immediate present, I suggest that yearning in Britten's Cello Symphony plays out over the course of the whole work, understood only as the compositional architecture unfolds. The overarching narrative of the Symphony is concerned with the move from D minor to D major. In light of the manner in which listeners conceive of harmony in vertical terms, this move is heard as an upward move. The striving agent in Britten's Cello Symphony thus yearns for an upward tonal move. This sense of yearning is experienced on a longer durational scale, and posited in the mind of a persona in the musical discourse. One might therefore argue, contrary to my title, that the sense of yearning is not embodied in the same manner as striving; rather it is primarily experienced conceptually. However, yearning is a somewhat nebulous concept, and while the precise pitch-based narrative (D minor to D major) is an elective reading, accessible only to a minority, one could put forward a case that the sense of a shift from minor to major (again perceived directionally) is a virtually-mandatory response, accessible to almost all. One might suggest that Pieter Wispelwey's (2010) reading of the shift from darkness to light in the Cello Symphony demonstrates an example of this kind of response; Wispelwey's language implies a more intuitive understanding of the Symphony.

Given that the work appears to actualize its object of desire—a shift from D minor to D major is achieved—one might question how and why a sense of yearning manifests, for, returning to the opening of this paper, I suggested that yearning manifests precisely because the things for which we yearn are often not achieved. Given that D major is reached, why then is there a sense of yearning at the close of the Symphony? While the music does elicit a sense of stark light in the final movement, forged in part by the hymn-like quality of the ending, the impression at the close of the Symphony is not one of optimism, but of an underlying tension. Referring to the ending of the Symphony, Arnold Whittall (1982, pp. 207-208) notes:

> [t]he tonic note, even the tonic triad, may be unambiguous, but the general harmonic character of the music is not so firmly focused. Contexts are never sufficiently diatonic or stable for one to feel that the structural weight of the D major triads could survive a determined challenge. And so the ending, though brilliantly coloured, is only precariously triumphant.

The Symphony ends with downward scalic motion: the perception of a sense of yearning in Britten's Cello Symphony is thus only truly possible because the object of desire remains idealized: the downward motion undermines the apparently stable D major.

6. Concluding thoughts: intra-agency

By means of a conclusion I introduce the concept of intra-agency. Although I have attempted to illustrate the manner in which senses of yearning and striving can manifest differently in music, I recognize that each individual listener's experience is unique and often indeterminate. While it is attractive to conceive of a model for understanding agency, I have shown that the senses of yearning and striving in Britten's Cello Symphony can be realized at multiple levels. The listener can embody a sense of striving; this may be perceived as the striving of the performer or projected onto a persona in the musical dialogue. Alternatively, the listener may not interpret this bodily knowledge, simply experiencing it. Yearning, I have suggested, is best understood as a large-scale interpretation that is not bodily, but instead is primarily conceptual. Yet this might seem to contradict many listeners' understandings of yearning as something that is "within" us, but impossible to articulate. Furthermore, yearning might have additional meanings if Britten's biography is taken into account.

I therefore propose the concept of intra-agency, existing as a kind of conceptual space that blends the plural agencies at play in a musical work: composer, performer, persona and listener. Intra-agency has resonances with Gadamer's thinking. Malpas notes, in response to Gadamer, that "[t]he artwork, no matter what its medium, opens up, through its symbolic character, a space in which both the world, and our own being in the world, is brought to light as a single, but inexhaustibly rich totality" (Malpas, 2009). To identify, conclusively, who it is that yearns and strives in any given musical discourse remains theoretically impossible: ultimately, listeners' perceptions of agential discourses are fluid. While I have proposed an argument whereby striving in Britten's Cello Symphony is bodily and yearning is conceptual, another listener might differently interpret the musical dialogue. I therefore propose the following diagram to show the fluidity of perceptions of agency (see figure 6). Might it be the case that intra-agency can be considered to correlate with the inherent subjectivity Gadamer and Cumming argue exists in any given artwork? After all, to close with Tennyson (1972, p. 645), Ulysses declares "I am a part of all that I have met."

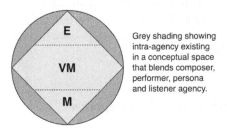

Grey shading showing intra-agency existing in a conceptual space that blends composer, performer, persona and listener agency.

Figure 6. Diagrammatic representation of intra-agency

Notes

1. Reyland's work is not yet published, but will appear in Nicholas Reyland and Edward Venn, *Music Analysis* (forthcoming).
2. I label motivic units in the same manner as Evans (1963).

References

BaileyShea, M. (2012a). Agency and the adagio: mimetic engagement in Barber's op. 11 quartet. *Gamut: Online Journal of the Music Theory Society of the Mid-Atlanti*c, 5(1), 7-38.

BaileyShea, M. (2012b) Musical Forces and Interpretation: Some Thoughts on Measure in Mahler. *Music Theory Online,18*(3).

Barthes, R. (1985). Rasch. In R. Howard (Trans.), *The Responsibility of Forms: Critical Essays on Music, Art, and Representation* (pp. 299-312). Oxford: Blackwell (Original work published 1982).

Cone, E. (1982). Schubert's Promissory Note: An Exercise in Musical Hermeneutics. *19th-Century Music, 5*(3), 233-241.

Cox, A. (2006). Hearing, Feeling, Grasping Gestures. In A. Gritten & E. King (Eds.), *Music and Gesture* (pp.45-60). Farnham, Surrey: Ashgate Publishing Limited.

Cox, A. (2011). Embodying Music: Principles of the Mimetic Hypothesis. *Music Theory Online, 17*(2).

Cumming, N. (1997). The Subjectivities of 'Erbarme Dich'. *Music Analysis, 16*(1), 5-44.

Cumming, N. (2000). *The Sonic Self: Musical Subjectivity and Signification.* Bloomington and Indianapolis: Indiana University Press.

Evans, P. (1963). Britten's Cello Symphony. *Tempo, New Series 66/67*, 2-15.

Gadamer, H. (1989). *Truth and Method*, Second, Revised Edition. (Ed. J. Weinsheimer & D. Marshall, Trans.). London: Sheed & Ward (Original work published 1975).

Hatten, R. S. (2009). Musical Agency as Implied by Gesture and Emotion: Its Consequences for Listeners' Experiencing of Musical Emotion. In K. Haworth & L. Sbrocchi (Eds.), *Semiotics 2009: Proceedings of the Annual Meeting of the Semiotic Society of America* (pp.162-69). New York: Legas Publishing.

Hatten, R. S. (2012). Musical Forces and Agential Energies: An Expansion of Steve Larson's Model. *Music Theory Online, 18*(3).

Larson, S. (2012). *Musical Forces: Motion, Metaphor, and Meaning in Music.* Bloomington: Indiana University Press.

Malpas, J. (2009). Hans-Georg Gadamer. In E. Zalta (Ed.) The Stanford Encyclopedia of Philosophy. Retrieved April 5, 2015, from http://plato.stanford.edu/archives/sum2009/entries/gadamer/.

Maus, F. (1988). Music as drama. *Music Theory Spectrum, 10*, 56-73.

Munk, J. (2011). *Agency, physicality, space: analytical approaches to contemporary nordic concertos* (Unpublished PhD thesis). University of Oxford, England.

Rebecca Thumpston

Nattiez, J. J. (1990). Can one speak of narrativity in music? (K. Ellis, Trans.) *Journal of the Royal Musical Association, 115*(2), 240-257.

Newcomb, A. (1997). Action and agency in Mahler's ninth symphony, second movement. In J. Robinson (Ed.), *Music and Meaning* (pp.131-153). Ithaca and London: Cornell University Press.

Tarasti, E. (1994). *A theory of musical semiotics.* Bloomington: Indiana University Press.

Tennyson, A. Ulysses (1972). In H. Gardener (Ed.), *The New Oxford Book of English Verse* (pp. 644-646). Oxford: Clarendon Press (Original work published 1842).

Walton, K. (1997). Listening with imagination: is music representational? In J. Robinson (Ed.), *Music and meaning* (pp.57-82). Ithaca and London: Cornell University Press.

Wispelwey, P. (2010). [Liner notes]. *In Britten Cello Symphony/Cello Suite No.1* [CD]. Onyx 4058.

Whittall, A. (1982). *The music of Britten and Tippett: studies in themes and techniques.* Cambridge: Cambridge University Press.

Editors

Costantino C. M. Maeder is professor of Italian Literature and Linguistics at the Catholic University of Louvain. He is Head of the Center for Italian Studies and of GLOBALIT, Louvain Research Center for Global Studies. As a musicologist, pragmatician, and semiotician, he publishes essentially on transdisciplinary topics, mostly on Opera, and Theater.

Mark Reybrouck is professor of music education and music psychology at KU Leuven – University of Leuven. His research is interdisciplinary and brings together insights from psychology, biology, semiotics and music with a focus on listening strategies and musical sense-making. His theoretical research involves foundational work on music cognition and perception, especially the biological roots of musical epistemology and the embodied en enactive approach to musical sense-making. His empirical research involves representational and metarepresentational strategies in real-time music listening tasks.

Contributors

Paulo C. Chagas is Professor of Composition at the University of California, Riverside, and currently Music Department Chair. A very versatile composer, Chagas has written over 100 works for orchestra, chamber music, electroacoustic music, and audiovisual and multimedia compositions. His music unfolds a pluralistic aesthetic, using the most diverse musical materials from different cultures, acoustic and digital media, dance, video, and audiovisual installations. Chagas is also a prolific author of books and articles focused on theoretical, critical and analytical reflections on contemporary music creativity, including musical semiotics, musical philosophy and aesthetics, electroacoustic and digital music. His writings incorporate ideas from ethics and philosophy, sociology, theories of media and communication, phenomenology, cybernetics, critical studies, and semiotics of classical music.

Isaac Chueke, conductor, pedagogue, scholar, is active in three continents. Holding a PhD from Université Paris-Sorbonne and an MA in Orchestral Conducting from the City University of New York, with studies also in Vienna and Rio de Janeiro, his research interests vary from issues as diverse as performance, aesthetics and cultural management. Following various artistic and educational posts in North America during the nineties, since 2002 he has regularly established a collaboration with Paris-Sorbonne as *Membre Associé* of l'Observatoire Musical Français (OMF); at the same institution he is also a co-founder of the Groupe de Recherche Musiques Brésiliennes (GRMB). He was awarded the title *Chevalier de l'Ordre des Arts et des Lettres* by the French Government and he also received a special distinction by Czech President Vaclav Havel. Head of the Music Department at Brazil's National Library in 2005, since 2006 he has been Associate Professor at Embap/Unespar in Curitiba.

Zelia Chueke (www.zeliachueke.com) dedicates her activities as performer and scholar to the study and practice of 20th- and 21st-century music. Being permanent researcher with the Observatoire Musical Français/Université Paris-Sorbonne (2003-2013), founder and head of the Groupe de Recherche de Musiques Brésiliennes (GRMB), she continues these activities with the new research body, the Institut de recherche en musicologie IReMus/CNRS, Paris-Sorbonne, BnF, MCC (www.iremus.cnrs.fr) where she was elected Associate researcher. Dr. Chueke is

Associate Professor at the Federal University of Paraná, Brazil, where she is Head of the research group entitled Studies and Practice of 20th- and 21st-Century Music (musica20e21.ufpr.br), where she was recently elected Director of the Graduate Studies Programme. Her project *International Exchanges on Music and Performance* gathers renowned scholars periodically at conferences and discussions available on line (www.iemtp.ufpr.br).

Maurizio Corbella holds a PhD in Musicology from the University of Milan, where he is currently appointed as a post-doctoral fellow. His main research interests concern film music, popular music and the theory of audio-vision. He specializes in the relationship between experimental music and (especially Italian) cinema, which was the topic of his PhD dissertation. He has published in international and Italian peer-reviewed journals (Music and the Moving Image, AAA-TAC, Comunicazioni sociali, Cinémas) and conference proceedings (ICMS-MRM Edinburgh). Together with Ilario Meandri (University of Turin) he is currently co-editing a special double issue of Music/Technology (Firenze University Press), entitled Music, Sound and Production Processes in the Italian Cinema (1945-70).

Ian Cross, initially a guitarist, has since 1986 taught in the Faculty of Music at the University of Cambridge, where he is Professor and Director of the Centre for Music & Science, and a Fellow of Wolfson College. His research is interdisciplinary, guided by the aim of developing an integrated understanding of music as grounded in both biology and culture. He has published widely in the fields of music cognition, music theory, ethnomusicology, archaeological acoustics, psychoacoustics, music and language evolution. Most recently, his research has focused on music and language as interactive media, showing that timing in speech and in music in interactive contexts is mediated by common mechanisms.

Paulo F. de Castro (PhD, Royal Holloway College, University of London with a thesis on the musical implications of Wittgenstein's philosophy) is a musicologist, a lecturer at Universidade Nova de Lisboa, and a member of the CESEM research centre (Lisbon, Portugal). He has published several books and essays, including the sections on the 19th and 20th centuries in a book on the history of Portuguese music. Alongside his activities as a researcher, a lecturer and a music critic, he was Director of the Teatro Nacional de S. Carlos and Chairman of the Portuguese Society for Music Research. His current interests as a researcher include the philosophy of music, topic theory, transtextuality and the ideologies of modernism and postmodernism.

Robert S. Hatten, Professor of Music Theory, University of Texas at Austin, is the author of *Musical Meaning in Beethoven: Markedness, Correlation, and Interpretation* (1994) and *Interpreting Musical Gestures, Topics, and Tropes: Mozart, Beethoven, Schubert* (2004). Articles on music and emotion, Mozart, and Schubert have appeared, respectively, in Music Analysis and Music Theory Spectrum (with Jenefer Robinson); *Mozart's Chamber Music with Keyboard* (ed. Martin Harlow); and 19th-Century Music Review. "Narrative Engagement with Twentieth-Century Music" (with Byron Almén) appeared in *Music and Narrative since 1900* (ed. Michael Klein and Nicholas Reyland), and "The Troping of Topics in Mozart's Instrumental Works appeared in *The Oxford Handbook of Topic Theory* (ed. Danuta Mirka). Dr. Hatten edits the book series "Musical Meaning and Interpretation" at Indiana University Press.

David Huron is Arts and Humanities Distinguished Professor at the Ohio State University, where he holds joint appointments in the School of Music and in the Center for Cognitive and Brain Sciences. Originally from Canada, Huron completed a PhD degree in musicology from the University of Nottingham (UK) in 1989. Over the course of his career he has produced some 130 publications, including two books. Among other distinctions, Dr. Huron has been the Ernest Bloch Visiting Lecturer at the University of California, Berkeley, the Donald Wort Lecturer at Cambridge University, and the Astor Lecturer at Oxford. In addition to laboratory-based research, Prof. Huron has over the past decade pursued field studies in Micronesia.

Jamie Liddle is an Associate Lecturer in the Arts Faculty of the Open University, UK; he also teaches piano within Stewarts Melville College, Edinburgh, Scotland. In addition to research and teaching he maintains an active performing life as both a pianist and a guitarist. Both his undergraduate studies and doctoral research were completed at the University of Edinburgh; his thesis focussed on irony and ambiguity in Beethoven's late quartets. His current interests centre on semiotics and topic theory, particularly Romantic topics in the music of Schubert, Mahler and Richard Strauss and the emergence of topics in 19th-century piano music.

Gabriele Marino (Cefalù, Palermo, 1985) studied Communication Sciences at the University of Palermo and holds a PhD in Language and Communication Sciences from the University of Turin. He is mainly interested in the sociosemiotics of music and the Internet. He collaborates with CIRCe (Interdepartmental Research Centre on Communication, University of Turin) and Episteme (research institute on social change and markets, Milan). He single-authored the book *Britney canta Manson e altri capolavori* (Crac, 2011). He is editor of the magazine "Sentireascoltare" and the journal of music studies "Analitica", and runs the social networks of "Lexia. Rivista di semiotica". His website is gabrielemarino.it.

Dario Martinelli (1974), musicologist and semiotician, is Director of the International Semiotics Institute, Professor at Kaunas University of Technology, and Adjunct Professor at the Universities of Helsinki and of Lapland. He has published six monographs and more than a hundred contributions to edited collections, studies and scientific articles. His most recent scientific monographs include: *Lights, Camera, Bark! - Representation, semiotics and ideology of non-human animals in cinema* (Technologija, 2014), *Authenticity, Performance and Other Double-Edged Words* (Acta Semiotica Fennica, 2011), *A Critical Companion to Zoosemiotics* (Springer, 2010), *Of Birds, Whales and Other Musicians* (University of Scranton Press, 2009). In 2006, he was knighted by the Italian Republic for his contribution to Italian culture. He is also the youngest winner of the Oscar Parland Prize for Prominent Semioticians, awarded by Helsinki University (2004).

Nicolas Marty is a PhD student at the Université Paris-Sorbonne, where he studies the listening to acousmatic music in its relation with the experiencing of time by listeners. This follows his master's work about a "natural" narratology for music. All of his research draws from his learnings as a psychology student. His interest in perception comes from his practice as a young composer. He is currently following Jean-Louis Agobet's instrumental composition courses and Christophe Havel and François Dumeaux' electroacoustic composition courses at the conservatory of Bordeaux. He was junior lecturer in computer music for the 2013-2014 spring semester at the Université Bordeaux III.

Maarten Nellestijn studied musicology at Utrecht University, where he received his MA in 2013. His research interests include minimal music, opera, music theatre, film, and other musical multimedia. He published on John Adams's and Peter Sellars's Doctor Atomic, and is currently writing about the interrelation of visual and musical rhythmical structures in Philip Glass's and Robert Wilson's opera Einstein on the Beach.

Mônica Pedrosa de Pádua, a native of Belo Horizonte, Brazil, is a voice teacher at the School of Music of the Federal University of Minas Gerais (UFMG). She has a Bachelor's Degree from that institution, a Master's from Manhattan School of Music and a Doctorate in Comparative Literature from the College of Letters, UFMG, with a dissertation on articulations between poetry and music in art songs. Mônica has been especially interested in the research and dissemination of Brazilian Art Song and is a member of the research group entitled "Rescuing Brazilian Song". As a singer, she has won awards in several national and international competitions, including the XX Artists International Auditions, in New York, and performs regularly as a soloist and recitalist.

Małgorzata Pawłowska, PhD, is a lecturer in Music Theory in the Department of the Academy of Music in Kraków, (Ear Training, Music History, Musical Analysis, Music Literature and Methodology). She graduated from the Music Theory faculty at the Academy of Music in Krakow (2006) and undertook some of her MA studies at the Royal Conservatoire in Brussels (2003-2004). She was awarded a prize at the national competition for her MA thesis "The Devil in 19th- and 20th-Century Music" (2006). In her doctoral thesis (2013) she studied the problem of musical narratology, taking into consideration musical pieces of different styles and genres inspired by the story of Romeo and Juliet. She also completed postgraduate studies in Culture Management in the European Context (2007) and has been very active in organizing international artistic and scientific events. She is a member of the European Narratological Network and The Polish Composers' Union. She has published many articles in Polish and international monographs and co-edited books within the field of musical signification.

Piotr Podlipniak is an assistant professor at the Department of Musicology at Adam Mickiewicz University in Poznań. His main areas of interest are the cognitive musicology, biological sources of human musicality, psychology of music and methodology of musicology. He is author of the book *Uniwersalia muzyczne* [Musical universals] (Poznań, 2007). In his musicological research, he refers to such academic disciplines as cognitive science, evolutionary psychology and cultural anthropology. He is an editorial secretary of the journal Interdisciplinary Studies in Musicology and a member of Society of Interdisciplinary Musicology.

Rebecca Thumpston completed her PhD 'Agency in twentieth-century British cello music' at Keele University in 2015. She co-organized the Society for Music Analysis Graduate Students' Conference at Keele in 2013 and was a member of the programme committee for the Royal Musical Association Study Day 'Studying the "Tonal" Avant-Garde: Methodologies of Twentieth-Century Music'

(Keele 2013). Exploring the role of the body in understanding music, Rebecca is currently co-editing 'Music Analysis and the Body: Experiments, Explorations and Embodiments' with Nicholas Reyland and Stacey Sewell for Leuven University Press.

Mieczysław Tomaszewski is professor of the Academy of Music in Cracow. He was born in 1921 in Poznań, where he was educated as a pianist. He studied philology at Nicolaus Copernicus University in Toruń and musicology at Jagiellonian University in Krakow. He received his PhD and a postdoctoral degree (habilitation) at Adam Mickiewicz University in Poznań. From 1949-52 he was director of the Pomeranian Symphonic Orchestra in Bydgoszcz, from 1952-88 the editor-in-chief and director of the Polish Music Publishing House, from 1960-66 a lecturer of music theory at Jagiellonian University, and since 1960 he has been connected with the Academy of Music in Krakow. The primary area of his studies includes theory and history of 19th- and 20th-century music, in particular Chopin's work, romantic song and Polish contemporary music as well as the ontology of musical composition and the aspects of intermedial and intertextual relations. He has published approximately 25 books.

Lea Wierød received her PhD in October 2014 from Aarhus Universitet, Denmark. The topic of her thesis was church songs with texts by N.F.S. Grundtvig, and its aim was to propose an intermedial approach to song analysis by combining literary and musicological methods. Lea Wierød is currently teaching Music History and related subjects at Aarhus University. In addition, she is involved in the Word and Music Association Forum, an international network for the study of musico-literary interconnections, and is currently coediting their 3rd conference proceedings.

Lawrence M. Zbikowski is Associate Professor in the Department of Music at the University of Chicago. He is the author of *Conceptualizing Music: Cognitive Structure, Theory, and Analysis* (Oxford 2002). He recently contributed chapters to *The Oxford Handbook of Topic Theory* (Oxford 2014), *Speaking of Music* (Fordham, 2013), *Bewegungen zwischen Hören und Sehen* (Königshausen & Neumann, 2012), *New Perspectives on Music and Gesture* (Ashgate, 2011), and *Music and Consciousness* (Oxford, 2011), and has also published in Music Analysis, Music Humana, Musicæ Scientiæ, Music Theory Spectrum, Ethnomusicology, the Journal of Musicological Research, and the Dutch Journal of Music Theory. During the 2010–11 academic year he held a fellowship from the American Council of Learned Societies and was also Fulbright Visiting Research Chair at McGill University.